More praise for
THE BISHOP'S DAUGHTER

"*The Bishop's Daughter* is a celebration of Paul Moore's life and of Honor Moore's honesty. Paul is a sympathetic figure, more human and fallible and somehow more noble than if we had simply been left with the picture of him as the powerful and renowned bishop of New York. . . . One feels that both Paul Moore and his daughter have been set free by this book. There is no shame left, and neither is there blame."
— *Los Angeles Times Book Review*

"*The Bishop's Daughter* is both a probing autobiography and forthright reflection on a man who, for all his flaws, inspired his daughter to understand him. Eloquently summing up her father's inner life, she comes to realize that his power derived from a shadowy existence that both tormented and inspired him. . . . *The Bishop's Daughter* . . . tells us much about the willingness of daughters and sons to confront complex emotional truths. We owe our fathers nothing less." — *Newsday*

"Moore backed away from his gilded pedigree . . . to become a champion of the poor, a civil rights crusader in the Johnson era, and ultimately Episcopal Bishop of New York. But the life of this charismatic reformer was also a reliquary of secrets, which his eldest daughter, poet and biographer Honor Moore, opens up with grace and urgency in her memoir. . . . Prose as emotionally resonant as a confession. It's brave to open up old wounds; braver still to help them heal." — *O, The Oprah Magazine*

"An indelible portrait of a charismatic religious leader. . . . At the dramatic heart of this engrossing family chronicle is the ultimately triumphant struggle of the daughter, who suffered her own sexual confusion and years of therapy to reconstruct her father's personal history in an effort to understand his behavior and thereby forgive."
— *Publishers Weekly*, starred review

"*The Bishop's Daughter* is an eloquent argument for speaking even the most difficult truths." —*New York Times Book Review*

"A powerful memoir of life with an accomplished but secretly tortured father. . . . Poet and playwright Moore, an attentive, sensitive narrator, performs an intensive, sometimes painful genealogical dig on her parents' backgrounds, their courtship and marriage, their work together in the church and their private lives, including many interviews with friends and male and female lovers of her father. . . . A moving prose poem about what it means to be spiritual, sexual and human."

—*Kirkus Reviews*, starred review

"[A] galvanizing portrait. . . . Entwining candid reminiscences with the fruits of often unnerving research, Moore creates a dramatic family history that casts fresh light on the civil rights, peace, and women's movements, and the corresponding evolution of the Episcopalian Church. But the blazing heart of the book is the revelation of her father's secret homosexual affairs. As Moore struggles to recalibrate her understanding of her confounding parents, she revisits her own relationships with both men and women. The result is a generous and thought-provoking chronicle of public altruism and private betrayal, high ideals and forbidden desire, love and forgiveness."

—*Booklist*, starred review

"*The Bishop's Daughter* is an unsparing portrait of a glamorous but elusive father and his daughter's search for the truth about his secret life and conflicted loyalties. What makes Honor Moore's memoir so arresting is the effect of the author's cool and penetrating gaze on her beloved subject. Before the life and book end, the god-like hero of New York's crisis years has climbed down from his pulpit to reveal the hidden tenderness, joys and fears of his all-too-human heart."

—Sylvia Nasar, author of *A Beautiful Mind*

"Eros and charisma. Are they linked? Or does the one masquerade as the other? Honor Moore offers a startling evocation of the malleability of sexual identity, her father's and her own, amid a vivid recollection of American church life at its high tide in the mid-twentieth century. The millions of

New Yorkers (and others) whose lives were touched by Bishop Paul Moore will read this book in wonder." —Jack Miles, author of *God: A Biography*

"*The Bishop's Daughter* is much more than another daughter's story; it evokes a time, a way of life, a habit of spiritual and political idealism. It reminds us of who we are as Americans, who we have been, who we really always were. Honor Moore speaks with the truest kind of love, both honest and compassionate, and allows us to accompany her—and she is an elegant and eloquent guide—on her fascinating journey of discovery and understanding." —Mary Gordon, author of *Circling My Mother*

"What is the nature of memoir, and how does it intersect with history? Honor Moore's rich and beautiful new book, *The Bishop's Daughter*, offers some answers to these questions. Moore's thoughtful investigations encompass the intimate history of her own family and the philosophical history of the Episcopal church; the great cultural network of the Protestant tribe, the ethics of twentieth-century marriage, and, finally, and most powerfully, the nature of passion. This is a gorgeous book, full of experience, wisdom and *caritas*."
—Roxana Robinson, author of *Georgia O'Keeffe: A Life*

"In part because it reveals an iconic and titanic figure, and in part because its author is a gifted writer with a capacious soul, *The Bishop's Daughter* must be a remarkable book. Spiritual, psychological, political and quirky, it is celebratory and revelatory too. . . . It movingly relates the inevitably bittersweet saga of the dashing Yale man, who finds faith, goes to war and lives, woos and weds the princess of his dreams; then sallies forth with her at his side to slay dragons and, sadly but truly, have nightmares. It is most memorably a frank, loving, faceted and fully realized portrait of an inspired rebel, visionary priest and passionate man who deserves no less."
—*Washington Times*

THE
BISHOP'S
DAUGHTER

ALSO BY HONOR MOORE

BIOGRAPHY

The White Blackbird: A Life of the Painter Margarett Sargent by Her Granddaughter

POEMS

Red Shoes

Darling

Memoir

PLAY

Mourning Pictures

AS EDITOR

The Stray Dog Cabaret: A Book of Russian Poems

Amy Lowell: Selected Poems

The New Women's Theatre: Ten Plays by Contemporary American Women

THE
BISHOP'S
DAUGHTER

A Memoir

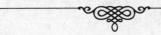

Honor Moore

W. W. NORTON & COMPANY
New York London

The lines from "Planetarium." Copyright © 2002 by Adrienne Rich. Copyright © 1971
by W. W. Norton & Company, Inc., from *The Fact of a Doorframe*: Selected Poems 1950–2001
by Adrienne Rich. Used by permission of the author and W. W. Norton & Company, Inc.

Excerpt from "The Tea Shop" by Ezra Pound, from *Personae*, copyright © 1926
by Ezra Pound. Reprinted by permission of New Directions Publishing Corp.

For information about permission to reproduce selections from this book,
write to Permissions, W. W. Norton & Company, Inc.,
500 Fifth Avenue, New York, NY 10110

For information about special discounts for bulk purchases, please contact
W. W. Norton Special Sales at specialsales@wwnorton.com or 800-233-4830

Manufacturing by Courier Westford
Book design by Helene Berinsky
Production manager: Anna Oler

Library of Congress Cataloging-in-Publication Data

Moore, Honor, 1945–
The bishop's daughter : a memoir / Honor Moore. — 1st ed.
p. cm.
Includes bibliographical references.
ISBN 978-0-393-05984-7 (hardcover)
1. Moore, Paul, 1919– 2. Episcopal Church—Bishops—Biography.
3. Anglican Communion—United States—Bishops—Biography.
4. Moore, Honor, 1945– 5. Fathers and daughters—United States. I. Title.
BX5995.M69M66 2008
283.092—dc22
[B]

2008001337

ISBN 978-0-393-33536-1 pbk.

W. W. Norton & Company, Inc.
500 Fifth Avenue, New York, N.Y. 10110
www.wwnorton.com

W. W. Norton & Company Ltd.
Castle House, 75/76 Wells Street, London W1T 3QT

1 2 3 4 5 6 7 8 9 0

For my siblings, each of whom would have another story

for my nieces and nephews and their children,

and to the memory of my parents

CONTENTS

Part III: REVELATIONS

Prologue

It is Easter, and in the darkness of the Cathedral of St. John the Divine the singing soars in descant, the gothic ceiling multiplying the clamor. And now, as if a great storm has ceased, there is no music, and in the silence held by five thousand worshipers, there come three resounding knocks. And as we wait, the massive doors swing open, an ethereal shaft of sunlight floods the dark, the roar of the city breaks the gigantic quiet, and there at the far end of the aisle, in a blaze of morning light, stands the tall figure of a man. My flesh-and-blood father, the bishop.

When I was a child, I accepted my father as a force of imagination that flared and burst and coruscated, an instrument of transformation. During World War II, he had survived a Japanese bullet and had a scar to prove it. "If my heart had been going this way instead of that," he announced once, rowing me across the lake in the Adirondacks, "you would never have existed!" Remembering his saying that now, I am startled. It was a joke of course, but it was also the text of a lesson that endured throughout our life together. My father had supernatural powers. His fate had determined my existence. I was something he had made and would continue to make. Physical independence from my physical parents was one thing—I got too big to hold my mother's hand, too big to ride on my father's shoulders—but it took me decades to escape the enchantment of my father's priesthood.

*   *   *

On Sundays and feast days, he became a giant in resplendent brocades lifting his arms as he preached. Or on Easter as a child, I am bedecked in my new finery, and there he is, dressed in white, accompanied by vested acolytes, sweeping along the dusty street on his way to the church; I get not a kiss but a blessing—his hand raised, fingers poised and moving through the air in the shape of a cross. At my father's first parish, the church was right next door; going to church was not a duty but a chance to be with the deepest part of him, to be inside his imagination. In the darkness at the altar rail, I would hold the wafer in my mouth, allowing it to become wet with the wine that burned down my throat. Take, eat, this is my body, my father would say. Just as I came to understand his splendid vestments were not ordinary clothes, I learned that during the Eucharist, the bread and wine were shot through with something otherworldly, something alive that vibrated and trembled, and when I watched my father, enormously tall, the color of his vestments blurry through all the incense in all the candlelight, it seemed to me he brought all this about, up there at the altar, enswirled in the fragrant smoke, the organ thundering, his voice carried by the King James language. It therefore made sense that when he sang Gregorian chant his voice would break and falter. He was being transported by what he called "the presence of God," a force much more powerful than his physical body. What happened to him seemed also to happen in me, behind my eyes, on the surface of my skin, and when it happened, I didn't think of how my mother looked with a baby on her hip, how my younger brothers and sisters shouted and screamed, or how awkward I felt at school. Instead, everything became comprehensible—simple, safe, and beautiful.

After the service, after removing the gold and the colors, after lifting the tiny white wafer as high as his long arms could reach, after administering wine at the altar rail and drinking what remained in the consecrated chalice, my father came home. Now wearing his black suit, he burst into the living room, where we all waited, the grownups drinking sherry, joking or talking seriously. I would run to him and he would bend and give me a kiss before going to talk to the others. Dressed in ordinary black clericals and the stiff white collar, he looked almost like other humans, quite normal, though taller than everyone else.

My father's extreme height made him seem even more distant than he might have had he been of ordinary dimensions. I thought his tallness had to do with the brocades, with the music, the candles, and the gold crosses that preceded him when he walked down the aisle, that it rendered him closer to God than those of ordinary height and therefore closer to enchantment. When I was a child, my father wore civilian clothes only on vacation or when he and my mother went to New York City once a week for their day off. When he dressed like ordinary men, it made me uneasy. I knew what the vestments were for and what his clericals signified. Wearing them, my father was clean and crisp, unsullied by everyday life. But when he wore a tweed jacket and a Brooks Brothers shirt, he became someone else.

The place where my father changed out of his day clothes was called the sacristy, and when we lived in Jersey City he took me there once, down a narrow hallway from the altar. It was a small, silent room, all dark wood that gleamed silkily in the parchment-yellowed light. There were closets that opened like gates and shallow drawers that pulled out evenly with a sound like exhalation. The warm air smelled like wax, bitter and smooth, and as I breathed I began to forget the color of daylight. Here, my father spoke to me in a grave voice and familiar things had other names. Getting dressed was vesting, a scarf was a stole, and the black sculpted hats were birettas. In the sacristy that evening, one of the other priests, a man who lived with us, looked at me with different eyes, as if he did not know me, and quietly folded his vestments. The boys who teased me when we played handball were quiet here, and so I bowed my head and didn't look at them.

My father showed me what incense looked like dry, and where you put it in the brass censer, which looked like a lantern with holes in it. He showed me the ciborium, the round silver box in which the bread was kept, white wafers that came to be called "the host" when he blessed them. He put on a cassock, buttoning it from his neck down to his ankles, and opened a tall narrow door to pull out a cotta, a white gathered garment with sleeves like wings. Hanging there were smaller cottas for the acolytes and the long cassocks, black for ordinary Sundays and red for festivals. In another closet were the golden brass crosses and candlesticks on long poles and fat creamy candles and a crucifix that was real gold, with a gold Jesus dead on it, and in a small cupboard with a caged door and a brass lock were communion "vessels"—silver chalices and silver plates kept separate, I thought, so they wouldn't lose the touch of God.

As my father opened the drawers for me, he explained the colors of the vestments splayed like the clothes of saints I later saw in Italian paintings. Red for blood to commemorate the deaths of martyrs, and red for fire to celebrate the day flames burned on the heads of the apostles without setting their hair on fire. Purple for Advent, the waiting for Christmas, and for Lent when Jesus went to the desert to pray for forty days before he came back to Jerusalem on a donkey, holding a palm as a scepter, a week before his death. Black for Good Friday, the day Jesus died and light went out of everything and every brass cross and icon in the church was veiled with black gauze. That day every year my father led all of us in the church in a procession to each of the fourteen pictures of Jesus carrying the big wooden cross on his way up the hill called Calvary where he would be crucified. There was a story for each picture: Saint Veronica wiped the sweat and dirt from Jesus's face, and his face appeared on her towel; Jesus stumbled and fell, the cross was so heavy. My father closed the drawer of black vestments and opened another: gold and white for Christmas, for Easter, and for Ascension, when Jesus rose up into the sky, to be in heaven with God, his father.

I believed I had been invited into the sacristy only because I was a little girl, that if I ever became a woman, I would no longer be allowed in, that once I became a woman the smell that would come from me would cause violence to God, as if when I became a woman I would have great stores of violence and sweat, enough to wipe out an entire town. The only female people who came into the sacristy were the women in the altar guild who wore flowered dresses and bowed their heads, or the nuns who wore black, and, my mother said, were married to Jesus Christ. The women in flowered dresses ironed the cottas and, after the priests doused the chalices in a bowl of water and polished them with white linen, put them away. The nuns, my mother told me, had no hair under the crispy white caps beneath their black veils; they cropped their hair like men, she said, in order to sacrifice their vanity to "the Lord." "What is vanity?" I asked her. "Looking in the mirror too much," my mother said.

Years later, my father told me that one Good Friday when I was little, after the three-hour service, after hearing him tell the story of the seven last words that Jesus spoke from the cross, of how a storm "rent" the walls of the great temple, of Mary watching her son die, I cried and cried. When he asked why I was crying, I said, Because Jesus died. I don't remember any of that, but I could tell you the whole story and as I told it I would see the darkness that descended as the rain fell, the light that broke through a gash in the clouds as the sky cleared, how it sounded when the young man on the cross said, My God, my God, why hast thou forsaken me. I would tell you about the old rich man, Joseph of Arimathea, who offered his own grave for Jesus at the last minute. I could make you see Jesus's face loosen as he finally died, and what I imagined Mary Magdalene looked like, sitting there on the ground looking up at him, the vials and pots of fragrant ointment on her lap.

In the sacristy, my father left being a father and a husband to become someone more like God, God who had a son but no daughters, God who had had a son without touching a woman. In the sacristy, as my father put on his vestments, I watched him become more like Jesus. When my father put on the long white alb and the colored chasuble over it, and knelt at the altar and raised his arms, he became more like Jesus still, someone without skin, without smell, without weight, in a separate dimension where everything shone from within and existed beyond any sound but music.

In the weeks before my father's death, the weather in New York was crystalline. It was April, and the leaves were coming in. There were a couple of days when we thought we could actually see the tiny pale green nubbles growing as we sat on the stoop watching people go by, imagining who they were and what they did. "We" were me, my father, and whatever other brother or sister was keeping watch now that the diagnosis was terminal.

I was teaching two classes. On Wednesday evenings I would read Fernando Pessoa or Paul Celan with student poets, and on Thursday mornings lead a workshop where students talked about each other's nonfiction. Mornings I walked my dog, returned telephone calls, and read student papers. The afternoons I was in charge of my father, I hurried downtown to his house on Bank Street. When he woke up, I might sit with him near the window in the front of his living room and help him go through his mail, tossing empty envelopes toward the wastebasket, which was, inexplicably, several feet away. It was like a childhood game, and when I missed, that old competitive glint came into my father's eye. But now when he aimed and threw, he missed too, and as I bent to rescue the torn envelope or crumpled letter, we'd both collapse into giggles. Some letters of course he wanted to answer. I'd make a call, regretting an invitation, or take a bit of dictation. Or I might say, "You don't need to answer this," and he'd look up in utter astonishment, and I'd say, "Do you really want to spend what might be your last months answering mail?" And then we'd both laugh, knowing there was no "might" about it, and that it would not be months at all.

"But what, but what . . ." he asked more than once, looking at me as if I knew every answer to every question.

"What, Pop?" I said.

"What's going to . . . happen!?" His eyes were very wide.

"What do you think is going to happen?" I would say, and I'd watch him think.

"I think I'll just . . . go to sleep," he'd say, relieved.

As April went on, he was less often awake when I got there, and so, after I checked in, I might wander around the Village, to buy flowers for the house, have a cappuccino, just get out. Afternoons were quiet on those intimate streets, and as I walked, I could feel my father's love for his life on Bank Street. He had been a fixture here for years, a giant of a man with white hair, tilting from side to side (he had a hip problem), often walking Percy, his tiny Yorkshire terrier. There was a café on the corner, and directly across the street, a one-story shop with tall windows and what looked from the outside like a vaulted ceiling. It must once have been a stable, I thought. Eventually I learned it had originally been a brothel. Now it housed a hairdresser who seemed always to have the most beautiful and exotic flowers in the room where he cut and styled hair.

My hair had gotten too long. There had been no time to have it cut, and now the weather was warm. I'd have my hair done in the room with the flowers, I imagined. One afternoon I went into the shop.

"Can you wash and blow-dry my hair?" The hairdresser looked at his schedule. "My father is dying," I said absurdly. "Can you wash my hair?"

"Is your father Bishop Moore?"

As he washed my hair later that day, he told me that his partner, the man sitting in the front room talking with a friend, the man in charge of the flower design company responsible for the amazing flowers, was a friend of my father's, and had recently stopped him on the street to ask him to have supper. "I'm dying, you know," my father apparently said. When we got out into the front room, the hairdresser said to his partner, "This is Paul Moore's daughter."

"Oh, I know Paul," the partner said.

The hairdresser said, "And you saw him the other day. What was it he said?"

"I'd rather keep it to myself," the partner said abruptly. I looked at the man's face. It was long and narrow and showed its years—he must have been about my age. What was my father's relationship to this man, I wondered. Did my father often have supper with his gay neighbors? When these men said, "Oh, I know Paul," how did they know him?

For more than ten years I had known that my father had had secret male lovers all his life, but in spite of that revelation inside our immediate family, the details of his actual gay life remained hidden. My father's bisexuality had become part of the way I thought about him, but it was not something we talked about, and that silence contributed to the pain and awkwardness of our life together. Now, in the weeks before my father's death, I had encountered a gay man who seemed to know things about my father's life that I did not. Had this man who arranged flowers loved my father's long body, longed for his extraordinary smile, listened to his sufferings? Would he ever talk to me about what my father was like as a gay man? Would I want him to? If my father's privacy was his privilege, what of his life was I, his daughter, entitled to know?

"I used to do Brenda's hair," the hairdresser said, breaking into my reverie. Brenda was my late stepmother. "And he," he said, pointing to his partner, the florist, "he used to do their flowers."

The last summer of his life, I visited my father in Stonington. The first morning was gloriously clear, and after we packed a picnic, we headed out, my father piloting me in his Boston Whaler across the Stonington harbor to a sandspit where we anchored in transparent shallows and wandered to a deserted beach. There we sat, he wearing the striped gondolier's shirt I'd brought him as a present, talking comfortably, looking out at the ocean, swimming, sunning. I asked if he remembered the time when I was tiny and we were at the beach at the foot of his grandmother's lawn in Massachusetts. We were swimming together, and he walked ahead of me out of the surf, and I was tossed and pulled under by a wave and rescued by a stranger. When I told him this story, my father apologized. He was always apologizing for things he'd done or not done in my childhood, as if by apologizing he might finally correct the brokenness of the past.

For years I had believed the past couldn't be mended, but that morning on the beach I felt we had finally come to some semblance of the relationship my father always said he wanted, a closeness I now understand I also longed for. In the past, after visiting him, it would take weeks to recover my balance—the chasm of silence between us seemed impossibly wide. I would manage to be courteous, but I was also distant. I was still in the process of identifying my wounds, and I wanted to avoid the rage that seemed always to descend if we differed. But this time he had made such an effort—a dinner party, a trip to my stepmother's grave—that I could not help but be moved. Before I left, I said stiffly how much I'd enjoyed our time together, and he looked at me, tears in his eyes, fighting emotion, and said, "I hope we'll see more of each other. It means a great deal to me."

I watch myself then, a woman in her fifties, in that small sunny room with her father in his eighties. There was so much unsaid between us. Would he ever talk to me about his love for the women he had married, of the nature of his love for men? Would I ever be able to make clear to him that it was safe to talk openly with me, that I wanted to talk about what had pulled us apart and also the complicated experiences of love that might bring us together? Of course I embraced him, and of course I gave him a kiss goodbye, but I couldn't surrender myself.

In the weeks before my father died, that restraint began to dissolve. At first it took the form of empathy, sadness that he'd never return to the Adirondacks where he'd gone every summer of his life (except one during the war), or that he'd never celebrate mass or preach again. As he got sicker, I spent more and more time at Bank Street, almost running from the subway station to the house. I didn't question this new urgency, I reveled in it. The longing seemed physical, and its satisfaction came in just being in my father's presence, taking in his weight, the shape of his head, his posture. And now I was losing him!

As I wrote in a journal each night, I could conjure him, almost, it seemed, bring back the years of our life together, images and dreams unfolding as I remembered. One day, about two weeks after he died, I started this book. "My father always wanted me to write about him," I wrote, and suddenly he came into view, enormously tall in silhouette on Easter morning in the cathedral doorway. I had turned away from my father, but he had never turned entirely away from me, and now, as the past opened, I was turning back to him.

Part I

———⧫———

FATHER

1

Prophet's Chamber

My father often told the story of St. Paul's conversion. On the road to Damascus, a Pharisee temple official and persecutor of Christians, then known as Saul of Tarsus, is brought to a halt by a sudden effulgence of such radiance, he is shocked to unseeing. Out of the swirling dust, the blinding light, the merciless heat, he hears a voice: "Why do you persecute me?"

"Who are you?" Saul responds.

"I am Jesus, whom you persecute."

It was clear always, when my father preached this story, that before his own conversion, he considered that he, too, had been Saul, a privileged young man, a good churchman, virtuous enough, suddenly broken open. In the years after he was wounded in the war, he came to believe God had spared his life so that he could become "holy." My mother reminded him of this when he learned, after recovering from his wound, that there was a chance he would not be sent back into combat. ". . . It is not your fault that you cannot fight now," she wrote during their wartime courtship, "and because your life was saved it seems to me it might mean that there are other things for you to do . . ."

My father was born in 1919, the beneficiary of vast wealth. He was a grandson of William H. Moore, who, as one of the Moore brothers of Chicago, had made a fortune in corporate mergers at the beginning of the twentieth century. William died in 1923, and my grandfather Paul, for whom my father was named, was a lawyer who sat on the boards of the companies his father and uncle founded; he also did some investing of his own. My father, the last of his four children, was a classic younger son. He was a beautiful child, but sickly as a little boy, awkward and incompetent athletically, especially in the wake of the accomplishments of his older brother, my Uncle Bill, who was a hockey star.

"When Paul was young," Bill told me, "he had seizures."

"Seizures?"

"You'd be sitting there at dinner and suddenly his head would be on the table. Jean Watson, who was his governess, once put a pencil in his mouth so he wouldn't bite off his tongue."

"Epilepsy?"

"I don't know what they were. He was just a weak little boy for a few years, and then, just before he went away to school at St. Paul's, he started to grow, and then he was all right."

In photographs prominent on the grand piano in the living room at Hollow Hill—the gentleman's farm in New Jersey where my father grew up and which I visited as a child—Bill wears a St. Paul's jersey, then a Yale sweater, and holds a hockey stick—a lance of primogeniture—and my father, a sweet-faced blond boy, poses with his dog, a golden retriever called Laddie.

As my father got older, his siblings, one by one, left for boarding school.

His older sisters, Fanny and Polly, went to his mother's alma mater, the Masters School in Dobbs Ferry, New York, and Bill to St. Paul's School in New Hampshire, and so, for five years, "young Paul" was the only child at home. He was loved, he always remembered, "too much"—not only by his mother, but also by the governess Jean Watson, who was Scottish and had taken care of all four children. After they had all gone off to school, Jean moved out of her room in the big house, but she continued to live on the property, knitting sweaters and socks for her absent charges, their pictures crowding the tables of the small house my grandparents provided, near the greenhouses.

"We were all she had," Bill said, "and there she was, alone in that house."

I remember the cookies she gave you if you stopped to visit, and my father's guilt: "I *must* go see Jean." I remember wearing the dark green sweaters striped with bright yellow that she knit for my brothers and sisters and me, and my mother packing away later gifts, blue sweaters and red ones, and sending them to children "who don't have as much as you."

My father's mother was also a source of guilt. He always described his relationship with her as "very close," but also, with some chagrin, as "suffocating."

"She had terrible headaches," he told me in one of the long conversations we had about her. "She was really an invalid for much of my childhood." In the diary my father kept at St. Paul's School, I don't find her taken to her bed, but when he's invited to go abroad the summer after Bill marries, he doesn't, because, he writes, "Mother, I am sorry to say, is still lonely and unhappy. I must do something about it." The happiness of his childhood was disrupted, he said in the oral history he recorded at Columbia University in the 1980s, only by his confusion about the "overwhelming" nature of his mother's love. On the other hand, it was his mother, he said, who was supportive of his decision to go into the church and "of any choice her children made."

Until he went away at twelve, my father spent falls until Christmas at Hollow Hill. He went to Peck School, a private school in nearby Morristown, and played with friends he kept for a lifetime, taking long walks and riding his horse on the farm's hundred acres, tending his dog, his pet roosters, playing tennis and golf. In January, the family migrated to Palm Beach, where they lived in an Addison Mizner villa, Lake Worth on one

side of the house, a wide ocean beach on the other. There, between fishing and boating trips with the "captain" and occasional golf with his
father, my father was tutored until the family returned home at Easter—
to Hollow Hill and to their Manhattan apartment on the eighteenth floor
at 825 Fifth Avenue—enormous, with three bedrooms, dining and living rooms, and a view of the seal pond at the Central Park Zoo. Evenings
"in town," he would walk down the avenue to visit his widowed paternal
grandmother at 4 East Fifty-fourth Street or accompany his mother to
the theater or the opera.

St. Paul's was an adjustment. At twelve, my father was small for his
age—his voice did not change until he was sixteen—and self-conscious
about it. How was he to become a man? Match his big brother, already popular with girls and certainly heading to Yale and a big college life? On the
New Hampshire campus, my father found himself, he wrote in his diary,
"a complete stranger"—none of his school friends from home had chosen
St. Paul's, and his brother, in his final year, held a privileged position as
a counselor to the younger boys. Not every student came from a family
as rich as the Moores, and while the school could hardly be described as
diverse—all male, all white, only a sprinkling of Catholics and Jews—
the quality of life in the stark, forbidding dormitory of sixty boys—"like
something out of an English novel"—brought a leveling. Each boy lived
in an alcove with a bed, a bureau, a chest, and one straight-backed chair;
minimal personal decoration was allowed.

The austerity of the sleeping quarters was in contrast to the extraordinary natural beauty of the campus, which had ponds for canoeing, playing
fields, forests and wetlands for bird-watching. My father soon came to love
the routine, the cold morning showers, how his wet hair froze as he raced
with a throng of friends to morning prayer in the Gothic chapel, past the
larger-than-life war memorial in the entryway, a naked youth dying in the
arms of a hooded Saint Gaudens–like figure. Once inside, he banged into
carved mahogany pews crowded with boys, landed in an assigned place,
then quickly knelt as the rector began morning prayer: "The Lord is in his
holy temple. Let all the earth keep silence before him."

The all-male world he found "a sort of magical utopian place." The
school was an escape from his mother and Jean, but it also represented
mental freedom, an entrance into the world of thinking and imagining. My father's striving to belong was soon relieved by a love of Eng-

lish literature, of Latin and Greek, and by an introduction to religion. St. Paul's was a church school, the headmaster was called the rector, and a half dozen of the "masters" were Episcopal clergy. My father took to the required sacred studies classes and to a master new to St. Paul's. Fred Bartrop was alcoholic, Anglophile, and, like many of the faculty, "a bachelor." Every afternoon at teatime, masters opened their quarters; my father and a few of his friends went often to Mr. Bartrop's, where their host, smoking his pipe, told them heroic stories of Christian bravery—Brébeuf, the French saint who had converted the Algonquins, burned at the stake by their enemies, the Iroquois; Saint Martin of Tours who stepped from his horse and cut his crimson cloak in half to dress a naked beggar; Saint Francis of Assisi throwing off his fine clothing and giving away his fortune, devoting himself to a ministry for the poor; the Anglican priests who ministered at the London docks at the turn of the century.

Sometimes "Bear," as they called Bartrop, spirited the boys away on a Sunday to St. John's Church in Portsmouth, New Hampshire. It was there my father first "vested" as an acolyte and walked in a procession ahead of the celebrant, there where he first experienced the Anglo-Catholic strain of the Episcopal Church—a practice different from the church he went to with his mother at home, where there were fewer candles, where brocade vestments were rarely worn, and where, like most Episcopal parishes of the time, the Sunday service was not a communion celebration. To my father and his small group of like-minded friends, "High Church," as Anglo-Catholicism was known, was threatening because it seemed close to the Roman Catholic Church that they had been brought up to consider alien. But it also had the allure of the forbidden.

My father joined the St. Paul's choir and was soon "acolyting" at school services. Under Bartrop's instruction, he became conversant with theology and the liturgy. "Bear" explained the Oxford Movement, which in the nineteenth century restored to the Church of England some of what had been torn away when Catholicism was repressed, first by the soldiers of Henry VIII and later by Queen Elizabeth's bailiffs—frescoed images of Christ and the saints, carved rood screens, confessionals and candlelight, the sensuality and color of vestments. The movement's tracts and the teachings of John Henry (later Cardinal) Newman awakened the moribund Church of England to the importance of the sacraments—Holy Communion and confession—as a means of growing personally closer

to God. Once, on a family trip to England when I was fourteen, we visited what remained of Rievaulx Abbey. When my father, standing on the
bright green grass amidst the rubble of stone cornices and broken arches,
pointed out where the altar would have been and described the destruction of the monasteries and the complexities of Henry VIII's conflicts with
the powerful abbots, my imagination raced, filling in color and sound as
his must have at Bartrop's fireplace.

By his fifth form, or junior year, my father and his close friends were
having tea or coffee at the Bear's several times a week. In a diary otherwise
marked by adolescent confusion, he is clear and certain when he writes
about religion, as when Dr. Drury, the headmaster, "made a spirited and
awfully good sermon," or when he found a High Communion service celebrated by a visiting priest unnerving: "It was well done, but I don't like
it." The idea of confession scared him, he wrote, but there was no question
that he would be among the boys who made appointments with Father
Wigram, a member of the Cowley Fathers, a contemplative order founded
during the Oxford Movement, when, at Fred Bartrop's invitation, the British monk visited St. Paul's the fall of my father's final year.

Since I always thought I knew the story of my father's conversion, I never
asked him to tell it. But six weeks before he died, at our last dinner out
together, I realized I wouldn't have another chance.

"He was a very, very old man," my father said, describing Father
Wigram. He emphasized the second "very" just as he would have telling a
story when I was a child, but now I was a grown-up woman and he himself
was a very *very* old man, his huge familiar hands frail but forcefully gripping the table where we sat in the dark paneled dining room of the Century Club. It was late October, he told me, and the leaves had fallen from
the trees, some floating on the surface of the stream which surged over a
dam beneath the Prophet's Chamber where Father Wigram was receiving
students.

"So you went into the room?"

"Yes," my father said quietly. "And we talked."

"About what, Pop?"

"Oh," he said, his eyes slowly blinking, "about everything."

As my father told the story, I could see the monk in his black cape, his black cassock, his strange "shovel" hat. My father had heard him preach at chapel and speak in his sacred studies class, but nonetheless, when he knocked on the door of Prophet's Chamber, he was apprehensive. How could he possibly tell anyone all the terrible things he had done? Why should he tell his sins to a man rather than directly to God? And he was confused, as he would later say, that his "religious emotion" came only "in spells."

"We talked," my father continued, "and then the old man said, 'I think God wants you to make your confession.' I couldn't believe he was asking me to do this!" Now my father was shouting: "No! No!" His voice resounded across the quiet dining room, his eyes blazing. "*No*, was what I first thought." He breathed fiercely and then he was silent.

"You were how old?"

"Sixteen." My father shuddering, that slender blond boy in family photographs, just shy of his seventeenth birthday, shuddering with terror or wonder. "It seemed too Catholic," he explained, "and the idea of sin was— scary, you know."

"Sex?" I asked.

"Oh, probably!"

I remember almost crying when I made my first confession at ten, kneeling in the small dark booth, a priest whom I knew solemn on the other side of the screen. My father was frightened not only because of the overpowering idea of disclosing his wrongdoings to a stranger, but also because when he was seventeen, even when I was ten, there was no order in the Episcopal prayer book for individual confession, the sacrament of penitence, in which God, through the medium of a priest, grants forgiveness for one's sins, an act called "absolution." In the Episcopal liturgy, absolution ordinarily took place in the context of the communion service, everyone saying the prayer of confession together; one kept one's sins to oneself and God. What Father Wigram brought to St. Paul's was indeed, as my father said, "Catholic"—it was a rite that Anglo-Catholic Episcopalians took from the Roman Catholic liturgy, translating it from Latin and adapting it.

I think God wants you to make your confession, said the monk in the room above the waterfall.

"And so I did," my father said. His calm surprised me. I had forgotten he was dying, and after his shouted "No!"s I expected a more dramatic cul-

mination. He continued. "I said my confession, and . . . and . . ." Then he
was speechless, tapping his head. As he searched for the word, I imagined
him staggering back from the old monk, everything changed. Now, as
my dying father, he was looking at me, his eyes shining. He had forgotten
what word he was looking for, and there was nothing on his face, a "nothing", that had the look of that dimension in which he was always alone.

But how did this momentous event happen in the life of a rich boy at
St. Paul's, in the life of this particular boy, my father? He had tossed off
my question about sex—"probably," but he went no further. Who was my
father as a boy? I wondered. And I remembered photographs: an impossibly
beautiful three-year-old posing with a Guernsey calf, a twelve-year-old in
shorts and a tennis shirt reclining with his golden retriever, the later snapshot of an impish beanpole of a teenager in a guide boat in the Adirondacks.
That night at the Century, my father told the story of his conversion as an
event that happened to that boy suddenly, dramatically, but as he recorded
it in his boyhood diary, the conversion was part of a larger narrative.

He was discouraged when he returned to St. Paul's for his final year. "I
haven't amounted to a damn up here & all because of being young—and
lazy." At first, as in previous years, what took him away from his despair
were afternoons rowing on Long Pond with Bartrop or bird-watching with
Mr. White, a master who was an amateur ornithologist—"marsh hawk,
yellow palm warbler, myrtle warbler, hermit thrush, seagulls, flickers,
greater yellowlegs . . ." But in spite of a "good" schedule of classes—Latin,
English, history, sacred studies—he was agitated by everyday boarding-
school life. When one of his friends got punished for having a Victrola in
his room, or when he burned with disapproval of another boy for being
"extravagant and weak," my father turned to Bartrop. But this particular
time, Bartrop had turned my father toward confession, a way into an independent spiritual life. Of the conversion that later gained such power, the
St. Paul's student wrote simply that "the father" reasoned with him "until
it was good." And that "impurities were straightened & the whole thing I
really understood better than I thought possible." It surprised me to read
that, after the confession, Father Wigram asked a question that would pre-
occupy my father for the rest of his time at St. Paul's and all through Yale:
"Have you thought of the clergy as a profession?"

"No," he had replied, but he noted in his diary that he could imagine
that answer someday changing. Both at school and at home when he was

in New York, he would seek out a confessor. During a weekend that fall, he went downtown to Trinity, Wall Street, only to find no priest—it was the wrong time of day. "A very disappointing thing, but I tried." Back at St. Paul's, he read Trollope—*Barchester Towers*—and James Russell Lowell's "The Cathedral," a meditation on the divergence between a religious and scientific way of life, and, at the end of January, commented that Jack Crocker, a visiting priest, had given a magnificent sermon: "It was truly inspiring. He is the kind of man that makes you want to become a clergyman. Incidentally I am in a quandary about that." During a long talk with his classmate Tony Duke about "life in general," he was reassured to discover his friend had the same ambivalence.

But my father's ambivalence never took him very far. On his seventeenth birthday, he was invited to read the lesson at chapel—"which was more fun than I have had in a lifetime"—and when his mother came to pick him up for the weekend of the Yale-Harvard game, he introduced her to Bartrop. In New Haven after the game, a visit to Bill's Yale room, and seeing John Gielgud in *Hamlet*—"marvelous"—he drove his mother home to Hollow Hill and, with difficulty, told her about the confession with Father Wigram. I imagine he feared she would realize, as he did, that his experience in the Prophet's Chamber marked his first real departure from home. He did not note her reaction, but apparently he'd asked her to send Bear a portable communion kit, and when he got back to school the following week it had arrived. After Bartrop died, it was returned—a small silver chalice and ciborium. I remember my father using it once celebrating a family communion in the Adirondacks, his large hands slipping the small silver cup out of its worn leather case.

That spring, his final term at St. Paul's, he was entirely taken up with the church: "The work goes on everywhere." he wrote in his diary. In Florida for spring vacation, he reflected that "being home & having a pleasant time makes me wonder about religion and I think less of the priesthood." But, as it would his entire life, the church retained its power: when he returned to school the week before Easter, he marveled that "Holy Week seems so for the first time," and on Good Friday, celebrated by a long service with meditations on Christ's last words, he stayed the entire three hours: "Bartrop did a magnificent job & the service meant everything wonderful." On Easter, after he and his friends Quigg McVeigh and Tony Duke accompanied Bear to a mass at St. John's in Portsmouth, his friend

Fred Herter confided that because of Good Friday and Easter, he had decided to make a second confession. "I have accomplished something thank God," my father wrote. In the next few days, he also successfully persuaded McVeigh. Confession seems to lead, he wrote, "to more belief and a new scheme of life, based on God." But his roommate Watty Dickerman resisted his evangelism—"afraid," my father was certain, "of strengthening his conscience."

The night before commencement, the service in honor of those graduating always ended with the rector saying a particular blessing: *Oh Lord, support us all the day long, until the shadows lengthen, and the evening comes, and the busy world is hushed, and the fever of life is over, and our work is done . . .* Afterward, everyone in the school, beginning with the youngest boy in the youngest class and ending with the most senior master, shook hands with each graduating boy in a solemn line in the cloister. "Almost everybody was sobbing," my father wrote in his diary.

Yale was as much a Moore tradition as St. Paul's. My father's ancestor George Beckwith had been a member of the original corporation, and his uncles and father and, of course, his brother had gone there. But none of this soothed the loss my father felt of the security of St. Paul's. His close friends had gone elsewhere, Tony Duke to Princeton and Quigg McVeigh to Harvard: again, he was a stranger. "The bottom has fallen out of my world with no end in view," he wrote in his diary; "religion helps but not enough, as I don't put myself out for it. I defeated last year with its problems . . . by keeping to & following out my ideas . . . Two thoughts today. I am not suffering from unpopularity which is lucky. 2: (this solves all) my end this year will be accomplished only by taking each affair & doing it well & good with prayer. The rest will come. I'll have no great uplift like new religion to help, but a good staff [of life] in old religion."

When my father reminisced with me about his years at Yale, he didn't talk about religion. He talked about his athletic incompetence; about taking Greek; about his secret society, Wolf's Head; and how he learned to drink. There were stories of being bailed out of jail by J. Press, the New Haven haberdasher; of driving a car up the steps of Widener Library on a Harvard weekend; of being picked up by the police at the end of his grandmother's driveway one summer in Prides Crossing. He was so much the "party boy" that his brother, Bill, was genuinely surprised when he began to talk about becoming a priest. But there is no doubt in the diary he kept at St. Paul's and a fragmented notebook whose entries begin in 1939 that while my father wrestled with the idea of a life in the clergy, he never questioned what happened to him that afternoon in the Prophet's Chamber.

In New Haven, as Bear had advised, he took himself to Christ Church, a renowned Anglo-Catholic parish. In spite of Bartrop's theology, the services at St. Paul's had been Low Church and plain; Christ Church was even more Anglo-Catholic than St. John's in Portsmouth. Its sung liturgy, thick incense, and black-clad nuns made my father wonder if he'd entered a Roman Catholic basilica by mistake. At first the "bells and things" made him so uneasy he begged off becoming an acolyte, but eventually he had a "mellow session" with the priest: "Just like with the Bear. This set me up considerably, as it is an anchor which I thought yesterday was not going to be any good." Within weeks he declared in his diary that his profession would be teaching religion, "probably at St. Paul's."

But he also felt an obligation to "do something for Yale," a tradition "drilled" into him by his father. For Bill, this had been easy—he was a varsity athlete—but for my father it was problematic. Working the first football match while auditioning for manager, he lost the sweatshirts the team wore after the game and knew then that he would never succeed. But, his father insisted, "at Yale you never quit," and so my father finished out the term. In the spring, he went out for rowing and won his crew "numerals"—the first athletic insignia of his life. "It meant more to me than most people would imagine." But eventually he gave up athletics and turned his attention to the Berkeley Association, the Episcopal student group of which he became president, and to Dwight Hall, the Yale community service organization, under whose auspices he was a Boy Scout leader. And he began to find intellectual excitement, first in a course on Alexander the Great taught by Professor Rostovtzeff, a distinguished classicist who "wove in the romanticism of the figure of Alexander into the economic and cultural life of the day." He continued Latin and Greek, but he ended up majoring in English. His drinking education, which he also took seriously, began with "Cuba Libres," rum and Coke, his first term in his freshman dormitory, with a group who christened themselves the Duck Club.

But no matter how much he drank on Saturday night, my father went to Christ Church on Sunday morning for "hung mass," as he and his friends called it. He was still grappling with Father Wigram's question: "Have you thought of the clergy as a profession?" By temperament, my father was passionate. He wanted to go "all the way for Christ," as he put it decades later in his oral history, but he didn't want to give up drinking, he didn't want to watch his language, and he didn't want to dress in black all the time as a good Anglo-Catholic priest would. His worship experience had been genuine ever since that first confession, but from time to time he considered the liturgy itself "a little much." He wanted to have it both ways: "I sort of despised people who were too puritanical about their religion . . . I thought it was sort of a good thing to be one of the boys and also to be a Christian." He served as an acolyte at Christ Church every Tuesday morning and joined Servants of Christ the King, a "rule of life" set out by the Episcopalian Order of the Holy Cross for young people, which required morning and evening prayer, daily meditation, confession four times a year, and retreats. His confessor was encouraging, but "he never sort of backed me into a corner and told me I was totally off base."

By the end of the summer before his last year at Yale, my father was seriously thinking of making a life in the clergy, and so he had a talk with his father. His brother Bill, now working in one of his father's businesses, would eventually become a banker; it was my grandfather's dream that if his younger son refused to go into business, he would become a lawyer. My father's sincerity about a religious vocation moved him not a bit. A young man in his position should take a year or two in business, my grandfather sternly advised, recalling that at Yale, after reading Browning and Scott, he'd wanted to become an English teacher, had even written some poems. But he'd gotten over it, as he was sure my father would get over this "ridiculous idea" of the priesthood. My father's overweening interest in the church was a "spiritual problem," which my grandfather advised he discuss with his grandmother, who had an interest in such things. She had traveled, studied Buddhism and Hinduism, had even met Mahatma Gandhi, and she and my father were very close.

In his diary after the conversation, my father berated himself for not being more definite. "I should have said from the start—I'm going to." But he also asked himself if his dream of the ministry was selfish. Could he characterize entering the priesthood as Christian "sacrifice" if not becoming a lawyer or a banker laid the entire burden of the family holdings on his brother? If it made his father unhappy? He even asked himself whether he was being unfair to himself in refusing his birthright. "Amusing thought," he wrote, "going to a directors meeting in a clerical collar."

That December on a retreat with Yale students, he led a meditation, his notes a neat outline in the same notebook in which he had recorded his conversation with his father. Like the beginning work of a poet that intimates what comes later, this early preaching foretold preoccupations that endured in my father's theology. Taking *The Pilgrim's Progress* as a text, he made a fable of his own story. A pilgrim struggles uphill from "the slough of despond." He stumbles and falls from weariness but ahead of him sees a column of rough wood rising from the ground. His eyes follow it up and recognize the cross. At twenty, my father had grown in the courage bestowed by his conversion three years before, the courage to live his own sense of possibility, its emblem—I might say metaphor—the cross. "His eye follows it up," he wrote in the meditation, "and then his burden is rolling away. He is free."

2

Guadalcanal

Who is the young man in uniform in the photograph framed in red? "Killed in the war" was a phrase that was repeated often enough when I was a child that it lost all substance: it was both serious—someone who died like that must have been a hero and gone straight to heaven— and not serious—there was no sense of what war was. Most of the other men my father had pictures of in uniform, including himself, were smiling, but George Mead was not. His dark hair is slicked back and in his dark eyes is a searching expression, as if he knew, when the photograph was taken, that he was moving toward his death. George Mead from Dayton, Ohio, lived across the hall my father's last year at Yale and became his best friend. Together, in early 1941, they'd made a snap decision to enlist in the Marines the day they saw a marine officer driving a convertible coupe across campus, the silver and gold insignia on his bright white cap glinting in the winter sun. When the officer stepped out of the car, my father wrote in his memoir, "the crimson stripe down the side of his blue trousers flashed in the sunshine." That was enough for him.

After two weeks fighting in the Solomon Islands on Tulagi, my father landed on Guadalcanal in August 1942, and his first evening there, asking after his friend, he was told that George Mead had been killed. "You don't know what a feeling that was," he wrote home. "He was such a superb person and so close. I'd been looking forward to seeing him for 2 weeks so we could laugh together about the various happenings. And God to think of him, of all people, dead. I still can't believe it." During a battle to control a village, fighting had become fierce—expected reinforcements didn't arrive—and one of George's platoon was wounded. "George, as was like him, rushed up to help him out," my father continued in his letter. "He bent over the wounded man and as he did the Japs opened up. It was instant death, thank goodness. But why did it have to be George?"

I always knew my father had been wounded at a place called Guadalcanal, and as a child I boasted about his medals. I liked to watch the surprise on the faces of boys at school when I told them my father, the priest who wore vestments that flowed to the ground, had been a hero in the war. Anything to mitigate the strangeness of being the daughter of "a priest." In Jersey City, where we lived close to two huge Roman Catholic churches, I explained that my father dressed like a Catholic priest but that the Episcopal Church was catholic with a small c and therefore priests could marry; in Indianapolis, where the churches nearby were Presbyterian and Methodist, I explained that in spite of my father's stiff white collar and bright purple shirt, he was definitely Protestant. It was in Indianapolis that I finally learned how my father had won those medals, what he'd really done in the war, just how close he'd come to death.

He won the Silver Star, the Marine Corps citation read, when, "upon seeing two of his men stranded on the opposite bank of the Matanikau River, and unable to withdraw due to their wounds, Second Lieutenant Moore, at great risk to his life, unhesitatingly swam across the river, continually swept by heavy Japanese machine-gun fire, and, with the help of his sergeant, brought the two men back to safety." For a later battle, he won two more medals, the Purple Heart and the Navy Cross: "Pressing forward in the face of a steady barrage of hostile machine-gun and mortar fire, Second Lieutenant Moore, by aggressive charges and skillful employment of his units, forced the enemy to retreat to the ocean's edge. As the Japanese fought desperately to survive, he stayed on the line with his platoon, directing its fire under terrific assaults by the enemy, and urged his men forward in a series of hand-grenade and bayonet charges, personally leading their successive attacks. In the final stages of the engagement, although critically wounded by a hand-grenade fragment and lying prostrate and helpless, he continued to encourage his men to keep attacking until he lost consciousness."

"I won the medal for the whole platoon," my father told a reporter the spring of 1943; he was home on convalescent leave after nearly five months in military hospitals. The journalist, and no doubt my father, took note of the contrast between the terror of battle and the terrace at Hollow Hill where they sat for the interview—Plowright, the butler, appearing with a tray of iced tea, quietly placing it on a table under a blooming apple tree as "the returned fighter" recalled his three months in the Pacific campaign, the five battles he had fought, the death of his best friend, the six men killed and four wounded out of his platoon of twenty.

As soldier and interviewer gazed out beyond the terrace at the gardener transplanting violets at the end of the lawn, at the "glistening furrows" of a newly plowed field, my father told the whole story. His recollections, the journalist wrote, "came crowding." Marching from 3 a.m. until six the next evening in terrific heat. One meal a day of canned C ration. Cold rain at night. No sleep, guns on both sides firing. The sick-sweet smell of dead Japanese on the hills, in the river, at water holes. If you were thirsty, you dipped your helmet in "shell hole water"—filthy and scummed with mosquito larvae—treating it before you drank with iodine and chlorine. "Until a man's temperature passed 104° he was considered well enough to pull the trigger." Sick marines in foxholes, weak from malaria, each holding a gun. Dead marines with flies on them. Japanese prisoners retching. My father leads an assault, his men running across a sandspit at the mouth of the wide, shallow river. Marines wading and mucking, bullets splashing beside them "like rain," grenades "swishing" overhead, the platoon getting smaller as boys are killed, and then he hears a low gurgle of blood and realizes he himself has been hit.

I knew that the big scars on my father's chest and back had come from a Japanese bullet that went right through him. I had an image—darkness, blood everywhere, a Japanese soldier standing over him with a rifle. But that is not how it happened. The sandspit was in the open and it was daytime, which was why, when my father rose to his knees to determine where the "troublesome" machine-gun fire was coming from, he got hit—from the front. I knew he got shot through the chest because in the Adirondacks when he rowed with his chest bare, or took us sailing wearing just bathing trunks, his scars were part of the event—his arms rowing, his head turning in pleasure to survey the expanse of the lake, his voice telling the story of how as an eight-year-old he'd been taught to sail when old Louie simply pushed him off from the dock, alone in the sailboat, no paddle, and said, Sail. But I can't keep my eyes from the scars. My father never told me what the battle was like, but he explained that the scar on his chest was small because that was where the shot had gone in, and that the large, cavernous splat which marked the skin on his back was where it had come out. Did the bullet, I wondered—it was a bullet, not the fragment of a hand grenade—go out my father's back and wound another soldier? And another?

"Contrary to most of the articles I've read," my father told the reporter, "I found that everyone is more and more scared with each battle until he reaches a point and then cracks."

"Dear Mother and Dad," he wrote three days after he was wounded, "No longer where I was because some yellow no-good lined up his sights and squeezed—" The shot had gone through his lung, an inch from his in-beating heart, barely an inch from his spine. "The bullet had my name on it, but I guess they spelled it wrong."

He was put on a stretcher and transported by jeep to a dressing station where he was given sulfa drugs and blood plasma. "They said if the jeep hadn't been there, I'd have bled to death before they could have moved me. When the war is over, I want to have a jeep to go fishing," wrote the twenty-two-year-old who fished for trout in the Adirondacks every summer, for blue marlin in Florida every winter. After the dressing station, the fallen fighter spent the night on a stretcher in a field hospital—"a hot stuffy dugout"—and early the next morning was taken by plane—breathing through his good lung—to a Quonset hut hospital in the New Hebrides. There he and tens of others waited for the hospital ship that would take them to New Zealand. It arrived on November 15, my father's twenty-third birthday, a bright white oasis entering the harbor, a giant angel, its name the *Solace*. I remember my father telling the story of being in the New Hebrides hospital for two weeks—how he watched through the windows as his fellow wounded were carried out and onto the ship one by one, how he marveled that he was being rescued on his birthday, how hard it was when he was not taken with the others but left behind, the only patient in the hospital, and given no explanation.

After the first days, he felt no pain, but he had a constant fever and a nightmare that woke him screaming every night: Tojo's Imperial Army making a frontal attack on his hospital bed. After ten days, the *Solace* returned. On the ship there was real food, he wrote home, and women nurses—like "beautiful music in a factory"—his own window out onto the Pacific, the excitement of steaming into the harbor at Wellington, New Zealand. I remember certain words. He got *malaria*. It was treated with *quinine*. For weeks his fever hovered between 100 and 103 degrees, and then, when his lung abscess kicked up, he was seized with violent coughing and a fever soaring to 105 degrees, days spent with his legs tied higher than his head so his lung could drain. Then the infection began to break, and he was "fine," by which he meant "no pain, good appetite, etc."

"You should have seen the oranges," I can hear him saying, his voice like his mother's, sliding up an octave of pleasure, his scar hit by the August sun as he rows across the lake.

But in daily family life, my father did not make a practice of talking as he had to the reporter, which is why, once when I was eleven, I made a terrible mistake.

It was September, we had just moved to Indianapolis, my father to become dean of the cathedral there; we'd arrived to some fanfare, and now he was called Dean, rather than Father, Moore. Eli Lilly was the chair of the vestry and my father had been his candidate—the old man had made his millions in drugs and collected his art and his rare books. Now he wanted the prosperous, social, "lily-white" cathedral, a landmark located on Monument Circle, at the very center of the city, to reach out to the surrounding community, poor white people from the Appalachians and poor black people from the South. A dentist in town, Gadi Lawton, who had been a "point" in the battle in which my father was wounded, gave an interview to an Indianapolis paper about the marine heroism of the new dean. My father was irritated that the coverage was about what he'd done in the war. By then he had made a name for himself at the downtown ministry in Jersey City, and it was that work for which he wanted to be known. The conservative Indianapolis newspapers, he growled, were more interested in the Pacific campaign and its convenient racist apparatus than in good housing, integration, and services for the poor. On the southern hem of the Midwest, Indianapolis was a segregated city mere decades from its legacy as a stronghold of the Ku Klux Klan.

I was in seventh grade, and I read the newspapers eagerly, considering my father's irritation false modesty. I learned for the first time that he had rescued the two men at Matanikau, that he had fallen to his knees, continuing to urge on his platoon until he fell unconscious. It made me look at my father differently to think of him as having saved lives, as having continued to give orders as he passed out, as having almost died. But Gadi Lawton, who had a big laugh and a great smile and who my father said was fond of climbing coconut trees on the base at Guadalcanal, also told another story about my father in the Marines. By now, there were four of us children at "grown-up" dinner after the three babies were put to sleep, and because supper at the big table in the dining room was always a theatrical occasion, I joined in when my mother started to rib my father about all the publicity, including Dr. Lawton's story. "And this big tall guy," I declared, affecting the joshing of a war buddy, "in a great feat of courage, ran across enemy fire . . . for a pack of cigarettes!"

I thought of this as having happened "long ago"—my heroic father, willing to risk his life not only for others but for a slightly sinful pleasure! But when I began the joke, my father, without a word, lurched from his chair, leaving abruptly vacant the seat at the head of the table where he'd just been merrily talking or carving the chicken. There was, after he left the room, not only vacancy but shocked silence. And I had caused it.

"Go after him," my mother said. I looked at her. I had never seen her so grave. "Go after him."

And so I left the dining room, my body so heavy with fear I could hardly walk, my brothers and sisters uncharacteristically quiet and solemn. What would I say to him? If only I could take back what I had said, I would have my father there in his chair, telling his jokes, awkward as he always was when he carved. The house seemed so big. I crossed the wide hallway and looked in the living room where we had evening prayer, but he wasn't there. Perhaps he had gone out. I looked toward the front door, which was open, the evening sun casting a shadow across the wide summer screen, the driveway outside, my heart pounding. And then I slowly climbed the stairs, made my way along the carpeted hallway to my parents' bedroom, and knocked. "Come in." He was sitting on the chaise longue near the window. As I went toward him, I could see he was holding his Bible open, one tissuey, gold-edged page between his long fingers, his hand trembling. Trembling myself, I approached. He looked like a stranger, broken there on the long chaise, his slender legs suddenly fragile in the loose black of his clerical trousers.

"I'm sorry, Pop," I said.

At first he would not look up, but when he finally did, I could see he'd been crying, and I'd never seen my father cry. I remember sitting down on one edge of the chaise, touching his legs. Even when I crawled up close, he didn't turn into my father again, he just strangely nodded his head. "His eyes still had the '1,000 mile stare,'" he had written his sister after seeing one of the boys he'd rescued. His own eyes had it right then, the thousand-mile stare. I was inside the stare now, meeting a man who was nakedly my father. The only father half close to this one I had ever seen was the man whose voice sometimes nearly broke when he preached about the Crucifixion, as he tried, I now understood, to bring into the church something of what he had learned in that faraway tropical place where he almost died. What was it like living inside this place where I saw him now, this place where, surely, he was always alone? I was scared, but even so, if he had allowed it, if he had cried again or put his arms around me, I would have tried to tell him, even at only eleven years old, that I wanted to know and understand what had happened to him, if only he would tell me about it. But all he could manage was, "I'll be all right." And then he touched me as a priest would a worshiper, saying he'd stay upstairs, that I should go back down to supper.

*   *   *

At the end of January 1943, three months after he was wounded, my
father was shipped from New Zealand to San Francisco. "Even the fumes
coming up in the ambulance smelt like lilac blossoms," he wrote home.
In April, he was back at Hollow Hill, where the lilacs were real, the nar-
cissus in bloom, the shrubs budded, his parents proud, the press calling.
The summer before in Tulagi, the comforts of life at home had come to
him in reverie—in a letter, he'd spun a picture of the family at Rockmarge,
his grandmother's seashore house, gathering for her birthday on a beautiful August evening for cocktails on the porch—"all clean and attractive
and fond of one another with Granny enjoying each minute of it all and
all of us making a justifiable fuss over her." In the distance, the offshore
islands glowed in the sunset, "a sail or two is white on the dark blue sea,
the pines a dark green, the lawn long and smooth." For supper, fish chow-
der and duck and gooseberry sauce, "the old family gags being cracked,"
his eighty-five-year-old grandmother unable to hear but smiling anyway,
opening her presents—the dressing gown from her school friend Miss
Enders, tea from some "queer Chinaman" to be "raved over and wondered
at." After supper, bowling in the alley in the basement with its "smell of
wood" and the next morning a swim from the beach at the foot of the
lawn and in the afternoon golf at Myopia, the club down the road.

But on Tulagi, he wrote in the same letter, "before the eye reaches the
water's edge, it must cross the beach and on the beach lie the dead." More
dead in the center of the golf course left by the British colonials, and hanging in the humid air, the familiar sickly fumes of human decay.

Now, at Hollow Hill, there was silence that was not ominous, no ocean
of Japanese destroyers to disrupt an evening on the terrace. At first he felt
relief and bland pleasure, felt, actually, nothing unusual. But one evening
in the book-lined library within days of coming home, having cocktails
with his parents, his father in the big chair, his mother dressed for dinner,
he feels "a strange lump" at the bottom of his feet; it comes up his legs, he
begins to weep, cannot stop "for half an hour." This happened again and
again, whether he was at home at Hollow Hill or in New York, staying at
the family apartment. The company of his parents; the concerned tenderness of his old nurse, Jean Watson; the memories of childhood—all of
this, when he needed clarity, became suffocating.

He was a stranger again, this time even to himself. Now a man of twenty-three, he had been a boy just a year earlier when he left for the Marines, his references juvenile: "How did Dick Tracy escape?" he had asked in a letter from Guadalcanal. He had been prepared for basic training by playing competitive games as a boy, but nothing had prepared him for combat: "On the third day, I was sitting in the midst of my platoon in position defending the C.P. [command post] when a sniper ran across the field below. We opened fire. It seemed like shooting clay pigeons." The man fell, and when they reached the body they found photographs of his children in his jacket. "He smelt violently for two days. My hands aren't bloodless." My father was aware of the power of language and allusion. *My hands aren't bloodless*—he knew his Macbeth; Shakespeare had been his reading on the transport ship. "The Marines changed him," his brother said. He was no longer even slightly physically soft, and the sweetness he'd had as a child was submerged in the Marine Corps manner of mental toughness. My father's new self was stronger, but also broken. Eventually, when he and my mother fell in love, he would confide in her, trying to describe what he called his "confusion." But only in talking to a fellow veteran of combat was there nothing to explain, nothing my father had to do to feel the elemental self he had discovered in battle, a self intimate with the nexus of life and death, where as a matter of course one thing is transformed into another.

Posted to Seattle after he recuperated, my father began, in memory, to observe himself as he had been that spring after coming home, his disconsolate staggering and meandering, those evenings out drinking martinis and smoking cigarettes, the arch, funny chatter fading when across the room he saw a marine in uniform standing at the bar. He'd go over to him, simply to shoot the breeze, maybe buy him a drink, and feel, he wrote, "closer to the stranger than to my own family." He began to wonder why he had been spared, why on earth the bullet had come so close to his heart and his spine without killing him. Between nights of drinking too much, of parties with navy enlisted women (WAVES) or Seattle girls, of mornings coaching the marine rowing crew, of his fierceness placing this or that "lad" on discipline, he began openly to think that perhaps he had been saved to do something else with his life.

He could dream all he wanted about becoming "holy" after the war, but now, as a marine hero, my father was called upon to give speeches, interviews, and talks in which he not only told, in an upbeat way, the story of his platoon, but also cheered on the war effort: "Out there," he would say, "we used to promise each other that any of us who got back would tell the people here what war in the Pacific is like, how tough it is. We thought that if people really knew what it's like, that would hurry production so that our job could be finished and the boys could come home." In time he grew tired of what he called "Guadalcanal trash" or "the same old thing"; the story he wanted to tell would not fit the blunt rhetoric of the propaganda offensive. When he was approached to write something about a Christian going to war, he quickly agreed. The invitation came from *The New Start*, the magazine of the Order of the Holy Cross, an Episcopal order of monks that sponsored Servants of Christ the King, a group my father had been part of at Yale. Here was an opportunity, outside the context of the war effort, to wrestle with his anguish over killing.

At his desk at the University of Washington, where he was commander of marine recruits, my father wrote from the private conscience of a young man who took the Ten Commandments seriously but who had killed enemy soldiers, whose best friend had died in combat with that same enemy, and who, he sometimes thought, had himself died. "Perhaps you have noticed the break that comes in a soldier's voice in the middle of a story," he wrote, "how his eyes turn away, or how his breath comes deep for a moment. Once in a great while how his eyes fill and his lower lip quivers! He may leave the room, or break a match hard with his fingers. He has seen the face or heard the voice of the dead in that moment . . ." Unable on active duty to use his name, he wrote anonymously and in the third person. He drew on his grief about George Mead's death, the fellowship he felt in his platoon, with other marines dead and living, with any young man who might approach battle. Without the fear he'd felt writing home, that his letters were too "depressing," he portrayed himself as a young man who had discovered at seventeen a desire for depth and meaning in a dramatic conversion, who had found in the experience of battle a spiritual resource that could take him forward into adulthood. After the piece appeared in the magazine, he was asked to expand it, and in 1945, thousands of a pamphlet called *A Marine Speaks of War* were published by the Church of the Advent, in Boston, still without an author's name.

It was not that my father wrote in the pamphlet things he had never said before, but that the person who was writing was different. The soldier writing home had easily described the Japanese enemy to his five-year-old nephew as "monkeys without tails" or to his sister as "yellow swine." But the first dead enemy the anonymous marine describes is a "pathetic little Japanese boy curled up by the side of a trail with beardless cheeks and small feet who did not seem like the fierce Japanese soldier he'd read about." Here, in response to the "violent shame" that came over him in battle, the marine admits that "we" are guilty too and "asks God for forgiveness." He acknowledges too that when "on a dark beach he heard that his closest friend had been killed trying to rescue another man . . . a burning anger was his only reaction . . . and a desire to fight."

The last winter of his life, I went to Bank Street to meet my father for supper. He was wearing blue jeans and a red plaid flannel shirt, and though he looked much younger than he was, he was unsteady and I held his arm as we walked to the restaurant. He had just received the news that his melanoma was probably terminal, but his spirits were high, and he was calculating whether in the time he had left he would be able to finish a new book.

"What is the book, Pop?"

He told me that he'd entered the priesthood not "to have people admire me" or "to do good," but because he always had a longing to celebrate the Eucharist. I had never heard him say exactly that before. In the book, he would talk about some of his most powerful experiences celebrating, and how the time and place where a particular Eucharist had occurred—Vietnam during the war, in a dry riverbed in India for a hundred thousand people, in Mississippi during the civil rights movement—illuminated its meaning. The restaurant was a small, dark French place in the Village, and as we ate our *moules* and our rack of lamb, he asked my advice. He had a few chapters, he said. If I were in his situation, what would I do? Would I go back and revise or would I forge ahead? "I have a year or two," he said. "I'm sure I can finish."

I could hardly bear it—I feared, we both feared, that he might not have that much time. "What would you do?" he asked. I told him that if I had a limited amount of time, I would keep writing. Now he was like one of my students, suddenly with a little encouragement full of inspiration. "What are you working on?" he asked.

"Poems," I said.

"I thought you were writing a novel."

"I put it aside." He nodded.

A little while later, he asked again with the same intensity what I would do in his situation. He didn't know he was repeating himself. "I would forge ahead, Pop, I really would."

"Okay," he said with relief. "That's what I'll do." And he began to tell me again about the dry riverbed in India, the hundreds of thousands of worshipers, and the time in the 1960s when, at a retreat with Roman Catholics, having spent an evening in discussion that ended in sadness that intercommunion was forbidden, the group spontaneously knelt for a Eucharist after my father, just told of the sudden death of a friend, broke into tears. "This is what matters to me," he said, opening his big arms as if at an altar, "you know?"

Sunday fell on the fifth day of combat on Guadalcanal. The Eucharist was celebrated by the chaplain, who was Roman Catholic. The service took place in blinding sunlight on a flat field near the beach where the dead lay, hundreds of dirty marines kneeling. "Mud was on their clothes, perhaps blood on their hands. The musty smell of the tropics and of the dead was in the breeze. Everything was rotten. Many men had seen close friends killed. All had gone through too much already. Some leaned on their rifles. Others had laid their pieces carefully beside them." This was a different voice than the one in which he'd described that morning in a letter home: "Catholic Mass near the cemetery with a tin roof to support the altar. Many dirty Marines as Congregation. The Priest wore an immaculate chasuble— probably the only clean thing on the island. One could hear firing in the distance." Writing as the anonymous marine, my father took the chasuble as an emblem. "They knew that despite their experience, the part of their soul that was God's would be white . . . Perhaps the simile is sacrilegious, but that first Mass seemed more like taking a bath than anything else. For those who had not been able to go to confession, this was our first real strong contact with the living God." And then, as the anonymous narrator of *A Marine Speaks of War*, my father came into the voice that years later marked his power as a preacher. "Living, that was it. God was alive, had been alive, would be alive, alive, alive. It is hard to tell what that would mean. There was a lesson. Man could fall sick, bleed, die, rot. But God was alive. God could not rot. God was clean and alive. The living God. The resurrection. When God did die, when Christ suffered the unholy indignity of death, it was for us, that we might overcome death." Reading the old pamphlet, I could hear his voice, his fist pounding the pulpit. Now "the boy was learning," my father wrote of himself. "He was growing hard to the sights and the feelings of war, but he was growing deeper . . ."

3

Inseparable

It was near twilight, the glossy time when you can't imagine the lake is ever bright blue or its surface ever roughened by wind, or that the wind can blow so hard in one direction you can't row against it. We were moving tranquilly, the prow of the old amber guide boat opening a path through black water, my father rowing, oars dipping one at a time, making the only sound in a silence so encompassing even occasional shouts from the shore seemed a form of quiet. He was wearing "ordinary clothes," was dressed like the Yale man he was, as if these were the same faded khakis he'd worn in New Haven in 1939, the same Lacoste tennis shirt, gray-green Shetland sweater the worse for wear, and worn white sneakers. I was ten, or maybe eleven, and it began as a game: Poppy, tell me about your old girlfriends! I expected to hear again about "Lois," whom he had dated in Seattle during the war, about whom my mother teased him mercilessly. He stopped rowing, let the boat glide, and told a story.

After the months in the New Zealand military hospital when he came home, my father found himself at parties with Jenny McKean, four years younger than he was, just nineteen, black hair to her shoulders curled under and so smooth that in photographs it looks polished. He had known her summers when he went to Rockmarge, and his parents and Jenny's were in the same social group; the McKeans lived in Beverly, just miles away. Through her father, Quincy Adams Shaw McKean ("Shaw"), Jenny was descended from Thomas McKean, who had signed the Declaration of Independence, and Louis Agassiz, the scientist. Her mother, Margarett Sargent, a modernist painter and sculptor who had exhibited in New York, was one of the first in Boston to collect modernist art, a fourth cousin of the painter John Singer Sargent, and a granddaughter of Horatio Hollis Hunnewell, a Boston philanthropist and horticulturalist who'd made a fortune in railroads in the years after the Civil War. By the spring of 1943, when my father began to court Jenny McKean, her family had all but fallen apart. Her mother, who had always had extramarital affairs with both men and women, was an undiagnosed manic-depressive who drank to medicate herself, and she hadn't had an exhibition in nearly a decade. Within two years she would enter a sanitarium, and within five she and Shaw would be divorced and Shaw married again.

My parents always said they first met at a dog show on the McKeans' lawn and first noticed each other in a Vermont drugstore. By 1943, when my father was back from the Pacific and recuperating, Jenny was at Barnard in New York, and one night, when he met his old friend Cord Meyer for a drink, Jenny was Cord's date. My father let his admiration be known by aiming a siphon bottle and shooting seltzer at her from across the table, all of them collapsing into laughter. Later he asked Cord if Jenny was his girl, and if not, he'd take her out. On their first date, my father took my mother to the St. Regis, where they danced to "I'm in Love with a Soldier Boy." Later, in the darkness of the Kretchma, a Russian café on East Four-teenth Street, they talked and talked and talked. "If a man can tell someone else of his fear," my father later wrote of that evening in a letter to their unborn child, "he lessens it." As he lit Jenny McKean's Chesterfield, his hand touched hers, and they fell in love.

"She was so beautiful," he always said, repeating the story. During the summer of 1941, he'd known her as just a kid, one of "the younger set," a group of friends who went to parties together; she'd been his friend Potter's girl, and they'd all called her "Nutty Brown" because of her tan and because her navel, exposed by her fashionable two-piece bathing suit, reminded someone of a nut. Now she was almost twenty, so sophisticated my father was shocked when she told him she was only nineteen. In a newspaper photo, they smile for the photographer, sitting on the banquette at LaRue, a favorite bistro; she is wearing shiny black and white stripes, and he is in uniform. "Marine hero, Boston socialite," reads the caption. The gunshot wound had healed enough for them to dance the fox-trot, and their long, searching conversations continued—his guilt at having killed Japanese soldiers, her shame about the mother who drank alone in a huge dark room hung with paintings of empty courtyards and white horses. "Everyone thought we were engaged," my mother said. She was certain that after his leave my father would choose a post at the Marine training program in New Haven so they could spend weekends together. But sometime in early July, they went for a walk at Rockmarge, down the willow path to the ocean.

"All of a sudden he looked at me," my mother remembered.

"I probably won't see you so much this summer," my father announced. "I've been posted to Seattle." After he told her this, my mother cried for two days.

Telling me his version of the story that evening on the lake, my father seemed a bit embarrassed, certainly full of regret. "I wrote her about a girl I picked up in a bar in Minneapolis," he said. "An awful girl. Everything Jenny wasn't. Coarse, uncivilized, voluptuous, a tart."

"He wrote to me in detail about a girl he picked up in a bar," my mother said.

"I wrote your mother continually," my father said, "until I got to Seattle, and then, after a while, I met Nona."

Nona. I looked out across the lake. "Like the song?"

"Yes," he said.

And then we both sang: *"Nona is like a dream come true / So sweet and unaffected.*" He told me more—about her family's enormous house outside Seattle, about tennis games and weekend dinner parties, how he might have married her if she hadn't been Catholic. An Episcopal priest, he explained, couldn't have a Roman Catholic wife.

The next time I heard about Nona Clark was in the dining room of the Pierre Hotel in New York. Gami, my father's mother, had taken us, my father and me, out to dinner at the beginning of my junior year in college. The waiters, in Raj costume, tried to feed us chicken curry. I think we all had lobster Newberg. I made some comment about a pretty blonde across the room looking at my father as if she knew him, and Gami, almost eighty, took up the teasing: "Yes," she said gleefully, "and you went to the St. Regis to meet that woman from Seattle who telephoned. Went to meet her, even though you didn't think you should!"

"That was after Nona Clark's husband shot himself," my father explained evenly. "She needed to talk."

I imagined the scene: hotel bar, a beautiful woman with red hair—he'd told me she had red hair—dressed in mourning, soothed by conversation with a tall young man she'd known as a marine before both married others. I next heard about Nona not long afterward when Luke, my first serious boyfriend, was drafted and broke up with me before enlisting in the Marines, a choice inspired by my father. It was 1966, and the Vietnam War was just reaching the consciousness of students like me. I had "lost my virginity" to Luke the summer before in his Riverside Drive sublet. (Of course, I did not tell my father I had slept with Luke—marriage was a "sacrament," premarital sex was a "sin.") In his pastoral voice, my father reassured me: he'd married my mother even though he'd gone to Seattle before they were engaged; and even though he'd gone out seriously with Nona Clark, he found that he was still in love with my mother. Seattle had been a choice, he explained—he could have taught in the East to be "near Jenny," but he needed "more life on his own." Perhaps, he suggested, my boyfriend Luke also "needed freedom from all his burdens." That my father considered my mother burdensome passed unquestioned into my mind, as did his characterization of me as part of what he called Luke's "knapsack of stones."

Planning a trip to Europe a year later, the summer before my senior year in college, I saw that I could pass through Geneva and asked my mother if she thought I could visit Nona Clark. The name had come up

again, and with it the sense I had that night on the lake that I might finally
come to know my father, though now it seems to me I also wanted to know
something about my parents' marriage. My mother encouraged me, but it
must have been difficult. Nona's name had come up again because, weeks
before, she had come for a drink on her way through Washington. "We,
I mean they, talked for an hour," my mother said, reporting with sarcasm
that she'd made a point of sitting next to Nona, whom she'd met only
briefly twenty years earlier. Apparently Nona never turned to face her,
looked only at my father, who sat across from her in the blue easy chair.
She'd called my mother the next day and apologized—her neck had been
stiff. To me, then, just twenty, "Nona Clark" was part of a distant past, but
of course my father and Nona had been involved fewer than twenty-five
years before, which I now understand is no time at all.

Nona was the only child of a lumber tycoon's son who had married
a Catholic and converted. Sheltered and adored at her family's estate in
the Highlands, Seattle's version of Tuxedo Park, she made her debut both
at home and in San Francisco and went East to Radcliffe. But the United
States entered the war, trains were commandeered for soldiers, and she
left college after her sophomore year. Soon the Pacific campaign brought
West the pick of Harvard and Yale, including my father. All his life, Paul
Moore had navigated New York and Boston parties where the same last
names, and sometimes the same first ones, had turned up for generations.
My father hadn't had many girlfriends, and even though he was power-
fully drawn to Jenny McKean, she was part of what he knew. From the way
he said Nona Clark's name, I could tell he considered her something else.
"I've met," he wrote his brother, Bill, "a typical girl of the Golden West."

When she opened the door, I could smell her perfume. She was tall, a
woman you would describe as willowy, with pale skin; her wavy red hair
was not long, but not short either. We sat down immediately, and she
leaned forward, her fragrance becoming more intense. "What about you?"
she asked. I'd been to Florence, I told her, and she asked what I had seen.
I said I'd seen the Brancacci Chapel, and she asked what I had liked about
it. I talked to her about the size of the figures and about the expressive-
ness in the bodies of Adam and Eve, how they bent in shame leaving the
garden. She asked if I'd seen Santa Maria Novella and I said yes, and if

I'd liked the Uffizi, and whether I had gone to Siena. Eventually I asked how she met my father. "I met Paul at a party," she said, "in Seattle." And then she smiled, breaking into a wistful melodic laugh, rose from the sofa, escorted me to a small bedroom, and left me to unpack.

Halfway through the week, Nona took me to a cocktail party where everyone spoke French, or English with an international accent. Our host, Nona told me en route, was a prince from Liechtenstein whose family had suffered "tragic losses" in the war. The party was at his "cottage," a substantial stone house on the outskirts of the city. The women wore silk suits and larger pieces of jewelry than I'd ever seen. The men were nothing like my father; they did not wear Brooks Brothers seersucker, and some of them had deftly trimmed mustaches. Nona introduced me as her friend from "the States," and once in a while the man or woman who shook my hand was a count or countess, and "very rich," Nona would later whisper. Nona was being courted by an international financier famously wanted by the United States government, and there he was, free to walk across the room, take her hand and kiss it. Since by then she had told me how sad she was about her husband's suicide, I was surprised when I saw her sitting with the financier on the veranda, a loose silk blouse falling off one narrow shoulder as she leaned toward him, then threw back her head and laughed.

Another night, Nona took me out to dinner. We sat in the back of her big car as the chauffeur drove us along the lake and through the countryside to a small village, and up a narrow street to a tiny restaurant with white tablecloths, upholstered chairs, the smell of flowers in the air. Nona was greeted as "Madame," I as "Mademoiselle." I wore the slender lime linen dress with a hot pink welting that my grandmother had bought me in New York. Nona was dressed in silk, gray or off-white, and I remember, because it was the first time I'd seen them, that she wore stockings paler than her skin—when she crossed her legs, I could see her freckles. She spoke about the men at the party, exiles, international businessmen. Her move to Geneva had been an adventure, she said. "But by coming here I wasn't escaping, you see. I was bringing my children to a totally new life— one that we could begin together, with our pain behind us."

She did not speak of my father until the last morning at breakfast on the balcony overlooking the city, the lake, Mont Blanc. The sky was hazy and the air warm. An intermittent breeze lifted strands of her hair and the shoulders of her sea green dressing gown. She had a way of looking at me with such attention that I was completely at ease. "You remind me a great deal of your father," she finally began. "The way we can talk. I remember so well talking to him—on those long summer days. He was a much better listener than most of the servicemen I met at the Officers' Club. Seattle is so lovely in the summer, and that one was no exception, even though the war was on and many of us had lost people in the fighting. Paul was one of many soldiers in Seattle then. We saw each other for a little more than a year, I think. We were even a little in love. I'm sure marriage to Paul crossed my mind, but he never mentioned it, and there was the war. My mother, who was a grande dame of sorts and quite a difficult woman, liked him a great deal, and I think would have let me marry him even though he wasn't Catholic. I don't know whether she was more impressed with his mother's Cleveland connections or his father's large interest in the American Can Company. But marriage certainly wasn't my primary concern, and most certainly wasn't his.

"We talked about books," Nona continued, "about Auden and Eliot. About the war and about our families. He never talked about Jenny although I knew there had been other girls—that there were other girls in the East. We played tennis, went sailing, swam, danced, went to parties." Nona barely paused as she told the story, as if by telling it she might regain who she had been before she married, before her husband's suicide altered her experience of life. "I remember," she continued, "sailing out to a little island we had off the mainland and taking a picnic and I remember a drunken songfest in a police station." And then she stopped talking and looked at me. My hands were on the table between us, and she took one of them. "Look, you can see the mountains rather clearer now; that's where I take the children skiing in the winter. You must come with us sometime. I'll give you a winter holiday."

I was being invited to look at my father in relation to a woman other than my mother. My father and Nona, dressed in tennis clothes, for instance. Picnicking and reading poetry to each other. They liked to talk, Nona said. He had said that, too. I did not report what my father had said that night on the lake, that he might have married Nona had she not been Catholic.

"Your father was very cruel to me," Nona continued. "I remember when he left. He was so happy that the war was over and that all the killing might stop. He wrote for quite a while, letters from Idaho, Chicago, and from New York after he got back. How he cared for me and missed me. But after about two weeks the letters stopped and I got a telegram: SORT OF SUDDEN. MARRIED JENNY MCKEAN STOP. I remember how I felt. I could not believe that Paul would do such a thing. There had really been no warning. My mother was fit to be tied. She thought it was absolutely inexcusable. I didn't know how to defend him to her, and I don't remember exactly what happened. I could hardly forgive him right then and there, but I will thank him for sparing my finding out from the newspaper."

My father a two-timer? My father one of those boys who suddenly break up with you? Never call again? What was I, his twenty-year-old daughter, to make of this information? What could I do to keep the story at a distance? Fiction. In the creative writing class I took the year after that summer in Europe, I wrote a short story using the events as I'd gleaned them from my parents, the events as I recount them here. But it contains no analysis or reflection. The instructor, who liked the story very much, also remarked that he found it "painful," but I didn't think about it that way. The occasional spats I'd witnessed between my parents had left no dent in my ideal, and Nona, after all, was part of my father's past and now, for me, a shimmering intimation, a private dream.

When I got back from Nona and Switzerland, it was August, and I went straight to the Adirondacks, bringing presents from Europe. I earnestly reported to my father the details of my visit with his old girlfriend, how movingly she'd talked about her husband's suicide. I did not tell him how much he'd hurt her, and I did not consider what my infatuation with Nona Clark might have reawakened in my mother, who was the same as she always was, buoyant, radiant, curious, given to the sardonic remark. In fact, everything was the same, all of us around the table, the shouting and joking and laughing, my father rowing across the lake or taking one of us for a sail, the family game of prisoner's base as darkness fell. It would be decades before I learned that the pain in my parents' marriage had nothing to do with another woman, that my mother's response to Nona Clark's stiff neck drew on something she knew nothing of, something sadder and more serious than jealous pique at the rudeness of her husband's wartime sweetheart.

*   *   *

When my parents married, my mother had a twenty-one-inch waist. The first time she told me this, she was pregnant, lying on a pale pink bed at Rockmarge. Out the big window the willows along the ocean path were moving in the afternoon breeze, my father's father in summer whites was walking across a lawn so vast it curved downward like the edge of the world, and the sunlight was doubled in its brightness because the ocean shone it back. My great-grandmother's house was the white of creamy chalk and too big to count the rooms of, so huge and grand that after she died no one in the family could afford to live in it, and so it was torn down, the oceanfront land sold off in pieces.

But the day my mother told me the measurement of her bridal waist, the house was still intact, and when I remember how she said it—"I had a twenty-one-inch waist when I got married"—I can see her young. She has grown to her full height, five foot nine, and carries herself with slight awkwardness, as if such tall slenderness might throw her off-balance. It was this precarious girl whom Benny Bradlee wanted to kiss when he took her to see *Now, Voyager*, but whom Bobby Potter kissed first. Evenings the summer she was fifty years old and dying, Ben and some of the others who had kissed her at the movies, now powerful men, came and sat with her on her porch in Washington, still making her laugh, still wanting her irony and the quiet way she listened and questioned once you got her attention.

When my mother was four, her mother stood her in front of George Luks, the Ashcan School painter, who made a portrait of her that looked like a Spanish infanta. Almost as soon as she could walk, she would dance even without music, spinning, laughing, spinning, and, when she stopped, drop to the floor and look up to see paintings whirling, the faux Italian furniture rising to the ceiling, edges of light falling out of kilter through the tall windows. They called her Dizzy. At twelve, she turned solemn, and soon after that, beautiful. By the time my mother became beautiful, her mother was almost always in bed in the room at the end of the long hallway, rousing herself for an infrequent meal or gin disguised in a teapot delivered on a tray. My mother talked less about her mother's drinking than about her inadequacy. "Mama never behaves as a wife to Papa. But then again she never has." It went without saying that "Mama" was hardly a mother either.

Once, in a letter to my father, my mother drew a cartoon of a family dinner in the paneled dining room at Prides, the big house where she grew up north of Boston, which was not far from Rockmarge. First she drew a rectangle, in the center of which she printed TABLE. Around the table, instead of stick figures, she wrote little blocks of narrative for each of her family. At one end sat "Mama in tears at table." From "Mama in tears," a penciled arrow swooped across the drawing and out a portal labeled DOOR. Also tugged from the table by departing arrows were her brother Shaw, sixteen, whose shouts had caused Margarett's outburst, and her sister Margie, who collapsed into tears and followed her mother out, which in turn caused Shaw to weep and also leave the table. "Papa" did not cry but rushed out "to comfort Margie." "Jenny" remained "stationary" and "tearless," her only company the maid, "in and out with more food continually."

As soon as she could, my mother fled to boarding school in Virginia, to the Madeira School. When she did come home, she sat with her father in the library talking hour after hour about what to do about her mother. Her sister, just a year older, escaped into a life my mother was too shy for. While Margie modeled, posing as a "socialite" smoking Camels for magazine ads, Jenny put on red-framed glasses and read. When she wasn't reading, she was at the stables wearing a tweed riding jacket with velvet lapels, a hard black hat, and jodhpurs tight at her knees. She laughed with the stablemen, mucked stalls, and threw the shiny smooth saddle onto her own mare. Before boarding school, she'd been a champion rider; a newspaper pictured her then, holding Me Too by the bridle, a silver prize cup in the other hand. My mother was a middle child, between her sister and twin brothers—Me too! she must have thought as she galloped the field close to the sea. When her horse took the jumps, she held her seat so easily she was sure she was flying.

After Madeira, she went to Vassar where she got A's until the morning she woke up unable to see. My mother always took her glasses off to have her picture taken, so there's no evidence she had bad eyes. When I think of her then, the Vassar hallway is dark, it's night, she is alone in her room, and all over are stacks of the books she's tried to lose herself in. The blinding illness never got a name, and it took a year to get her sight back, not to feel the pain in her head like fists pushing from behind the eyes. She was still recovering, rooming in New York with Ben Bradlee's sister, Connie, when Paul Moore returned from Guadalcanal the spring of 1943.

They became inseparable, nights in the city, weekends away. It was sweet for my father to bring a girl home to Hollow Hill, to the slate-roofed country house built just after his parents' marriage, white stain sloughing from its brick walls so they become pink, clipped hedge, pruned shade trees, lawns just turning green again. The Moores had horses and dogs and played family games of croquet. Cocktails were in a library walled with my grandfather's leather-bound Scott and Tennyson, Browning and Keats, where he sat, taciturn in an armchair placed like a throne, its back to the center window, and where my grandmother, dressed for dinner in a long velvet skirt, made cheerful, pliant conversation. How sweet to show Jenny the rock garden, the roses, the house he'd so missed. *The bullet had my name on it, but I guess they spelled it wrong.* Now, with his girl, he climbed the stairs to his childhood room with its four-poster and the sailfish he'd caught in Florida mounted above the fireplace, then he ushered her to the guest room where the bed had a mirror headboard. There he kissed Jenny McKean in the midst of his mother's antiques and colorful decor, so different from the dark Italianate solemnity of the house she'd grown up in. "I love all the luxury," she wrote him.

Years later, when my father was married to Brenda and no longer romantic about his marriage to my mother, his tender sympathy vanished and he began to tell stories of her ambivalence and extreme emotion. As always he was a vivid storyteller. At his parents' house after their engagement, in the room with the mirrored headboard, my mother sits at the dressing table, a mirrored vanity painted with deer and trees. She is quietly looking at herself, making sure her hair is smooth. Giving her nose and cheeks another rush of powder, moistening her lips with one more swish of raven red. My father has his dinner jacket on. "Come on, Jenny, it's time to go downstairs." She continues to sit, pushing a coil of hair into place, looking at her face from the right, from the left, cursing to herself that she wears glasses, deciding not to wear them, that it's not so important to see. Suddenly she begins to cry and my father doesn't know why. He'd bought her a gold dress for their engagement party in Boston the week before, and her proper grandmother had let her know she disapproved, but "Jenny, you looked beautiful, everyone said so," he now reassures her. She can't stop crying, and he gets a little frightened. Finally my mother says she simply can't face all the people downstairs, and, to my father's astonishment, when he puts his arms around her, she hits him hard, with her fists. When my father told me this story in the early 1980s, his voice driven by blame and judgment, I didn't understand why, more than a decade after my mother's death, in the bloom of his new marriage, his retrospect had no compassion for her.

My mother kept scrapbooks, and after my father died, I knew I would return to them. But I was surprised, going to Bank Street when the house was being taken apart, to learn that he had saved wartime letters. I was even more surprised at how many there were. Hundreds, enough to overflow one box into another, and another. Bound into packets with string. I first saw them at Bank Street, dusty, the August after my father died, and later, taking inventory at Stonington, I found more, in frayed shoe boxes stacked in old liquor cartons. My father's letters home from battle, more than a hundred pages; letters between my parents, from Seattle and later, nearly two thousand pages. Eventually all of them ended up tidily Xeroxed, and I had my set bound at a copy shop. It was in these volumes that I began to look for the beginning of the story of my parents' marriage unrevised by the decades, commentary that introduces them in their early twenties, between the beginning of their romance in the spring of 1943, through the conversation on the willow walk and my father's year in Seattle, up to my birth in late 1945.

New York, 1943. The Katharine Dunham dancers, Paul Robeson's Othello, Rodgers and Hammerstein's *Oklahoma!* A "set" of friends with last names like Aldrich, Cutler, Fowler, Whitman, and Potter. My mother's prose fairly clatters with high heels and stylish suits, and I can hear the talk: an exclamatory rush of endearments—"darling," "dear"—a particular manipulation of the pitch of voice and vowel, an aversion to the direct expression of emotion. I remember these people as tall, as well dressed, as possessing esprit in the use of language and gesture. Those who haven't died are now very handsome people in their eighties, faded images of the younger selves who vividly enter my imagination as I read the letters. Engagements announced, babies born, leaves given and withheld, casualties, deaths, so many deaths—a war widow, friend of all of them, whom no one can console. The fighting is so part of their lives that in the letters it seems at a remove, but also present, insistent.

When my father left for Seattle the morning after the encounter on the willow walk, he sent my mother flowers. "They meant so much," she wrote. "They are nectar to the nostrils and reach my navel." My mother was sitting at her desk in New York. She wanted to apologize. "I might not have showed too much character . . . I am sorry to have interrupted you by humming, to have acted so violently physically as well as mentally . . . I am so really sorry that I made it so hard for you to say goodbye, and hard for myself." My father had tried to kiss her goodbye and she had become "violent." Think of her, barely twenty, the daughter of that mother, a mother who once, my mother confided in a letter to my father, stumbling toward her drunk, threw a telephone receiver, by mistake hitting my mother, breaking the skin on her lip, leaving her mouth bruised and bleeding. Take all that into account when you read what she writes: "I wanted to hurt you—anyone . . . I thought of writing you a letter and saying 'Steer away from women, Paul, you might break someone else's heart.'"

"There was a fault of ignorance on my side, a fault of naïveté on yours," my father replied. "Perhaps they went together. Perhaps I was ignorant of your naïveté and you of my ignorance."

For my mother, though, "the hurt remains physical," and she tells my father everything. Of flirting "like a wild thing" with Davy Challinor, a former beau whom they both knew—listening with him to "waltzes in a music store booth—yesterday drinking mint juleps at the Stork and teadancing—not to see if I could get out of myself again, but to see if it would soothe the raw edges." She has "no regrets," she writes, but her bravado is stiff with pain. She envies my father, in a new place "where listening to 'I'm in love with a soldier boy' will not make your throat dry . . ."

Eventually my father admitted that before he left, he'd felt nothing for her at all; that he had not missed her the week he spent in Washington, but that on the train West, the countryside flying past, he'd realized he felt "less alone" with her than with "anyone I have ever known." And then, plaintively, "Forgive me Jen, will you?" My mother countered that he "felt nothing" because "as the days went by, my weakness made you strong, I needed you more than you needed me and so the magic for you was gone. But still for me the magic persists . . ." In response, my father accused her of being "subjective & inverted & rather unhealthy." He didn't mean to sound "stuffy," he wrote, but seriously, "there's no point in worrying the scar tissue."

My mother responded with memories: "the weekend at your house and family bridge and the mirrored headboard for the first time—And Sunday night when we read aloud flower catalogues and you looked so rumpled and young and boyish in your blue shirt and you seemed clumsy like I was, and I wanted you so badly . . ." And then, when they were at her family's at Prides, "unexplainably, it happened . . . as if there were a string from one end of my body to the other and the string broke and every part of me was flooded with something warm and exciting and true." No wonder my father chose Seattle over New Haven. No wonder he wrote my mother that she was naïve. The downstairs guest room at Prides, its walls blue French silk with a silvery jacquard, was called the Silk Room. In letters after they reconcile, they will refer to what they did there as "silkrooming."

In the last years of her life, my mother became a writer and published *The People on Second Street*, a memoir about our years in Jersey City. When she knew she might die, she began another book, about her childhood and her marriage; in the weeks before her death, she burned much of her writing, but not a passage in which she described herself as having "an intense sexual drive." She made the admission as if it were an affliction, a deformity, something she had always contended with. It was there already when, at twenty, she wrote my father: "I was just going too fast and you got scared."

4

Holy Matrimony

Neither could stop writing, and after months of correspondence, my father invited my mother to Seattle. Her brother Harry was stationed there and her mother was visiting him, so she could go along without rousing gossip among their friends. My father was nervous. He'd arrested one of his men because he refused to see his wife, didn't dare face her; did he dare face Jenny McKean in this new situation? They had always seen each other in the context of their friends and family—here in Seattle they'd be on their own. He wrote her all these fears—she should know he took his job seriously: "Without dramatizing it . . . there is a responsibility to the men these future officers will someday serve." In spite of his uneasiness, he prepared for the trip—he had his college car, a Buick convertible he called Bovette, and he saved ration cards for gas and for liquor so he could give her a good time. "It doesn't seem possible I'll see you within a week," he wrote, unable to keep from voicing another fear: "I don't see why the hell you shouldn't come out & I don't see what it has to do with MARRIAGE. Don't misunderstand . . . If you misunderstand, you'll get sore, so don't."

My mother *was* thinking of marriage, and their reunion the first night was so romantic, so close to what she had dared to imagine and hope for, that she told him how she felt. But my father lost his wallet, and along with it all his carefully hoarded ration cards—not only could they not drive up into ski country as they'd dreamed in their letters, but it rained all four days, which kept them indoors. Even so there were dinners and parties, among them a cocktail party given by a cousin of my mother's at her grand house in the Highlands, where Nona Clark's family also lived. Of course Nona came to the party, but my father never told her that he had been involved with Jenny McKean, the beautiful black-haired girl in the Bergdorf Goodman suit whose glamorous mother was a painter. "Mrs. McKean approached me," Nona told me, "and said 'You have the face of an artist.' But Jenny and I never spoke, not one word."

When he saw my mother off at the station, she was what my father described as "stingy" with her goodbye. Reading my mother's postmortem letter to my father, it's clear why:

> Did it ever occur to you that it might be more to the point to stay in
> your own room at the U. and take a nap if you are in a bad mood,
> instead of rationalizing your tangents of disposition by saying to me
> "God, you're so in love with me," or "I really hate you tonight"? Either
> say in a nice voice that you want to nap or be quiet—and I will leave
> off pleasant chatter, and lay a cool hand on your forehead. I don't
> blame you for your moods, but we weren't in a house, I was too
> rested to take a nap myself and didn't relish sitting in a bathroom.

Though my father finally apologized for his rudeness, my mother asked that he not write her again: "If you ever come East let me know, and we can have a good time with nothing else in mind. So love & happy hunting, sweetheart." In his reply, my father seems chastened:

> I have never said anything substantial because I knew the wind
> would blow it away & didn't want to kid either you or myself there-
> fore I never could REALLY let myself go . . . here's a last and deeply
> sincere apology for letting you down & being so abominably self-
> ish . . . I am glad VERY glad you took the initiative to chop. I never
> had the will-power & didn't want to anyhow . . . Maybe I can't love.

I have a photograph of my mother taken in the library of her parents' house. She is wearing a long-sleeved velvet dinner dress, dark red is the color I imagine it, and she is tilted toward the tall young man who sits next to her, leaning in toward her. The picture is in one of the red frames in which she loved to hang eight-by-tens of friends' weddings, and it ended up in the boxes of things that came to me after she died. The young man is Artie Trevor, with whom my mother went out for several months after her disastrous visit to Seattle. In the photo, Artie Trevor has a long face and a lanky body, but he looks more like a grownup than my father did in his twenties, his flirtatious smile one of bemused delight. "I would have married him," my mother said once, "if it hadn't been for your father."

Twenty-five years later, after my parents began to live separately, my mother and Artie Trevor fell in love again. I know this because she wrote then to tell me there was someone in her life, and though she didn't reveal his name, she later identified him. She was writing me this, she explained, because she wanted me to know that my father had not been her only lover and because she wanted me to be free to have sexual happiness. After she died, I hung the picture of her with Artie Trevor in the house in Connecticut, which I then shared, on alternate weekends, with my father and Brenda, my stepmother. I hung the picture because it reminded me of my mother alive and happy: her hair long and loose, the shine of her skin against the dark velvet, the angle at which she held the cigarette between her fingers, her confident smile. "How could you," my father once said, months later when we were fighting, "hang that picture of your mother and Artie Trevor? Didn't you know it would hurt my feelings?"

It did not occur to me then that a photograph of my mother with Artie would hurt my father's feelings—after all, he was in a happy new marriage

and things with my mother had ended badly. But writing now, older than
he was when my mother died, I understand that what goes unresolved
never loses its power. My father was hurt because my mother's romance
with Artie Trevor occurred the first time he felt he might lose her, and now
she was dead and he had lost her for good.

Studying at Barnard, living on the East Side, and engaged in a busy social
life, Jenny McKean was becoming, as a friend of her mother's said, "vital,
amusing, charming, and beautiful," and you can see it in a picture taken
of her and Artie during those months. Among the tattered letters, I found
a cache of Artie Trevor's, written to my mother in 1944 after he left for the
Pacific in July. He calls her Muffin and she calls him Bunny. Though her
side of the correspondence does not survive, his indicates that among the
subjects they seriously discussed were the possibility of a world organization of nations, their mutual friends including my father, Artie's adventures on shipboard, and that she sent him presents and books, including
C. S. Lewis's *Screwtape Letters*, which she later sent to my father. Artie was
besotted. "Why," he wrote on July 22,

> can't you remember the difference between Little Necks and Cher-
> rystones? Why do you get all A's and deny you're a great brain? Why
> do you have sad eyes? Why do you wear sneakers at cocktail parties?
> Why do you always walk behind people? Why do you read the Real
> Estate page in the Sunday paper? Why do you say, 'say something
> nice' when I am saying something nice? How can you perform this
> great series of marvyisms? For I am undone by them. They make you
> the original wonderful heart along with 9,000 other you-nesses—

Her new beau gave my mother confidence and she wielded a bit of it
with Paul Moore. When he wrote that he'd be back East soon, she replied,
"I hope I can stagger my lovers so I will have time for U. I don't know
where Nona gets this jag that you are so superior on the sofa. I thought
Artie was better than you once I got him trained. He didn't get carried
away so quick as u. SO I had a better time." That she had initiated the
break this time was exhilarating. "You have to toe the line, do the woo-
ing, it's your gamble, you have to think clearly, if you do or don't want to

is your business. It's your worry, your problem, your project. So the tables have turned." My father had little ammunition with which to return fire: "There's a rather cheap little secretary who works down at the gym called Dixie, who may provide a little trouble . . ." My mother's riposte: "Why don't you have something with Dixie. It would be good for you."

There were many ostensible reasons for my father's "vacillating" about marriage to Jenny McKean. After my mother's death and his remarriage, he was apt to defend his early caution as a response to her "instability," which was how he characterized her emotional intensity, and at the time my mother heard gossip that "Mrs. Moore" didn't want her son to marry Jenny McKean because of Margarett McKean's "lesbian reputation, affairs, drink etc." Of course, my father was used to pathologizing women's disappointment, accustomed to feeling guilt for letting them down. Even though his mother was now active in museum work and was running Hollow Hill, he still felt in her the depression that always had made him vulnerable to her love and need. It had intensified with the war. My father saved and labeled "revealing" a letter he got after a visit home before he went overseas. "Things very near my heart were hard to say," his mother wrote, "but I am glad we had those 15 minutes in the dark in your room . . . Deep love passeth all understanding, words are superfluous . . . What a poor instrument speech is. I think the look in one's eyes does express the soul, don't you?"

But what of his own sexuality—the homosexual desire of which he was already aware? I find no tidy quotation to prove those sexual secrets were an element in the chaos of his courtship of my mother or of his life in Seattle, to suggest that among the WAVES, the Nonas and Dixies and Loises, there were nights with men. The only clue to a possible conflict, and this from Nona Clark, was that during their evenings together he was drunk more than he was sober. Later he told me he'd had "those feelings" for as long as he could remember, but let us take my twenty-four-year-old father at his word. Eventually he found himself in love with my mother, his misgivings about her and his other desires subordinate to his quest for a partner in the life he was becoming more and more determined to pursue, a life in the church.

And what of my mother's willingness to turn back toward a man who had been so indecisive when she had no shortage of more ardent admirers, Artie Trevor in particular? Her consistent flirtation and sexual provocation in letters to my father had gone largely unresponded to, at least in his letters that survive; my father's tone was alternately adolescent—off-color humor and penciled cartoons—and romantic or earnest. Sexual banter came naturally to my mother—she was used to her mother's seductive nature, which, intensified by alcohol, sexualized the atmosphere in which she grew up. In a way my father was perfect—he had a manner that was sweet and kind, but also, like her mother the artist, he was a mysterious, mercurial person who sought relief and steadiness in the unseen. Nor was he overtly cruel as Margarett could be, and he did not rage at my mother as her mother did, but he did drink too much and he did have moods. My mother was used to being preoccupied with Margarett's well-being at the expense of her own, but she had also learned to dismiss other people's moods and move on. While she associated Margarett's late conversion to the Catholic Church with her mother's desperation and mental illness, my father's interest in the church seemed to express an intriguing part of him; instinctually my mother felt he had discovered something in his belief. Before long, her need for someone with whom to share a serious approach to existence would become more important than virtuosity "on the sofa." The source of that new seriousness would come not from inside their relationship, but from outside. It would come when my mother joined the Episcopal Church.

"I never asked you about God," she wrote my father after their first breakup; in her grief, she longed for something that could help her emerge from her sadness and from the volatility of her family, Margarett in particular: "Mama has taken up hiding sherry under the bed in the silk room— wet tumbler found rolling round the floor. It was hideous having her in the drugged condition at Saturday breakfast. I have lost the antagonistic attitude and am merely terribly terribly sorry." Months earlier, before the trip to Seattle, she had visited the chaplain at Columbia. At home afterward, there was, by coincidence, a letter from my father: why didn't she get "organized about religion." She should go see Gordon Wadhams, the priest at the Church of the Resurrection, on East Seventy-fourth Street, the church where my father went in New York: "Father Wadhams is deeply spiritual, damn brilliant, sense of humor . . . He really KNOWS what the score is & can explain better than anyone I can think of what the

Church is all about." In her prompt reply, my mother was self-conscious: "I would rather go to the man at college than someone I have no connections with . . . Probably the old shyness, but I can feel the sweat on the palms already . . ."

I always assumed my mother had a pro forma Episcopalian upbringing—I knew about Margarett's dramatic departure from old-fashioned Boston Unitarianism, but I assumed Shaw, my mother's father, was at least an occasional Episcopalian. Here my mother explained that Senny, the Irish Catholic governess, was "the only person who ever told me there was a God even." Her father, whom she described as "nothing" when it came to belief, had feared that Margarett would "convert all of us" to what he considered a predatory religion. Nonetheless, Senny had taken my mother and her sister to Sunday mass, given them Catholic prayer books, taught them the Hail Mary. The Episcopal Church therefore always seemed to my mother "sort of fake Catholic—they took communion and didn't believe the same thing . . ." She was embarrassed to admit that in matters of the spiritual life, she was as naïve as my father had always accused her of being:

> . . . It has often worried me because I detest ignorance more than anything else, and even if I do not get faith I care for the knowledge. And ignorance of that is apt to scare you, at least it does me, for you think you are alone in your ignorance and that it is therefore shocking. I believe in a child's sort of wonder way, but that is all and it is not much good, for it holds little comfort—the fear became more when I knew you—I suppose because I knew you didn't have the ignorance—and I was scared of little things like going to church with you for fear I shouldn't know what to do—for I know and understand the Catholic Mass but not the other . . . But I didn't dare tell you. And I'm sure I never would have dared to had you not asked me to. I am very grateful that you did. It all sounds sadly childish as I read it over. Baring the soul like that makes me feel very emotional and you very near.

My father replied immediately, eager to put her at ease—the letter, different in tone from others, is striking for its maturity, for the clarity of his handwriting (which usually tended toward the curlicued and illegible), and for the solemn directness of its language. He wrote her to continue with the

Columbia chaplain if she wanted to, but that he believed Father Wadhams had the capacity to "make the most awkward attempt of anyone to speak to him about anything seem completely natural . . ." He advised her not to worry about dogma just now, explaining that he believed "Catholicism of some sort would be far more congenial than benevolent, vague, love-thy-neighbor Protestantism." Protestantism was what Columbia offered, and it was analogous to the plain Episcopalianism in which my father had been raised. He wanted Jenny to join him in the Anglo-Catholic strand of the Episcopal Church, which had enabled him to make such an emotional connection with God.

Amazingly, given the conversations they'd had about the war when they first courted, this was the first time they talked about what was so central to my father's life. Now they brought to their correspondence a language that could place the events of their life together in a larger, reso-nant context, and the effort changed and deepened their relationship. "If one believes in the creed as it is written," my father continued, "there is no way out of believing as a Catholic: the Mass, Confession, a disciplined life of prayer." For an intellectually gifted young woman born into a compli-cated family and a world of foxhunting, dog breeding, art collecting, and assured marriage to one of the limited array of young men in her tribe, the possibility of belief and a life of prayer seemed to offer a more adventurous opportunity for meaning and constancy. But it was not until her definitive rejection of my father after Seattle that she took his advice. She found her way one Sunday in April 1944 to the Church of the Resurrection, and to Gordon Wadhams.

In early June, newly baptized and confirmed an Episcopalian, she wrote to my father, breaking their months-long silence. He had once told her that experiences never seemed more real or wonderful than when they were shared. Now she too had had an experience that needed sharing, and since he was partly responsible, she had decided to write him about it. She'd made her first confession: "I practically flew the nine blocks home I felt so pure. And then this morning early was first Communion and after-wards we all went down to the Parish Hall for breakfast. Father W. had told us that meal would be as wonderful and should mean as much as receiving the Sacrament and until now I did not quite see why."

My father's reply was immediate. "I was very touched by your writing, and, more than that, tremendously happy that you have found your way to the Church. The feeling you described of light-footed purity after the sacrament of penance is one of the things that seems so valid and authentic an experience as to justify in itself the existence of the Church . . . The whole business of the Church, prayer, the Eucharist, etc. never came home to me until after my first Confession in the fall of my 6th form year." He went on to explain his commitment to the Anglo-Catholic tendency in the Episcopal Church: "There is a fire and a challenge to it, a sense of humor in most of its disciples, a warmth and human quality, and above all a definite and strong framework on which to build and on which to learn . . . I am awfully interested in all this of yours . . . How did you go about 'breaking the ice' about which you had so much trepidation?" He signed the letter, simply, "God bless you, Paul," as if, in this role, he were a person other than her sometime suitor.

My mother also wrote Father Wadhams—true to her upbringing, a thank-you note—and he immediately replied: "The more I review the events of the past few weeks—your coming to me, your quick, but I am sure real, grasp of spiritual values, your confirmation and all that has followed—the more aware I am of God's hand in all this and of your happy prospects in the life of grace. I know that as your understanding grows, so will your sense of dedication to our Lord and to the work he has called you to." He suggested that for fifteen minutes a day she undertake "non-critical, breath-catching reading" of *The Imitation of Christ* and *The Confessions of St. Augustine*—"both classics, indispensable."

For the moment, the spiritual work my mother was called to was in her family: "I think," she wrote my father sometime after her confession, "that compassion would be a better approach to Mama and Margie"—her mother was weighing the decision to go into a sanitarium; her sister, twenty-one with a small child, was contemplating divorce. Both circumstances were threatening to my mother's already tenuous sense of security. Eventually her life in the church would not only leaven her dealings with her family but profoundly affect her intellectual life, as her curiosity and enthusiasm drew her to apply her considerable intelligence to evolving a theology and practice, to making spiritual metaphors from her own life. By the time she and my father married, she was as much Gordon Wadhams's protegée as he was, and she took her religious vocation every bit as seriously as he did. While she pursued a life of service in partnership with him, her spiritual life was independent and entirely her own. It was as if two artists, one a painter and one a sculptor, had decided to marry and live together—the relationship would be one of mutual criticism and inspiration, but the work would remain separate.

While my mother was writing him about her first confession, my father wooed with another letter of apology for his behavior in Seattle. "There was a tenseness and a rush and too many hotels and restaurants for clear thinking & acting. I'm made up in such a manner that when something gets a little too involved to see completely clearly," he wrote, "I'm rather inclined to obey the emotion that says 'to hell with it.' Not an admirable trait." He was taking responsibility, but my mother's reply was harsh: "Isn't it high time you did?" In his next letter, my father met the challenge—"Your letter also made me very nostalgic and lonely—we did have a grand time, what?" In his nervousness, he affected leading-man rhetoric: "To coin a phrase, my dear, it's water over the dam." It took a long sequence of sentences for him to come clean: "You know, life is a very funny business. I hesitate to tell you this, but I think you'd get a laugh out of it—I'm rather jealous about your dating"—after which he conceded to his rival: "If Trevor is the gentleman in question you have my highest approval. I think he is probably one of the best people who ever drew the breath of life."

His letter had the desired effect. Even before she saw Artie Trevor off in early July, my mother was making her way back to Paul Moore. In June she noted it was nearly "four months since our brief kiss in the Seattle station" and that she was now "just plain not sure" whether "all or nothing" was a good "scheme of things."

"Thanks for your change of heart," my father replied, assuring her that he was "trying like hell to get rid of the 'I' that has been too big for a while." In an August letter, my mother asked who he had "kist" since their breakup, and in response to his list of five women, explained that she started "going steady" with Artie in the spring, but that he hadn't "attacked" (i.e., kissed) her until just before he left. Of his newest girl, my father wrote, "I've been datin' Lois pretty heavy & having a grand old time. She is not an intellectual giant—just a big healthy and rather attractive animal. Grand for the summer months as Nona is not enough of an extrovert for warm weather . . ."

But even Lois didn't keep him from writing my mother nearly every day, much more frequently than ever before, and on September 1 he tele-

phoned collect, and they talked, nervously, for ten minutes—telephone
time was rationed and often a long-distance call did not go through:

> . . . You probably wouldn't believe it, but I was nervous as a cat
> waiting in the little booth, and then a long time with no answer.—
> and then finally U. It was like hearing a familiar lilt of past seasons
> —seasons that were so much fun and so good that the memory of
> their passing is sad. But the beautiful difference was that your voice
> was not a memory. And I love to hear you laugh. The reason I was
> useless was that I was nervous and giggly. But maybe you liked it too;
> I hope so . . . I could kick myself for being nasty out here. Oh well—
> won't go into that again . . . I want to see you more now than ever
> before . . . Maybe I'm crazy but I don't think so.
>
> There's a full moon caught in the branches—can you see it motor-
> ing home through Chebacco Woods? Shining over the lake by the
> old ice house? Or are you coming home along the shore to catch it
> whitening the swamp land between the road and the Knowles and
> glistening the harbor beyond?

But he mailed the letter without enclosing money for the call, and in a
subsequent note enclosed with the check, he was suddenly self-conscious
about the openness of his letter: "Hope you weren't surprised and/or
shocked by my somewhat unusual lack of casualness."

"Of course I wasn't shocked by the post phone letter," she wrote, "It's
high time you started slinging a little crap like that. Everyone else does (in
my long list)."

"Play hard to get," was the only advice my mother ever gave me about
men, but if she was playing hard to get here, she misfired. My father wrote
back, barely controlling his rage. "I write as nice a letter as I know how &
the only reference from you is 'It's high time you started slinging a little
crap like that' . . . My feelings aren't bruised very easily, but don't you think
that's a little callous?" He'd considered calling her. Had she sent a letter he
missed? Abject when she read his "blast," my mother wrote an apology on
a narrow card, as if now unworthy of a full sheet of paper:

> I wish you were
> home now. NO letter

was lost, I really am
sorry, I have no ex-
cuse. Darling, really
I want to write nice
things I don't know what
got into me. I'm not
trying to butter you
up. Please call up so
I can apologize again.
I wish we were to-
gether now, I mean it.
Please say it's all right.
I'm a shit when you
have taken so much
from me in the last
months. Call me, darling . . .

But she called him, and he immediately forgave her while admitting he
was so angry he hadn't felt like writing:

. . . pure hurt, and the old impersonal feeling that comes with it—
and the loneliness . . . You see, your letter sounded as if you thought
me insincere, and I thought you knew by now that I express sen-
timent of that kind so rarely that it could not be insincere . . .

A week later, he wrote he now had "no romantic feeling" for Nona, who
had made it clear she cared for him, and offered to "cease all honkin'"—
that is, necking with others—if my mother wanted him to. Two weeks
later, he tried to call again ("I wanted to hear your throaty, pulsating
voice"), and in his next letter reported his landlady had kidded him about
Lois but quipped that "of course the girl in the East is the one." When he
explained his disapproval of war marriages, the landlady was matter-of-
fact: "Just go where you heart leads you." Back East, my mother dreamed
they were married and wrote my father that sitting on the sofa in the
library where they first necked, she thought of him. My father's reply
sounds like Jimmy Stewart: "Your letter was awful nice, Jen. Don't fight
any feelings. I'd hate to admit how eager I'm getting to see you. Gee whiz,

if we can't be as attractive to each other on the spot as we are in our letters, to hell with it."

The story my father told of deciding to marry my mother did not change from the time I first heard it as a child. He loved to tell it, casting it always as inevitable and very romantic. After he had been in Seattle for a year, he had leave before a change of assignment. On the journey home, which took more than a week, he wavered—"Over Idaho, yes, I'll marry her. Over South Dakota, no. Over Ohio, yes"—until he saw the New York skyline and the yes became definite. Within nights of his return, sitting across from her in a nightclub called Fefe's Monte Carlo, he proposed. Telling me the story, he left out Nona Clark, who also got love letters postmarked Idaho, South Dakota, Ohio, even New York. And he left out the war, how he drank too much, how battle returned to him in dreams. But both of them, as my mother put it in a final letter, had "buried the hatchet."

It was an element in the arc of my father's romantic narrative that my mother was startled when he leaned across a table at Fefe's Monte Carlo and proposed, startled and incredulous: he was drunk, so drunk she insisted he call her in the morning to confirm he meant what he said. She was deep into an exciting term at Barnard which she wasn't eager to abandon—an International Studies seminar, Blake to Byron, Religion and Contemporary Social Issues with Ursula Niebuhr, and a graduate history course, Europe 1914–1944. But she did quit Barnard, and her version of the courtship narrative was always tinged with regret, even after she'd gone back to get her degree and graduated with her first baby, me at nearly one year old, on her hip: "I wish I had taken a year to work at *Life* magazine, or something," she wrote during her first pregnancy. Thirty years later, during the first weeks of her final illness, I was sitting next to her hospital bed when, out of the blue, she said, "Do you think you'll get married?"

"I don't know," I said.

"Don't," she said. "You love your independence too much."

There was barely a week to celebrate before my father had to report for duty, teaching at the Officers' Training School at Quantico. On November 15, his twenty-fifth birthday, settled in temporary quarters, Paul Moore sat down and began a letter to his fiancée: "This is the first time I've had to write and the first time ever on paper I'm able to relax completely and tell you how I've missed you, how I love you and how I've missed you & loved you over the last 9 months." He closed the letter with his fondest hope. "And so, my darling, will we always be able to talk? We can pray that we always will wish to talk."

"Your wonderful letter was amBROOOOSIA after a hideous day in the pouring rain," my mother immediately replied. "It is so wonderful to get a letter from you where no one feels frustrated and there is nothing lacking. I get more excited every day about being with you . . ."

As my father adjusted in Virginia to workdays that started at 7:30 a.m., my mother, in New York, planned their precipitous wedding, to be held on November 26. Since her own mother was in a depression, she had only her prospective mother-in-law, whom she called "Mother Fan," to turn to. Later she would tell me that during those weeks Fanny Moore became "the only mother I ever knew." The affection was mutual. As my mother spent more and more time at Hollow Hill, whatever misgivings the Moores had about their son's choice vanished. In New York she was rooming with her sister, and, Margie remembered, "All that week we ran into people on the street and invited them to the wedding." When the enormous engagement diamond arrived, my mother got my father on the phone to open it with him. He had some pangs about not putting it on her finger himself: "We've missed so much of the little fun things of getting married."

Denied special leave, my father was late to the rehearsal dinner the night before the Sunday ceremony, and the wedding "orchestra" was a pickup combo pulled in for the evening. But my mother wore her grandmother's 1881 slipper satin wedding gown, quickly altered to fit her, and, observing tradition, got dressed, surrounded by her girlfriends, first posing in lacy silk underwear, hands on her hips, one thrust forward, grinning for the photographer. But as much as it was a wartime wedding, as much as it was a gathering of friends, as much as it was the culmination of a dramatic courtship, my parents' wedding was the performance of a sacrament. "In times such as these the fact of being bound to each other often seems ever a greater miracle," Mrs. Niebuhr wrote my mother.

It was the wish of both my parents that the wedding service be a nuptial mass, and Gordon Wadhams sang the liturgy as the pungent fragrance of incense filled the small church, the newlyweds receiving communion. The longest wedding anyone had ever been to, friends joked for decades. Father Wadhams was so enthralled he swore in his post-nuptial letter that if these vows didn't hold he'd renounce his orders, a promise my parents told as a story every time his name came up. For him, a celibate who would later leave the Episcopal Church for Roman Catholicism, the union between my parents transcended the quotidian, even the mortal. "I shall never forget what it was to turn about, look down on you two kneeling there," he wrote. "What yesterday gave of promise—this, I think, no one of us can tell. Promise—not only for you two, but for the Body of Christ, the Church." These young people were his handiwork, "two persons, of a mind about things that matter, penitents, disciplined communicants, willing in the presence of 'this company' to witness to their faith in 'the means of grace and the hope of glory.'"

In a photograph taken in the back of a car after the ceremony, my father is grinning, leaning back in dress blues, and my mother's smile is blindingly radiant. They are chauffeured from the church to the Cosmopolitan Club, and when they enter the ballroom, the guests turn and applaud. You can hear the festive tenor of the talk just by looking at the tiny black-and-white photographs, young women with hair brushed back and up and pulled behind their ears like Betty Grable's, skirts to the knee that flattered waists and buttocks, mule pumps with languorous silk flowers flopping over open toes, young men in uniform or dinner jackets. Mother Fan had brought flowers from the Hollow Hill greenhouses to render the Cosmopolitan Club ballroom pretty if not luxurious. In one snapshot, my parents' grandmothers are deep in conversation; they had known each other for thirty years, but not until that evening did they enter into something that might be called friendship: "Will you call me Ada?" Mrs. Moore asked. "If you will call me Marian," my mother's grandmother replied. All four parents were there, and, Margie said, "It was the most lovely wedding."

Sometime that day, my father took time to send the telegram to Nona Clark she described to me twenty years later, and that same day, somewhere on the Pacific, Artie Trevor sat down in his berth to respond to my mother's letter announcing her engagement to his old friend. "The news of you and Paul is the most really good thing that's happened in the war . . . Something I could never quite understand about you two was why, being so completely in love . . . you apparently made yourselves so miserable. I love the picture of Paul, who really hates any scene or effort, coming charging across the continent full of fire and determination." He didn't want her to have any guilt: "I think we both agreed that my interest in the

third economic conference of the Baltic states would never exactly fasci-
nate you and surely you can't forget that sort of hunted glassy stare of mine
that used to appear when you mentioned the church."

As the band played the marine hymn, my tall parents stepped out
onto the dance floor, and later my father cut the wedding cake with his
Marine Corps sword and fed a frosted square to his laughing bride. The
next morning, the newlyweds embarked for their first residence, a low
white outbuilding on a Virginia plantation, close to the Marine Officers'
Training School—the property, called "Beauclair," had belonged to George
Washington's brother, so they said they were living on the plantation of
"the uncle of our country." To get there, they flew to Washington. They
tried to be discreet, but when my father took off his Marine Corps cap on
the plane, wedding rice spilled on his blues and the other passengers burst
into applause.

5
Firstborn

My parents' honeymoon cottage in Virginia came with seven cats that shrieked in the night throughout the four months they lived there. There are photographs, but the cottage in Fredericksburg is far more vivid in my mother's needlepoint. Her mother's painting had given her ambition to be a writer—she'd written short stories at Vassar—but my father's mother, who ran an exemplary house, gardened, and did needlepoint, inspired my mother in the domestic arts. I imagine her embarking on the project, drawing a picture of the cottage, cats stationed like sentries out front and in the bushes, having the image transferred to buckram, ordering wool and needles, asking her mother-in-law for a demonstration. The stitching took twenty-five years. "Oh my God, I'll never finish," my mother would say every summer in the Adirondacks as babies climbed onto her lap and she put aside her needle and wool. Summers passed, and still the honeymoon cottage lay in an embroidery bag, unfinished, my mother its Penelope. When she began to stitch, cottage and cats appearing, my parents' marriage was new, her new husband home each evening. What was my mother's dream? What did she imagine as she knotted and stitched white for clapboard and cat, brown for tree trunk, green for grass, blue for patches of sky. Why did it take her so long to bring the cottage back into view?

When my father carried my mother over the threshold and dropped her on the wedding bed, it collapsed, but omens aside, the four months in Fredericksburg seem to have been a honeymoon—in letters afterward, both spoke of their surprise and delight in being married. Before seven, six mornings a week, my father went off to teach at the officers' school in Quantico, and my mother fed the cats, which they had named for the mothers of their friends, and figured out what to make for supper. She had never cooked nor had any instruction in cooking. "I didn't know how to keep house," she always said. Her mother could tell what was wrong with a sauce someone else prepared, but she did not cook herself, and she could not lay a shirt, collar first, on the ironing board and tell her daughter where to start pressing. Raised with servants, my mother and her newly-wed friends made housekeeping a frontier, a protest against their parents' outmoded way of life, which my mother described in her letters as "so pre-war." Both my parents believed that if they lived differently, they would have a happier married life than either set of parents. "I want you to promise not to feel that I'm lonely and unentertained at all in Quantico because being able to make you even half happy would make me completely so," my mother wrote my father a week before they married.

The cottage at Beauclair was a baptism by fire for my mother, the housewife—there was no hot-water heater, no furnace. My father chopped the wood, my mother boiled water for baths, shaving, and laundry and did the first cooking of her life on a woodburning stove—heat came from that stove and one other. After my father left for work and after her chores, my mother, alone in the cottage filled with wedding presents, wrote thank-you notes, pasted photographs and letters in the scrapbook, did needle-point, and took a stab at the laundry. Close friends like Quigg McVeigh came to visit, as did my mother's brother Shaw, and, at Christmas, her father—Margarett had finally entered Four Winds, a sanitarium in Kato-nah, New York.

After two months, when the war had not ended, and when it was clear that in April my father would be posted again to the South Pacific, my par-ents decided to conceive a child. If it was a boy, it went without saying that he'd be named Paul Moore III; the possible daughter was named Honor before conception. I was always told I was named after no one in particular but that each of my parents had a friend named Honor. "We just liked the name," they said. But it was an unusual name, and it attracted the young man who'd almost lost his life in battle, the young woman idealistic about what she might accomplish in the world. "I could not love thee, Dear, so much, / Lov'd I not Honour more" were lines they both knew, lines that would be quoted in scores of telegrams friends sent at my birth. Like the cavalier speaker of Richard Lovelace's poem, my father would soon be "going to the Wars." But in addition to its suggestion of an ideal, the poem is a clear statement of a theme that would bedevil my parents' marriage. What was the "honour" that my father, always off to various wars, would love more?

When I had a birthday away from home, my mother would always call: "How does it feel to be twenty?" she might say, but with an edge that assured me both that the world was filled with the unexpected and that during the year of my new age, I should anticipate wonderful things. And then she'd say, "Something riveting is on its way to you," and I would feel a surge of excitement as she continued with news of home. The call might end with another reference to the birthday package, and a characteristic hint of insecurity—"I hope you like it." After my mother died, my father took over these calls. Usually he'd throw in a reference to my being his "first born." There was always a lot of charge as he said that word, his voice rising on "first" and culminating in "born," but I didn't know what it meant to him. I thought it was just something affectionate to say, or later, when things were combative or awkward between us, a way of keeping me at a distance while referring to a time when neither of us was ambivalent. In our therapy together decades later, I learned that my parents' decision to have a first child had indeed been tied up with my father's relationship to war; as he put it in his memoir, published in 1998, I was conceived because "we had some romantic notion that if I were killed, at least I would have left behind a child."

The war wasn't over when my father's term at Quantico ended, and my mother was two months pregnant; since he had three weeks' leave, she accompanied him to San Francisco, where he would embark again for the Pacific—the destination, then secret, was Guam; the mission, also secret, training for the invasion of Japan. They registered at the Fairmont, and, the first night, dined and danced at the Top of the Mark. After a few days in San Francisco, my father planned to take his new bride to Santa Barbara to meet his sister Fanny, whose husband had died in the war right before their wedding, and to visit his bachelor uncle, Leonard, in Los Angeles. But when he reported at marine headquarters, he was informed of a sudden change and never got back to the hotel. In the hour he had before departure, he sent my mother carnations. "The lady said, 'We have only one red one, it will look silly with all the pink ones,'" he wrote. "I want the red one," he insisted, bursting into tears. A single red bloom punctuated the pink bouquet.

Their first letters crossed: "I waved at you in the sky at about 4 . . . I have been haunted by the fact that I omitted saying goodbye to the commandant," my mother wrote. "A gripping embrace to him." Reading, I was amazed at my mother's sexual candor. "God bless my darling daddy," she concluded. "I am now crying." As the transport flew over the Mark, my father waved through the window. "Today has seemed like a day anywhere when I will see you. Still don't know where we go or when." His apprehension was leavened by memory of their new life. "You know darling, the more I think of it, the more wonderful the last four months was. What amazes me is that we did so much and came so far in getting together. It is so much a part of me now that even without you nearby, I can't imagine what not being married was like." And, "I find myself talking about marriage all the time. It gives one such a pleasant full feeling to talk about it, about the vagaries of women folk and the sanity of men—about how 'Jenny does this' or 'we do that.'" The letter reached my mother in Santa Barbara, where she had gone alone to visit Fanny and her two little boys. "I wish you were here so we could neck. I am hep as an old cat," she wrote back. But facing a return to the mentality of war, my father left aside talk of sex, longing simply for her companionship: "Last night someone killed a bird for no reason, and I wanted to talk about it to you—about the disgust and revulsion of seeing it and how that feeling was like the old experiences of two years ago . . . One must start some time and I suppose this was as good as any time to start hardening and coarsening and preparing the outer toughness . . . necessary out here." Part of that "coarsening" involved what my father viewed as a military attitude toward sex—enlisted men, married or not, could sign up for dates with single women. He recounted a generic conversation:

> "Where's your date, Mac?"
> "I ain't that hard up."
> "Boy, I will be when I'm going on my 27th month."
> "That's no way for a married man to talk."
> "I saw your name on the list, you can't snow me."
> "Hell, they're all alike in the dark."
> "If you can get 'em in the dark."

Was my father's lack of response to my mother's seductive talk due to awareness of military censorship, simple discretion, or something else? "He seems so indifferent," one of my sisters said on reading the letters. But that is not what my mother felt about her husband's desire. She reported to a girlfriend at the time that their physical relationship was "very passionate"—her personification of his "commandant" and references to her own arousal bear that out. "Had slight insomnia because there was no Daddy to smell," she wrote the day he left. "I have moved over to your bed which is one of the more vicarious forms of pleasure I have yet encountered . . ."

After Santa Barbara, my mother took the train to Los Angeles to visit my father's Uncle Leonard. Leonard Hanna had roomed with Cole Porter at Yale, and now he collected Impressionist paintings and invested in plays and movies. When my father was at Yale, he had arranged for my father to visit the set of *The Philadelphia Story*, and the memory of shaking Katharine Hepburn's hand sent my father into wide-eyed nostalgia even late in life. That spring Leonard was leasing a villa in Bel-Air; he picked my mother up in his "drive-yourself," a long black Buick convertible with

red leather seats. In her immediate letter to my father, my mother delight-
edly described a master bedroom with shocking pink walls, the bed eight
feet by eight feet, gold cupids on the headboard. The enormous magnolia
blossom on the breakfast table was a gift from "Judy" (the actress Judith
Anderson, in Hollywood filming Jean Renoir's *The Diary of a Chamber-
maid*), and the first night, Leonard took my mother to supper at Mike
Romanoff's with glamorous friends, including the actor Monty Woolley,
another Yale friend of his and the star of the movie *The Man Who Came
to Dinner*. Until an evening bout of morning sickness drove her from the
table, my mother's pregnancy had been a secret she wanted to keep, in
spite of my father's protests—"I don't understand why women want to
keep these things secret!" That Monty Woolley now celebrated my existence vindicated him, and my impending birth became something my
father talked about to anyone who would listen. I was "Honor" between
my parents, but the proposed name for a daughter was kept secret from
everyone else.

My mother now wrote my father daily letters. "Honor" first kicked
when she was in the dentist's chair, and she was so startled by the sensa-
tion—"like a bubble bursting near your naughty. It's all too fascinating!"—
that she asked her sister-in-law, Bill's wife Mouse, pregnant with her third
child, if what she'd felt was a baby's kick, "and Mouse said it's Honor for
sure!" But as time went on, she also worried: How long would it take her to
recover from the birth? Would the war really go on for two more years? If it
didn't, perhaps they could paint the crib together. "Yes," my father replied,
"the talk is two more years." He can hardly bear the boredom of his desk
job, or of Guam itself in spite of its physical beauty and temperate climate.
Only friends coming through by chance—among them, Tony Duke and
Artie Trevor—lift his ennui. "We just heard of Germany's surrender with
complete lack of excitement," he wrote on May 8. "It seemed extremely
natural that there should be no excitement, but when one reflects a little
it is quite amazing. People say 'Did you hear the Germans surrendered'
& you say 'Yeah' Period. It seems very far removed from us." He became
romantic describing Paul Muni in "A Song to Remember," a movie about
Chopin.

The music ran through it and was part of it . . . No experience—
even our experience of listening for an hour or two to music—is

complete unless you are with me my sweet. Jenny, we must live
high and strongly. We can't let the rattling of the days get in the
way of what we both see once in a while. We see it clearly. It
stands straight. It is tall. It is finely polished. And from it we look
up and see, and we look down. Should we stay on it and with it
always we may sometime become part of it. Please help me, darling,
to keep alive to what we both must do. I'm so vacillating. So weak.
I need you, my darling. I need you so badly. Keep praying for us.

As he had in Seattle, my father escaped the routine in cycles of drinking and remorse; he'd write my mother of a binge, then remonstrate with
himself, "You must really think me a sinner by now—now that you know
what one is committed to in this business. I hope you never slip the way
I have."

My mother's doubt pulled at her confidence in their marriage. "I have
been mentally unfaithful to you. Tell me, darling, if you ever have me? It
would make me feel better. I have been bitchy and feel disgusted & superficial. Please, have you ever? Have you? I really do love you though today
I worried. Have you ever worried? Don't get mad, darling, please." And,
later, "I am all upset about God—my mind wanders in church and I don't
think I can ever be a Christian. I am so uncharitable. I wish I could get
that from you—you are so wonderful that way. I am crying now so had
better go to sleep . . ." In a third letter, she wrote that her insecurity was
exhaustion and that she needed something to do; she looked forward, she
wrote, to going back to Barnard in the spring.

"Come a little preoccupation, your scales of gloom will clatter down,"
my father replied. "Possibly Honor's clattering out will help too. Well,
it all adds up to a compromise. Unlike what we thought when we were
young"—they are twenty-six and twenty-two!—"we can't have and experience everything, and so 'tis better to chew and savor the pâté we have
than to yearn for caviar . . . a normal person smells a beggar's dirt, someone else might see the splendor of his ultimate humility. The poor are happier than the rich, etc. etc. Gee what pedantry, apologies."

By early May, my mother was back from California and living with my
father's parents at Hollow Hill, Mouse her only contemporary. In spite of
her affection for her mother-in-law, she was frustrated. "I have been on the
verge of hysteria with Mother F. and I have avoided writing you till my

mood got better. Instead it is worse . . ." When Mother Fan opened and read two of my father's letters to her, my mother, furious, packed a suitcase of my father's clothes and moved them to the apartment she'd just found in New York. My father took less offense at his mother's intrusion. "If she had a little sleep and a little love, she'd be better." He was more interested in talking about their future. "Oh Jen, you don't know how I'm counting on our life together in the church . . . the more time is spent on useless years of war, the more I get hungry for the years to come . . . We have the whole of a wonderful world to look to—I pray for us every time I pray, Jen, as I know you do too. I feel closer to you then."

At last, after weeks at a desk job and a stint as a battalion operations commander, my father was given a rifle company, which meant doing, he said years later, "what we now call creating community." Because of censorship, he could not write my mother that he and his company were in the jungle, training to invade Japan, and were about to break camp and board ship for final maneuvers. My father had just emptied his tent—the little table with its photographs of my mother, of their wedding—when there were rumors that the atomic bomb had been dropped. "It seemed like something out of a fairy tale, scuttlebutt that somebody'd started as a joke." In New York, my mother sat down to write him: "It has just come over the radio about the US bombing in Japan with the bomb the size of a coconut that releases atomic energy. I guess it's nice in a relative way that we learned how to do it first, but still I wish it hadn't happened. I am sure we will destroy ourselves." When my father and his company heard for sure, they were still camped in the jungle, still preparing to embark for Japan, spread out in case they were attacked. "It was after lights, taps . . . and things were quiet," he later wrote, "and then we heard, way off in the distance, some rifle shots and machine gun fire, and we thought perhaps a group of Japanese had come out from the jungle . . . And then these sounds got closer, and we heard weapons going off near us, nearer and nearer and nearer, and finally, in the unit next to us . . . and then we heard that the Japanese had surrendered."

It would be six weeks before my father reached New York. "If you get home before Xmas, would you want to study for half a year and then go for a nice Mummy-Honor-Daddy summer?" my mother wrote, excited about finishing college and studying piano before getting pregnant again. "I'd really like to study and be Daddy's helper & typewrite . . . I want to see you

again standing in front of the mirror in your skivvies and shirt tails with
your heaven legs . . . I want to dance on board ship somewhere too. I want
to dance like mad." She was putting finishing touches on the apartment,
had moved in the bassinet she ordered from the Women's Exchange, the
mustard yellow Regency chairs, their furniture and paintings. "Your apartment in New York is superb," her brother Shaw wrote my father. "Huge,
airy, somewhat Moorey, with a flavor of McKeanishness, but not enough
of either to really ruin it."

In early October, when my mother read that the Third Marine Division in Guam was being broken up, she wrote asking my father to delay
his return, not to come home right after the birth. "It doesn't mean I'm
being callous or hard boiled, but the stronger I feel the better time you'll
have . . ." My father's reply was categorical. "You *are* being callous & hard
boiled. Even if I didn't want like hell to see you, can you imagine how long
you'd stay in California if your first child was sitting in New York & you'd
never seen it?!" On the twenty-first of October, from the transient center
in Guam, he wrote that he was about to set sail on the USS *Wayne* for San
Francisco. On board my father met an old friend of his brother's with
whom he played chess, between solitary hours spent in his bunk reading
and writing a letter to his unborn child, which he dated October 25. *Look
at the date above*, he wrote. *You see it is your birthday or a few days before, or
even after your birthday. There is no way for me to know, because, as you have
heard tell many times, I am at sea, knowing that you, our first child, are about to
be born into the family of Jenny and Paul Moore.*

Just three years before, my father had been at sea heading for points
unknown in the South Pacific. *Guadalcanal Diary*, a movie released in
1943, was based on a book by a reporter who followed a platoon of marines
to the battles of Tulagi and Bloody Ridge. On a ship coursing the Pacific,
the platoon awakened one morning to marvel at the sudden appearance
of a flotilla of American battleships. "We rose at dawn," my father wrote of
that same moment, "to see a vast armada of warships, transports, destroyers, cargo ships, cruisers, battleships, aircraft carriers . . . It was a strangely
moving and beautiful sight." He had only a few quibbles with the movie—
"You don't see the Jap & you don't run shoulder to shoulder 6 men deep,
obviously," he wrote my mother, but "the scenes on the transport & in
and around the bivouac area (camp) etc. are good—dialogue authentic."
In the film, in recess from what my father described as the "hardening"

of preparation, the young men are physically easy, even tender with one another, reclining intertwined on the sunny deck, resting on each other's bodies, the training-strengthened arms of an older soldier cradling a dozing private, no more than a boy. More than once, in letters to my mother, my father expressed regret that in order to enforce discipline, he had to reprimand a young marine when he would rather "take him in my arms and comfort him."

It was on board such a transport in the Pacific Ocean that my father learned of my birth. On the morning of October 28, 1945, in New York City, Gordon Wadhams took my mother to the Harkness Pavilion at Columbia Presbyterian Hospital, where I was born in the late afternoon. The next day, on board the USS *Wayne*, my father got a telegram announcing the birth of "Honor Moore," her weight as "7 lbs. 5oz." Someone had a bottle of champagne and cracked it open, and my father and his firstborn were toasted all around. Later, in his bunk, my father resumed writing the letter. Now, knowing his first child was a girl, he began to outline his ideas about love of men and of women. *A woman*, he wrote, *should know men not only from her own point of view* but also *as they are of themselves. If she does not understand men without women, her relationship to men—as sister, daughter, lover or wife—will be inadequate. The strength of relationships between women and men, and their potential weakness*, he explained, *lies in the interlocking of womanly and manly characteristics.* As a result of the meshing of those differences, the love a man and a woman have for each other *becomes its own entity . . . hiding within it the true nature of a man's love and a woman's love.*

When I read the letter for the first time, I already knew of my father's love for men and his refusal to speak about it in any depth. As a result, I brought to the letter a particular frame of reference—my father as a young man struggling to communicate conflicting desires to his unborn child. Nonetheless, I was astounded when, at the bottom of a page, I read, *Let me tell you a story or two, first about the love of a man for a man.* Quickly, I turned to the next page, where my father's crooked, spirally handwriting began a narrative. *Charles Tokavich lived on a farm in upper New York. His family did not own the farm, they worked on it. Before the sun arose in the freshness of Spring, his father—* And there the letter ended. Charlie Tokavich was not a name familiar to me, but there is a similar name in my father's letters, a buddy from Guadalcanal whom he made sure was transferred to his unit in Seattle. Did he love this man? Desire him? Earlier in the letter, my father described the stormy ocean, attributing to it *constancy and sameness, no matter that lightning and thunder fling themselves against her.* His child might wonder why he spoke at such length of the sea: *Perhaps when you finish reading you will understand.* My father never finished writing his story of a man's love for another man, but I think I do understand. What he didn't tell would have illuminated a distinction he was beginning to make between his love for a woman, my mother, and his love for the man he called Charlie Tokavich. To tell that story he required the tumultuous companionship of the night ocean, but in spite of the ocean, the task undid him. How could he explain to his newborn daughter that he loved her mother and would love her, but that also inside him was another kind of love, a forbidden desire that was part of how he understood himself?

When my father arrived in New York almost two weeks after my birth, my mother and I were ensconced with a baby nurse in the apartment on East Seventy-third Street that my mother had so carefully furnished. As my father reported it, my mother was quiet as she took him to the nursery, turned on the small bedside lamp, and showed him the tiny girl. "I thought I should feel something enormous, but I didn't feel anything much," he wrote. His second night home they had a huge fight, "about nothing." Suddenly my mother was in tears, in a fury. He had reached first for the baby rather than for her, he had not been there to take her to the hospital, was not leaning over her as she had dreamed he would be when she came out of anesthesia.

During the summer, while my father was still away, my mother had written him a desolate letter full of doubt and fear: "I never knew it would be as awful as this—I have felt so terribly alone the last week I have almost gone crazy . . . I need you so badly . . . I'm afraid I kidded myself that everything's a whole lot easier than it is, and that somehow by a little wrangling you could have your cake and eat it too—I want my daddy to hold me in his arms,—darling—will you be good about drinking when you get home—I really don't love you then and I worry about it."

For my mother to explode with fear on his return was probably inevitable, but my father, full of romantic anticipation, was also exhausted. Guam had not been an abandonment like Seattle, he protested. He had not chosen it; he had no power over the war. But the more he tried to excuse himself, the more alone my mother felt, the more desolate, the more angry. My father relived the moment she shouted on the willow walk, the night he announced his departure for Seattle and she hit him with her fists. He was frightened. "I did not appreciate the baby or know how to act with her," he wrote. "I had been too self-centered to thank Jenny for all she had done." My father composed those exculpatory sentences for a memoir published decades after my mother's death. I can extrapolate the apology my mother might have offered from the note she wrote explaining the terrified letter of the summer: "Oh Bliss—I slept 12 hours last night and really feel like a new woman—I'm pleased because I know now I can blame all those hideous thoughts on fatigue."

Within weeks of his return, my parents were planning their new life. My father visited the bishop of New York, the first step in the process of becoming a priest. He had no idea what he would do once he was ordained. Perhaps he would teach, even become the rector at St. Paul's School—there were rumors he'd be asked. Or maybe he would write. Gordon Wadhams wanted him to go to Oxford or Cambridge for seminary, but my parents decided it would be too difficult with a one-year-old, and my father's father, who now accepted my father's vocation as a priest, was eager that they remain in New York. Eventually my father enrolled at General Theological Seminary, the Episcopal theological school on Ninth Avenue in Chelsea. Since he could not enter until the following fall and since my mother would be finishing at Barnard that spring, she encouraged him to take courses at Union, the interdenominational seminary near Columbia, where the great theologians Reinhold Niebuhr and Paul Tillich were teaching. "I favor Union for a year to get a slant on the Liberal set," my mother wrote. "You're not the type to get carried away by them, but there's such a thing as knowing about it." In the end, my father studied at Union with both Niebuhr and Tillich and, eager to understand the forces that had brought about the war he had just fought, signed up at Columbia for courses in historiography and in Modern European history with Jacques Barzun.

My father had first heard of Niebuhr and Tillich from Truman Hemingway, an independent farmer-priest whom he'd met just after he finished St. Paul's. Once, as a child, I was sent to stay at his farm in Vermont— the Hemingway daughter, Honoria, was one of the inspirations for my name—and I remember looking down from my cabin on the hillside into a valley of fields, seeing the old priest on a tractor, haying. "There were always three or four people staying there," my father remembered. "A couple of kids like myself"—he'd worked there the summer before Yale—"and maybe a priest who was getting over being an alcoholic . . . getting over having a nervous breakdown." Father Hemingway was not only "holy," as my father put it, but aware of political and social movements and of religious radicals, contemporary practitioners of the kind of activist Christianity Father Bartrop talked about. Therefore, in spite of the fact that he still practiced the family Republicanism and had voted for Dewey in 1944, my father was not averse to my mother's suggestion that he be exposed to "the Liberal slant." My mother's religion professor at Barnard had been Niebuhr's wife, Ursula, and they had become close enough that she had invited the Neibuhrs to her wedding. Afterward, Mrs. Niebuhr wrote my mother she suspected that "probably you share various feelings & beliefs—you & your husband—very akin to mine. Someday I hope we'll be able to meet and talk theologically." They did so during the spring of 1946. When classes started, Paul and Jenny Moore were among the young theological students at the Thursday night gatherings the Niebuhrs held at their apartment in the Union Quadrangle.

My father, a generation younger than Niebuhr, educated in literature and not philosophy, and fresh from battle, had no faith in the capacity of human intellect to formulate solutions to problems like war: "First of all, the world is such an unalterable, stirred up, gory, neurotic, prejudiced, emotional, unstable mess that there is going to be hell to pay for all of us during our whole life and no post-war planning can create peaceful happiness in the near future." The war had inspired their friend Cord Meyer to attend the UN planning meeting in San Francisco, but my father, loyal to the conservative tradition in which he had been raised, was not so idealistic. "There is no permanent value in building more and more economic, diplomatic, social and political cages for the lion or human beast; rather he's got to be trained from the inside out, then the cages are immaterial. So—let the diplomats & hot-shots decide their treaties." For him, there was only one solution: "Our job, as Christians, is to think & pray like hell so that God can someday enter the lion's heart."

Niebuhr certainly believed in the efficacy of prayer—he became famous for one in particular, the Serenity Prayer. But his meditations were more than addresses to the divinity—in them, and in his books, he was working out a nuanced theology that encouraged an ethically and spiritually based activism to bring about political and social change. "Wisdom about our destiny is dependent upon a humble recognition of the limits of our knowledge and our power," he wrote at the time. "Our most reliable understanding is the fruit of 'grace' in which faith completes our ignorance without pretending to possess its certainties as knowledge; and in which contrition mitigates our pride without destroying our hope." At the Niebuhrs', my father entered a conversation in which "sin" was acknowledged and discussed, not only in the context of theology but also in a framework of philosophy and history. Unlike anyone else then in my father's life, Reinhold Niebuhr was in the business of integrating the horror my father had just experienced into a livable world.

But Paul Moore, young, idealistic, and a sensualist, approached religion with different needs than the mature, scholarly theologian. Niebuhr would be instrumental in pioneering international cooperation among the Protestant denominations, and he had argued for America's entrance into the war, not because he believed that war had virtue, but because having witnessed the devout of Germany, his ancestral country, twice fail to restrain the villainy of its rulers, he believed a faith divorced from history, from actual time, could not serve the interests of justice, peace, and community. To Niebuhr, the luxuriant Anglican liturgy my father loved seemed an escape from the urgent conflicts between belief and action at the heart of his thinking.

After exposure to Niebuhr and Tillich, whose course on Luther he took at Union, and to Jacques Barzun, my father was wary of General Seminary. How could this medieval quarter so far downtown rival the high rigor and stimulation of Barzun's teaching at Columbia? How could a faculty of British and American Anglicans possibly measure up to the fervor of the Niebuhr evenings at Union, of studying with a figure such as Paul Tillich? And what, after the intensity of his own spiritual evolution at St. Paul's and Yale and in the war, could the parochial chambers of a denominational education offer beyond a credential for ordination? My mother, for her part, planned to model herself on Ursula Niebuhr, who continued to teach while finding it "a most expensive hobby . . . my family & health have been the most heavily taxed." But in spite of her one-year-old, Jenny Moore was full of plans. "There are so many things I want to do, like Plato, piano, sewing & having a [second] baby & maybe social work school . . .

I wonder if I can get away with not being a solid housewife nurse with the fellow seminarians—I can always find out from Mrs. Niebuhr."

"Find out," Mrs. Niebuhr replied, "if your husband wants a cushion or a stimulus, and model your life on that."

One day, on a walk to show my mother the seminary, my father introduced her to the dean, "a tall, gaunt, slightly stooped man, who looked like an English earl played by Edward Everett Horton." Hughell Fosbroke peered over his horn-rimmed spectacles at Jenny Moore. "We do not like women at the seminary," he said, "but we will, I am sure, absorb you." My parents found the incident hilarious; it would be decades before my mother understood that the dean's remark exposed a strain of Anglican theology and practice to which even the most progressive clergy, including her husband, were subject. For the time being, though, she and my father dined out on the story, appalled at the regulation that forbade single seminarians from marrying until after graduation. As it happened, the dean who told my mother that General Seminary didn't like women was my father's most memorable teacher. When he lectured, he took his students viscerally into an ancient desert world. As he spoke, my father wrote, "we stood with Moses, trembling before the burning bush, sensing the numinous presence of the god of Abraham, Isaac, and Jacob, in his confrontation with the holy, the total otherness of God."

6

Becoming a Priest

Inside my room, the early morning air is almost violet, the slats of the crib rising like stalks in the grainy near-dark. Or downstairs in the kitchen, the brick walls painted white, only a small amount of light coming in through the windows, half-windows that face the street so the room is in shadow, and I am sitting at the table, watching someone's shoes walk past every once in a while—a woman's pumps, a man's oxfords. Or shyly in the doorway I stand, Ernie, my nanny, behind me, the living room crowded with grownups, the smell of cocktails and perfume, my mother wearing dark red lipstick, my father turning toward me.

And so I have come into the story.

At first Ernie takes care of me, lives with us I think, as my parents begin to bring me up in the way they are used to—children looked after by nannies, parents at a distance. My father is at seminary, my mother taking courses in theology at Union and in social work at the New School. In most of my early memories I'm alone, or about to be alone—my mother one morning at the door of my room, and then gone. There are photographs in which I am on her lap, even one I recently saw for the first time, in which I am in her arms and we are smiling, smiling into each other's eyes. But I don't remember touch. The clothes I wear in most photographs are pressed linen, the shoes polished, the socks neatly turned down. In one I wear a pale coat that looks to be velvet, with a white fur collar and cuffs, a matching hat; I am not smiling in that photograph—I look anxious. Soon Ernie, the nanny, is no longer there, and someone we call Gagy comes a few days a week.

We are sitting in that half-underground kitchen and the chair she is sitting on is too small for her. She is a big, tall woman with long brown hair she collects and swirls into buns she secures with hairpins at either side of her face. Bright blue eyes and big round arms, big cheeks and a small mouth, big thighs that make soft hills under her apron. She was only in her forties, though I thought of her as old because of her large size, because of how she wore her hair, which I couldn't stop looking at, especially early in the morning when I might catch her with it down or at night when she pulled her hairpins and it fell to her shoulders. She'd come from Norway at eighteen, from a large family whose Norwegian names lullabied off her tongue like an awkward, beautiful alphabet. Always when she spoke Norwegian, I imagined a small house outside a town near the ocean, green grass between the rocks on the shore, the water bright blue all summer, a place where it was dark most of the day in winter and houses were lit with gas and candles.

"You ate all your spinach!" She is praising me.

"Yes," I say, "and I want more."

"Oh, Honor!" she proclaims, as if my eating spinach were evidence of something extraordinary. And after I finish the second helping, I ask again; I'm still hungry, but for the praise.

"I want more," and she gives me more. "Are you married, Gagy?" She laughs because she knows I know she has three children. She had loved her husband very much, she tells me, and one morning had woken up, turned toward him in their high bed, and found him dead.

"After that it was very hard," she says, looking at me with a serious expression on her face. "I had to go out and work. I had to go out and work to take care of my children."

Or I am a bit older, and she takes me to visit our landlord, a painter, who lives upstairs. I remember the tousle of his gray hair, his mustache and glasses—he was painting enormous dark skies with billowy clouds and tiny sand-colored houses. It was the first time I'd seen a desert and I remember thinking it must be Bethlehem: where are Mary and Joseph? I breathed in the smell of his paints, scrutinized the tubes twisted and messy with color in the wooden box next to his easel. Soon I could go upstairs alone, and he would stop painting and tell me the little houses were made of adobe and the big skies were not in the Holy Land but in a place called New Mexico. I found his name strange, Houghton Smith, and his wife Laura's long, nearly white hair was piled on top of her head. I thought she was beautiful. I had been directed to call them Mr. and Mrs. Smith, but after a while she said, in her Southern accent, her pretty mouth laughing, "Call me Laura." In a painting Houghton Smith did that hangs now in my apartment, one of those sky-and-clouds paintings is on the easel in his studio, a Roman head sits on a bookshelf, and out a window is the reddish tower of the seminary chapel that I could see from my crib.

Every day my father disappeared into that red-towered place; some-times from my window I would see him, early in the morning, leap across the street, unlock the gate of the seminary wall, and he'd be gone. Soon I knew that in the Gothic buildings where comings and goings were governed by the bell I could hear from my crib, my father was becoming a priest. He had written my mother of the urgency of his desire to make this life in the church, an urgency that came, it seemed, out of a terror of returning to civilian life: *Please help me, darling, to keep alive to what we both must do. I'm so vacillating. So weak.* He remembered his convalescent leave, the desolation that could pull him from a nightclub table of laugh-ing friends across the room just to say hello to a marine stranger, his need to drink and drink and drink, even though, as he wrote my mother, he considered drunkenness "sinful." Now there was the possibility all of that torment could be swept away, he himself transformed.

My father was prepared for the excitement of a community of worship —morning prayer that began at 7 a.m. and evening prayer at the end of the day. The revelation was that one made the effort not for one's own "subjectivity" but as "heavy work which you rendered to God as a duty and as a form of Thanksgiving day by day." And he had not anticipated the intellectual ferment he encountered, how his engagement with his vocation would make learning a passion, make what he'd been thinking about ever since St. Paul's come vividly alive—I can hear his excitement as I read transcripts of the oral history he taped forty years later. Not only Old Testament, which Dean Fosbroke taught with "force and drama," in the context of Freud, of Marx, of "current intellectual trends," but also Dogmatics, which Dr. Stewart taught as the chronology of the development of Christian doctrine, always placing it in the context of its origins. In a class called "Liturgics," my father's knowledge of the Anglo-Catholic liturgy that had once made him uneasy deepened. And he learned to withstand the ebbs and flows of his faith: as one of his professors said, "It might be harder to believe in God on a cold rainy morning." As he had been at St. Paul's, my father was part of a community of men that was virtually monastic. Unlike at Yale, where he was constantly striving to prove himself and partying to relieve the stress, or the Marines, where the requirements of being an officer held him apart, he was one of many, a seminarian among seminarians. And now, also, he was married, with a child.

Once, after supper, my father swept me up into his black seminarian's cape and across the street for evensong. I remember the starry sky, the cold darkness as we climbed the stairs to the seminary and stepped along the grassy path to the chapel. I could already hear it, something like the rushing of wind, the coming of a storm. We were late, and as we slipped into the pew in the candlelit church full of men, I understood that the rushing sound was singing. Without women or children, the rumbling voices of priests and seminarians, resounding against the stone walls of the small chapel, were otherworldly, even God-like. I was scared and so I leaned against my father, nuzzling the black cape still fresh from night air, but he didn't look down at me or put his big hand on my head. Now he belonged to something else, this big and strange sound, so deep and loud it made me shake. I could hardly breathe as all the men together spoke words I couldn't yet understand. *And with thy spirit. Ah-men. Alleluia.*

My father was holding his prayer book, speaking and singing, his voice disappearing into all the other voices. I tried to speak along with everybody else, hold on to Poppy, keep him from rising, from flying up into the darkness. The room was slowly swinging in the candlelight, and suddenly the organ stopped playing but the men kept singing, and, as if the earth had dropped out from underneath us, the thunder of their voices lifted off, leaving behind the shiny dark wood of pews that smelled of lemon, the feel of my small body, the hardness of the floor. "The church is the house of God," my father would tell me later, but that evening I was just beginning to talk. I could almost make out what they were singing, but I didn't know what the sounds meant stretched out by the music, in the sway of those voices and the strange excitement of candles and incense.

After that night, I looked at my father with new curiosity. He was no longer different from my mother just because he was the father and she wasn't. He was in touch with something that couldn't be seen but was also real. When he left our apartment, he visited a place where utterance had a use beyond ordinary talk, was something frightening and beautiful. Across the street in the dark, inside the red tower, in the honey light of the candles, was a landscape like a dream, a place to which my father belonged and from which my mother and I were excluded.

It was at seminary, I would learn after his death, that my father had his first full affair with another man—a priest, an instructor also married, his name unknown to the friends of my father who told me the story. Had my father imagined having a wife and baby would erase the conflict he'd felt since childhood? Had he imagined what an extended sexual affair with another priest would be like, how it might lift the barricades between sexuality and spiritual passion, perhaps illuminating each? Was it at seminary that my father's secret and the shame it brought entered his spiritual struggle, became, as it were, an angel to wrestle with? I imagine him then, in his twenties, working to keep that part of himself firmly enclosed within the walls of the seminary and held just as safely in a separate compartment of his life.

A memory. I am nearly three, and my little brother and I are awake. He is wearing diapers and rubber pants. I am old enough to walk, but I thump down the narrow stairs behind him, both of us on our bottoms. We crawl along the carpeted hall to our parents' closed bedroom and scratch at the door till my father lets us in. The cloud of my mother's black hair is on the pillow, and she holds the sheet over her face. My father talks, though I can't remember what he says and he doesn't let us onto the bed. Maybe he starts a game. I am worried about my mother, who doesn't move, but then she does move so she isn't dead. But she doesn't speak. My mother is hiding. Had they been fighting? Usually my mother was radiant, smiling, her arms open, already saying something funny, my father laughing with her. Her hair was so black on the pillow. Why couldn't I just touch her? And why do I remember this? Did I already understand there was something sad and difficult between them or did I just want to see her face?

Eventually, as my mother grew out of girlhood, she began to feel my father's distance as a sexual complication. Having entered into a marriage of their time, my parents had no language to explore what was wrong with their erotic life. For my father, it was certainly too complicated and painful to consider that his secret existence had an impact on his desire for my mother, or that something she was not even consciously aware of might come to affect her desire for him. Instead, they began to feel disappointed in their intimate life. My mother, being a woman of her time, considered the problem hers, and my father, a man of his time who knew the consequences of revelation could destroy his life, kept his dangerous secret. Decades later, I would learn that by the time we moved to Jersey City, each was visiting a "shrink" in New York—my mother for her "frigidity," my father to come to terms with, if not change, his sexual nature.

But at twenty-six and twenty-two, they were fueled by the energy and spirit of idealism as they embarked on a new life they took seriously, not only as a mission but as a partnership. My father counted on my mother— *Please help me, darling, to keep alive to what we both must do*—and he also supported her aspirations. And she looked to him: "The more I think of it the less I want to be detached from what you are doing," she had written, pregnant with me. Wasting no time, she and some of the other wives formed a group to protest the exclusion of wives from the guest lectures held at the seminary. Finally women were admitted, provided they "didn't ask questions."

My parents soon made friends, among them Kim Myers, who was

the first to make them aware of the radical ministries in the postwar church that would inspire my father's ministry and my mother's intellect. C. Kilmer Myers, whom I called "Father Myers," had black hair and pale blue eyes and was older than my parents; he taught my father "Patristics"— that is, the history and teachings of the church fathers. He had graduated from Berkeley Seminary, the Episcopal divinity school in New Haven, where innovative theologies from Britain and Europe were being integrated into American Anglo-Catholic practice. In the late 1930s he had spent a postgraduate year at Maria Laach, a monastery in Germany at the center of a movement within the Roman Catholic Church—called the liturgical revival—that was challenging the church to make its rituals relevant and compelling to the man on the street. It was at Maria Laach that some of the work was done to revive pre-Augustinian liturgies that were eventually reintroduced at Vatican II, innovations that led to greater participation by ordinary people in the liturgy. At the end of the war, Father Myers went back to Europe to serve as the Anglican chaplain at the Yalta Conference, offering morning prayer and Sunday services for Roosevelt and Churchill. Now in New York, he was afire with the ideas of the French worker priests, Roman Catholic clergy who went incognito into factories in Paris, Lyon, and Marseille to bring "the word of Christ" to workingmen. First insulted and abused by workers who saw the church as part of the ruling elite, these laborer-priests, receiving no stipend from the church, gained credibility when they took on not only real work but the vulnerabilities of workers—it was when one priest lost his job that his fellows accepted him. Eventually, in the anti-Communist climate of the early 1950s, these priests would be recalled to conventional parish work, but in 1946 their mission was a great innovation in the mission work of Catholic clergy.

Having two children under three (my first brother was born between my father's first and second year at seminary) did not keep my mother from joining my father one afternoon a week to work at St. Peter's Episcopal Church, a failing parish near the seminary. Kim had become priest in charge there, with a mandate to make the parish relevant to people in the then decaying, impoverished neighborhood. He eschewed the missionary notion of bounty to the poor; his idea was to enter the actual lives of the people who lived near the church, often by working with children. My father tried to talk seriously with his group of boys about "life," but when that failed, he organized a baseball team and acted as coach. The work was reminiscent of what he'd done with kids at the St. Paul's summer camp and also of his "ministry" to young marines during the war. My mother had no previous experience to draw on. The people they met, she wrote, were "Puerto Ricans we had seen on doorsteps, some Negroes, and children of those white families too poor to move away."

By the summer, one afternoon a week had expanded into a full-time program. My mother and other faculty and student wives organized a nursery school for neighborhood children on the seminary grounds, and through the principal at the local school, my mother started a girls' club in their apartment—the girls couldn't, one of them explained, join a club that met at St. Peter's since their families were Roman Catholic. In a scrapbook there's a photo of the girls, arm in arm, wearing lipstick, tight capri pants, kerchiefs tied at their necks, curly fringe bangs and hair pulled back. By the end of the year they'd made enough money at dances to buy everyone a blue satin jacket with her name in lacy machine-embroidered script.

There was one place in New York where these new ideas about the role of the church were already being put into practice. My parents were reading *The Catholic Worker*, a monthly newspaper started by Dorothy Day and Peter Maurin in 1933 and sold at a cent a copy. A community of Catholics living in voluntary poverty, the Catholic Worker movement was, by 1946 when it came to my parents' attention, a network of communal houses and farms that ministered to the destitute, so called to distinguish them from those who took a vow of voluntary poverty. My parents had come upon the paper the first year my father was in seminary and were among those who invited Dorothy Day to address the student body. "She came to the arched gate of the seminary," my mother wrote, "in ill-fitting, shabby clothes (from the hostel's clothing room, she told me later)." My mother escorted her to the room where she was to speak and was amazed when Dorothy asked for her prayers: "It made her nervous to make a speech." She spoke of her bohemian past (which included romantic pursuit by Eugene O'Neill), of joining and resigning from the Communist Party, of converting to Catholicism out of gratitude after the birth of her daughter.

"Afterward she thanked me for my prayers and said they had helped," my mother wrote. In spite of some embarrassment at their "fancy" furniture, she and my father invited Dorothy back to the apartment for a drink—she came to the apartment but refused the drink. "She said she couldn't bear the burdens of alcoholics and drink herself." The evening began a long friendship—Dorothy Day's grandchildren got some of Jean Watson's sweaters. My mother was "stunned by her simplicity." To the daughter of an aristocratic, glamorous Boston modernist and her tweedy husband, Dorothy Day was "a wind from another land—strong, warm and a little frightening."

In this wind, my parents began to understand what they might be looking for after seminary, a circumstance in which the strong partnership that cradled their marriage might thrive. Reading my mother's frayed copy of Dorothy Day's *Loaves and Fishes*, I found a passage that exactly answered my father's dispute with his contemporaries who believed the world could be changed by creating *economic, diplomatic, social and political cages for the lion or human beast.* The Catholic Worker hostels and farms were run by volunteers, money appeared out of nowhere in response to prayer, and people in need were helped. "We were trying to overcome hatred with love, to understand the forces that made men what they are . . . to change them, if possible, from lions into lambs," Day wrote. "It was a practice in loving, a learning to love, a paying of the cost of love . . . we were not a community of saints but a rather slipshod group of individuals."

Paul and Jenny Moore would soon become part of another "slipshod group of individuals" and attempt their own "practice in loving." By the time my father was in his third year of seminary, he and my mother were convinced they wanted to work in the inner city. "It just didn't feel right," my father said in the oral history, "to take a job in a posh suburban parish. It might be right for some people, but it wasn't right for me." For both my parents, a particular afternoon the fall of 1948 became emblazoned in memory. They were walking along a seminary path when Kim leaned out of his office window and suggested they find a parish where they could do downtown work full-time; by now "they" also included Bob Pegram, a priest from Virginia who taught classics at the seminary.

Within days the discussion was more about how than if. They dispatched letters to several big-city bishops, and eventually Bishop Washburn of the Diocese of Newark offered Grace Church, Van Vorst, in Jersey City, and the summer after my father's graduation from seminary, on July 1, 1949, we moved to 268 Second Street, blocks from where the movie *On the Waterfront* was filmed four years later, and just as gritty. I was almost four, my first brother Paul almost two, and my mother eight months pregnant with my first sister, Adelia, named for my father's beloved grand-mother. The ministry included three priests, Kim Myers as priest in charge, my father, and Bob Pegram—my mother was the fourth member of the team.

My father, who had imagined himself the headmaster at St. Paul's or alone in a room writing books, found himself, with two friends, an intrepid wife with whom he had conceived a life of partnership, and two tiny children, at the threshold of what would be the formative adventure of his career. Like the Marines, which had made him a man but a man he could not have imagined himself becoming, Jersey City would define him as a priest. Though I hardly remember the crowded church and the crush of priests and bishops, I saw my father ordained to the priesthood the fol-lowing winter in Jersey City, on December 17, 1949; he celebrated his first Eucharist that Christmas.

In the years we lived in Jersey City, having been born into my grand-parents' world of monogrammed linens, tea every day at four, country houses, full-time servants, and chauffeured cars, I became a public school pupil among girls whose Polish and Irish fathers worked the waterfront and factories of Jersey City or whose African-American parents, born in the South, had come North in the Great Migration. "Family and friends asked us with varying degrees of tact how long we would stay in such an area with a family," my mother wrote. "We told them we didn't know." Dor-othy Day offered immediate instruction. When my mother, overwhelmed with the children, the house, the church, asked her what to do about the contradiction between Christian service and an orderly household, she replied sharply, "Lower your standards."

When I remember *The Catholic Worker*, printed on newsprint and illustrated with dense woodcuts by the Quaker artist Fritz Eichenberg of Christ huddled in the breadline at a soup kitchen, of Christ as a worker or a farmer, I think of my mother, employing her considerable wit and imagination to base a household on Dorothy Day's ideas and doing all the work with very little help. In the narrow brownstone rectory, we lived on the second floor and Kim Myers and Bob Pegram on the third. The first floor was common, and in the manner of a Catholic Worker house of hos-pitality, the doors were thrown open. We had what we came to call an "open rectory." Poor men with nowhere else to go and breath thick with whiskey drank my mother's homemade soup on the front porch. Families burned out of their apartments outfitted themselves in the "clothes room" in the basement, leaving a child or two to stay with us until the church helped them find a new apartment. All of this was made possible, even necessary, by the pursuit of an ideal that flowed from a belief shared by the team at Grace Church of what being a Christian meant in a modern city—and it included political and social action in behalf of parishioners evicted, jailed, or excluded from illegally segregated federal housing projects. The supper table was crowded not only with random hungry kids or men from "the porch set," but priests maybe from India or Africa, activists from England or France, the curious among my parents' East Side friends, or college volunteers. The conversation, to which I avidly listened, asking questions like "What is Communism?" was a weave of politics, religion, wisecracks, and laughter; and the meal, cooked by my mother, was introduced by my father or Father Myers or Father Pegram saying grace, all of us holding hands, thanking God for what we were about to eat. There was always enough; as Dorothy Day said of such tables, "Everybody just takes a little less."

Soon I was old enough to stay up with the grownups on Christmas Eve. After supper, oyster stew which my mother made with great pride, Father Myers and Father Pegram and my father would leave to vest for the service. Let's say it's the first Christmas Eve I am allowed to go to midnight mass. My grandmother has come for the night and friends from New York, and we all wait until about nine to go over to church. The purple that has shrouded everything the four weeks of Advent has been replaced by glistening white; white flowers from the greenhouse at Hollow Hill arranged by the altar guild, with holly, adorn the steps up to the altar, and the almost life-size crèche to the left of the nave is no longer empty. Carved from wood and beautifully painted, Mary and Joseph are there, and the baby, and the shepherds and the animals—the three kings won't arrive until Epiphany, on January 6. The real hay is from my grandmother's farm. Everyone is wearing their best clothes, and the church is full, the smells of perfume and aftershave mingling with the fragrance of the evergreen that thickens the roof of the crèche, and as we walk to our pew, there are whispered exchanges of "Merry Christmas!" and "God bless you"—the Williamses and the Skippers and the Walkers, who are black, the new Puerto Rican families, and the white old ladies who still come to the church even though there have been so many changes. And I see some of the people who worked here in the summer, and the nuns who have come to teach Sunday school.

Soon Father Penfield is playing the organ—Christmas carols! "Once in Royal David's City," "Angels We Have Heard on High"—"Silent Night" will come later. Now the processional: first the acolytes in their red cassocks and white cottas all solemn, carrying a cross or a candle; then Father Myers and Father Pegram and maybe a visiting priest, all in vestments; an acolyte swinging a censer, the smell of incense. And, of course, my father, the tallest, looking gentle and solemn. "His face changed after he became a priest," Nona Clark said decades later. "It became clear, clear with his purpose."

On this particular Christmas Eve, I watch my father climb the pulpit. "Merry Christmas," he says, which is strange since it's something he would also say outside church, and this raises laughs of quiet delight in the congregation and soft intakes of breath; my father smiles in response. And then, as he begins to speak as a priest, his tone changes and he is preaching. Tonight the sermon is just like a story. Mary is pregnant and lives with Joseph, the father of her child, right near here, but because he has lost his job, they are without a home, and because they are black the motel had turned them away. They are cold and afraid and her time is near as they walk the dark, empty streets until they see an old garage, its door ajar. There Joseph finds an old lantern and a kerosene heater in the corner—and a few old pasteboard boxes and some rags, rags blackened with motor oil that have been used to repair a car. Stretching out his long arms, my father tenderly describes Joseph settling Mary onto a pile of those rags, and he looks down at us, and then, lifting his face, he says, emphasizing certain words: "And as a bright STAR appeared in the SKY, the baby was born. Jesus was BORN." And, he continues, "the CHRIST CHILD was laid in a box of those rags, by the light of the strange old railroad lantern."

I could see Mary and Joseph—I could see the shadowy, cold garage, the battered lantern, the kerosene heater. My father was both someone else entirely and just as I knew him; and the story seemed completely true, happening right here in the neighborhood where we lived in the tall, narrow rectory.

I understood miracles—my mother read me the lives of saints, of martyrs, and my father had told the story of Saint Christopher, who carried a child across a river, his weight growing heavier and heavier until Christopher could hardly walk, terrified he might stumble and drown, and drown the child. But he did not stumble or allow the child on his shoulders to fall into the turbulent, stormy current, and when he reached the opposite shore, the child leapt from his shoulders and, standing there in the darkness, was suddenly illuminated, revealed as the Christ child. This Christmas night it seemed that my father, by telling the Nativity story in a new way, had himself created a kind of miracle. He had made me see and smell and feel. When I told him how much I liked his sermon, he looked down at me and smiled.

I don't remember when I did not carry a sense of the miraculous. I expected such marvels, and I looked for them. In our dining room one day, on the wall, there appeared a piece of paper that looked like the mottled black-and-white cover of a notebook. My mother said that if I stood and looked at it, Jesus would appear. The dining room was toward the back of the house, closed off from the living room by a pair of sliding doors. Tacked to these doors was the black-and-white piece of paper, and I stood there and looked at it, certain the Christ child or the man he became would appear to me, as he had in my father's sermon, as he had to Mary Magdalene at the empty grave on Easter morning. I was alone there, and I stood, waiting, but no matter how long I looked and waited, I couldn't see him. My mother rushed in and out of the room doing housework and I stood there. I couldn't see Jesus. I couldn't see Jesus's face, but I kept standing there, looking, because my mother had said, There he is.

7

My Jersey City

When my mother was home, my favorite place was the kitchen because there were always other people there and I could watch her talk to them and try to do it myself. One day Tom Venable was leaning against the washing machine, which was to the left of the window in the kitchen. Outside the window was a metal fire escape, and beyond the fire escape, the parish hall. Tom Venable was wearing a uniform, an army uniform, a greenish brown get-dressed-up uniform, all pressed. It was a sunny morning. His skin was creamy brown and he talked in an almost Southern accent, although his family lived in the neighborhood. He was back on leave, just about to go to Korea, where there was a war. We had air raids at school, but there was no talk about war, even at supper. There was talk about the unfairness of how poor people lived, and about how prejudice kept black people, whom we called Negroes, from getting places to live, jobs, enough money. I asked my father about Korea, and he explained there was a war there, against "the Communists"—and Ledlie Laughlin, a seminarian, explained that communism with a small *c* was good, people working together without a boss, but that with a capital *C*, Communism had leaders who lied and put people in prison for saying what they believed and that Russia and China were Communist with a big *C*, along with other countries they had conquered.

But that comes later. Now I am in the kitchen, and Tom Venable is smiling and talking. My mother is at the sink with her arms in soapy water and I am standing there, tilting back on my heels looking up into Tom Venable's smiling, handsome face. He couldn't have been more than twenty; probably I asked him his age, and he certainly told me it as I tilted, listening as he talked to my mother and to me, answering our questions so buoyantly. "I like the buttons," I said, looking at his jacket. And he smiled down. "What grade are you in?" He had a way of slapping his hat, an army hat that folded, against his thigh, and laughing. He used words like "sharp" and was very polite to my mother. After a while, he left, and I watched him out the window, jumping down the front stoop, stopping a second to pull his hat from his trouser pocket and place it, so it looked "sharp," on his head. He was on his way to the war, I thought to myself. Would I ever see him again?

When my father was still in Guam and my mother pregnant with me and they got romantic in their letters, they would muse back and forth. One conversation had to do with a house in the country. Would they have a little farm in Vermont? Would there be meadows and mountains, or ocean? My father wrote my mother a letter that was a story: *Let's go for a picnic, Mummy!* he had little Honor say. And then while he biked into town for hamburger, my mother made *sandwiches of cold chicken and lettuce & juicy tomatoes.* They'd pack grape juice for me and beer for them, and maybe fresh peaches. They'd have to lug the heavy sail-bag out of *a sea-smelling closet,* but soon we'd all be in the boat. *The big whiteness of the sail leaps up from the crumpled cocoon,* my father imagined, *and soon the last fog has lifted, leaving sky-bright water, clear firs and bright flicks of white houses. Everyone's pretty excited, especially Honor. The lines are coiled, the life jacket wound around Honor . . . Daddy runs up forward . . . there is a breathtaking lunge, and we are off, bounding along, gunwales awash, breezes blowing.* At exactly 12:45, they reach *Needles Harbor, as Honor calls it, because she first learned about pine needles there. It's a nice place to swim and there's a blueberry patch and a dog. Then while Honor looks for shells, Mummy & Daddy lie in the sun together or read aloud.* But by the time I was born, and old enough to ask to name a harbor, we were living in Jersey City, and my father was making stories out of other materials.

Recently a friend of mine, a young man in his twenties, read the book my mother wrote about Jersey City and said, "I think it was terrible of your parents to live in a place like that with all those children." I protested: "It was the best time of my childhood." My parents did not, like Dorothy Day, live in voluntary poverty, but the life they made in Jersey City was modest compared to how they could have lived, and they made a commitment to try to share the lives of those they ministered to. In their New York apartment on Twenty-first Street, they'd installed wedding presents, monogrammed linen, inherited paintings and furniture. But for the move to Jersey City they packed most of their things in crates they stored at Hollow Hill. "We wanted the house to be a place where people could feel at home." With a child's logic, I didn't expect Jersey City to be like Hollow Hill, nor did I expect to be attended to by my parents the way I was by Gagy, or even by the extra grownups who gathered around the dinner table every night. By the time I was older, I shared my parents' dedication—notes I took on "my" Jersey City are filed under the heading "Utopia."

I want to remember Grace Church as a dream of what is possible among people. When I think of how I listened in the kitchen or around the supper table, I can say, Yes it was. I learned from the extra grownups, but I also learned from my parents, as every night they talked—my father and Father Myers about what was happening with the fair housing campaign, my mother about the book she was reading—*Cry, the Beloved Country* about South Africa, *The Diary of a Country Priest,* or a new book by Charles Williams, the English novelist who also wrote theology. Listening to those conversations was how I learned who my parents were, and knowing what they were thinking about made the more intimate times—

my father telling us stories, my mother reading me *Black Beauty* when I was sick—all the more extraordinary.

But for the most part, I made my own way. Having themselves been cared for by servants, my parents had no model for paying the kind of attention one might now expect—they had seen their parents at meals, just before bed, all day long only on vacations; round-the-clock caring was done by others. And so my mother, with only Gagy when she and my father were away and someone to clean once a week, did the best she could while doing everything else, while my father, when he wasn't out calling, at a meeting, or next door at the church, charmed and delighted us or explained things. It took my mother a long time to learn what a child needed—till number six or seven. I had no words to protest how alone I felt, and I'm not sure my parents would have heard me. They were on a mission.

The summer we moved to Jersey City I was four, my brother turned two in July, and my first sister was born the end of August. Gagy came once a week from the Bronx by subway and Hudson Tube and stayed for a night or two while my parents had their day off in New York. They'd stay at "825," the apartment on Fifth Avenue that belonged to my father's parents. For that thirty-six hours, my father was the Episcopal chaplain at NYU and my mother continued her social work courses at the New School. They saw Gami and, at night, their old friends, and they saw their psychiatrists. My father needed the time off—he was intermittently so tired that some mornings he stayed in bed late, and sometimes when he had a cold, he'd get pneumonia. Without being told, I understood he got sick that way because of the war, that the wound in his lung had made him weak. I couldn't know then that less than a decade is no time at all, that my grown-up father was at hardly any distance from the wounded marine.

Of course my mother was also tired, but she didn't look it. "I'm exhausted," she would say with emphasis on the middle syllable, so it sounded like a joke—she loved to make everyone laugh—and go right on with what she was doing: throwing leftovers into the soup for the men who came to the door, greeting everyone in the kitchen, which was the center of the rectory like the altar was the center of the church, feeding the baby in the high chair, others of us running in and out, then cooking supper. Every night at the table were her husband, her three children, and Father Myers and Father Pegram, not to mention whoever came to stay for a day or two—evicted, burned out, recovering. "Come for supper," she would say with her dazzling smile. We had fish on Fridays to mark the day Christ died, and my mother always looked for other ways to integrate ordinary life with the story being told in the church next door; it was there that I could go to find my father celebrating mass in the morning before I went to school or when I came home, saying evening prayer, the black letters forming words across the white pages as he read the lessons and psalms.

Once, on my parents' day off, I told Gagy I couldn't sleep if I was by myself and so she let me take a nap with her on my parents' bed. But her closeness scared me. If I allowed myself to fall too close to Gagy, I wondered illogically, would my mother ever hold me again? The light in the room was yellow because the shades were pulled down, and I tried to fall asleep, keeping my body separate from Gagy's, and then it came to me, something so frightening I was convinced my insides had turned upside down. Gagy was sleeping, and I watched her breathe, a quiet snore coming from her nose, her hair loosening from its pins. I whispered her name, my voice so scared it was too soft to wake her, but now there were tears on my cheeks. And then I was shouting her name, and she was turning toward me, that serious expression on her face, which made me feel I was asking too much. "What's the matter, Honor?" The sound of her voice made me cry harder. I wanted nothing more than to be just like her, feet on the ground, head in the air, but I felt as if I were permanently upside down. "You're just dreaming," she said when I explained.

"No, no! I'm not." I tried to stop crying. "Gagy, Gagy, when I grow up, will I be like you?" I wanted this awful upside-down feeling to go away, to be able to stand upright.

"No," she said. " No." She was stroking my cheek with one of her big soft hands. "You won't be like me," she said, her blue eyes narrowing a little, "you'll be beautiful."

Why didn't my mother ever say that?

The Good Friday I was five, I was wearing a velvet dress with a wide lace collar. The color was somewhere between turquoise and sky blue, and I loved it. As a toddler I'd had blond curls, almost white, my father said, but by the time I was told about them, they were long gone. This particular Good Friday, I was lying on my bed at Hollow Hill, looking at the ceiling and stroking my long hair, standing in front of the mirror that ran the full height of the bathroom door, feeling narrow and maybe even beautiful, turning my head to the side, running my fingers down a straight strand all the way to the end, where it curled a little.

"We're going to get your hair cut," my mother said, coming briskly into the room, "and then we're going to the movies." It was so unusual to be alone with her that I pretended not to care when the long pieces of hair fell to the floor as she and the hairdresser talked about the shape of my face. *The King of Kings* was the name of the movie, and it was about Jesus, about what had happened to him this day all those centuries ago. I remember the dark parish hall in the church my grandmother went to, the smell of my mother's perfume, and the color of the movie, pale gray, the shape of Jesus in his long white robe moving toward us, on a donkey, waving a palm, the crowd, faces I could barely make out. I knew Jesus was going to die, and I couldn't help crying when the men whipped him and pushed a wreath of thorns onto his head that made his forehead bleed, and when the soldiers nailed him to a cross.

At home there were no long mirrors, but I had a bedroom to myself; it had lots of light and wallpaper with bunches of cherries on it. After supper, my father would come in to tell us a story—my brother would crawl onto my bed, my little sister, and we'd all lie there. Once he asked each of us for a character. My brother asked for an eagle named Daniel and my sister for a rabbit named Peter. I asked for a fairy princess with long blond hair named Josephine, and in the first story Peter and Josephine soared away on the wings of Daniel the eagle. After the story (there was a new installment every night), the others would leave and I'd wait to sleep until Mommy came to kiss me good night as she always did. In the morning, I'd wake up, sit up in my bed, and look around the sunny room, the bunches of bright red cherries popping as if they were real. The house was mostly dark—"like something out of Charles Addams," my mother always said— but this room was so light and wide that sometimes a guest would sleep there too, in another bed. It also had the biggest closet in the house, and so my mother kept things there—winter clothes, Christmas tree ornaments, extra sheets.

It must have been morning because it was light, and it must have been before I went to kindergarten the January after I turned five. My mother was taking something out of the closet and I asked her a question. I was facing her and she had her back to me. She didn't stand up, so I asked again, and she answered and I didn't understand what she said and she asked me to be quiet but I asked again, and suddenly she turned, shouting. There was a sharp sting across my face, the sound of a slap in the air, so hard it made my head turn. It hurt and I was crying. That's all I can get back. It was a simple moment, and it broke something. Clouds suddenly darken and roll in across the sky, and the sky breaks open with thunder. In the lightning you see everything, but before the image goes to your brain it has vanished, so you see nothing but a warning. It could happen again, is what I suppose I felt, looking up at her. And it did happen again, more than once.

"I can't cope," my mother said, putting the Coca-Cola she was drinking down on the table. Everyone laughed—another joke. I remember that moment because "Coke" almost rhymes with "cope" and I didn't know what "cope" meant. We were sitting around the kitchen table before we had a dishwasher and everyone was in stitches. It was afternoon or a night after supper. I'd gone to school, stood with the other children in the basement corridor looking down at my shoes, at the ochre tile floor. My mother was twenty-six, twenty-seven? She had already cut my hair off, and then she turned and slapped me. Before that I had my body to myself.

Once, in the Adirondacks, long after my mother's death, my father and I were taking a walk. It was a wet day and so the green of the forest was uninterrupted by splotches of sun as we walked the trail, so narrow he was ahead and I was behind. "I want to apologize to you," he said, "for not intervening when Jenny fought with you. I was going to a psychiatrist at the time who said not to interfere—mothers and daughters. But I was wrong, and I'm sorry about it now." As he talked, images came into my mind of the house in Jersey City, which I still remembered as a happy place, all the extra grownups I could talk to when he and my mother were so busy. I remembered the soup on the stove and that Tony Duke presented the household with a dishwasher after being put to work in the kitchen on a visit. It's the white enamel of the dishwasher that came back when my father apologized, then the marbleized linoleum kitchen floor, and the narrow stairs that led upstairs. I remembered my fear, I even remembered looking in the mirror after one of those fights with my mother. But I no longer felt anger toward her, just a kind of sadness for her confusion. Why didn't my father feel that sadness? I had moved on from that pain, and now I had no mother. I didn't understand that my father actually felt sadness for me.

"You would come to me," he said, turning on the trail, "and I would so want to comfort you, but I couldn't." He was making a gesture with his hands, a gesture interrupted, a pulling back. That day on the trail was not the only time my father apologized; he would do it every few years. Now I understand that he really was trying to make it right, trying to get closer to me even though he knew that I needed to stand up for my mother. He didn't tell me what I have now put together reading the wartime letters—that she had hit him too, that he too must have been afraid of her violence, and that his own fear may have been another reason he didn't protect me.

Once, soon after the morning in the room with the cherry wallpaper, my mother and I were both at Hollow Hill and she was driving me somewhere, explaining what a saint was. She often read me the lives of saints from books by a woman named Joan Windham, but now she was telling me about a young girl in France who became a saint, Saint Thérèse of Lisieux. My mother explained that Saint Thérèse had learned "self-forgetfulness" and "simple obedience" and that coming to know about this saint had made her ashamed of her bad temper. Her temper was a sin, my mother said, and she was praying to get rid of it. I looked out the window at the rush of trees. I didn't understand that she was trying to apologize to me. Some of the girls at school had parents who beat them "with the belt" whenever they did something wrong, but when my mother slapped me in the room with the cherry wallpaper and her face got red, it was as if she was not herself. That must be her temper, when she wasn't herself. And also sin, I thought. Temper, I mouthed. Sin, I thought, looking at her long fingers curled tight around the steering wheel.

Public School 37 was housed in a big yellow building about seven blocks from where we lived. It's still there, smaller than it looked then, but still yellow, and with cutouts still pasted on the insides of the windows. There must be children there, though certainly the old wooden desks have been replaced by the bright pale ones, and the wooden floor has been covered with linoleum or tile and the blackboards replaced with green ones. Fifty years ago, the floors were still wood and the desks still bolted to the floor, though in the kindergarten room, to which I first went, there were no desks at all, just chairs we moved into a circle, or pushed to the walls when we were, for instance, learning to curtsy.

I remember a girl named Carol Suzicki and I remember her yellow frilly dress that flared like a lampshade and her bright glossy black patent leather shoes. Joanie Rostenkowski had on the same kind of dress, only pale blue, and the same kind of shoes. The dress I was wearing was lavender and white checks with embroidery across the chest, a present from Gami, who told me the embroidery was done by hand and called "smocking." On my feet were brown oxfords and white socks. My dress didn't stick out and my hair wasn't curly like the other girls'—it was short, straight, and almost black, with bangs. It was the first day of school, and we were standing in line. Carol and Joanie were speaking English, but I couldn't follow what they were talking about, boys, ball games, what they were doing after school. When I went home I told my mother I wanted dresses like theirs, but my mother said their dresses were nylon, as if nylon would burn a girl like me, a girl so different from them, a girl with dark straight hair. The teacher, Miss Hart, was tall, her gray hair tightly curled. She wore glasses with shiny jewels in them and red lipstick. Teaching us "left" and "right," she said, bow to the left, curtsy to the right, which is how, if I am disoriented, I still remember left and right.

My parents had no experience of a school like this one. My mother was tutored at home until the age of fifteen, when she went to boarding school at Madeira, where you could bring your own horse; and my father, before St. Paul's, had gone to a private school minutes from Hollow Hill with children who also lived in enormous houses and were served by butlers and maids. My parents wanted us to be free of the limitations of the way they had grown up; they wanted us to lead happier, more expansive lives. Both had been self-conscious about privilege since they were children. There is a story my father told over and over until it became iconic: seeing the poor as he rode in his family's Rolls-Royce, he dove to the floor because he was so ashamed. So send your children to public school, send them to school with the other children in the neighborhood, send them to the same school as the Negro children they play with.

But P.S. 37 was not in our exact neighborhood, and there were very few black children there. Most of the children in our neighborhood went to P.S. 2, but P.S. 2 had no toilets—you peed through a hole in the floor. And so I walked the six blocks to "37" escorted by Stella Skipper, who was in sixth grade. In exchange, she came to our house for lunch. She wore her hair back and straightened and her skirts longer than I did. She had a scar on her knee, and because her skin was brown, the scar was almost white. It looked like a mouth, a mouth that was almost laughing, but laughing meanly. Sometimes she wore stockings and so the mouth of her scar was stretched and flattened by the nylon. At lunch in our kitchen when my mother or Gagy wasn't looking, she'd whisper that the scar was going to "git" me. She must not have liked walking me to school, but it wasn't possible for her to complain. I couldn't either. How could I complain about someone with brown skin?

By the time I was in second grade, my brother Pip was in kindergarten so I became the older one, walking a child to school. He was shy at school, but at home he was a wild, funny, forceful boy with a blond crew cut and big dark blue eyes who moved much faster than I did, always running, making my mother laugh, rabbit-punching my arm, or giving me Indian burns on my wrists. After school, I played mostly with him and his best friend Ralphie Walker, who became my boyfriend when I was seven or eight. We used to stand in the corner between the kitchen and front door and kiss. He was younger than me, his skin was the color of dark wood, and he had dancing eyes with dark brown irises that made their whites really white. Usually he would be making jokes with Pip, but I would get him to be quiet so we could kiss, on the lips; afterward there'd be wet stuff all over my mouth and chin. And then what happened? Back to handball in the front yard, the concrete broken and heaved up so the ball sprang back at an angle from the high brick wall. I remember feeling my whole length as I jumped and that you made a fist and hit the ball, a pink rubber one you'd buy for a quarter at the candy store. We'd play as dusk came, Pip and Ralphie and I, and maybe the Monroe boys, and sometimes I'd win, leaping to the ball, punching it as it zoomed off the wall, stretching my body up into the darkness. Soon there was a time when Ralphie teased me but never kissed me, so Alan Monroe became my boyfriend, a white boy with a crew cut, a little taller and older than I was, with a slow way of talking. I remember us kissing in front of the door to the church, my arms bent around him, bright flannel squares of my shirt at the edge of my sight.

The afternoons we didn't play ball, we rode pretend horses; mine was a palomino. At Hollow Hill where there was a television, my brother and I watched Hopalong Cassidy movies and the Lone Ranger and Roy Rogers. Playing on Second Street, I was Dale Evans, and the horse came to life as I drew her over and over in my notebook when I was bored at school, her mane flooding back as she galloped, pursued but never caught by the boys on their stallions, who shouted, wielding their cap guns until it was time to go home for supper, gallop up the path to the door, where old men waited for my mother's soup, dozing or snoring in the retreating light. Good night, Mr. Gould, I would say. Good night, Mr. O'Hara, as I stumbled over their legs, holding my breath to keep from smelling the fumes of alcohol and filth that thickened in the small vestibule.

Every summer, my mother packed the scrapbook materials she had thrown into boxes all winter and took them up to the Adirondacks, where she would sit on the porch sorting. Now the scrapbooks are stored in a cabinet there. One day last summer, I went up there for a few days to look. I wanted to sort through the visual record, discover how I'd feel all these years later. I had been back to Jersey City a year or so after my father died for the dedication of Bishop Paul Moore Place, the stretch of Second Street between Jersey Avenue and Grove Street where Grace Church is situated. Everything looked very small as I wandered down the gentrified streets from the barely recognizable station where the subway line is now called PATH rather than the Hudson Tube. The ceremony was small, people from the old Grace Church families gathered for a celebration of old times. An African-American woman quite a bit shorter than I was who looked to be in her sixties came up to me. "Hello, Honor." It was Stella Skipper. Pretty soon her sister Joyce joined us and we got to laughing, and I said to Stella, "You know you had a scar on your knee and you used to tell me it was going to hurt me," I said. She laughed and I laughed. "Really," I said, "you scared me." Affectionately she punched my shoulder and we stood together for the ceremony, watching the deputy mayor climb a ladder and affix the bright green street sign as a photographer took pictures. After some speeches and coffee, the ceremony was breaking up. "Honor," someone was saying. I turned. It was Stella. "I'm sorry about the scar."

As I leafed through the photographs, I saw my parents young, looking to be no more than children, my mother making funny faces, my father with his arm around her. Or my mother serving soup surrounded by black children and looking efficient, her glasses crooked on her nose, and in another picture, my father sitting outdoors, wearing his vestments looking solemn, encircled by children, all of them black except for me, someone's puppy on his lap. In weekly staff meetings my parents and the two priests became a team, learning to work together and strategizing, my mother set on keeping them honest, always challenging, never content unless she was satisfied they were at the heart of the truth. Pam Morton, who worked there later, found her probing questions unnerving. "What kind of questions?" I asked. "How do you *really* feel," Pam told me, " over and over." Like my parents, Pam had been brought up never to disclose what she really felt. But there were also plenty of laughs. In another photograph, a souvenir from Coney Island, my parents and Kim Myers and Bob Pegram all embrace each other, my mother's smile blazing.

Each spring, Grace Church sent out an annual summer appeal for funds to their well-heeled friends and relatives, my father contributing from a small foundation he had set up with some of his inheritance. "We found there was no program for the children," read the text the first summer, "and so we set about creating one." As soon as school was out, before we went to the Adirondacks, we children were dispatched to Hollow Hill with Gagy, and the "summer staff," idealistic young seminarians or college students, moved into our bedrooms. When the summer program grew to seven base-ball teams and winter events and meetings outgrew the parish hall and our living room, the church purchased a brownstone down the street. The parish office moved out of the basement, and after the top floor of the new house was converted into a convent, an order of Episcopal nuns moved in, taking over Sunday school and confirmation instruction, and some of the pastoral work with women my mother had done all by herself.

When I was nine, I was taken to the Brearley School in New York where the daughters of my parents' old friends, the Potters, went. I was to be "tested." I remember the wide hallways and that all the kids were girls and all the girls were white. I remember the big gymnasium. I did well on the tests. My parents felt vindicated and proudly told friends and family that my knowledge was competitive with that of girls my age at the best private school in New York. I stayed at 37 one more semester, and then my parents moved my brother and me to a church school in New York, a short ride away on the Hudson Tube. Pip and I became friends on the subway to and from St. Luke's. In the mornings friends of our parents drove us to school, but we took the subway back by ourselves. Since we came home at about three, there were very few people on the train, and we got to know the engineers. Sometimes we would stand in the front car gazing out the window into the long, dark tunnel as the train sped under the river, a red light, a green light blinking in the pitch black.

The fifth-grade class at St. Luke's was all white except for one African-American boy whose name was Colin, but I had a crush on Jay. He was blond with a close crew cut and big eyes, and he had a girlfriend, Jill, who was small and thin with dark dark hair and skin so pale it was almost blue. She talked to Jay like my mother talked to my father, in sarcastic, oddly pronounced endearments, and he leaned his body up against hers like a Slinky. In class, he and I often raised our hands at the same time, and gave the right answers. After a while, he came up to me and said, "You are smart" or "What do you think about that story Father Weed read us this morning in chapel?" I liked the serious way he talked to me. About the third week of school, the fifth grade went, with the sixth, seventh, and eighth grades, to the church camp in Connecticut for a week, all the teachers and all the students. On the bus, I sat near a window and, without my asking, Jay came and sat next to me. I showed him my drawings of horses, and he said he liked them. He talked about where he used to live, in North Carolina; his father was a priest, too. It was a three-hour trip and suddenly, trees whooshing by outside, he said, "I want you to be my girlfriend." "Okay," I said, allowing a smile to creep up behind my face. It seemed strange he said that since he was Jill's boyfriend, but I was so happy he liked me, I said nothing.

When we got to the camp, we went to the bunkhouse and I unpacked my things onto my cot. Jill was there, and Temma, who had long blond braids. I was quiet, hardly able to contain my excitement. "I'll meet you in the barn at the dance," Jay had said, and so, when we got there, I went straight over to him. The music was starting. Jay was standing talking to Jill and some others, but I continued walking, then stopped right in front of them, looking expectantly at him, but he didn't turn his head toward me for a long time, then Jill looked at me, and then Jay said, "Jill is still my girlfriend," and, laughing, they walked away.

As I stood there, I felt my stomach push against the waist of my skirt. Temma was suddenly right beside me, saying something consoling, and then we walked toward the long table with the food on it—spaghetti and salad, stacks of paper plates and napkins, paper cups with red punch in them. I pretended I knew what I was doing, that I had never for one second expected Jay Leach to be my boyfriend. The music was a song called "Sixteen Tons" and across the room I could see Jay and Jill talking—and then they were dancing to another song, hopping around to the music. Jay was narrow like my brother and Jill's hair flowed down her back. I looked down at my hands and opened one of them. It was wide. I will never have narrow hands, I thought to myself. I will never be able to see the veins under my skin, my cheek flesh will never retreat, allowing a narrow face. I will always have a round face. I will never have a twenty-one-inch waist.

8

Four-in-Hand

My grandmother runs down the steps of the vast entrance hall, her arms open, and I fall into them, and she kisses me and says, "Oooooh, how good to see you," her voice rising in pitch at the word "see," light through the French doors at the other end casting shadowy shapes on the Persian triclinium carpet that enlivens the room's entire vastness. We turn into the living room, light playing off tawny pinks and yellows and buoyant greens, the blues of curtains and slipcovers, English paintings on slate blue walls, on creamy walls, a tiny bronze horse, the silver cigarette box, a Chinese snuffbox, chairs and sofas to sink into, sunlight through Palladian windows illuminating porcelain, glinting from silver, from silver-framed photographs, from polished tables, side chairs, the grand piano.

Even in memory I am rescued by that space and light, by the give of the beds, by the food that came straight from the farm, by Nellie the cook in the enormous kitchen, her fiery brown eyes laughing as she pulls the cookie jar across the counter and says, "Peanut butter or chocolate chip?" After supper, after reading my book, I'd slide between the silky smooth monogrammed sheets and look out wide windows at the trees turning black against the pale summer sky, watching it all darken until I slept.

When we lived in Jersey City, Hollow Hill was where we children were sent with Gagy for frequent weekends all year or weeks in June or July—refuge for us, a break for my mother from all the cooking and housekeeping at home. My father and mother hardly ever came with us. After he began to work with poor people, my father became embarrassed by Hollow Hill. Its pleasures made him uneasy: how was he to integrate "all of this" with what he had seen in the war, what he saw now in Jersey City—the burnt-out tenements, families evicted from their apartments, black families from the South, Spanish-speaking families from Puerto Rico, men unable to find jobs, nothing for the children to do, young men going to jail or into "the service" in Korea. To me, Hollow Hill was proof of the world's abundance—wasn't there enough for everyone? Every week Patsy drove the farm truck to Jersey City, delivered flowers, butter, cottage cheese, milk and eggs, fresh chickens and vegetables—so much my mother often gave bottles of milk and cream away.

When my parents did come with us, we saw them only when we visited cocktail hour in the library where the air smelled of bourbon, gin, cigarette smoke, and Chanel No. 5 or Je Reviens. My grandmother would be in velvet and my mother likewise transformed; free of changing diapers and cooking, she looked like the young queen in her wedding pictures, her hair glossy, a supper dress of velvet or taffeta, her lips dark with Raven Red, on her hand the big diamond engagement ring she never wore in Jersey City. Long legs crossed, a lit Chesterfield between her fingers, her low laugh made you long to be in on the joke. My father also dressed up—oxford cloth shirt, bow tie, tweed jacket—would be leaning forward, or pulling back with a laugh, Camel in one hand, his drink in the other. "Oh, Jenny," he might be saying. I would kiss my mother and smell her martini, then lean across to kiss Pop, then Gramps, and then Gami, who would be doing needlepoint—signs of the zodiac for the dining room chairs, or squares of Aesop's Fables for a dreamed-of rug—while nursing one of her two nightly Gibsons. There was never conversation when we children raced in, just oohs and aahs. The grownups ate in the library because Gramps had Lou Gehrig's disease, although what he had was never discussed or explained. My grandfather didn't talk much and he didn't wear shoes—just many layers of socks, his feet on a pillow on the floor. I remember no voice, just the slow smile with a curve like a banana and the glass of bourbon clasped in his hand.

Almost as soon as I knew anything about grown-up life, I knew my grandfather was a lawyer and businessman, that he had "disapproved" of my father's decision to become a priest, but that my grandmother had encouraged her second son in his unconventional choice. My father's older brother remembers the controversy differently. He says that my grandfather was perfectly supportive of my father's decision to go into the church, but wanted him to work in finance for a year "to learn about what he had." My father believed the family's money was limitless, that there was no reason to learn anything about it—the chief thing to do with it was to use it for the human good. "A cross of gold," Bobby Potter told me. He was my father's lifelong best friend. "That money was always his cross of gold."

Gramps seemed so weak sitting there in his big chair that I couldn't imagine him intimidating my father, who was so tall and seemed so transcendently powerful. By the time I understood such things, the argument between them had gone underground; all that survived were signifiers. My father's study in Jersey City was hung with a silver cross given to him by a Greek Orthodox prelate, my grandfather's library adorned with talismans of another kind: the chrome model of a jet presented to him on his retirement from the board of Republic Aviation, the company he had a hand in starting; an inscribed photo of President Eisenhower enshrined in a silver frame, rendering my parents' proud votes for Adlai Stevenson fragile protest against something permanent. My father so dismissed his father's accomplishment that I was surprised when I saw evidence of it. I remember solemnly watching a television documentary about Republic Aviation with Gramps—the tale of his investment in Seversky, who

invented the low-wing metal aircraft, how the enterprise nearly bank-
rupted him, only to conclude in triumph.

More important to me was evidence I found the Christmas I was seven
or eight, behind a painted screen in the dining room. The sleekly polished
mahogany box the size of a small suitcase bore a brass plaque which identified it as a gift to my grandfather from the National Biscuit Company,
which Great-grandfather Moore and his brother, Hobart, had assembled
from a dozen local bakeries that had names like "Uneeda Biscuit" and
"Lorna Doone." In the box was a gorgeous array of every kind of Nabisco
cookie. Day after day, I returned to it, stealing first a Lorna Doone, then a
sugar wafer, then as many Oreos as I could remove leaving no trace.

My grandparents' enormous and beautiful brick house rested in a hollow on a hundred acres of pasture and forest. There was a pond where
mallard ducks and geese swam, an ample vegetable garden, stables, barns,
and three enormous greenhouses where flowers grew all year round. At
Hollow Hill, my grandmother oversaw a Noah's Ark of a farm populated
by a herd of Guernseys, flocks of hens and attendant roosters, bantam
cocks, pheasants, pigs, turkeys, horses, and a kennel where she bred
championship dalmatians. From a perfectly ordinary country road, you
turned through discreet brick gates at a sign that said Hollow Hill and
drove down a driveway past the stables to the house—lawn, apple trees,
a pair of larger-than-life wrought-iron dalmatians painted to look real, my
grandmother's Buick convertible with her initials on the doors.

If you walked in the front door of the house and passed through the long
entrance hall, you could go out the French doors onto the terrace where a
pair of apple trees had been espaliered to form a canopy for shade, fuchsia
plants hanging from their branches in the summer. The terrace gave way
to a lawn that ran the entire width of the house; edging it was a perennial
border about five feet deep—I remember delphiniums and snapdragons,
phlox and baby's breath, artemesia and lady's mantle—a cutting garden that
never ran out of blooms. From the terrace where my grandmother served
tea every day at four, your eye fell to a half-moon flight of brick steps that
dropped to a lower lawn, descending to another set of steps, and another.
When Gramps still walked, there were three holes for golf—putting greens,
sandtraps, and the rest—ingeniously placed on the descending levels of
lawn and on fields across the road near the tennis court; by playing the
holes three times in different configurations, you'd get a nine-hole game.

But for me the stables at the top of the hollow were the center of life there. They were built around the courtyard where my father had learned to ride and where I and every grandchild first sat astride a pony, Christie, the groom, holding the bridles and instructing in his Scottish burr— press in your knees, hold in your heels, sit up straight. There were stalls for twenty horses, but when I was riding there were many fewer: Jackson, a chestnut gelding; Bill, my father's seventeen-hand thoroughbred named for his brother; Mademoiselle, a smaller bay mare I usually took when Christie and I rode out every morning I was there, hours along bridle paths through the forest.

When I was very little, Seaton Pippin was still alive. Gramps had inherited his father's Hackney farm down the road from Hollow Hill, and Pippin had been its equine prodigy. Gami, and later my father's sister Polly, drove her to Best in Show five years running at Madison Square Garden. Years after making a bronze portrait of her, Katharine Lane Weems, the animal sculptor, wrote of seeing Pippin again: "She has real glamour now & temperament & stage presence like a prima donna. She needs no check rein & makes the other hackneys look like machines. She has won 65 championships & more blues than any living horse." Of the sculpture, my grandfather exclaimed to the artist in a letter, "What we want is Pippin & you have given her to us." After Pippin's farewell competition, the band played "Auld Lang Syne" as she circled the ring, a giant horseshoe of flowers around her neck.

On the other side of the stable, beyond the tack room and office where blue ribbons hung thickly over the desk, was the carriage house. It was always dark inside, coaches and landaus and rigs of all kinds resting there, barely visible in the light that made its way through the windows at the top of the wide doors. The ceiling was high, like a church, the doors and window frames were painted dark green, and the floor was a pale tan, almost yellow, of bricks arranged in a zigzag pattern, the room fragrant with fresh paint and varnish. I remember the huge spokes of the wheels, and once when Gami showed me the carriages, Christie opened a brougham door and took my hand, helping me up and inside where I sat back on the chamois upholstery and breathed in the old air. The coaches were shipped to Hollow Hill from Prides Crossing after my great-grandmother died, their lacquered exteriors like sleek skin, the colors painstaking—dark, dark green, tan, bright white—the brass lanterns and locks brightly polished.

Gami didn't explain what she meant when she said proudly that this was the "brougham" that belonged to "Great-grandfather." He had died in 1923 at the age of seventy-five, but his wife, my father's adored grandmother whom we called Great-granny, had lived till I was ten. Great-grandfather seemed like a character in a fairy tale. He had raced the coaches, Gami said, "four-in-hand." The only driving I'd ever seen was when Christie harnessed Sally to the pony cart and my grandmother drove me around the farm, her hands on the reins, once in a while letting me drive, carefully guiding my fingers to the proper position or demonstrating how little pressure it took to send Sally to the right or left. Once, visiting my uncle and his wife, both then almost ninety, I complimented them on the enormous brass-trimmed mahogany bucket in which they kept magazines.

"Do you know what that is?" my Uncle Bill asked.

"No."

"A feed bucket. Your great-grandfather had one of these for each horse."

"And these went to England when he raced?"

"Believe it or not."

There was a photograph that turned up whenever we moved—four horses, one of them gray, the white-haired driver in a top hat holding all four reins in one hand. "That's your great-grandfather," my father said once at Bank Street. In the years leading to the First World War, Great-grandfather took his brougham across the Atlantic to race in England—grooms, trainer, horses, harnesses, all of them on a ship—and in 1911 won the private coach division, racing from Hyde Park to Richmond, his coach pulled by horses named Minerva, Hinocker, Abigail, and Bismarck. A photograph in a faded newspaper clipping makes clear why he was a champion—horses galloping, coach hurtling forward, the tall, powerful driver calm in the midst of a furor, in charge, it seemed, of all the force in the world.

Great-grandfather, whose name was William Henry Moore, established the family wealth, making the millions that purchased Rockmarge, the creamy mansion on the sea, the Stanford White house on East Fifty-fourth Street, and Hollow Hill, his wedding present to his youngest son. What my grandfather inherited made it possible for him to live in great luxury not only at Hollow Hill but in two apartments at 825 Fifth Avenue, an Addison Mizner house at Palm Beach, and to purchase, with five friends, the fifteen-thousand-acre hunting and fishing camp in the Adirondacks. The inherited wealth of the women who married Moores was supplemental— it was the fortune her husband left that Great-granny passed on when she died; plenty remained after her thirty years of enterprising widowhood— world travel, the collecting of Chinese paintings, Persian artifacts, and Babylonian cylinder seals, and her funding of the construction of museums at Persepolis and Corinth.

Great-grandfather, namesake of his grandfather William Henry, was born in 1848 to Nathaniel Moore and Rachel Arvilla Beckwith Moore of Pittsfield, Massachusetts, and grew up one of two brothers in a large Georgian house in Greene, east of Utica, New York. These Moores first appear in public records in the person of Alexander Moore, who in the year 1708 was admitted as a "freeman" to the municipality of New York City, his occupation entered as "sadler." Later he would be elected tax collector, then a tax assessor in the East Ward, and would serve as a vestryman at Trinity Episcopal Church on Wall Street. On the Beckwith side, the men were Congregational ministers in Litchfield, Connecticut, and Rachel's grandfather, George, a fellow of the Yale Corporation. Rachel, whom her daughter-in-law, my great-grandmother, described as having a mind "almost masculine in its exactness and clearness of judgement," had been sent as a child to live with her aunt after her mother died and her father remarried; it was in that household that she met Nathaniel, a fifth-generation descendant of Alexander, who would become "a merchant and a banker" and six times Greene's justice of the peace. Less is made of my great-grandfather William's career at Amherst College than of the job he held after his freshman year "holding a surveyor's stick" for a local railroad that, as a financier, he would one day fold into a single company, the Delaware, Lackawanna & Western Railway.

Because of "ill health" William left Amherst after two years, and en route to California, where he planned to join cousins, he stopped in Eau Claire, Wisconsin. Apprenticed there to a lawyer, Mr. Bartlett, he worked, as was the custom, for no salary but room and board. In letters throughout 1871, he begs his father to make good on a promise "to support me"—he has an offer from a "reputable" Eau Claire man, recently returned from Montana in search of partners, to come into business with him there. From the end of the Northern Pacific Railroad, they would ride horses into Montana, where they would start "a ranch for horses and cattle." His father, conservative, devout, and fearful, refused his request—"It hurts me terribly for you to even dream I am dissipated," William wrote back. He apparently stayed with Mr. Bartlett, because in 1872 he was admitted to the bar in Eau Claire, after which family legend tracks him to the Great Plains, where, as my father told the story, he became friends with Sitting Bull, who cautioned him to leave the West. By the time of Custer's Last Stand in 1876, my great-grandfather was safely in Chicago, ensconced in the firm of Edward Alonzo Small, a corporate lawyer, and married to the boss's daughter, my father's adored grandmother Adelia, who was always called Ada. After Small died in 1883, William's brother, Hobart, also a lawyer, became his partner, having married Ada's sister, Lora.

Working with their father-in-law, the Moore brothers became fiercely clever at adapting the intricacies of Illinois corporate law to the advantage of their powerful clients—Pullman, American Express, Vanderbilt, and Frick among them. Great-grandfather proved so sharp at assessing stocks that he was called "Judge" Moore, and when the nickname endowed him with juridic legitimacy, no one protested: he seemed like a judge, keeping his own counsel, never giving an interview. This trait served him well as he and his brother began their own investing. Standard Oil, created by Henry Flagler and John D. Rockefeller in 1870, was a "vertical" trust, which meant that one company owned all the resources needed to get the product from the ground to the consumer. Eventually Great-grandfather and Uncle Hobart assembled "horizontal" trusts. They would raise money, purchase a small company, improve its performance, thereby driving up its stock price, then use its profits, along with loans they took as needed, to buy out its undercapitalized competitors. As soon as possible, they'd charter a new company made up of the smaller ones, offer its stock, realize multimillion-dollar fees or stock equivalents, join its board, and turn over the company to executives they handpicked. Frazer Axle Grease Company was their first promotion, followed by the American Strawboard Company, purchased "to control the manufacture of strawboard and wood pulp," and New York Biscuit, the forerunner of Nabisco. But their promotion of the Diamond Match Company, which they bought and rechartered in Connecticut "to control the manufacture of matches," put the Moore brothers on the map.

Imagine a time when safe matches were an innovation, the paper book match brand-new. In the nineteenth century, when wooden matches went into mass production in England, they were manufactured with sulfur and white phosphorus, a toxic chemical that caused "phossy jaw," a deterioration of the jawbone, contaminated the bones of the workers who made them, and deformed the skeleton of any child who mistakenly sucked on one. Matches made with sulfa and "red" phosphorous were finally introduced in Europe in the 1850s, and by the 1890s in the United States, Diamond Match had developed a method for mass production of these safer matches, including book matches, whose patent the Moores purchased from Joshua Pusey, the Philadelphia lawyer who invented them because he disliked the bulge that boxed wooden matches made in his waistcoat. Under their improved management and with their absorption of smaller match companies, the Connecticut company's profits began to rise, and the Moores, taking advantage of the more sympathetic laws of their home state, expanded the capital available to them by forming the Diamond Match Company of Illinois. In early summer 1896, when it was announced that Diamond executives would travel abroad to seduce and acquire European match companies, Diamond's stock began a spectacular ascent on the Chicago Exchange.

"His brother was named Hobart?"

"Yes, Hobart. He tried to corner the market on matches and almost ruined the whole thing," said my uncle.

"Really?"

"It's all right here." He got up, disappeared into another room, and returned with a large red bound book. DOWNFALL OF MOORES, reads a headline, and written in pencil across the clipping, orange and crisp with age, August 4, 1896. Great-grandfather was at Rockmarge for the summer and calmly playing golf at the Myopia Hunt Club when a butler approached across the putting green, carrying a silver tray on which lay a telegram announcing the disaster. FAILURE OF DIAMOND MATCH MAGNATES A SURPRISE, read another headline in the red book. "The fable," my uncle, the retired banker, said, "was that Hobart, in Chicago, drove the speculation, and that Grandfather had to leave his vacation to repair the damage." In family lore, William was the thrifty, responsible one, "Hobie" the profligate, given to such extravagances as hiring a train to transport a party of friends to Hot Springs for a week of pleasure. "My dear Papa," my grandfather wrote his father in August 1896, "I am very sorry you lost your money. But we will not forget the good times we had, and shall have. Mamma told me all about it. Mamma and I feel very badly, but we can be brave though in trouble."

Reading the clippings in the scrapbook Uncle Bill gave me, I was able to piece together the story. When Diamond announced a deal with Bryant & May, the British match company, Diamond stock was at $148, but during the following weeks, reports in the financial press of Diamond's negotiations with the governments of Austria and France about acquiring their match manufacture caused the stock to soar. The brothers' declared intention—to control the world match market—seemed within reach. In a wild surge of speculative buying, the price of Diamond stock went as high as $400. The word "on LaSalle Street" and among the investors Great-grandfather and Hobart had recruited assumed the brothers had access to enough cash to back the stock, and that their expertise was up to the task. Brokers continued to buy shares at high prices, which held the stock to the mid-$200s, and Hobart flooded the banks with shares priced at $170, unaware he and his investors were purchasing that very stock at $230. Soon a nervous investor broke rank, buying five hundred shares at the higher price (long) as one of the Moores' investors and five thousand at the lower price (short) for his personal account. Forthwith the banks refused to lend any more cash, and on August 3 Moore Brothers declared itself insolvent. DOWN WENT DIAMOND MATCH STOCK, read another headline in the red book, LIKE A PUNCTURED BALLOON.

The Chicago business press attempted to head off full-scale catastrophe with reassurances from the financial establishment: BANKS ARE FULLY PRO-TECTED, one such headline asserted, and in the article Great-grandfather's friend the meatpacker P. D. Armour was quoted: "I cannot see any signs of a panic over the Diamond Match matter. There will be no effect upon other securities." Armour was one of the investors assembled by the Moores to promote Diamond stock.

"Will the Moores succeed in getting out to the squeeze all right?" the reporter asked him.

"As to that I cannot say. It is, of course, their own matter. But as to the probable effect upon other interests I don't think there is the slightest cause for apprehension."

In fact there was plenty of cause for apprehension. It seems unlikely that Great-grandfather knew nothing of Diamond Match's forays in Europe, but it is possible he was ignorant of the extent to which Hobart, in supporting the stock's ascent, had strained the brothers' resources and the goodwill of their investors. At the end of the crash, the Moores themselves were out six million Gilded Age dollars, not including debts of four million they owed ruined investors. (The equivalent of $254 million in 2006 dollars.) After the telegram on the golf course, Great-grandfather apparently caught a train to Chicago. A newspaper sketch places him at the center of a cabal of Chicago financiers around a table, Mr. Armour to one side. CAPITALISTS TAKE MEASURES TO PREVENT THE SPREAD OF TROUBLE, a headline read the next day, reporting the group's decision to shut down the Chicago Stock Exchange (it stayed closed for three months, sending shock waves through the New York and London markets). Great-grandfather hung fire: "We are a long way from financially dead," he declared. "We'll be on top again."

In my imagination, these events unspool as a sequence of images that underplays the scandal's reverberation through my father's generation of Moores and on to mine. My father boasted, even marveled, as he told the story: the intensely green golf course, the gleam of the butler's silver tray, the making and losing of a fortune, the closing down of the Chicago Stock Exchange, the triumphant recovery. But decades later, reading disintegrating clippings in the red book, I began to understand the Republican fealty in generations of Moores: why my uncle the banker, turning a blind eye to a president playing fast and loose with spending, still voted Republican in 2004; why my father's lurch to the Democrats appalled his father; and why, perhaps, my father, when he was young, "always" thought of the burden of his vast inheritance as "a cross of gold."

I don't know how much attention my handsome, six-foot-tall, cleanshaven great-grandfather paid to William Jennings Bryan, but at least one Chicago financial daily had fun with the collision between "Judge" Moore and "the boy orator from Platte." The run-up of Diamond Match stock happened in the wake of Bryan's famous "Cross of Gold" speech which he had delivered at the 1896 Democratic Convention in Chicago that July. "When you come before us and tell us that we are about to disturb your business interests," the congressman from Nebraska declaimed, gesturing to supporters of the gold standard, "we reply that you have disturbed our business interests by your course."

My grandmother explained the gold standard to me one afternoon as she drove me around the farm in the pony cart. It was a hot Septem-

ber day, and the pony was walking as we passed the grape arbor near
the greenhouses and she assured me that every dollar bill had equivalent
gold locked up in Fort Knox. She would not have agreed with Bryan, who
was battling the gold standard because it meant tight money and tight
money made interest impossibly high when small farmers in the West
and South tried to get short-term loans to tide them over until harvest—
a common situation in the mid-nineties which caused farms to fail and
laborers to lose their jobs. "Free silver"—that is, a money system based on
both gold and more plentiful silver or just on silver—would make money
more abundant and therefore easier to borrow. At the convention, Bryan
directed the consideration of "gold bug" Eastern Democrats to the fate of
farmers and laborers, or, as he put it, "the producing masses." When he
was triumphantly nominated, the Democrats became the party of "free
silver" progressives set against the gold-standard Republicans, who had
nominated William McKinley, a conservative congressman from Ohio.

Republican capitalists like my great-grandfather supported McKinley
and vehemently opposed "free silver," but Bryan's New Testament-laced
rhetoric was irresistible to those who shared his condemnation of Gilded
Age economic injustice: "You shall not press down upon the brow of labor
this crown of thorns. You shall not crucify mankind upon a cross of gold,"
he said at the convention, and the standing ovation went on and on. Great-
grandfather was exactly the sort of man Bryan assailed when he declared
"the attorney in a country town is as much a businessman as the corporation counsel in a great metropolis." But, like Rockefeller and Carnegie, Great-grandfather saw himself as an architect of American commerce
and American production, and considered his enormous fortune legiti-
mate remuneration for the stability these enhanced companies brought to
American commercial life. He founded a tradition in our family that my
father inherited; my grandmother explained it all to me one afternoon at
Hollow Hill, a Gibson in her hand: We were stewards of the money we
were fortunate enough to have. It was ours to live on, ours to share with
others more in need than we, ours to pass on to our children.

McKinley was no match for Bryan as an orator, but his candidacy was
promoted by big business, and one of the oil industry's great tacticians,
the Ohio mining tycoon Mark Alonzo Hanna, was his campaign manager
and raised an unprecedented three and a half million dollars from corporate stakeholders who believed that government should serve industry

and that industry was best represented by its owners, men like Hanna himself, who famously articulated his point of view in a letter he later wrote to a young Republican candidate: "You have been in politics long enough to know that no man in public office owes the public anything." In the meantime, uneasy Democratic financiers abandoned Bryan, leaving him with a campaign purse of only fifteen thousand dollars, but tireless and inspired, he traveled sixteen thousand miles, carrying his own suitcase, holding forth from the backs of trains, hotel balconies, and townsquare bandstands, illumination by pink flashlight powder and calcium light canonizing him the savior of farmer and laborer. Hanna, on the other hand, unbridled by ethics or altruism, boldly tailored campaign literature to particular constituencies, ominously recalling for voters the bloodshed and chaos of the Homestead and Pullman strikes of the early 1890s and warning that a President Bryan would bring anarchists and socialists into the government. Republican campaign funds were deployed to get out or purchase the vote and trains hired to bring hundreds of voters to Canton, Ohio, where McKinley sat on his front porch instructing his visitors on the virtues of the gold standard and promising each workingman "a full dinner pail." By the end of the campaign, Hanna had positioned "free silver" as bounty for the idle—"something for nothing"—and McKinley was on his way to victory.

But not soon enough to blunt the impact of Bryan's rhetoric on the fortunes of Diamond Match. By late July, when the stock was hitting its highs, the markets began to respond with what came to be called the "Bryan panic"—if free-silver policies were enacted, loans based on the gold standard would not be repaid with currency of gold-standard value and those who had borrowed to buy stock at speculative prices would be ruined. Investors riding the surge of Diamond Match stock became abruptly cautious: "Purse strings were closed with a twang," wrote one reporter, "vault doors snapped on loads of money."

We are a long way from financially dead. We'll be on top again. Greatgrandfather's prediction was correct. William McKinley was elected in a rout, William H. Moore repaid his debts and earned back his fortune, and fourteen years later William's son Paul, my grandfather, married Fanny Hanna, Mark Hanna's niece, who, wearing a white dress, had sat on McKinley's knee during more than one of his porch perorations. Mark Hanna, in effect, had feathered his niece's nest; McKinley's election was no small element in the restoration of Great-grandfather's fortune; indeed Republican monetary policies allowed him to continue creating trusts, untrammeled, at least until McKinley was assassinated in 1901 and succeeded by Teddy Roosevelt, the first president of that surname to thin the flow of money into the pockets of the rich.

The Moores' recovery took four years. Rising phoenix-like from the ashes of Diamond, the brothers restored their stature by organizing two new companies. Nabisco was achieved by reorganizing New York Biscuit as a trust called the National Biscuit Company. The new company, capitalized at $55 million, promptly absorbed its competition, three trusts that between them owned 114 cracker bakeries. The Moore brothers' second company, American Tin Plate, capitalized at $50 million, brought them dizzying gains when it was one of the companies subsumed in the consolidation of U.S. Steel by Andrew Carnegie, J. P. Morgan, and others, one of the great feats of the Gilded Age. For the formation of Nabisco and American Tin, each brother reportedly received a total of $16 million ($409 million in 2006 dollars) in stock "for the cost of cigars smoked making the deal," as one reporter put it.

In 1900, as Great-grandfather was in the midst of negotiating the Moores' participation in U.S. Steel, the climate in Illinois turned against the consolidation of companies. In a dramatic gesture, he asserted himself. Every clerk and lawyer at work on the new company, and his family if he had one, boarded a hired train to New York, accompanied by every desk and file, every ticker-tape machine and glass-faced bookshelf. Work did not slow, ticker running even on the journey, and when the train arrived at Pennsylvania Station, employees and equipment were taken to a handsome two-floor office space, families were moved into houses and apartments and the unmarried into boardinghouses. William and Ada— by then their three sons were at St. Paul's and Yale—put up at Collier's Hotel, where they resided until a Stanford White house at 4 East Fifty-fourth Street was ready—on one of his trips to New York to oversee the New York Biscuit Building going up on Tenth Avenue, William purchased the half-built house, commissioned and abandoned by W.E.D. Stokes, for $325,000. Hobart stayed in Chicago, as William took on New York, and by the time Great-grandfather died in 1923, his handiwork included not only Nabisco and U.S. Steel and the American Can Company, but a seat on the founding board of the Bankers Trust Company.

It was in a conference room high up in the old Bankers Trust building on Wall Street that my father passed on a sliver of his cross of gold to me, a portion of his grandfather's legacy which had passed tax-free to the third generation. The spring before my twenty-first birthday, there was a solemn meeting with two bankers who were well aware that I was William Moore's great-granddaughter. I wore a suit, stockings, high heels, perhaps even gloves, having flown down from Boston on the shuttle to meet my father, who flew up from Washington, where he was then suffragan bishop. I felt as if I were being initiated into a rite that would finally make me truly a Moore, at last as much my father's daughter as my mother's. Sitting at the table, the bank executives explaining disbursements and trusts in sonorous voices, I felt like a princess. I did not consider the money a license for my own independence, but rather the source of some greater, more mysterious obligation. Suddenly it seemed more important to contemplate what would happen to me. What would I do with my life? What *could* I now do with my life? All I thought to do right then was to buy a car, a Corvair my cousin Alex ordered for me, customized with dual pipe exhaust.

My father sat calmly and proudly through the meeting. As we left the bank, he had only one piece of financial advice. "Never lend money to friends," he said. "It's better to give it away."

My father gave money away to support the ideas and people he believed in, and he usually gave it anonymously. His philanthropy was the only financial aspect of his life that he was conscientious about. He taught me that giving away money was virtuous, that spending it was fun, that holding on to it was unnecessary. What he didn't teach was what his father had begged him to learn—financial literacy that would have enabled him both to engage in philanthropy and maintain his fortune. But my father's ethics conspired with a spirit that loved luxury, and he thumbed his nose at paternal authority. The bromides that the very rich traditionally passed on to their legatees—Never invade principal. Live with moderation, on your income—seemed to my father limitations on his freedom and irritated him as much as any curb on corporate profit had exasperated his grandfather. As he grew older and the dollar lost value, my father's philanthropic capacity decreased. His relationship to money always remained uncomfortable. In spite of his genuine concern for the poor, he seemed unable to grasp the idea of frugality—what his mother called being "Scotch."

But the very qualities that enabled "Judge" Moore to build the fortune which made my father's life and work possible—we didn't live on a parson's salary—gave him the power and independence to take political positions that owed more to William Jennings Bryan than to Mark Alonzo Hanna. When New York City went bankrupt in the 1970s and corporations began to depart their old New York headquarters for sprawling glass buildings in the suburbs, my father launched a campaign. He was by then bishop of New York and his bully pulpit crowned the nave of the Cathedral of St. John the Divine, built with robber baron money on Morningside Heights at the borders of Harlem. As his grandfather would have, my father met with associates who supported his enterprise—in this case, friends, also in high places, who were willing to help him hone the message and set the stage in the newspapers. From the pulpit on Easter Sunday 1976, six feet five in a flowing white chimere and a scarlet rochet, pounding the lectern, my father denounced the dog-eat-dog methods employed for decades by those who emulated tycoons like William H. Moore. "Hope is dying," he asserted. "The rats are leaving the sinking ship; businesses are leaving the city." Instead, he exhorted, companies should help their wounded city rise from the ashes of the burned-out tenements that lined the streets of the Bronx. Correspondence with the Easter story of Christ's resurrection was no accident.

The sermon was widely reported, and my father received letters from captains of industry, some of whom changed course and remained in the city. His brother Bill, named for their grandfather and chairman of the board of the Bankers Trust, reported that his fellow bankers had taken to calling each other "Brother Rat," but also complained in a letter to my father about the sermon's rhetoric: "I wish you would speak rationally once in a while." The *New York Times* coverage, on the front page, jumped to a photograph of my father preaching from the granite pulpit of St. John the Divine. The praise of New Yorkers leaving the cathedral was amply quoted, as was disagreement. It was not the first time, nor would it be the last, that my father's detractors remarked that such a tirade was hardly the sermon they expected from a bishop, especially on Easter Sunday.

9
The Oldest

Keep children off the streets! Giant benefit field day at Mary Benson Park! shouts the flyer for the kickoff of the 1951 summer program at Grace Church. On the next page of the scrapbook is pasted a formal photograph of a group of people, white and black—documenting an "interracial rally" held Friday, November 16. Hear Walter White, famous negro leader, reads the flyer pasted opposite, mimeographed on pink paper. On another page, a photograph of a bishop in a miter and full regalia, my father to one side, Father Myers to the other: "the Bishop of Haiti," my mother noted below it, "procession to open Field Day."

That year a *Life* magazine photographer spent weeks at Grace Church, and pasted in the scrapbook; his cinematic black-and-whites bring back teenage boys wearing Grace Church baseball uniforms, pigtailed girls jumping rope, double Dutch. I remember jumping between the two ropes, keeping the beat with a chant, Dotty Gaston at one end, Stella Skipper's sister, Joyce, at the other. I remember finding a five-dollar gold piece on the sidewalk, then losing it down a street drain next to the church, and I remember wearing bright gold wings and a long white gown each year as one of a dozen girl angels in the Easter procession.

My mother kept everything. The Vacation Bible School (July 16–21, 1951) achieved full attendance, a production of *Rear Window*, cast with neighborhood people, was performed in the parish hall, directed by my parents' friend Freddie Bradlee, an actor from New York. That year, 1951, the 133 baptisms performed at Grace Church during the two years since we'd arrived was "as many as between 1932–1949," reported a note in my father's handwriting, and a carefully pasted headline declares EPISCOPAL BOYS WIN BASEBALL TITLE; beneath it a photo of the team, the assistant mayor presenting a trophy cup. As I turned pages, years passed, 1951, 1952, 1953: I was as enthralled as if I were watching a movie. The *Life* article never ran, but Grace Church was attracting national attention among Episcopalians. "Anyone interested in changing the Episcopal Church in those days passed through Jersey City," a student of my father's work told me. "Grace Church was the working model for an Anglo-Catholic city parish."

Every half volume or so in the scrapbooks, Jersey City memorabilia was interrupted by pages on which my mother had aligned sheafs of telegrams that applauded the newest addition to our family. Inevitably the greetings were followed by photographs of an infant in the gauzy family basinet, one of the older children standing nearby, beaming with pride. Visiting the rectory on Second Street recently, seeing the rooms that seemed large when I was a child reduced to their actual proportions, I could hardly believe that in 1955 it housed a family of five children with one on the way, in addition to one of the priests; Ledlie Laughlin, who had replaced Bob Pegram, lived in the biggest third-floor room. My sister Rosemary was born in 1952 in Jersey City, but for the next birth, my mother moved to

Morristown Memorial Hospital, for which my grandparents had donated the land. In the shiny new hospital, ten minutes from Hollow Hill, three of us arrived by natural childbirth, my mother breathing as she'd learned at the La Maze classes she took with my father, who was in attendance in the delivery room. For her first four births, my mother was given anesthesia; this new method thrilled her. She was enthusiastic as she always was about a new adventure, and I never heard her mention pain, only the pleasure of being awake as the baby came, my father right there.

In the years of my childhood, I looked at family photographs as if I were part of an athletic team racing for a championship, the Cartier 18-carat gold bangle, engraved with the baby's name and birth date that my father gave my mother for each new child, a kind of trophy. How many brothers and sisters would I have? How many would it take to win? Now, looking through the scrapbooks, seeing us strung across a lawn or crowded artistically onto an outdoor flight of stairs, I find our sheer numbers literally incredible. But in 1954 when George, the fifth of us, was born, I knew of no other family than one in which children kept coming and coming. I was used to the rationed attention I got from my mother, and for decades no therapist's questioning cracked the shell of my idealism. "Honor says the family is an institution," my mother wrote to her friend Pam Morton when I was in eighth grade just after Susanna, number eight, arrived. "The wonderful remark was 'Poppy and you have made the family a little church, so that's why Poppy can call the church a family.'" What was my mother thinking when she declared she wanted a family of nine, enough for a baseball team or a small orchestra?

As I became an adult I had my theories, based on her declared adoration of babies: "Susanna is dreamy and my milk floweth. I'm so relaxed I can hardly boil an egg." Clearly, having children gave her something she didn't get elsewhere in her life, in her marriage, something that was taken away when a baby became a child. I'd never heard her express a syllable of doubt before I read another letter to Pam, written in 1957: "I've been through moments of wishing I had no children, or 3 children, or ought not to have had children—but am slowly regaining my equilibrium—they sure are demanding . . ."

It was an August afternoon working on the scrapbooks in the Adirondacks, photographing, taking notes, that my defenses dissolved. The chronicle of Jersey City had just resumed after the birth of George, when it gave way to pages announcing another birth, of Marian, my third sister and fifth sibling. I would have been ten, in my first year at St. Luke's. These decades after the fact, the banks of telegrams and notes of congratulation seemed an assault. Suddenly my mother's jokes about the baseball team and my father's certainty of the infinity of his inheritance seemed sad and arrogant rather than affirming of some courageous mission. Again I asked myself what on earth they were thinking. What did my parents' friends, who stopped at four or five children, think as we went on to seven and eight? How could everyone keep sending congratulations? What I hid away or disguised with humor as a child suddenly came clear in an image of myself as a girl of ten coming to terms with the loss of any hope of uninterrupted attention. *They sure are demanding.*

In the years after my mother died, when my father began to revise his view of her, he always insisted that the number of children had been my mother's idea. He spoke of her suicidal postpartum depressions, his efforts to stop after five, six, seven. Close friends of my mother's disputed that she was depressed after her children were born, and I dismissed my father's blaming her for our numbers as refusal to take responsibility. It wasn't that they never had unprotected sex: they boasted of their use of birth control, their membership in Planned Parenthood, the timing of births—we came every two years. When, seventeen years after my mother's death, I learned of my father's secret life, it came to me that his allowing my mother as many children as she wanted might have been compensation for what he was unable to give her. How much I'd like to ask now what they were really thinking! If they were thinking. How much I'd like to have again the pleasure of them I had when I was little and there were just four or five of us, my father at supper in the Adirondacks wiggling his ears one at a time or telling a story, my mother's radiant smile, darkness rising on the lake.

I had planned to work until supper and it was midafternoon. As I shut the scrapbook after Marian's birth, I could hear the living voices of my brothers and sisters, the answering calls of their small children, little feet running along the boardwalk, splashes and shouts from the lake. It was never comfortable for me to take my baby brothers and sisters in my arms, and I never had my own child. Because I was afraid, I now understood, so confused and sad and angry every time another came. Every time another came, I repeated to myself. Who could I have told? I put aside the book, my eyes closed, and the past pulled me into an exhausted sleep.

*   *   *

The summer of 1955, Grace Church had seven baseball teams in city tour-
naments, and when I came home from St. Luke's on the Hudson Tube, I
still stumbled over the legs of the homeless men who sat on the porch, still
answered the phone for "Father Moore" when the police called the rectory
to announce one of its boys had been arrested or that someone needed a
bed for the night. One boy who hung around and loved to play with us
had been arrested and gone to jail. The office typewriter had been stolen,
and when the police investigated, the trail led to him, and so, when Stella
scared me with her knee or I got into a fight with one of Ralphie Walker's
sisters, I kept it to myself. Some things had changed. Father Myers left to
take a Lower East Side mission in Manhattan, and when his replacement,
Jim Morton, married Pamela Taylor, they moved to an apartment in St.
Christopher's House, as the newly purchased brownstone down the street
was now called. My father and the other priests now had real offices there,
and in the rectory there was another bedroom for us.

My parents were starting to consider even more change. I didn't realize my father's bouts of exhaustion were becoming more frequent, that
his recurring pneumonia now seriously worried both my parents. My
mother had come into her own at Grace Church, but now that she had
a brood of children, she was beginning to feel the strain of the twenty-
four-hour open rectory. In a letter she wrote to Pam Morton when we left
Jersey City, she imagined living differently: "I'm more & more looking
forward to using my porch-set, telephone-answering, door-answering
energy, to spoil Paul and the children." She and my father had already
made a stab at expanding the time we spent as a family. Just after my
sister Rosemary was born, they bought an old house outside Kent, Connecticut, where we spent the weekends my father didn't have to preach,
and weeks in the summer when my father's siblings used the Adirondacks. One summer all of us stayed two months—my father's doctor
had diagnosed him with "cumulative fatigue" and the cure was eight
weeks of rest. My first sister Adelia, then called Dee, and Pip and I took
an art class at a farm down the road, and every afternoon all of us piled
into the car and drove a long dirt road to a swimming hole in the Housa-
tonic River, formed when a long-ago flood washed out a bridge. Often
my mother stayed home with the baby, or to take a nap. Later she would

say that Kent had been no vacation, all six children to cook and clean
for, for help just a high school girl from town.

In my own room in Kent, which was on the first floor away from the
others, I spent the summer reading Hawthorne's *Twice-Told Tales* or a
book about King Arthur and dreaming. That fall was my first year at St.
Luke's, and when the teacher suggested we write a story, I bought a blank
book with a black-and-white cover and began something I called "a
novel." Suddenly there was a way to say what I was thinking—not to my
friends or anyone else, but as my father did in stories, and as my mother
did when she joked or recounted an anecdote, relishing each word. The
notebook is lost, but I remember the story, and that the teacher read it
aloud to the class two days in a row. A girl whose mother and father were
killed by Indians when she was just a baby has been taken in by another
family. She has no idea her mother and father are not her real parents, but
every night as she lies on her hard bed, under a bearskin blanket, next
to the two little girls she thinks are her sisters, she tries to understand
why she alone of the children has to haul wood and cut up vegetables and
weed the garden and carry dirty clothes down to the brook for washing.
Mrs. Leifert, the teacher, was tall and skinny with salt-and-pepper hair.
She wore glasses and spoke with a Southern accent. I didn't like her then,
but I think now that she was very intelligent and that what I didn't like
was her nervousness.

The classroom was a converted parish hall, and I sat in the back near
the piano with Temma, as Mrs. Leifert stood reading from my black-and-
white notebook. *It was very cold and dark,* she read, *and as Abigail fell asleep,
she started to dream about her real mother, who had blond hair. In the dream
she was sitting on her mother's lap; she wondered who this lady was, who was
singing to her. And then she woke up. Pa was standing next to the bed. Get up,
he said. And she got up. He handed her a pail. Go to the well and fill this up. She
started to put on her coat. You don't need a coat, he said, and pushed her out into
the hallway toward the stairs. Her feet were bare and white and there was snow
on the ground. Abigail pretended the snow was warm instead of cold as she ran,
that the burning was fire instead of ice. The dog barked and she could tell that Pa
was watching her from the door. When she got to the well, she had to feel for the
hook at the end of the rope and she found it and hung the pail there. Very slowly
she let the pail down, but then suddenly it fell off the rope and she could hear it
bang in the bottom of the well.*

It was ice, Mrs. Leifert read, turning the page, *The light was coming as Abigail ran back to the house and pushed open the door. Pa was standing at the fire. Where's the water? Abigail shivered. Pa, she said, the well was frozen and the pail fell. She was very scared and started to cry as he turned from the fireplace and came toward her. Her feet were so cold. Come here, he said. The bricks on the hearth hurt her feet, almost blue with cold. She knew what would come next and watched Pa unfasten his belt. The buckle shone in the light of the fire. He made her lie down across his knee. Abigail could feel the strap burn into her skin,* Mrs. Leifert read, *as Pa hit her again and again.*

I simply listened. I don't remember what happened in the room after Mrs. Leifert put my black-and-white notebook down, promising to keep reading as I finished new installments. I didn't write anymore after she read it, though I knew that in the end, like Sara Crewe in *A Little Princess* which I had read at Hollow Hill, Abigail would escape and, returned to the embrace of her blond-haired mother, who had not been killed after all, forgive even the cruel foster father she called Pa. Of course, in my own life, my mother had black hair and it was she who inexplicably hit me, not my father. I think I was waiting to write the ending before showing the book to my parents, nervous that what Abigail had endured might tell them more about me than I wanted them to know.

I had begun instruction for confirmation with one of the nuns at St. Christopher's House. Her name was Sister Ora Mary and she was very tall. I knew that the better I did in confirmation class, the more I would understand about my father, so I worked hard on the Ten Commandments, the sacraments, the lineaments of theology. At my father's ordination, the old bishop had laid hands on my father's head, reading prayers that made him a priest and able to celebrate mass. Now Bishop Washburn would lay his hands on my head, and I would become part of the last supper, drinking wine and eating bread like the disciples. (All of us, my father preached, were, in different ways, disciples.) My mother and I had shopped for my confirmation dress, but the Thursday before the Sunday ceremony she'd left for Hollow Hill to await a new baby, and the day before my confirmation, my father called from the hospital with news of Marian's birth.

My two godmothers came to the service—my father's sister Polly and my mother's friend Sylvia, her roommate when she was pregnant with me and my father was away at the war. Aunt Polly gave me a red leather Bible and Aunt Sylvia a red leather prayer book—each stamped in gold with my name and the date. My dress was white and frothy, of dotted Swiss organza, and I felt like a bride sitting there in the front pew as candlelight made the incense gold and the organ rumbled, it seemed, from somewhere beneath the amber floor. At the altar, acolytes in red cassocks and white cottas genuflected, stood up, then genuflected again. Because I had fasted, the white of their cottas burned my eyes.

When it was time for the actual confirmation, the acolytes moved a large thronelike chair into the crossing, and Bishop Washburn took his seat. I could hardly wait. There had been a rehearsal, and so even though I was trembling, I did exactly as Sister Ora Mary had instructed, genuflecting as I left the pew, my father at the edge of my vision as I carefully walked forward and knelt on the cushion in front of Bishop Washburn. *Defend, O Lord, this thy child with thy heavenly grace*, he began. I bowed devoutly as I had seen my father do, and the bishop lowered his hands onto my veiled head . . . *that she may continue thine forever* . . . I closed my eyes, so I could listen. Forever? Yes, forever. I was starting to cry. His hands vibrated, seeming, as heat came through them, to hold on to me as if I were earthbound and solid, but they were also heavy and comforting because they were so big and my head was so small. *And daily increase in thy Holy Spirit more and more*, I could hear him say, his hands getting heavier and heavier, *until she come into thy everlasting kingdom*. And then he said Amen and lifted his hands, and I sprang to standing, as if without effort, everything shimmering. Surely this was God, I thought in that moment, the heat and heaviness in Bishop Washburn's hands, the lightness I felt as I stood up.

Days later, I played a princess at St. Luke's in a play our drama class had written. We were studying ancient history, and the play was called *Do the Scales of Egypt Balance?* Our drama teacher, Mrs. Melchior, who had red hair and eyeglasses with bluish lenses, was a real actress and the wife of an opera singer. I was to play Maru, the pharaoh's daughter. The week before the performance, the Hudson Tube went on strike, but my grandmother came to the rescue and Pip and I moved into the apartment on Fifth Avenue with Katherine Burgoyne, who had retired as my grandmother's upstairs maid. When I told her I needed a costume, she nodded, reassuring me, and the night before the play, she appeared with a lavender silk dress she had made specially. It had a slit skirt and a matching headband with a lavender flower attached that flopped beautifully over my ear. I hadn't thought I could ever be so happy, even though my mother couldn't come see the play. She was at Hollow Hill recuperating from Marian's birth.

Jill played the pharoah's wife, and we had gotten over our conflict about Jay Leach; she was now one of my three best friends. When I went to spend the night at her house, I'd go to her dancing school and watch the class, all in white ballet-length dresses, dance the mazurka. Her father was a theatrical press agent who wore a suit and tie to breakfast; her mother also worked and her sister was reading *The Catcher in the Rye*, a book I hadn't heard of. My friend Debbie played my sister; she had changed her name to Shai—because she was a dancer, she said. Her mother was divorced and a writer who lived with another woman, a singer named Charity Bailey, who was black and the first American woman I ever saw dress in African clothes. I was intrigued by the parents of my St. Luke's friends even though I didn't quite understand them—they worked, they didn't seem to go to church, and when I visited, they asked me so much about myself I was too shy to talk.

My friend Temma was the daughter of painters. The first time I spent the night at her house, we knocked at the door of her father's studio, which was really just a room in their house. His overalls were smeared with paint and he smiled when we came into the room. He had curly black hair and dark brown shiny eyes that were also a little wild. The air smelled of oil, and stacks of paintings were leaned against the walls. I remember dark colors and shapes that looked almost like people or leaves, the paint so thick it seemed to have a life of its own. I remember dirty rags on the floor, the floor splotched with color but swept clean. Temma called her parents by their first names; her father's name was Leland, and she called him Lee; her mother, whose name was Luisa, she called Ulla. Ulla was from Iceland and spoke with an accent. She had a narrow pinched face, and she painted with brighter colors than Lee did. Supper was soup and rough bread and some cheese and then stew and salad; the plates were brown and heavy. Once I went to Temma's for Passover—Lee was Jewish. His parents were there, and we ate horseradish and lamb, and read aloud the story of the Jews being spared by God.

St. Luke's, on Hudson Street, was a dozen-block walk downtown from where Temma lived on West Sixteenth Street, past the fishmonger and past every kind of store you could think of, buses racing by as we walked,

workmen shouting as trucks lurched against the gray stone curbs and
cars zoomed along, their horns honking. My second year, sixth grade, St.
Luke's opened a new building, which had bright new classrooms, a vast
art studio, a carpentry shop, a gym, and a cafeteria. I had always painted
and drawn at home; now I had an art teacher who was a real painter—she
of course said yes when Temma and I asked if we could collaborate on "a
mural." On the pristine floor we unrolled a six-foot sheet of brown paper
and planned our farm—a barn, chickens, cows, trees, horses, a girl carrying a bucket from a well toward the house.

Temma knew how to do such things—we drew first, then painted
boldly with saturated tempera colors. I learned to imitate the freedom of
her drawing, so different from my own restrained accuracy, to see that a
cow or a tree you drew would never look exactly like a cow or a tree, that
what you were after was a version of the cow or tree that was funnier or
prettier or scarier than life. When we finished, which took weeks, our
great work was hung on the classroom wall. What would we paint next?
We could do anything! During shop class, drawing on a piece of fresh
pine, I outlined a toy for my baby sister Marian, a wooden duck whose
shape I cut out with a handsaw and painted white, with an orange bill,
attaching wheels I also painted orange, to approximate feet.

I became a reader, checking out five books at a time from the new St.
Luke's library, taking them home to read in my room. *Misty of Chincoteague*.
The Black Stallion, *Pippi Longstocking*, *Jane Eyre*, anything to do with horses
or girls or enchantment. On the top floor at Hollow Hill, I found shelves
full of old books. I read ten in the Oz series, and a series about girls during the American Revolution—*A Little Maid of Old New York*, *A Little Maid
of New Orleans*—my favorite was the one in which the heroine found the
Marquis de Lafayette in her family's farmyard and helped him hide from
the British but also from her family, secretly bringing him food and water
in the hayloft. My book list was the longest in the class, and I also won
the contest in which you had to recite "If" by Rudyard Kipling, whose
stories *The Jungle Book* my father had read us when we were little. Mrs.
Rice taught arithmetic by improvising "brainteasers"—begin with the
number 37, add 3, divide by 4; she'd spin numbers for as long as twenty
minutes, no pencil and paper allowed. Sometimes my St. Luke's friends
came to Jersey City. One spring night when Temma came, the church
had rented a sound truck to publicize a four-day preaching mission to be

held the week before Easter. Temma and I huddled in the seatless back of the station wagon, and when Father Morton was tired of announcing through the loudspeaker, we sang, our eleven-year-old sopranos piercing the night.

There is a green hill far away
Without a city wall
Where our dear Lord was crucified
Who died to save us all.

One night that spring, my father announced that there would be a family meeting after supper in the room with the cherry wallpaper. We had never had a family meeting. What was next? I wondered as we gathered, the three oldest of the six children, my mother then thirty-three years old, and my father thirty-seven. I was eleven, the other five of us ranged down to a year and a half, and my mother was pregnant again. We were moving, my father announced. He had been "called" to Indiana, where he was to take his mission of social justice to the Midwest as dean of a cathedral. I was already crying. Yes, they assured us, we would go to the Adirondacks; we wouldn't move till August. Yes, Indiana was in the West and the land was very flat—I imagined there were buffalo, the open plain. No, we wouldn't have weekends at Hollow Hill, but we would have our own big backyard. Yes, we would miss Gami and Gramps. And, of course, we would miss Gagy, but she would come visit. And so would our friends, Ralphie, who was almost part of the family, and Jill and Temma and Shai. What about Jersey City? What about the important work, the summer staff, the neighborhood? Father Laughlin would stay on, Pam and Jim would move into the rectory, the work would go on as before.

I understood only that a "call" had come; the word made it sound as if the summons had been issued directly from God; Indianapolis is where God wants us to be, my parents said. The only cathedral I knew was huge, St. John the Divine, and the dean there was Jim Pike (later the controversial bishop of California). Being a dean, I realized, was close to being a bishop—this higher position put my father even closer to God, I concluded. It was only in reading his oral history that I learned his health had been a factor in the decision. The sickness his doctor called "cumulative fatigue" had lasted beyond that long summer, and it made the intensity of

Jersey City and its round-the-clock requirements too much for my father. He'd been getting stale, he said, arguing with Jim Morton and Ledlie's ideas: "We tried that five years ago, it didn't work." Indianapolis offered a life that he and my mother hoped would mend his health, that she hoped would give her time with her children. But I understood none of this that evening at our family meeting, and each new realization of what might be impossible in this strange place called Indianapolis brought another wave of tears.

Sometime in mid-August, my brother Pip—newly called Paul—and I set out with my father in the station wagon. We would arrive with the moving vans, and after a while, when the new baby, who turned out to be my third brother Daniel, was a little older, my mother would follow by plane with the other kids and with Gagy, who would stay for a while to help us get settled. By the time we pulled away from Second Street, my imagination was focused on the West. My mother stayed behind in Jersey City to check last-minute details, and then Pam and Jim Morton walked her to the Tube. "I loved our walk to the subway & remembering the Rectory dirty & dark, with kids playing ball in the yard," she wrote to Pam.

Because Paul and I were alone with our father, the harness of family left behind, the trip had the feeling of adventure. As we drove out through the Holland Tunnel, I asked my father to tell the familiar story of how his father had put the entire family in the Rolls-Royce the first time they took the tunnel into New York, preferring, should the engineering marvel collapse, that everyone die at once. I tried to read the book I'd brought along, but I couldn't keep my eyes off the road and my father driving West. Just before lunch, we came to the edge of New Jersey and signs announced the Pennsylvania Turnpike. "We'll go all the way to the end of it," my father told us. How wonderful, I thought, the idea of going to the end of something. Indiana meant Indians. It meant wonder, ending as it did in an *a* like a woman's name. We spent the first night near Pittsburgh with a St. Paul's friend of my father's, arriving at dusk in time to swim in a pool, sleep in a room with windows that looked out on an endless lawn and a weeping willow—maybe this is what our new house would be like!

The second night we spent with the Meads, the parents of my father's friend George who had died in the war, and after lunch the third day, we

were on Route 40, driving through small Indiana towns with names like
New Paris, every few miles a vegetable stand that sold string beans and
corn. By late afternoon, we pulled up at 3665 Washington Boulevard.
"The Deanery" was an enormous Tudor-style house set in the center of
a large lawn on a bright boulevard which had been the shadiest street
in town until the Dutch Elm disease killed all the trees. It was very hot
and humid, but the house, which had very high ceilings, was cool, even
though there were wall-to-wall carpets, something I'd never seen before.
The big kitchen had an island of matching cabinets down its center and
two ovens set in the wall, a separate laundry with a laundry chute. There
was also an enormous dining room, an eating porch—and the house had
seven bathrooms!

On the floor of the living room which ran nearly the entire width of
the front of the house, my parents would lay Great-granny's Chinese rug,
place Aunt Lily Hanna's Victorian settee and chairs, and hang Fritz Eichenberg prints that had started life as illustrations in *The Catholic Worker*.
There would be many things in the house that I had never seen before,
things stored at Hollow Hill before we moved to Jersey City. My mother
always swore that Gami, despairing we'd ever return to a proper life, had
given away several crates of their wedding-present glass and china. We
were now living in the luxury on which I thought my parents had reso-
lutely turned their backs. The polished walnut paneling in the house, the
light color of the refinished pews at the cathedral, the haute excellence of
the boys' choir all seemed temporary, something we were pretending at
between acts of the real play. But my parents seemed to take to this odd
place as enthusiastically as they had to Jersey City. My father had a secretary who sharpened his pencils and typed his letters and sermons, and his
workday ended when he drove home. My mother now had more time for
her six children, her seventh infant; she would make her way as an ordinary clergy wife rather than a teammate. Also, she wrote Pam Morton, she
and my father were relieved to be out of range of Hollow Hill and Gami's
hovering presence.

Before school started, my mother took me shopping to the largest,
"best," department store in Indianapolis. She stood at the counter in L.S.
Ayres and got a temporary charge account and the saleswoman called her
Mrs. Moore. There were no stores like this where we lived in Jersey City;
we went to the Wonder Store where blouses cost a dollar and your feet were

measured with an X-ray machine, and our dressy clothes came in large flat packages from "Best & Co." in New York, sent by my grandmother. So this was the first time I'd gone shopping for serious clothes with my mother. Over her protests at its narrow cut, I chose a navy blue and black plaid skirt with a matching vest. I undressed and stood in front of the mirror in my underpants and undershirt, first putting on the crispy white blouse the sales lady brought, and then, as she and my mother watched, trying the skirt. It would not pass my hips. "Put it on over her head," the sales lady suggested, but my mother pulled it off and handed it back to her. "I think it's too grown-up," she said abruptly. Moving had been difficult for my mother. She wrote to Pam of those early weeks:

> I have had . . . a real dark night of the soul, from which I trust I am now emerging. I became terrified that I was or would become some-what nuts, and couldn't seem to get any perspective. Every single characteristic, achievement, act, experience, relationship of the past few years was suddenly reviewed in a very black shadow—with only bad motives apparent etc. I had always thought I was aware of the pitfalls (for the soul) of Jersey City, but it became obvious that I was only aware of them in the most superficial manner. As I looked back on it I was guilty of the worst kind of pride in so many areas. I suppose anyone could have told me, had I sat down and listened. Once I realized that God was kind and would only show me these things briefly and then let me pass on, and once I real-ized that I was under a terrible strain for a long time . . . I felt some-what more able to cope. I was helpless with the children—mostly of course because all seven were at their most demanding . . . I'm sorry to inflict this on you but must share it with Christian friends . . .

In Indianapolis, my mother was closer to us, but my father was further away. In another letter my mother reported to Pam that when my father was home he was really home, but that he was gone a lot of the time. "Paul seems really revived by the change, and when he gets tired, is able to snap back after a night's sleep." Like other fathers, mine now disappeared to work early in the morning, but he was also out a few nights a week and most of the weekend; Monday was his day off. Like ordinary children, my brother and I walked to school at seven-thirty, our younger sisters fol-

lowing an hour later. School was P.S. 66, a large brick building five or six
blocks away. When you got to Thirty-eighth Street, a traffic boy held his
arms out, and when the light turned green, you crossed, which seemed
exotic after New York and the Hudson Tube.

My seventh-grade homeroom was filled only with white children, and,
unlike at St. Luke's where we'd all worn black tights and turtlenecks, the
girls wore sweaters that matched a straight or pleated skirt, and loafers or
"tennis shoes" or "saddle shoes." The boys wore button-down shirts and
khakis, and they had crew cuts. How would I fit into this? At the first
recess, I stood next to the window overlooking the school playground
with a girl I'd met—we were both watching the kids running across the
yard. She had a wide face, long straight hair, and blemished skin and she
was the only girl who had befriended me that first day. Suddenly she said,
"I don't believe it, a nigger at 66."

I had never heard anyone use that word because in my family it was
an obscenity, and so when I heard that word out loud, I suddenly did not
know where I was. The strange girl standing in front of me, the odd landscape with its porched houses, lawns, straight skirts, and football games,
humidity so heavy I could hardly breathe. I looked down at the yard and,
yes, there was one black boy outside, wearing a striped shirt, running at a
diagonal from one end of the yard to the other. I knew I should say something to the girl, whose name was Ellen Massey, but my heart was pounding and now I could barely see her. I said nothing, and in that moment,
I betrayed Ralphie Walker and Tom Venable and Stella Skipper. In that
moment I deserted my father and mother. I believed that if I told them
what I had not done, they might direct me to confront Ellen Massey, and I
did not have the courage to do that. I knew already that to be popular was
everything in seventh grade at 66, and I knew that in order to be popular,
I would have to leave Jersey City behind.

My father, of course, did not altogether leave Jersey City behind; in fact,
he had been brought to Indianapolis to create at the cathedral, a beautiful
Indiana limestone church on Monument Circle in the center of the city,
a downtown ministry inspired by his work in Jersey City. John Craine,
the bishop, his predecessor as dean, had remodeled the church, built its
endowment, and attracted a powerful and wealthy vestry. My father was
receiving a salary and he was free of fund-raising; all his energy could
go into the actual church work. The difference was that he was not alto-

gether in charge. While the bishop supported his work, the vestry were his official employers. About a year into his ministry my father decided to begin efforts to integrate the congregation; the neighborhoods closest to the cathedral were racially mixed or entirely black, but that parish, except for one Negro couple, was, as my father said in his oral history, "pretty much lily-white." Unlike in Jersey City where the church was next door and its doings part of my daily life, the cathedral was a twenty-minute drive away, and we went there only on Sundays. From my experience with Ellen Massey, I had learned that we were in enemy territory as far as race was concerned. I didn't know my father understood that until, during his second year at Christ Church, he spent a weekend in retreat with the vestry at the diocesan conference center in the hills of Brown County, south of the city.

My father had been thrilled by the invitation. He looked forward to real conversation and more teamwork with the leaders of the congregation, but instead of affirming what he was doing in the parish, the vestry confronted him about the presence of new black parishioners at Sunday services. Why was it necessary to bring "them" into Christ Church? There was, they reminded my father, a Negro parish nearby. "I kicked over into the role of group therapist unconsciously as we went around the room," my father remembered in his oral history. He tried to get them all to speak their minds, and after everyone had spoken, he said, "I don't know what to say. I really feel very strongly that the church has to be open to all people. I haven't done this carelessly." He reiterated what he had made clear when he was hired, that he was a member of the NAACP and committed to social action, and that he had Bishop Craine's support. It turned out that when he was chosen, none of them had heard of the NAACP and couldn't anyway imagine that a man with my father's pedigree would hold such radical opinions. Now they associated my father with what was being reported in the news. That autumn Governor Faubus of Arkansas had used the National Guard to keep black children out of Central High School in Little Rock, and in response President Eisenhower had sent in paratroopers and federalized the National Guard to enforce the law. What would the government do next? The Christ Church vestry had concluded the NAACP was a Communist front and that my father had been sent to turn the cathedral into "a nigger church."

The only member of the vestry absent from the retreat was Eli Lilly, its chairman, who supported my father's work and who, by virtue of his success in turning his grandfather's drug company into a powerful pharmaceutical corporation and becoming the city's great benefactor, occupied the pinnacle of Indianapolis society. The weekend retreat had traumatized my father, and he was still shaky when, days after the confrontation, his secretary announced that Mr. Lilly was at his office door.

"Excuse me, Mr. Dean"—that was Mr. Lilly's familiar name for my father—"could I have just a few minutes of your time? I know you're very busy." My father was immediately disarmed: "Here I was," he remembered later, "just a green kid . . ."

"Of course, please sit down."

"Well, I've just got one thing to say to you . . . There will never be a Little Rock on Monument Circle. You can paint the cathedral blue with pink polka dots if you wish, and I will stand behind you. Good day, sir." Mr. Lilly held this position even though his own company at the time hired no black chemists. Later he created a million-dollar endowment to support my father's work in the diocese—a consortium of downtown parishes to organize inner-city initiatives—and soon the parish voted in a new vestry, younger, more progressive, and enthusiastic about my father's ambitions for the cathedral's ministry.

My mother was negotiating her role as the dean's wife. The first fall, she and the wives of the two other priests in the parish were asked to provide centerpieces for the tables at the parish bazaar, which she reported with a cacaphony of exclamation marks to Pam in a letter. A year later, though, a vestry wife asked her to lead a prayer group, and she wrote Pam asking for suggestions of readings about the desert fathers, the early Christian mystics.

Indianapolis was not a cultural backwater. When I was in high school, my father could take me and a friend to a Bergman or Fellini film at the Zaring Egyptian Theatre, and for a deli sandwich at Sam's Subway afterward, and my parents' friends invited them to musicales held by patrons of the Indianapolis Symphony: "the Budapest String Quartet in the Fesslers' living room, my dear," my mother wrote Pam. By our third year in Indianapolis, when I was a freshman in high school, my parents had found a community of like-minded friends, great people, based on whom my mother formed a theory that Democrats in conservative states like Indiana were required to have real endurance. In 1958, Martin Luther King Jr. came to speak downtown, and in 1960 Dorothy Day came to stay for a week and gave a talk at our house, and once my mother took me to a discussion about "the Beat Generation" at All Saints, the Anglo-Catholic parish where she went for confession.

My father's work was gaining national prominence and hardly a year went by when he wasn't nominated for bishop somewhere, but we were settled and no one, including my parents, had any desire to move. All of us who were old enough were beginning to have gangs of friends, and my father's spells of illness were less and less frequent. "I sometimes wonder," my mother wrote Pam, "how anyone can be as happy as we are."

Part II

DAUGHTER

10
Light and Dark

In my memory, Jersey City was dark and angular. Even when the sun shone, the darkness remained because of the sharp shadows cast by the church. In the front yard where we played handball, bright pavement always had a black shadow right next to it, and inside the church it was always dark—even when the parchment lanterns were lit, the light they gave seemed to come from darkness. I hear my father's voice: "The light shineth in darkness; and the darkness comprehended it not." There cannot be light without darkness. The house in Indianapolis did not have darkness, and neither did the church with its almost-blond pews. In the car, when we drove to church, the streets were too flat and quiet. There was never traffic, nothing jostled up against anything else.

My mother wrote to Pam Morton that I was "plugging along," an accurate description. What I remember is anxiety about my body and my mother's inability to reassure me. The hips that had resisted the skirt in the L.S. Ayres fitting room had continued to swell, as had my breasts, and I got my period at twelve, four years earlier than my mother had. Knowing that I was not the lean, boyish girl my mother was in teenage photographs, I thought I was fat, and so when I had my yearly checkup, my mother told the doctor I ate too much and asked if he could do something about my weight. He had me tested, and when the results came, he prescribed pills for an underactive thyroid. To curb my appetite, he prescribed Dexedrine, which I took in one form or another for the next ten years, unaware until I was in my twenties that it had any effect other than as a diet pill.

My mother wrote Pam Morton that she was "on a campaign to let Honor emote her ill feelings (which were endless)." She had not realized, she explained, that I'd "resented the years in Jersey City" and had felt too guilty to complain. In tears, apparently, I protested the "friendlessness of it, the hectic-ness, etc." I don't remember resenting Jersey City or the invitation to spill my feelings—only enraged battles out of earshot of the other children, in the downstairs half bath with its aubergine fixtures, over my body, the hair in my face, my "messy" room. But my real complaint went unidentified by both of us. It was a mother I missed. When would I ever have her to myself? When would we walk together as we had once in Kent when I was eight or nine, down Route 7 having a serious talk, to an antiques shop where she bought me a vase for my collection? "It was very rough," my mother wrote. My father didn't intervene, but once when Gagy visited, she brought laundry upstairs after overhearing one of the battles. "Neaten your room, Honor," she said. "Things will go better for you."

My mother, of course, had not had the kind of mother I wanted, who drew her out or questioned her: caring had come from Senny, the governess. On principle, my mother had decided to raise her children herself, but our numbers soon outran her idealism, and the constant nanny each of my parents had taken for granted was left out of their adventurous equation. My mother was inventing the wheel as far as her approach to mothering was concerned, and I was the first parenting exhibit. How could she admit that every time she had a new baby, her eldest child suffered? I don't think it occurred to her. As for my father, he was gone before breakfast; his thorough absence—the church where I could always find him no longer next door—diminished my life. At St. Luke's, "Honor" had written a novel, painted a mural, and acted in a play. She'd ridden the subway and walked the streets of New York with friends who wore black leotards and danced the mazurka. At 66, the girls wore Peter Pan collars and practiced cheerleading moves, and Honor didn't know what to do with herself.

It was all my mother could manage to make lives for seven children in this alien place. Mrs. Lee, who was black, came to help each day, and once in a while Adeline Walker, white and single and a secretary at Eli Lilly and Company, who decades later became an Episcopal nun, babysat in the evenings. To give herself more time "with the children and Paul," my mother experimented by hiring a cook. Mrs. Pendleton, the wife of a Baptist minister, came for a few months, but having a black woman wearing a uniform and serving and clearing made my mother uncomfortable and she soon went back to cooking herself, assigning clearing and washing to one of us, a poster with jobs and days of the week taped above the kitchen sink. The little ones ate early, then my parents had cocktails, and then my father officiated at evening prayer, all of us together in the formal living room, kneeling on Great-granny's Chinese rug in front of a table with a cross and candles on it. After prayers, everyone under ten went to bed, and then, "Mommy" and "Poppy" at either end of Grandma Kean's polished mahogany table, we all sat down to supper, Paul telling jokes, me finishing fast so I could have seconds, all of us, my mother in the lead, laughing as we mimicked the way my father ended the Lord's Prayer: "The POWer and the glowree . . ."

My favorite teacher at 66 was Mr. Walker. My mother joked that I was "in love" with him, but my admiration was not romantic. He was Southern and theatrical in his immaculate pale yellow linen jacket, striped shirts, and bright ties, and he wore his auburn hair in a pompadour. He was older, but perhaps only in his forties, the kind of single man I knew as "a bachelor." I remember him talking about Lincoln, and the day when everyone brought in clippings about the Russians launching *Sputnik*. But at 66 most of the classes, compared to St. Luke's, were like the Indianapolis streets—too wide and flat. What we read in English class came out of a big textbook; when I drew in art class, the subject was prescribed; and when I made a mural it was assigned, a map of Indiana, delineating its counties. Nor was there any discussion in Mr. Walker's current events class about what we talked about at home. Little Rock, Eisenhower sending in the 101st Airborne to enforce *Brown v. Board of Education.*

I did not bring those subjects to school: I knew what had happened to my father with his vestry, what Ellen Massey had said about the boy in the school yard at 66, and that no black people lived near us on Washington Boulevard. Evidence was mounting that what had been at the center of things in Jersey City here put us in danger. I just had to look at the paper, grainy pictures of white men and women outside the high school in Little Rock, their mouths distorted by shouting, arms raised to hit or throw rocks; the young soldiers with grim faces; Negro children just my age, their heads bowed, heading into the school. The papers had noted in announcements of our arrival that my father had been vice president of the New Jersey NAACP, and people were learning what the Christ Church dean stood for. It was while researching this book that I learned that my father, to gain trust, purposely kept his sermons apolitical those first Indianapolis years—pastoral and close to scripture. I noticed the difference, but I thought he'd simply changed, the way I believed I had to.

I didn't know then that my father had once been a racist and anti-Semitic, as was accepted both by the class into which he had been born and by the era in which he lived: the starkness of his bigotry still shocks me. From the Marine Corps, he wrote to my mother, baldly, that he hated Jews—he had a bunkmate who was Jewish. Of course there were no black people in his marine unit; the military wouldn't be integrated until 1947. My mother's attitudes changed earlier than my father's. During the war, she read *Strange Fruit*, the book about lynching by Lillian Smith, and wrote my father: "I know you feel differently than I do about such things. We have to discuss it." The change in my father, from being a racist and anti-Semite to being an antiracist, came with the same simplicity as his original conversion. He grew to know and, to his surprise, to love the Jewish marine. The end of his racism came later. "I saw Jesus Christ in the faces of the poor," he once explained. When he worked with neighborhood people at St. Peter's Chelsea, their faces were black and brown. Everything flowed from that:

. . . You couldn't go next door to visit a little kid who came to your
Sunday-school class, find him living in one room with eight brothers
and sisters—to say nothing of rats—and just pat him on the head
and say, "Jesus loves you." You had to do something about the conditions you saw. And when you started doing something about the
rats, then you got to the landlord; you tried to organize a rent strike,
as we did. A family got kicked out, and lived with you for several
months, until they found another home. Why was it so hard for them
to find another home? Because the public housing project discrimi-
nated against blacks, and let only a few of them in. What did you
do about the public housing project? You went to City Hall. There
you got a lot of promises but no action. What did you do next? You
went to Washington. And sooner or later you got involved in wider
politics—all starting with that little boy. That is literally the way
it happened to me. And shortly after I went to Jersey City I became
a Democrat—having been a Republican through my childhood, and
not having thought through social issues at all when I was at Yale.

Change for my father was simple; it happened to him, and it was irrevers-
ible. He expected no less of the men on the Christ Church vestry, and I
was his daughter. I turned aside my fear and set about making friends.

Andra lived two blocks away, and I went to her house to spend the
night and watch television—my parents objected to television and we
didn't have one. Andra was an only child, and her parents went out or to
bed early, leaving us by ourselves. She was tall and quiet, and studious
like I was. Her father was a doctor who was bald and wore wire-rimmed
glasses, and her mother, who fastened her auburn hair in a chignon on top
of her head, wore flaring ankle-length skirts. When I arrived after supper,
we'd make pizza from a mix in a box; after you'd blended in water and flattened the dough, you opened the tiny can of tomato sauce, spread it across
the pie, and sprinkled on cheese from a packet of cheese. As it baked, we'd
settle on the sofa in the glassed-in porch where the TV was.

During the second or third commercial, the pizza would be ready
to eat. The movie began at eleven-thirty and was introduced by Frances
Farmer, dressed in a stiff evening gown, and sponsored by Flanner &
Buchanan, the funeral home. A long time later reading her autobiography, I'd learn that "Frances Farmer" had been Frances Farmer the movie

star, and that her bland affect, which I thought Hoosier courtesy, was the consequence of a lobotomy. Still later, I would learn that the *New Yorker* writer Genêt, as Janet Flanner, had been the daughter of an Indianapolis undertaker. Late, late late, and even late late late, we watched old black-and-white dreams of the night—Greta Garbo in *Camille* and *Ninotchka*, the sad face and awkwardness of Lon Chaney Jr. as Frankenstein's monster, *Dracula* with Bela Lugosi in a black cape, pale face, dark-penciled eyes. As he lifted his arms, his body dissolved, leaving a bat tilting off into the night sky. Andra and I had long serious talks, and one year, for Christmas, she gave me my first book of modern poetry, *Selected Poems of Ezra Pound*, a skinny paperback, the stark black-and-white of the poet on the cover. In my parents' bookshelves, I'd found *Other Voices, Other Rooms* by Truman Capote and *The Ways of White Folks* by Langston Hughes, but I'd never read a poem that didn't rhyme, or that had only two lines, or whose title seemed to have nothing to do with what it said. A poem I liked in my new book was called "The Tea Shop," but it was about a woman getting older. *She does not get up the stairs so eagerly; / Yes, she also will turn middle aged*.

Shortridge, the high school, was even closer to our house than 66 and "integrated," but in the cafeteria, where you slid a brown tray along a steel rail to get lunch—chili or hot dogs or burgers, fish sandwiches on Fridays—what you saw was not what I had lived in Jersey City or at St. Luke's. The Negro students sat together in one part of the huge room, the white students elsewhere; you and the Negro girl sang together in A Cappella Choir, but you didn't seek each other out at lunch. The presence of Negro students was a "percentage" broadcast in whispers; the figures as I remember them were 30 percent when I was a freshman in 1959, more than 40 percent when I graduated. The black population of the city was growing, Negroes were moving further uptown, their neighborhoods breaching the Crispus Attucks boundaries and spreading into the district served by Shortridge. (Attucks, named for the black man who was the first American casualty of the American Revolution, was a historically Negro high school of which Oscar Robertson, the great basketball player, "the Big O" drafted by the Cincinnati Royals in 1960, was the most illustrious graduate.) As more Negroes came to Shortridge, many white families moved north and east into the Broad Ripple district—"Ripple" was Shortridge's historic rival, and it was all white. Other whites left the tree-lined streets near Thirty-eighth Street, selling comfortable 1920s houses to buy land north of the city limits and build one-story ranch houses, sending their children to the brand-new high school the county had just built, and taking business they'd once transacted on Monument Circle to Glendale, the shopping center where Ayres and Block's, the downtown department stores, built their first suburban branches. My classmate who pointed out the "nigger" in the schoolyard at 66 was not, I was learning, unusual in her attitudes.

The Indianapolis people who became my parents' friends—Catholic and Jewish intellectuals and activists who were Democrats, other East Coast transplants—shared their point of view about race. Some of them had gone to Shortridge themselves and, like my parents, identified their neighbors' sudden moves to the suburbs as what sociologists called "white flight," and believed it should be resisted. Like my parents, their new friends read the moderate *Indianapolis Times* and reviled the conservative Eugene C. Pulliam papers, the *Indianapolis Star* and the *Indianapolis News*. Like us, they subscribed to the *New York Times*, which arrived a day late, and which I considered the journalistic version of the Supreme Court— a corrective. Even as my father kept his sermons at Christ Church tame, he let loose out of town. In a speech to the women's caucus at the General Convention of the Episcopal Church in 1961, he declared it "really ludicrous that we presume to call ourselves Christians, when it can be a major issue in a northern urban parish in the year 1961 whether a Negro can serve as an usher," and, protesting the church's failure to do anything about the growth of slums, added, "the real purpose of the church can be quite brutally shown to be a religious convenience for those who can pay to live in the suburbs." My parents' new friends were people with whom they discussed these issues, people who voted for Stevenson in 1956 and, with my parents, for Kennedy in 1960.

At home I had no doubt where I really stood on the issue of race. I cared about my father's progress in bringing Negroes into Christ Church—first into the congregation, then the choir, the ushers, and the Sunday school. I understood by his tone of voice that he had been, as he later put it, "traumatized" by his experience with the vestry. It scared me when he was frightened, but it reassured me when he talked about the million dollars Mr. Lilly had given for the cooperative downtown ministry, the opening of a mission storefront out near the speedway. I thought of Mr. Lilly as my father's protection. He was a shy man and I barely met him, but we were welcome to swim in his pool "anytime." Going there was like entering a little piece of Hollow Hill, leaving the flatness, winding up a hill to the large white stucco house, its walls thick with glossy-leaved euonymus, reaching the large, round old-fashioned swimming pool, also painted white, a few leaves or petals of the big magnolia tree floating on its fresh-water surface.

We didn't join the Riviera Club, where a lot of our friends went, because it didn't admit Jews or Negroes, and we weren't taken to the amusement park, which was also segregated. There were two private schools in Indianapolis, Tudor Hall for girls and Park School for boys, but many of the old Indianapolis families had gone to Shortridge for generations and sent their children there, considering loyalty to their alma mater a badge of honor. I met some of the children from Park and Tudor and from the Catholic schools at Mrs. Gates's dancing classes, which were also all white but which allowed Jews. There, Mrs. McMurtrie, dressed in a flared black dress cinched at the waist with a wide belt, taught us to fox-trot, waltz, and tango; we knew she and Mrs. Gates had determined a new dance might last when she instructed us in a decorous version of it—in eighth grade she taught us the stroll, her elegant black-pumped foot incongruously executing the backward lunge.

To her friends in the East, my mother boasted about Shortridge, which had a daily newspaper and offered French, Spanish, German, Latin and Greek, history, social studies, math up through various advanced versions of calculus, biology, physics, and chemistry. I argued with my boarding-school cousins who thought it was strange that we went to public school. I told them about Dr. R. Ruth Richards, whom I had for biology, who had a doctorate and should have been teaching at a university, and about Mrs. Henrietta Parker, my chemistry teacher, who had worked on the Manhattan Project, though with her shiny blue eyes, her white hair stylishly caught up in a bun, she hardly looked like someone who would build a bomb. I started Shortridge in an eighth-grade "special class" that offered a faster pace of learning and a curriculum that included typing and French. We met in one room on the third floor of the enormous redbrick four-storied building; special class was not as freewheeling as St. Luke's, but it was more fun than 66 and a respite from football and cheerleading. I and my new friends there prided ourselves on being "intellectual," and for my oral report I spoke on Robert Frost. When I went back to Shortridge the following year as a freshman, I knew my way around the building. My friends and I all signed up for Latin and choir and were placed in the "g" ("gifted") classes that separated children of the middle class, including a large population of Latvian immigrants, from those less well prepared, usually black children or the children of the white families who had come up from Kentucky or West Virginia. Junior year, because our sophomore Latin class excelled, our Latin teacher, who was named Josephine Bliss and raised cattle on a farm, started an intensive class in ancient Greek that met every morning. My father was thrilled, regaling me with stories of his Yale class in Greek scansion in which he had received a failing grade from Eugene O'Neill Jr., son of the playwright.

Before I knew what a "social club" was, I heard whispers in the halls of invitations to teas given by WOW (Women of the World) and GALS (G is for the good girls that compose us, A is for the angels that we are, L is for the love we show each other, S is for the sex we rate by far) and acceptances to the two elite clubs—you could only pledge one of them. Subdeb and Euvola, I was told as if it went without saying, had a quota for Jews and, like the other clubs, excluded Negroes altogether. But when I saw the tiny black and gold pins—black enamel with the club's name in gold lettering—that you wore on a sweater or shirt close to the tip of your left breast, I burned with longing. "What a pretty pin!" I might say, though when I saw "pledges" approach "actives" and offer them candy in the halls, I pretended not to notice. Sometime in October, two of my friends from eighth grade and I were asked to pledge ARC ("All are considerate"). It was a club of dubious ranking, but I did not hesitate; now I had an acceptable answer to the question, "What are you pledging?" Now I too carried a bag of candy in my purse, risking punishment if a teacher caught me offering it in the hall or demerits from the club if I failed to remember an active's favorite.

My mother ridiculed the whole procedure—the four hundred pennies I had to collect, the skits I had to concoct for the Tuesday night meetings, and my desperation to belong: "Honor is always saying she isn't 'popular,'" she wrote to Pam. She didn't understand that she'd always been "popular," having been born to the tribe with whom she played tennis, swam, rode, and went to boarding school—children of her parents' friends, who in turn were the children of their parents' friends, all the way back to the *Arbella* and the *Mayflower*. Much later when we were grown up and living in New York, a woman I'd admired from afar at Shortridge, who'd been a prom-queen candidate and a cheerleader, told me how her mother had managed her successful campaign for popularity, choosing clothes that would show off her hourglass figure, designing and sewing the formal gowns she wore to dances, coaching her in strategies of flirtation. My parents had removed their names from the New York Social Register to protest its racism and anti-Semitism, but the elite to which they'd always belonged would always be there for them to return to.

Andra picked me up at seven-fifteen and we walked to school. Down Washington Boulevard, across Thirty-fifth Street, over to Pennsylvania Street, and turn left. The school with its playing fields and terraces occupied a full city block. At the curb, kids who drove parked their cars, doors open in warm weather, hit parade spilling out onto the street. From the corner of my eye I saw Carol Stout, a cheerleader who had pledged GALS, Jolee Benfield, a Southern girl with blond hair and sparkling brown eyes who had pledged Subdeb, and Toni Grant, who'd pledged WOW. "She's stacked," was what the boys said about Toni. I'd watch furtively as she walked from one car to another, her skirt tight, wearing stockings— "hose"—and flat delicate shoes—"flats." I was sure no one saw me, the girl who wore glasses, the girl with straight brown hair who got A's. Toni didn't seem to care much about A's, and her hair was honey blond.

Jim Spencer was a senior, and late one May night, I sneaked out to meet him. He had a girlfriend, and maybe he ended up marrying her, but he was the boy that Faye, an ARC active, recruited when I complained I'd never "made out." I was a little scared when she told me that her secret boyfriend Mac, the grown-up study hall teacher who drove a green MG, would pick me up at 2 a.m. Faye was quiet and her hair was brown; the popular girls, the cheerleaders, had hair turned fluorescent blond from swimming at "Rivvie" and eyelashes carefully blackened with mascara; they wore straight skirts that were never too tight, pleated skirts when they wanted to relax: Faye always wore very tight skirts. Jim wasn't popular either, but his girlfriend with her careful bouffant was not the kind to sneak out in the middle of the night to drink and neck under a highway bridge with someone else's boyfriend. His skin was sallow and he had a chipped tooth, but he had looked handsome posturing in pale blue brocade in *The Doctor in Spite of Himself*, the Molière play the school did that year, and for which I'd done props.

Exactly on time, Mac pulled up in his tiny green convertible, I slipped from behind the bushes, carrying a blanket, and Faye opened the door for me. In the clearing under the bridge, Jim was waiting in his pickup truck. We spread the blankets and sat down as if for a picnic, and then Mac opened a pint of Seagram's 7 and we drank. We laughed for a while—I was waiting, the way you wait before a dentist starts drilling. Suddenly as we were all talking, my eyes dodging Jim's, Faye and Mac knotted themselves into one of the blankets and fell away. Then Jim leaned forward and kissed my forehead; I couldn't look at him. He touched my chin with his hands, guided it toward him and kissed my mouth. When he pulled back, he didn't look at me, and then he kissed me again, shooting his tongue in through my lips and swishing it around. His mouth tasted stale. The whiskey bottle caught the dark light as his hand crept under my sweater and toward my breasts, as I resisted the deliciousness of the feeling of his fingers there, wanting and not wanting him to stop. Soon I was lying down—my clothes still on—and he was on top of me. I wondered as we kissed what Faye and Mac were doing, certain Faye knew how to do what I didn't. Along with the talk about who was pledging what club and what percentage Negro the school now was, there was disapproving gossip about who went "all the way"—frightening rumors, if a girl suddenly disappeared, that she had left school to have a baby, not, as she'd claimed, to live with her lonely or rich or sick aunt in St. Louis.

It was almost light when Faye shook me awake and I pulled myself from Jim's arms and got back into the boot of the MG. I had told Elly, the Dutch exchange student who was living with us, that I had to study late and would sleep on the porch. It was almost 5 a.m. when I fell asleep there, pulling around me covers from my bed upstairs, still tingling from the weight of Jim Spencer. Since I had to be at school at eight for the biology bird-watching trip, I set the alarm for seven, but when the hot sun woke me, I was hung over and the clock said five of eight. Without a shower or packing a lunch, I raced to school. The rented bus was still there, its engine idling, and Dr. R. Ruth Richards was standing at the door with a list in her hand, a faint smile on her face, as if she knew exactly what had made me late.

Therefore, with angels and archangels, and with all the company of heaven . . .
My father is speaking the prayer that begins the most sacred part of the

communion service, the prayers through which the bread comes to stand for Christ's body, the wine, his blood. On my knees with the girls' choir, I join him: *Holy, Holy, Holy,* we sing, the closest I come to being an actual part of what my father does. Had I been born a decade later, I would have been an acolyte, but in 1960, only boys were acolytes, and only men were priests; the girls' choir sang the family service at nine-fifteen, the boys the more important service, at eleven. I do not even imagine the possibility of any of this changing as I work to sing like a boy, reach a high soprano behind my eyebrows, a pure, beautiful voice that seems to come from no body at all.

John Fenstermaker was playing the organ, and I was "in love with" him. At Shortridge he had given piano recitals, and my friend Laurie, who was a pianist herself, told me he might one day have a concert career. When he took his bow on the stage of the auditorium, I couldn't clap hard enough. You could tell he was exhausted as he bowed, but also embarrassed by our praise. I agreed with Laurie—soon he'd be playing piano concertos with the symphony downtown at the Shriners' Murat Temple. Right now, though, he was at the organ, and I was just feet away, in a row of girls singing, long purple robes covering our Sunday best. He was slender, even slight, with brown hair and big brown eyes. He'd never spoken a word to me, but right before he graduated just weeks ago, I started saying hello to him in the halls, and eventually he'd acknowledged me with a crooked, sleepy smile.

All glory be to thee, Almighty God, our heavenly Father. My father is now reading, genuflecting, standing, genuflecting again. He is at the altar, his back to us, bass repetitions of organ notes seeming to lift him from kneeling, candles flaming insistently upward. Now he strikes his chest three times as three times he repeats, *Lord, I am not worthy,* the enormous cross appliquéd across the back of his chasuble falling and rising as he prays and kneels and stands again. Soon it will be time to move from the choir pew to the altar rail for communion. *For in the night in which he was betrayed* . . . The disciples wait in the garden, in the dark. Someone asks Saint Peter if he knows Jesus, and Saint Peter says no, he does not, and in the brightness of the sanctuary my father lifts the bread with both his hands high over his head. *And when he had given thanks, he broke it* . . . I am so close to the altar I can hear the wafer crack apart and see my father's hands open to touch all the bread and all the wine, as he continues the prayer. Now he is giving communion to himself and to the other priests, first bread and then wine.

So rapt was I that when the acolyte lifted his hand, gesturing to the choir to come forward, it was as if he were some sort of angel. With the others, I sidled carefully out of the choir pew and made my way reverently to the altar rail. Slowly I knelt, and my father moved toward me, the color of his chasuble blinding, and when he paused before me, his eyes and voice betraying no recognition, he pressed a white wafer the size of a quarter into my outstretched palms: *Take and eat this in remembrance that Christ died—*

John Fenstermaker was playing an interlude, Bach, something I recognized from my mother's Wanda Landowska record, and as I crossed myself I tried to look as pious as he did, hoping he would look up and see me kneeling there, as Father Bolles, whose son I babysat, stood in front of me, not allowing his eyes to see me either as he extends the cool edge of the gleaming chalice to my lips, tipping it so I can drink the wine. *This is my blood* . . . Sweet and aromatic, it burns in my mouth and rushes down my throat, and as the organ grows softer and then louder again, I see John Fenstermaker lean back, allowing the music to take him. I cross myself.

As I rose to my feet, a hot emptiness clamped each side of the back of my head. John Fenstermaker began to blur, and I could hardly feel my hands; it was as if I had left them behind in that vibrating goldness. I turned and walked toward the pew, deliberately, as if I might fall if I wasn't very careful. When I slid back into the pew, my eyes lowered, I crossed myself again, bowed my head, which was now throbbing fiercely, and leaned into my open hymnal, the page cool against my forehead.

John Fenstermaker went on playing Bach, then Saint-Saëns, and eventually I lifted my head and watched the congregation move up the stairs from the crossing and through the chancel. *Crossing. Chancel.* The words now seem alien, but at the time they were as familiar as "kitchen" or "bedroom." Mrs. Bolles and Mrs. Rountree, the wife of the curate, moved slowly toward the altar rail, and I could hear their husbands murmuring, *Take, eat . . . Drink this in remembrance . . . of me.* Now John Fenstermaker played chords I knew would end in the minor key of my mother's favorite hymn, and there she was, passing in front of me, her head bowed. I began to sing, hoping she would hear me:

Let all mortal flesh keep silence,
       And with fear and trembling stand;
Ponder nothing earthly minded,
       For with blessing in His hand,
Christ our God to earth descendeth,
       Our full homage to demand.

That August, before we left for the Adirondacks, my mother organized a party with the mothers of two of my friends, and I asked her to invite John Fenstermaker. We set up the food and record player on the eating porch where I'd slept the night I sneaked out with Jim Spencer, and opened the French doors so the guests would spill out onto the terrace and into the fenced yard that enclosed the wooden jungle gym my father had assembled from a kit. Everyone brought 45s, and we danced to Fats Domino and Lloyd Price and Brenda Lee. John Fenstermaker arrived, and soon he and I were slow-dancing to Pete Fountain, arms slung around each other's necks, barely moving. I could hardly believe it: I wanted a kiss, and we did kiss, slowly and sweetly. He didn't call the next day or the one after that, but a month later, when I wrote my friend Christine from the Adirondacks, he was who I was dreaming of: "I play Pete Fountain every 5 minutes. Anyway I always wish I were still dancing with him."

11
Thou Shalt Not

The spring of my junior year, a new girl arrived at the school, unheralded, from another part of town, or from out of town—no one knew where. She was very tall and she wore her skirts three inches above the knee, years before anyone heard of a miniskirt. Her mother made her clothes, altered what she did not make, and understood that her daughter's looks were an asset. Cassandra understood that, too. Her mouth was beautiful, and, she said, "my nostrils flare." She wore mascara and tinted her blond hair and her mother didn't object. Mrs. Diehl was heavy and dark-haired, wore glasses and navy blue dresses. Mr. Diehl's face seemed startled into a daze of perpetual confusion.

Cassandra always wore stockings, her garter belt was lace, and her underwear looked like a movie star's. I couldn't take my eyes off her legs, which she made a point of crossing and uncrossing in class, the tight nylon making a zipping sound. She was going to the Kentucky Derby, she told me; she planned to find a man there, and her parents had agreed to drive her. They were her awed spectators, and she looked so unlike them, she could easily separate herself. She made a game of it that weekend, she told me, pretending her father was her chauffeur, her mother the woman her real mother sent along to look after her. The hat she wore to the Derby was straw with a sweeping curvy brim, and she did "get" a man, an older one. He bought her a mint julep, and they smoked at the bar. She'd already gotten one letter from him and she thought she might write him back. She wanted to get out, she said. That's why she needed a man. She was not going to live in a squat brick house on a not-perfect street in the Short-ridge High School district of Indianapolis, Indiana. She was going to live in Europe.

"Why don't you get your parents to send you to boarding school?" she said. "You'd be much happier."

One day, soon after I met Cassandra, I asked my father what he thought of my legs. We were standing near the entrance to the dressing room of my parents' bedroom. "They're a little thick," he said. I thought of Cassandra. "I have legs," she would say, unbending one, then the other into the air. "And I'm going to be a model." And then she would take me into her dreams: "Cassandra, I'll call myself," she said, "just Cassandra." It didn't faze her that she was utterly ignored by the popular crowd—she consid-ered herself above them. All they wanted was marriage and a big house out near where Eli Lilly lived, the oldest, most elegant part of town. Cassandra considered that life simply the grown-up version of Shortridge. "I'm get-ting out," she'd repeat, "and so are you." I assumed I'd go East to college, but for now, despite what my father said about them, I wanted to admire my legs the way Cassandra admired hers—as if their perfection could be assigned a monetary value and she was aware when their stock climbed.

I was afraid to take her home. I thought my mother would be able to see what I saw and that she would then understand how much I thought about sex, that I had gone out in the middle of the night and let Jim Spencer put his hand inside my bra and had liked it even though it scared me. That in eighth grade, when I had Dorie McGee and Lucinda McCann over for the night on alternate weekends, we played man and woman, that I'd rubbed myself along Lucinda's pale body as she pushed against me until the light changed. The day Cassandra came for lunch, she was wearing pastel colors, a short skirt, a little top, and my mother happened to be in the room with the celery green carpet, the room with the small white bed where Lucinda and I had curved in the dark. But I didn't want to touch Cassandra, I mused. I wanted to be like her.

"How do you do, Mrs. Moore," she said, shaking my mother's hand. We had lunch at the table in the kitchen nook.

"And where do you live, Cassandra?" my mother asked in the formal voice she used when she was meeting a new grownup.

"My parents have acquired a house on Central Avenue," Cassandra said brightly, cutting a small piece of her tuna sandwich, slipping it into her mouth. I thought her parents rented the house.

"What a wonderful name you have," my mother said.

"Thank you," Cassandra replied. "I'm named for my great-aunt."

"And where does she live?"

"She died last year in New Orleans." I had never heard of this aunt. Cassandra had always told me she'd been christened Sharon and changed her name herself at the age of eight. Now she was complimenting my mother. "This is a splendid house. Just splendid!"

"It's big enough for all my children," my mother answered. Luckily the children had an earlier lunch hour, and it was quiet. Cassandra had eaten only half her sandwich.

"I've enjoyed meeting Honor," she said when we got up to leave. "She's different from the other girls at school. So"—and she paused—"refined."

Later I asked my mother what she thought of Cassandra, and she said, "I think she'll do very well with men."

Cassandra became my teacher. When Danny Michaelis flirted with me and I was standoffish because he was a year younger, she told me I was crazy and instructed me to invite Danny to her house the following Friday night and tell him to bring Philip Prentiss, also a year younger. "We'll listen to music," she said grandly, "and have some lemonade." When I arrived, she said she'd sent her parents away, and we went down to the basement to light the candles. "You sent your parents away?"

"Yes," she said. "They do what I say because I am beautiful."

When Danny and Phil rang the bell, Cassandra raced upstairs and I followed, watching her smooth her skirt before she opened the door. "Good evening," she said. "Hi," the boys said, grinning, twitching from one foot to the other. "We're going to retire to the rec room," she said. And then she opened the door to the basement, fluttering her long fingers, and led us down the stairs. Danny had big shiny blue eyes and pale hair, and Phil was so tall he stooped. We all sat down on the leatherette sofa, and Cassandra turned out the lights, but not before she put on Dave Brubeck and gave each of us a tall glass of lemonade—with a little whiskey in it, she said, just a little! "My father has an extensive jazz collection," she said ceremoniously. I remember Danny and I falling back into the sofa cushions, his hand under my skirt, awkwardly pressing aside the elasticized suspenders of my garter belt. I could hear Cassandra kissing Phil, who, I was sure, had taken off his glasses. Danny and I kissed, and then he looked at me in the near-dark, touching my hair tenderly, as if I were a puppy. He wanted to be my boyfriend, and he wanted to take me to my junior prom. I kissed him again so he'd stop asking. In the light of day, I was on the honor roll, a second soprano in the A Cappella Choir and the Girls' Ensemble, the president of the National Thespian troupe, and finally pledging Euvola. I couldn't take a younger boy to the prom. I had to wait for someone else to invite me—I had no idea who.

But no one did invite me, and so, instead of going to the prom, I spent the evening at a slumber party with the other dateless girls, filing and polishing our nails, watching television, and speculating as to what would happen with the prom-queen elections. Our class had been the first to nominate a Negro prom-queen candidate, Gwen Solomon, and at the prom I missed, she won the crown in a landslide—while the white students were choosing between Cynthia Mauck and Hilary Stout, the Negro students voted as a block. It was 1962, and the civil rights movement was having an influence at the school. A club called the Human Rights Committee had been formed and earlier that spring had organized a panel to discuss integration. Asked about love between people of different races, John Allerdice, one of the most popular boys in the school, said that if he fell in love with a Negro woman, he would marry her.

"It's what I really felt," he said in 2006 when I talked to him on the telephone. But, he said, he was not sure he would have said it if he'd known there would be consequences for his family. The Allerdices, who lived just blocks from us, were shunned by their next-door neighbors and harassed by hate calls; cherry bombs were tossed from cars that roared past their house in the middle of the night, and a cross was burned in the front yard. "It was a small one," Mrs. Allerdice said with a laugh, recounting the story of her own revelation; she had come to agree with her son, and with her husband, who had returned from World War II with a hatred for bigotry of any kind. When John ran for senior-class president, he pledged to do something about civil rights at Shortridge, and when he was elected, he and Gwen and Steve Hopper, who had been junior-class president, and Obie McKenzie, who was black and a track and basketball star, decided to gather some Negro and white students at John's house to talk.

There was a feeling of new recognition as each of us arrived that afternoon. I didn't know then about the hate calls, but I had a sense it was a risk for the Allerdices to have the gathering at their house, and that coming to the meeting was something none of us would have done without the leadership of John and Steve and Obie and Gwen. By signing on, we exposed ourselves in a way no one at Shortridge ever had before. Suddenly I was able to look at Obie and Gwen as I had my Negro friends in Jersey City, without fear. And Steve Hopper was not just the nice-guy junior-class president, but someone who had thought in silence about race, just as I had. John and Steve had been converted by the civil rights movement, but also by knowing Negro kids in music groups and on sports teams. The year before, Shortridge's basketball team, which had just two white starting players, had nearly won the sectionals, the first stage in the statewide basketball tournament, and the all-white cheerleading squad had urged on the black players, flinging their arms around them in the ecstatic moments after a game was won.

Kennedy was president, and two years before, black students in the South had intensified the civil rights struggle by sitting in at lunch counters. John Allerdice was still a boy, short with sandy blond hair and bright blue eyes; he had a way of disarming you by making a funny face or a silly noise, which he did before he started to talk that afternoon, so that when he got serious, we were all still laughing. I don't think he mentioned the sit-ins or Kennedy, but he talked about Gwen's election and how absurd he'd found the reaction to what he'd said on the Human Rights Committee panel. He thought something good might happen if our class divided up into committees of both races and did some real things. Sitting next to Martha, one of my friends from eighth grade, I fought tears. John was saying that if we all just got to know one another, people's way of thinking might change, and then the school could change. We went around the room, each of us talking about how we felt about race. We decided to keep meeting, to bring in new people each time we met, and, as time went on, the numbers grew.

John and I had been chosen to be American Field Service Exchange Students, and at the end of June he left for the Philippines, and I for Lahore, in what was then West Pakistan. By the time I got back in September, although I didn't know it, Mrs. Allerdice had been forced out of her partnership in Mrs. Gates's dancing school; they'd lost business because of her position on integration. And the week school started, Martha and I each received the blank note card from Euvola that signified we'd been blackballed. No reason was given, but we had gone to John Allerdice's meetings and, because Martha had been away at a language program in France and I in Pakistan, we had not been in town to work on the club's yearly dance, a requirement for pledges. I was crying in bed when my father knocked and came into my room. He was in a fury. "It's absolutely outrageous," he said. "How dare they punish you for bringing distinction to the school!" "I wasn't here to work on the dance," I whimpered. "To hell with the dance," he shouted. "They're not worth half of what you are!"

That fall, the school did *The Pajama Game*, and I was the producer. Standing up in "auditorium," I asked everyone to bring in used oatmeal cartons. We needed them for the pajama factory scene—with large ones and small ones, we could make the sewing machines. We'd paint them brick red. Anyone who wants to help build and paint them would be welcome. Cassandra played the vampish Gladys Hotchkiss, wearing her own fake-leopard capris and matching vest. Having thrown myself into the theater, I felt only a slight pang when I saw my former Euvola "sisters" wearing their tiny oblong pins. By the time spring came, none of that mattered anymore. John and Steve were going to Kenyon College, Martha was going to Vassar, Christine to Smith, and Marie Roberts and I had been accepted at Radcliffe. We sent a press release to the *Indianapolis Times*, and they printed the list—fifteen of us were going East for college. Graduation was at the state fairgrounds, and I went to the Club 30 Dance—the senior prom—with John Allerdice, and Stan Kenton's band played.

The dance was at the Indiana Roof, where the Ziegfeld Follies had once performed, and in a darkness illuminated only by the revolving splashes of a faceted, mirrored ball, we demonstrated our expertise in the fox-trot and waltz, the tango and lindy, which we'd learned so well from Mrs. McMurtrie, dances on the brink of becoming, at least for us, hopelessly out of date, a fact Stan Kenton acknowledged with a jazzy, too-slow version of "Let's Twist Again." The hula hoop craze had prepared our hips, but we hadn't expected old-fashioned Kenton to measure up to what went on at the Peppermint Lounge, the pictures in every magazine of Chubby Checker in his big-shouldered suit, of Jackie Kennedy crouched and twisting. Most of my friends and I stayed in touch, but I lost track of Cassandra until, five years later, a Shortridge friend sent me a copy of the *Indianapolis Star* Sunday magazine: there she was in full color on the cover. The model known as "Cassandra" was in town for a few days at the home of her parents, Mr. and Mrs. Rodney Diehl. She was visiting from Paris, where she'd lived for several years and where she was pursuing a career as a fashion model.

After graduation, I had a job at Elko Lake, an Episcopal camp in the Catskills. There were eight girls in my bunk, all from Harlem, the Bronx, or Brooklyn, all but one Negro or Puerto Rican. Mornings I took them to the lake, which was a hundred yards from the cabins; there they boated or swam. I made sure they got to meals, to afternoon activities, evening performances and marshmallow roasts, the dances where they taught me "the Pony" and "the Mashed Potato." Also, I was the counselor in charge of directing extravagant productions of musical comedies in the barn, a shortened *Music Man* and *My Fair Lady* for which I wrote scripts from memory and whose songs a counselor named Charlie Wyatt pounded out on an upright. But when night came, I forgot about my charges. I had fallen in love with Chris, who took care of the boats.

In the almost-dark, I could see a man walking toward the small cabin at the edge of the lake where Chris lived. I had put my campers to bed, and through the quiet I could hear their giggles. Although he took care of the boats, Chris never put on a bathing suit—he just sat on his cabin steps, watching as we swam with the kids, but jumping up to help if anyone wanted to take out a canoe or a rowboat. I must have ended up at his table at supper, or next to him at an evening event, and gotten him to talk. He was very quiet, different from all the boys at Shortridge, except maybe John Fenstermaker. He wore sandals and tattered jeans and T-shirts, and he was not eager to please. He was very tall—more than six feet—and a hank of sandy hair fell across his forehead; he had hazel, almost green eyes. I first smoked hashish with Chris Fleming that summer, and we both drank red wine from a jug, as we (mostly he) talked about Camus, Karl Marx, Beethoven, and Stokely Carmichael.

Among the few black counselors was Randolph Revere, older than we were—perhaps in his late twenties, even his thirties. He was an artist, and, he told me months later, homosexual. (At the time I hadn't yet known anyone who was homosexual, though, with some sixth sense, I knew that my teacher Mr. Walker and some of my parents' male friends, like Freddie Bradlee, would probably never get married.) I used to look at Randolph, scrutinizing his buoyant smile, never sure it was entirely revealing. He smoked a pipe and had gone to Howard University in Washington. When he responded to the ordinary jokes we told, his laughter had a gravity ours lacked, emerging, it seemed, from a worldliness we younger counselors— mostly white and heterosexual—had no way of understanding. I think Randolph had told Chris to read *Giovanni's Room* by James Baldwin and that Chris had then told me to read it; unable to find *Giovanni's Room*, I read *Another Country*, all the time imagining Randolph in that world with Rufus and Leona. Like a Baldwin narrator, Randolph had an attitude toward being black that fed an intellectual exploration of what it meant to be a Negro in America. I had encountered that cultivation only in the few Negro college students who came to Jersey City to work on the summer staff—thoughtful about changes they might help bring about—but, unlike them, Randolph seemed cautious around white people, and that made me shy.

It was after supper, or after whatever camp event took up the evening, that I would see Randolph heading for Chris's cabin near the lake. I began to imagine that Randolph was in love with Chris, and that Chris considered their relationship important—in other words, there was no running across the field to join them. I have come to know that feeling. Even with gay men I'm close to, there have been times I've been present

at the beginnings of a seduction, at first a participant in joking and rep-
artee, only slowly realizing, as the heat between the men intensified, that
a ritual was in play from which I was shut out. At seventeen, I viscerally
recognized this, everything slowing down, everything quiet except my
own heartbeat, my too-loud breathing; it also happened when my father
was with other priests or men in the church. And so, when Chris and
Randolph walked toward the cabin on the lake and I stood there watching, what I felt was not new but it was also unnamed and unnameable. I
turned away, perhaps lighting a Marlboro and smoking it as I crossed the
field to the women's washroom, turned on the light, looked in the mirror
at my face, and, taking off my glasses and adjusting my mouth, burst into
tears. After I saw Randolph the following autumn in New York, I reported
the visit to my father. Randolph, I wrote, "is (confidentially) a homosexual
and has had a great many slumps out of guilt feelings because of this . . . It
depresses me to see him . . . because his situation and way of life, e.g. periodic slumps etc. are so inevitable it seems to me, in his position. I really
want to say all the time that everything will be all right—but somehow I
can't believe that it will—at least not for a long time."

But at Elko Lake, I did not yet have that clarity, and so I kept my complicated feelings to myself, looking forward to the nights that I would be
the one to walk with Chris toward the cabin, to sit with him, both of us
smoking Marlboros, talking, listening to the latest Charlie Parker, lent to
him by Randolph, perhaps taking a puff or two of hashish as I tried to
imagine how I might get this big quiet man—he seemed a man, not a boy—
to take me in his arms. Sometimes, though, Randolph would be with us,
or Maria. Maria was Chilean, but she had no accent, and though she was
barely older than I was, she was taller and seemed "sophisticated"—she
went to Hunter College, in New York. I was anything but sophisticated.
In the one tiny black-and-white I have of myself and Chris, my badly cut
hair in angular almost-curls stops halfway to my shoulders, I am wearing
Bermuda shorts and the color of my white shirt peaks out from the crew
neck of my sweater. I have on my glasses and am standing at a tilt, a cigarette between my fingers, my smile garish with need.

Those evenings when we were all there, Maria would move across the
cabin and greet Chris with a little smile, her short black hair perfectly
brushed back, small gold earrings in her pierced ears, capri pants fitted
to perfect buttocks that sloped up to a narrow waist. If her blouse had a

low neck, it looked like an accidental departure from modesty. Narrow
wrists. Espadrilles on long slender feet. I gazed down at my sneakers.
Chris bent toward her and smiled, and I put my attention elsewhere. Or
walked toward them, overhearing Maria, who talked, if not with more
intelligence than I did, certainly with greater seriousness about who she
was and wanted to become. What book were they talking about? What
music? At seventeen, in spite of having necked, Danny's hands deliciously
sliding up my stockinged thighs, there was something I didn't understand.
As I watched Maria, I saw that she understood that thing.

I can't remember any particular conversation Chris and I had, or what
I said or asked. We must have talked about the civil rights movement,
about what I had seen the previous summer in Pakistan, the beggars with
amputated limbs, young men crowded into un-air-conditioned theaters
to watch Rock Hudson and Doris Day with Urdu subtitles, balconies of
the same theaters filled only with women in saris or salwar kameezes,
a veil pulled across their faces so you could see only their eyes. I might
have tried to describe Lahore, the wide boulevards, the almost translucent
dome of the Badshahi Mosque, the reflecting pools of the Shalimar Gardens, the strangeness at the border with Afghanistan where bearded tribes-
men strode the dusty road carrying rifles, their eyes glittering, women in
black chadors visible on the battlements if you looked up. Or we'd talk
about poetry—Pound and Eliot, or Neruda, whom he had read and I had
never heard of. That summer of 1963, we must also have talked about the
importance of the coming March on Washington, and after it happened,
marveled at what Martin Luther King Jr. said on the steps of the Lincoln
Memorial or the fact, stunning in light of the brutal attacks on civil rights
workers and demonstrators all that year in the South, that there had been
no violence. I would have boasted that my father had marched, explained
that he'd thought it too dangerous for a girl, so had taken my brother Paul
and not invited me.

When I was away, my mother always wrote, once, maybe twice a week—
usually reporting on the activities of the family, which then seemed a
vigorous, energetic conveyance that slid easily along, carrying all of us.
Rereading her letters I saved, I see that they are rarely intimate or confid-
ing and that the pronoun is usually "we," as in "We're so proud of you."

But my battles with her continued. I struggle with acne and she writes a friend in Cambridge to recommend "a skin man." "I know it irritates you to go to doctors but it does seem to make sense," followed by, "Paul & Dee & Rosie & I are going to hear the Beatles tomorrow night!" She complains I'm not a good enough correspondent: "I'm going to be very cross if you don't write me this month," or "The only thing to remember when life is such fun and so full is the other people—Gami, Gagy, Grandma Kean, etc. I never say this kind of thing to you, but do keep older people who do need attention in mind . . ." Didn't she understand that I had homework, work at the theater, a new world of friends? Coming as they did, in her declarative handwriting, two or three times a week, many of her letters went unread.

But my father, when he managed to write, often reflected. In the slim packet of his letters that I still have, I find a handful written to me in 1963 at Elko Lake; in each, he acknowledged the tardiness of his reply and promised he'd try to improve as a correspondent. That summer, while campaigns for integration were in progress all over the South, my father, in the thick of the struggle in Indianapolis, watched clergy friends like Kim Myers and Malcolm Boyd become politically active, often joining demonstrations in the South. In Indianapolis at the cathedral, he was host to "the Mayor's Commission on Human Rights" in its meeting with "the Indianapolis Social Action Committee," a newly formed Negro civil rights group. Two weeks later, he wrote that at a later small gathering with Negro leaders, the mayor had granted all their demands: "Round #1 for our side!" At the beginning of July, he visited me at Elko, en route to the Adirondacks with Gami and a raft of kids, and afterward wrote again:

I just loved seeing you at Elko and meant to write you right
off. I was so full of it—but! Never seen you better or more "ful-
filled" than you seemed that day. Your enthusiasm was infec-
tious . . . I could sense that you had a "pastoral" concern for your
girls and that you were having a ball with the other counselors. I left feeling, again, very very proud of you and all you have
done and especially pleased at the kind of things you find pleasure in. That is the secret to happiness—if there is one—"to
love the things that Thou commandest" . . . This is pretty much
God-given, but if you get involved in this sort of thing early in

your life, you can form and develop your tastes along that direction & it does deepen and last. I know. I remember going to
the St. Paul's School Camp at your age & loving it . . . the seeds
of what later was life at Jersey City were planted then . . .

In a letter toward the end of the summer, he confided that he was being
considered for a new position in the Diocese of Washington, D.C.—a suffragan, or assistant, bishop who would expand the diocese's connections
with the inner city. "Mommy is gripped," he wrote. I was "gripped" too.
When I got to the Adirondacks after Elko Lake, the talk was of the likeli-
hood that he would be elected. How thrilling it would be! In a Washington swept with the progressive spirit of the New Frontier, my father's ideas
about the church and the city might have national influence. I was now
considered "a grownup" and was allowed to join my parents at cocktails.
Suddenly my father was listening to me as if I had something to contribute
to the work he was doing. How had "race relations" been at the camp that
summer? I spoke of the counselors from the South who were white but
also in favor of integration. My mother asked questions too, sitting there
with her needlepoint, the Penelope rendering of their honeymoon cottage.
What courses would I be taking at Radcliffe?

These Adirondacks talks took place in "the Links"—a small room off
the dining room named after one of my grandfather's New York clubs. We
called it "the Animal Room" after the taxidermied menagerie left behind
a half century earlier by the previous owners—a bear cub whose fur was
thinning, a blank-eyed fisher climbing a tree. My grandmother had hung
chintz curtains and with the same material covered the cushions on the
wicker chairs; on the walls hung stuffed heads of antlered buck shot by my
grandfather and the friends with whom he'd originally bought the camp.
This was the place where nothing changed, the only place I could still have
three meals a day with my parents. Now, though, I also joined in grown-up
conversation. I wanted to hear from my father about the March on Washington, about his dreams for his work there, but I wanted him to be my
father, too. "So how are things?" he asked one night when my mother left
the room to call the children to supper.

"Great, Pop," I said, standing there looking down at the old backgammon board, twirling the ice in my gin and tonic. "Supper!" I could hear my
mother calling. Whenever he asked what seemed to be a personal question,

it made me uncomfortable: how could I tell him about being in love with Chris? I was supposed to be excited about going off to college, but actually I was scared, and I didn't know how to start that conversation.

My discomfort was swept away as we returned to Indianapolis and I started packing for Cambridge, preparing to leave home. My mother asked her brother's wife Linda to meet my plane and settle me in at Radcliffe. I was used to accommodating: the last of us, my eighth sibling, Patience, was sixteen months old, and my mother had to get the other seven "booted and spurred" for school. As Aunt Linda drove away, I stood on the steps of my dormitory and waved, but when I climbed the stairs back to my room, I felt myself a stranger, my body awkward, my clothes wrong—my mother had gotten a family friend, good at sewing, to help me make them. I was barely aware of my mother's Boston Brahmin genealogy, the generations of uncles and great-uncles, of grandfathers and great-grandfathers who had gone to Harvard. My direct descent from Louis Agassiz, the husband of Elizabeth Cary Agassiz, Radcliffe's first president, had been treated as a joke at home, so in my own eyes, I was a public school girl from the Midwest, a rube among private school dorm mates who talked about professors as if they knew them or were promoted out of freshman courses with something I'd never heard of called "Advanced Placement." In my admissions interview, I'd said that my summer in Pakistan had inspired me to consider international relations or the history of the relationship between Christianity and Islam, but really I didn't know myself well enough to know what I wanted to study. My mother might ask what courses I planned to take as if I knew, and my father was always ready to have a serious conversation about the relationship between an aspect of Christian theology and the ideas of the civil rights movement, but neither of them thought to guide me in my academic plans.

Nor did I think to consult an advisor. I signed up for a survey course called "Epic and Drama," for anthropology, for Horace and Catullus (I wanted to continue my Latin), and for a biochemistry course that climaxed with Watson and Crick's discovery of DNA. It was in Horace and Catullus that I had the first glimmer of what an intellectual life might bring. Translating a Catullus love poem, the professor, a devastatingly handsome young classicist named Steele Commager, pointed out a passage in which the poet had placed the name of the beloved, "Lesbia," between the adjective and noun that the poet used for the bedclothes. Thus, as Commager put it, looking out the window to emphasize his profile, the lines replicated, almost sculpted the tryst. It was the first time I entered a poem.

My first Sunday in Cambridge, I went to the eleven o'clock at Christ Church in Harvard Square—after all, church was where I'd always spent Sunday mornings. The pastor there, my father had told me, was "an old friend" and "a good man." The church was built of wood, painted gray, and dated from the American Revolution, but even before the service began, it was clear the liturgy was Protestant; it was morning prayer, not mass, and there were few candles, no incense, no colored vestments, none of the Anglo-Catholic elegance I was used to. I wouldn't have said it then, but I missed my father: church was how I felt close to him, the place where he was present and constant. I shook the rector's hand and introduced myself as I left the service, and one evening the following week, I went to a Harvard-Radcliffe supper in the parish hall. But I didn't go to church a second Sunday. On September 17 a telegram arrived from my mother: "Poppy elected." We would be moving to Washington.

My parents were wildly excited. Many of their old friends were in the Kennedy administration. My father had gone to outing class (day camp) on the North Shore with "Mac" Bundy, the national security advisor, and my mother to Madeira with his wife, Mary. Their old friend Cord Meyer was in the CIA, and Ben Bradlee, who was married to Mrs. Meyer's sister, Toni, was in Washington at *Newsweek*. When they went to Washington on their first house-hunting trip in October, a friend of Cord's on the White House staff arranged for them to see the president. As young men, my father and Kennedy had known each other in Florida, and Kennedy had also been a close friend of George Mead, my father's friend who had been killed at Guadalcanal. My mother wore a sapphire blue suede dress, and when they shook hands, the president complimented her, "You're terrific," he said, with a broad grin. After a few minutes reminiscing and chatting in the Oval Office, they walked outside to the Rose Garden and stood in the sunshine, "Where are the children?" Kennedy asked, laughing. "We'll bring them the next time," my father said.

The last time I went to church in Cambridge was on November 22, 1963. I had been in a biology lab when the professor came into the room and announced that the president had been shot. I raced up Garden Street to the dorm, then after supper went out alone. The streets were dark. People of all ages were either standing still and crying or walking fast and silent. There were hardly any cars. I did what I knew how to do, I went to church. In Jersey City, even in Indianapolis, the church would have been filled. My father would have improvised a vigil or a service, but this barren eighteenth-century structure, though open, was dark and practically empty. I knelt down. The message of Kennedy's inaugural address—"Ask not what your country can do for you; ask what you can do for your country"—had resonated through my adventures in Pakistan where I'd thought of myself as sort of Peace Corps volunteer in training. In letters home, I had described the exotic architecture but also the one-party political system that masqueraded as democracy and the vast numbers of beggars. I had met Peace Corps volunteers there—a woman who worked in a mental hospital where patients were kept in cages with dirt floors, like animals in a zoo. I wrote home in horror about the former professor she'd found sleeping naked on straw—through her efforts, he now had a desk and a lamp and a bed and books, pencil and paper; soon, recovered from the long, mistaken incarceration, he would emerge into society. I wrote too of the tall ex-marine who was building a school in a remote village. What would happen to him now that Kennedy had been killed?

On Sunday morning, in our nightgowns at the dormitory television, my friends and I watched as Jack Ruby lunged forward with a gun and shot Lee Harvey Oswald. Later that week, my mother flew, as planned, to Washington with my sister Adelia, her third trip to look at houses. In the airport, they saw U Thant, the secretary-general of the UN, and Adlai Stevenson, leaving Washington after the funeral, and on the way in from the airport, they passed Arlington Cemetery. "It was dark," my mother wrote me, "so all you could see was a flickering flame on the hillside with the Lee mansion all illuminated behind it." Early the next morning, they made a special visit to Kennedy's grave. "It was covered with wreaths and flowers with cards from all the royalty & heads of state," my mother wrote, "and Mrs. Kennedy's little bunch of lily-of-the-valley was right next to the flame. Pictures don't do the site justice . . . a beautiful wind-swept hillside."

My father's letters did not take up the assassination except to say that the time was "rugged" and that he'd been sick in bed. After a meeting of a national church committee, he'd stayed over at a retreat house in New York, to meditate on what lay ahead. "It is wonderful to be ALONE and quiet for two whole days," he wrote me,

to snooze, read, think, & or pray when you feel like it. You
feel like a snake shedding skin after skin of worries, nuisances,
obsessions and distractions. And it makes it possible to at
least be open to Our Lord—to sort of clean your glasses so you
can see Him once more. I hope you go on a Retreat sometime
if you have a chance: the first time is a little fidgety but after a
while it seems so natural as if you could live no other way.

I think it has helped me put Washington in perspective too.
The Bishop business presents itself in so many ways: even being
a Suffragan (and thank God I am to be that) has a certain glamour
to it, and this hides what it really means. And being in Washington
is exciting, and this hides what it really means, and having a
position of more superficial influence hides what it really means.

Here on the Retreat though I think it has come through clear
and simple and is no different than being a Christian basically
except the stakes are higher because more people will be dragged
up or down because of one. But what it is is loving, loving, loving
with all your might—everyone you can—and returning again and
again to God's love to go out & love some more. And to somehow
work it out so the Church is streamlined to show God's love which
is so simple & yet so terribly exciting.

As I read that letter now, coming upon it as if for the first time, I think
of my father, then forty-four, entering this new stage of his ministry and
actually being nervous. "I always marveled at your father," a powerful
friend of his once said to me. "He was so . . . modest." When I was eighteen, I wouldn't have found that description of him as startling as I did
three years after his death when I had the conversation with his friend.
From childhood, I can remember a modest man, a father who spoke to his
seventeen-year-old daughter as someone he could rely on: ". . . I will need
all of your help from time to time. Please pray for me about this when you
think of it."

I wonder if I did pray for him—I was excited for him, and I missed
being part of everything at home, but my loneliness and prayers had to
do with Chris Fleming, who was at college out West. In the photograph
of me in the Freshman Register, a kind of catalogue of new Radcliffe girls
distributed at Harvard, I look pretty enough, but at the time I had no

confidence in my ability to find a new boyfriend, and so my love life was waiting for Chris's letters, which came, and which I answered, waiting for the next one in his fascinating, awkward handwriting: "Oh Honor, I have so much to say, yet how can I? Keep writing and we'll get around to talking one day," he wrote. Or "I feel sad and resigned somehow, but happy." Eventually I had a sequence of blind dates, and sometime in December, when I began to work in the theater, at the Loeb Drama Center, Harvard's theater on Brattle Street, Chris faded as I met the boys who acted in *King Lear* and *Julius Caesar* and the epic *Oresteia* we put on at Sanders Theatre.

After freshman year, but before exams, at a cast party, I met Ben Sachs, an upperclassman whom I had never seen in the hallways of the theater and whose name I had never heard. He appeared so suddenly and was so attentive I could hardly believe he really existed. I was wearing a black dress I had just bought, piqué with a deep ruffled V down its back. After we talked for a while, Ben asked if I'd like to leave, and he took me to his sports car. This is a dream or a movie, I thought, as he drove me into the country and stopped at the edge of a vast park where we lay down on a lawn and necked. After that night, we began to go out, and one Sunday in his narrow college bed, as I looked at his face above me, my desire turned to terror as he fell toward me. "Don't come home pregnant," my mother had warned before I left for college. That evening, walking up Boylston Street toward Radcliffe, I told Ben that if he could tell me I was special to him, we could "go all the way." A month later, my second summer at Elko Lake, he appeared unannounced in his Alfa Romeo to tell me I *was* special, but I barely spoke to him. Like a mating bird that returns each year to the same body of water, I had taken up with the boy who succeeded Chris in the cabin by the lake.

Rick Warner drank beer, in contrast to Chris's jug wine. And he was not interested in conversation. Instead, with his buddy Ted, also blond and slightly kinder, and Maria, whom Ted was dating, we spent evenings in the cabin, lights out, Chris's bohemian austerity replaced by college pennants. Rick was pushing me to "give it to him," and when he was on top of me or wound around me, I wanted to. But, my bold declaration to Ben aside, I didn't believe it was possible to "go all the way" without getting pregnant, this in spite of my mother's detailed descriptions of how her diaphragm worked. And anyway, what would this mysterious thing called "going all the way" feel like? I wanted Rick to break through my resistance, but whispering "Not now," I'd push him away, hoping he'd ask why and help me figure it all out.

Chris's sister, a counselor that summer, had told me Chris was now "serious" about a girl he'd met at college, but I asked nothing about her when he came for a visit and we took a canoe out on the lake at dusk. He was shocked I'd spend time with Rick, who talked only about cars and who ridiculed the Negro children at the camp. I was ashamed. I couldn't, of course, tell him that I liked what Rick did, putting his fingers inside me, lying on top of me. Later that night I saw Randolph and Chris walk across the camp's great lawn after supper, and after breakfast the next morning I saw Chris deep in conversation with Maria in the driveway. Before he left, though, he said I should visit him at his family's house in Connecticut at the end of the summer. That day at lunch, Rick didn't speak to me. At first I thought he was preoccupied, but he wouldn't even look at me, and when I took my girls to the lake to swim, I saw him give Debbie, another counselor, a little spank on her bikinied buttocks. Debbie, Ted told Maria, had given Rick what I would not.

By the end of the summer, the war in Vietnam had entered a new phase. The Gulf of Tonkin resolution had passed in early August, and for the first time, the United States was bombing North Vietnam. When I visited Chris in Connecticut on my way back home, we resumed our long conversations on the town beach, smoking Marlboros, Chris tossing pebbles into the desultory surf of the Long Island Sound. Now he was concerned about the draft, and the war was what we talked about, not his girl out West, or my continuing feeling for him. The last time I saw him was in New York in 1970. I was organizing Black Panther defense, and we had a drink. In Chris's life, radical politics had replaced hashish and James Baldwin, and now he was far more militant than I was. Two years later, I ran into a girl I'd known in college; she'd had an affair with Chris Fleming. He'd live with her for a while, then disappear. She thought he was building bombs.

The year I was finishing Radcliffe, out of the blue, I got a letter from Rick Warner. He had seen an article in the newspaper recounting my father's civil rights work. Now he understood why I had led him on but refused to "put out." I thought I was better than him because my father consorted with "niggers." He was glad we had never gone all the way.

12

In Public

After we left Jersey City, my father began to write. Of course he always wrote sermons, which he saved, folders and folders precisely dated, beginning with his first, written for preaching class at the seminary, but the earliest image I have of him writing a book is in the Adirondacks, in the Links, which had windows overlooking the lake and another set giving onto the boardwalk. He would be sitting at the game table, from which he had removed the old backgammon set, his tiny Olympia portable in front of him. We were not to interrupt. He wrote after breakfast for two hours or so. We had to wait till he was finished to be taken, one or two of us, fishing, rowing, or climbing a mountain to stand vertiginously on the granite summit as he pointed out, depending on how clear it was, Blue Mountain or Mount Marcy, Tupper or Cranberry Lake, or where the Whitney Camp was. And waiting, we would tiptoe past the screen door, his blurred figure bent over, no sound but his intermittent pecking at the typewriter.

I had no idea what he was writing—he didn't really talk about it, only mentioned that he was "doing a little writing about Jersey City," but I was curious, and once in Indianapolis when he wasn't home, I opened the door of his study, a tiny room under the eaves, down the hall from my bedroom on the third floor, and, looking at the papers on his big desk, found some pages. What I read was not something written by the father I knew, nothing like the stories he told when the little ones snuggled up with him on the big bed, or even the stories he told to make a point while preaching; these were something not written by a priest or a father, but by who Paul Moore was when he was alone. Typewriter print on white pages, words crossed out and corrected in his scrawly, crablike handwriting, something about a Negro boy in the city, a memory I know is accurate because I found the manuscript in a file almost fifty years later, a story titled "City Boy": *Stickball—the broom handle whizzes, the rubber ball zips to the sidewalk, and the boys run every way in their fedoras and double-breasted jackets flapping against naked chests.* I put the pages down quickly, not then understanding what I read as an answer to any of the questions I'd had about my father ever since I'd followed him upstairs after joking about the war and found him crying. When his book came out, though, I did not find the Negro boys playing stickball in their fedoras, their double-breasted jackets flapping against naked chests, or any story that would help solve that mystery. The book, called *The Church Reclaims the City*, was something else altogether and had evolved from lectures my father gave in England.

The summer I was fourteen, my father taught for two weeks at St. Augustine's College, an Anglican institute at Canterbury Cathedral. This was the occasion for our first family trip to Europe, the three oldest and a boy cousin to keep my brother company—we spent two weeks driving around France and wound up in Canterbury, living in a tiny row house across from the ancient cathedral. The text of these lectures, which led with the theological idea that Christ's ministry to the poor and suffering required the church's involvement in social action, attracted the Seabury Press, the publishing company of the national Episcopal Church. My father had imagined a book in which his ideas about the church and the city would be interwoven with "sketches or stories based on fact," like the fragment I'd found in his study, but *The Church Reclaims the City*, which appeared in January 1964, the month he was consecrated in Washington and the month we left Indianapolis, was a manifesto, an analysis, and a guide—how might others go about doing what had been done in Jersey City and Indianapolis. "The title was NOT my idea," I remember my father saying. "The church never HAD the city, and it still doesn't." He was disappointed that the book was not the literary project he had envisioned. The chapter my mother contributed, "The Clergyman's Family in the Inner City," was more in the vein of what he had wanted to write, and he was jealous of its success. It attracted so much attention my mother began to write a memoir, *The People on Second Street*, which she published four years later. My father was not fated to become the kind of writer he dreamed of being, not destined to articulate, with the intimacy fiction requires, the way he saw the world. That more personal voice would instead animate a half century of pastoral counseling and meditation guidance, and he would become a great, even legendary, preacher. With his ideas published and his election as a bishop with a mandate to address social issues in a poor and mostly black city at the moment the civil rights movement was engaging the nation, Paul Moore was set on the course he would follow for the rest of his life.

My mother's letters that January were a frenzy of arrangements—who would stay where for the consecration, what needed to be done to the house bought for them by the diocese at 3400 Newark Street in Cleveland Park, near the National Cathedral where my father's office would be. We would rent nearby until the house became available the following summer. As my mother packed up in Indianapolis that fall, a new concert hall opened, and there was a week of gala evenings—a round of concerts, guest soloists playing with the Indianapolis Symphony, performances by the Ballet Russe de Monte Carlo. "The amazing and SAD thing," my father wrote to me, "was the numbers of people we had come to know & love. I almost cried . . ." A planeload of those friends came to Washington for the consecration, wearing "Moore for Bishop" buttons.

The consecration was on the Feast of the Conversion of Saint Paul, January 25, as my father's confirmation had been at St. Paul's School thirty-three years earlier. The presiding bishop of the Episcopal Church made the trip out of love for my father, but he was so ill with Parkinson's disease he could not speak, so his place as celebrant was taken by the bishop of Washington, who would be my father's superior. Among the other consecrators were Bishop Washburn of the Diocese of Newark, who had confirmed me and ordained my father to the priesthood, and John Craine, the bishop who had brought us to Indianapolis. His presenters were Father Pegram and Father Bartrop, "Bear" from St. Paul's. The cathedral, which can seat three thousand, was practically full, not only of the Washington powerful and Episcopalians eager to see their new young suffragan, but of priests from all parts of my father's life who saw his election as a step forward for the new social militancy of the church, of friends from Indianapolis, and of people from Jersey City I hadn't seen since we'd played in the street, walked together to P.S. 37 or taken the Hudson Tube to St. Luke's. My aunts, uncles, and cousins were there, all of the family sitting in the choir up front near the altar, and, of course, Gami, devout and proud.

With a thundering blast of the organ, the procession began, daylight through the stained-glass windows splashing color on the white marble interior, the Indianapolis boys' choir singing Henry Purcell as crucifers, priests, and acolytes moved down the aisle, and then the bishops, and finally my father, the tallest, his face lifted and solemn. "Almighty God, to whom all hearts are open, all desires known, and from whom no secrets are hid," the celebrant began.

I had left home, and also the solace of hearing those sentences over and over, words I had so often heard my father speak. Now we began to sing "In Christ There Is No East or West," a hymn I had sung ever since childhood, which was now an anthem of the civil rights movement within the Episcopal Church. There was a silence when Father Myers, whom I had not seen since Jersey City, climbed the pulpit and began to preach. "Bishops must cast off their expensive clothes," he declared, "and appear again among the poor, the first children of the church." I looked at my mother, at my brothers and sisters, and I looked at my father, whose expression didn't change. Since the days in Jersey City, Father Myers continued, he had prayed that Paul Moore would one day become a bishop, but now, now, he wept for him: "It is a dark world in which you are to be a bishop," he said, looking at my father. President Kennedy had been assassinated, an Alabama church had been bombed, there were violent confrontations between demonstrators and police in the South. "But you are a strong man and filled with Christ's love for men. I count it a wonderful act and a sign of hope for the church in this place to have called you to be one of its bishops."

The attending priests dressed my father in his chimere, the long-sleeved white undergarment only bishops wear, and after my father recited the "Promise of Conformity to the Doctrine, Discipline and Worship of the Protestant Episcopal Church"; and after the celebrant spoke a prayer reminding us that the night before Jesus chose the twelve apostles, he had prayed until dawn; and after the celebrant asked, *Almighty God, giver of all good things*, to replenish my father with *the truth of thy Doctrine and adorn him with innocency of life, that by word and deed, he may faithfully serve thee;* after all that, my father himself put on the gleaming bishop's habit and proceeded to the crossing, the place where the transept meets the nave, where each of six bishops, all at once, laid his right hand on my father's head. Then, in the minor-key ninth-century melody "Veni, Creator Spiritus": "Come, Holy Ghost, our souls inspire," sang the bishops, and the congregation responded, "And lighten with celestial fire . . ." By laying their hands on his head, the bishops brought my father into the apostolic succession, the line of Episcopal (from the Latin, *episcopus*, for bishop) descent that began with Saint Peter. Now my father was part of something that went back almost two thousand years, and he was part of it forever. On the same head from which his large ears stuck crazily out, the same head I'd held on to when I was little and riding his shoulders, my father now wore a miter, the pointed brocade hat bishops wear, and from those same shoulders flowed a cope, a white brocade ceremonial cape with a great gold cross across the back of it.

I don't remember when I started to cry. Was it when we sang "In Christ There Is No East or West"? When I first saw my father in that procession, his face lifted? Or when Father Myers began to preach and I felt all the aspiration of Jersey City return to the present? And what made me cry? Was it the force of that past returning with all its unresolved power, or was it the confrontation with a life outside this family, my own unknown future?

There is a photograph taken that day, black-and-white, an eight-by-ten glossy shot by a public photographer after the service. I remember the coat

I was wearing, wine red bouclé with a leopard collar. I was also wearing a black fake-fur pillbox and glasses with dark frames. The photo was not posed (like my mother, I never posed for pictures with my glasses on), and I don't remember its being taken, only seeing it years later, the expression on my face driven, removed, not focused, as if I were being commandeered by something forceful and interior. My mother looked beautiful; somewhere there is a picture of her that day, too, wearing what seems in black and white to be black velvet, a hat, the tracery of its veil across her forehead, her smile radiant. She and my father and, I suppose, all of us were standing in the National Cathedral, greeting people. His vestments had been put away, but he was wearing his chimere, long-sleeved, white, and reaching the floor, and his face had the freshness of a bride's. From a distance, I watched people greet him. Friends kissed him, others solemnly shook his hand; a stranger, a man, knelt to kiss the bishop's ring that his mother had given him, big and gold and set with green onyx. (My father had never worn jewelry, not even a wedding ring.) I remember the white marble of the columns and the black wrought-iron gates, but I don't remember being part of any constellation of people, and I was unable to stop crying. People I had known all my life were saying hello to me with a new formality—I was now the bishop's daughter, and so, when I sensed someone might be looking at me, I tried to compose myself, and when that failed, tried to find an acceptable cause for the tears: happiness for my father, sadness at leaving Indiana, the power of the service. But really I was looking this way and that, searching without knowing it for the nonexistent person who might understand this weeping of mine and comfort me. I don't know how I stopped crying because what I remember is that I couldn't stop, standing there, attempting to recover myself in the cold marble terrain of the cathedral, wearing stockings and high heels and that ugly coat, my beautiful father smiling and greeting people, my beautiful father dressed all in white.

Like many cathedrals, the National Cathedral is not a parish church, so my parents decided to become members of St. Stephen and the Incarnation, an activist parish on Sixteenth Street at the edge of black Washington; they wanted to be part of the real life of the District of Columbia. St. Stephen's rector, my father's seminary friend Bill Wendt, had run a Grace Church–

like parish on the Lower East Side in New York, and he had brought the model to Washington. St. Stephen's would be a parish home, ballast for my father's new life in which the task of navigating the split between his ministry and his privileged origins would become more intense than ever before. His job was to minister to the poor, to address social issues in the district, but he lived in a big Cleveland Park house. He was a radical, but because of the family he had come from, his wealth, and where he had been educated, he had natural access to the establishment, what he called "the power structure." These contradictions confused social Washington. The wife of a prominent cleric confided to my mother that hostesses were mystified as to "where the suffragan Episcopal bishop of Washington fits in on the city's political and social ladder," but assured her that it was "'a very low rung'—you're way down, along with low judiciary."

Weeks later, my father shared a platform with the high judiciary, speaking with Chief Justice Earl Warren at the National Council of Juvenile and Family Court Judges. It was his debut in the press. "In a blunt address," Dan Morgan of the *Washington Post* reported, "Bishop Moore said that the main reason the courts, agencies and churches fail is that they are not honest with children . . . Children who come before the courts have been made cynical 'by too many police [who] use the rubber hose first and ask questions later.'" The judges, my father explained, would do better if they separated themselves from law enforcement and aligned themselves with the people. Too often, he said, "the judges are remote, the police are venal, the churches are closed during the week, the teachers are too busy, and the parents are drunk." No matter what his rung on the social ladder, my father would not restrain his politics as he had the first years in Indianapolis.

Of course this was a different time. Days before his consecration, the Twenty-fourth Amendment to the Constitution was ratified, upholding "the right of citizens of the United States to vote in any primary or other election for President or Vice President, for electors for President or Vice President, or for Senator or Representative in Congress" and outlawing the poll tax. And shortly after that, on February 10, the first civil rights bill, which struck down the Jim Crow segregation laws, passed the House of Representatives, triumphing over a Senate filibuster on June 10 and becoming law on July 2. By then my father had found his way into the local civil rights movement. At a rally at Howard University, he had heard a speech by Walter Fauntroy, pastor of New Bethel Baptist Church and a colleague of Martin Luther King Jr. in the Southern Christian Leadership Conference, and weeks later, when Governor George Wallace of Alabama, as a segregationist candidate, began to rack up strong showings in Democratic presidential primaries including Indiana, Fauntroy invited my father to be the white cochair of the Coalition of Conscience, a new interracial group of clergy and community leaders that would address social issues in the District of Columbia.

A welfare mother found dead in the street with her children inspired the coalition's first action: picketing Robert Kennedy, then still attorney general, to persuade him to reverse Senator Robert C. Byrd's ruling that no household with a man in residence could receive Aid to Families with Dependent Children. The District of Columbia did not then have its own government, and Byrd's committee governed the city. Robert Kennedy agreed to a meeting. The situation demonstrated the limitations of my father's access to power—knowing the Kennedys socially was advantageous because, my father wrote, "it means you can usually gain access to them, but it makes one hesitate to question their sincerity." In spite of Kennedy's cordial welcome to my father that day as a man of the cloth, a brief acknowledgment of mutual friends, and a substantial conversation, the meeting brought no change.

In Cambridge I was reading my mother's letters, bulletins from their new Washington life: "Poppy met Hubert at some Civil Rights do the other night and was mad for him." She used Senator Humphrey's first name for theatrical effect; what she didn't let on was how challenging she found the formality of Washington dinner parties, how difficult it was to negotiate the subtle folkways of this complicated new world, to tolerate indifference in a dinner partner when she talked, for example, about liberalism in Indiana or sending her children to public schools. "My ogling at powerful figures turns to irritation when I am snubbed," she later wrote. Actually, she and my father had not succeeded in finding integrated public schools, and after a term, my sister Adelia transferred out of the neighborhood to a more diverse high school: "It wasn't real," she said of the all-white junior high school she left. As always, my mother was indefatigable in plugging her children into new lives. "Susanna is going to a nursery school three days a week in Potomac, Md.," she wrote Pam, and when she realized I'd have some weeks in Washington before leaving for my second summer at Elko Lake, she arranged for me to work for Birch Bayh, the liberal Democratic senator from Indiana for whom I'd campaigned in Indianapolis in seventh grade.

The force of the civil rights movement continued to build. On March 30, 1964, Mrs. Malcolm Peabody, the white wife of an Episcopal bishop and the mother of the Democratic governor of Massachusetts, and Mrs. John Burgess, the wife of the Negro suffragan bishop of Massachusetts, were arrested in an antisegregation demonstration in St. Augustine, Florida; their picture, the Brahmin Mrs. Peabody, white-haired and dressed just like Gami, with her Negro friend, appeared in papers all over the country. In Cambridge, I heard upperclassmen at dormitory dinners debate civil rights; by May, several of them were packing for Mississippi, for the voter registration campaign the Student Nonviolent Coordinating Committee (SNCC) was planning for the summer. My father wanted to go to Mississippi, but he hesitated because of the physical danger—you could see it on television, jerky images of police beating Negro men and women with billy clubs, terror on the faces of the demonstrators as they tried to flee, blood on their clothes and skin when they could not get away; "Bull" Connor directing firemen to aim hoses at protesters in a Birmingham city park, some of them children; policemen dragging young black people gone limp with passive resistance into paddy wagons, the implacable anger on the faces of the white people who stood by, giving the finger and shouting. My father was aware that in the South no one in favor of integration was protected by the law, and so he was torn, and more vulnerable than many because he had a wife and nine children. But this struggle had formed his adult life and his ministry, and he kept feeling he belonged there.

Sometime in July, he went to a service at St. Stephen's, and in his sermon Bill Wendt preached from a New Testament story in which the disciples fish all day but come back with nothing. "Launch out into the deep, and let down your nets," Christ encouraged. In spite of himself, my father took the story as a sign. He spoke to my mother, and within twenty-four hours was on a plane to Jackson, Mississippi, to join an ecumenical group of clergy working on voter registration. During the two weeks he was there, bedding down with other clergymen on a cement floor, he went from door to door asking people to register to vote. The atmosphere, he told us when he came home, was like war. He performed communion outside the bombed-out Freedom House in McComb, its front wall torn off, the altar an ironing board; he preached on the spur of the moment at a tiny Baptist church way out in the countryside "to people who were really preaching to me." The wine was grape juice served in plastic cups, and the host was just bread, but it was one of the great Eucharists of my father's life, a transforming experience—a tall white man rising to preach to a congregation, all but a few of them black, swaying awkwardly during the singing of spirituals, music that was unnatural to him but which he loved, which made him feel connected to these worshipers for whom the church was a real source of strength. The ironing board as altar in front of the bombed-out house was an easy transformation, perhaps bringing to mind the mass at Guadalcanal, the white sheet draped across a simple table in the jungle clearing; but to replace wine from a silver chalice with grape juice in an individual "plastic cup or something of that kind" was quite alien: how far was a silver chalice from family silver, communion wine from a good vintage at his father's club? And so, to understand what happened to my father in Mississippi in 1964, I think of him receiving grape juice from a plastic cup and, in that moment, surprised, humbled to find the sacrament there.

All kinds of barriers were coming down. He told us about a white man, "Red" Hefner, a native Mississippian and an Episcopalian, whose oldest daughter had been Miss Mississippi. When he tried to organize conversations between the whites at his church and Negroes he had come to know through selling them insurance, the family was ostracized, and he was fired from his job. When my father went to visit the Hefners, he had to do it at night, changing cars in the dark to avoid detection by the Klan. After their first drink in the basement family room, Klansmen circling the house, Mr. Hefner apologized for the dangerous circumstances. "I can't get any of my friends to come to meet you, so I've asked the FBI!"—and so the party for the visiting bishop was the Hefners, their younger daughter Carla, and the FBI men who had been assigned to protect them. This was as much of the story as I knew until the summer of 2005, when I visited Carla Hefner, now living in Sussex in a great country house and married to a British M.P. Later that summer, she told me, the Klan firebombed their house, and the family moved to Jackson, but even the high school there was too dangerous, and so my father arranged for her to attend the National Cathedral School, and eventually her parents moved to Washington, going to work for the Civil Rights Division of the Justice Department. "What did my father mean to you?" I asked Carla, touring her gardens forty years later. "He saved our lives."

After Mississippi, my father flew into Newark on his way to meet my mother and the younger children at Hollow Hill, and when he arrived at the airport the newspapers were full of the riot that had torn through Jersey City the night before. He called Grace Church, and Father Luce, the rector, asked that he and my mother come right over. That night my mother took charge at the rectory she'd left seven years before, and my father and Father Luce walked toward the neighborhood near the hospital where the riot had taken place the night before, the provocation, police beating a black mother. As the sun set and a crowd began to gather, my father heard a voice out of the darkness, "Hey, Father Moore, how you doin'?" Before long he was in the midst of young men he'd coached in baseball as kids during the days at Grace Church. What began as a joyous reunion soon changed: police cars began to circle, and soon a Coke bottle was thrown, and then another, and then "police repeatedly charged the crowd, waving their night sticks, needlessly harassing innocent bystanders, and firing their pistols, all while the mayor disregarded a highly responsible delegation of young people, clergy of all faiths, and civil rights leaders, who had sought to be mediators early on."

My father was now commuting once a month to Mississippi where the National Council of Churches was continuing the work started by the Mississippi summer, an effort called the Delta Ministry, of which he was chair. I was back in Cambridge for my sophomore year, and though I had decided to major in English, my passion was the theater. By December, I was stage-managing *Utopia Limited*, an obscure Gilbert and Sullivan operetta about a sort of Victorian-era Peace Corps. The director, who seemed already professional to me, was just a class ahead. Timothy S. Mayer had a lean, handsome face, dark, usually dirty hair that fell to his face and that he pushed back as a nervous tic, and dark-framed glasses that were never quite level on his nose. Until he stood up, you didn't notice his hunchback, an enlargement of his right shoulder, and you quickly forgot it, so caught up were you in his fantastically sophisticated, showbiz way of speaking. He had learned to direct at a semiprofessional Gilbert and Sullivan summer theater on Cape Cod, taking on full productions by the age of sixteen, and he had no trouble maneuvering chorus lines or encouraging a tall sophomore actor, my classmate John Lithgow, to sing despite the fact that he didn't have what any of us considered a singing voice.

*   *   *

Before I entered the room for the meeting, I'd fallen in love with Luke's smile, which I'd seen through a crack in the half-open door on my way up the stairs. "Hi, baby," Tim said, "this is Marston," and the tall smiling man shook my hand. "I'm Luke Marston." It was the spring of my sopho-more year, and Tim, deploying inordinate charm, swoops of rhetoric, and a Machiavellian talent for barter, had persuaded the Harvard Gilbert and Sullivan Players to break from their eponymous repertory and allow him to direct *The Threepenny Opera.* Luke was the producer, I was the assistant director, and Tim managed to get a married Radcliffe junior he'd seen in an Adams House one-act and who lived on Beacon Hill to audition for the role of Jenny. She arrived wearing black, and in a rehearsal room at the Loeb, bare except for a grand piano, Luke and Tim and I watched, David Schloss at the piano, as she took possession of the role. When the show opened in May, Susan Stockard, whom Tim delighted in calling by her married name, Mrs. Channing, took Cambridge by storm.

As I established myself at Harvard, my father's life was becoming more public. In January, the SCLC had taken its voter registration campaign to Selma, Alabama. By March, continuing mass arrests at the Selma court-house prompted Martin Luther King Jr. to put out a call for a march from Selma, fifty-four miles to Montgomery, the state capital. On Sunday, March 7, 1965, as marchers attempted to cross the Edmund Pettus Bridge, the route out of Selma, they met a wall of state police and sheriff's deputies, who beat them back with nightsticks and tear gas. On March 9, defying a federal restraining order, King led another march across the bridge, but turned back when troops again blocked the way; that night, James Reeb, a Unitarian minister from Boston, was beaten to death as he left a restau-rant in Selma. Now King put out a call to the movement at large to come support the marchers.

Kim Myers was already in Selma, and of course my father wanted to join him, but as supporters responded to King's call and the threat of vio-lence escalated, it was clear that a presence in Washington was crucial. It became the task of the organization my father led with Walter Fauntroy, the Coalition of Conscience, to convince President Johnson to send fed-eral troops to Selma to protect the marchers—as they pressured the White House for a meeting, the coalition organized a demonstration across from the White House in Lafayette Square, setting up microphones and signs and banners on the portico of St. John's Episcopal Church, whose conservative vestry had somehow been persuaded to allow the church to be used as protest headquarters. It was the first week of Lent, and, by coincidence, my father was scheduled to preach each afternoon at St. John's. The worshipers expected a simple Lenten meditation from their new bishop; instead demonstrators crowded the pews, and my father did his best, first preaching to the St. John's devout and later engaging the eager, tumultuous crowd in a strategy session. President Johnson had not offered a meeting, and so the demonstrations continued, the crowd growing all week, as my father and Fauntroy and their steering committee debated: Should they continue with speakers and rallies? Or do something more militant and radical—"like lying down in front of the White House"?

Since James Reeb's murder, Selma had become the epicenter of the struggle, and from all over the country, buses filled with demonstrators and clergy, some of whom had never participated in a civil rights action, rolled toward Alabama for the march that was sure to occur. President Johnson, under pressure from both Northern and Southern supporters, continued to hold back from federalizing the National Guard or sending troops, and the coalition continued to insist on a meeting. My mother wrote me of the excitement: "The week of negotiations with HHH & LBJ were incredible with HHH's office calling at 8 AM & then [Assistant Attorney General] Nick Katzenbach on the phone & all sorts of local leaders." On Friday, March 12, she and my sister Adelia, then fifteen, sent me a telegram: TRY TO COME DOWN SUNDAY BIG RALLY ABOUT SELMA MISS YOU CALL US SATURDAY AT 7 LOVE. Sunday was the day fifteen thousand gathered in Lafayette Square in support of the march, and my father was asked to speak. He followed Fannie Lou Hamer, the Mississippi voting rights activist, whose speech, he said later, was the greatest sermon he'd ever heard. My father had written a "carefully reasoned Anglican counter-attack" to the president's rationale, but as he mounted the podium, he threw aside his notes "and just took off." Standing on the podium, posters in the air, the White House behind him, he spoke: "The bodies of white men may be at liberty, but to the extent of their prejudice their souls are in chains. The bodies of Negro Americans are in chains, but those who are in the movement are the freest men in the world, for their souls are free."

Busy with *The Threepenny Opera*, I did not fly to Washington, but my mother wrote me to buy *Newsweek*. My father had been photographed, as "a leader of the new breed" of clergyman, for the cover. The story, written

by his old friend Ben Bradlee, was a report on what the magazine christened "the Church Militant."

The day after that Sunday demonstration, President Johnson finally
agreed to see a dozen leaders of the Lafayette Square demonstrations,
including my father. The meeting was in the Cabinet Room, and my father
was seated right across from the president. First Johnson invited those
present to say a few words; in the fifteen minutes allotted, each speaking
a minute or so, the group laid out an argument for federal troops. "Poppy
has notes of their meeting with LBJ," my mother wrote, "the latter talked
70 minutes without stopping!" The president told them about his youth
as a poor student, his work teaching destitute Mexicans, his courtship of
Lady Bird. Bill Moyers, then the president's young press secretary, was
dispatched to find the appropriate citation from Isaiah—"Come now, let
us reason together . . ." My father lost the notes he took that day, but he
always remembered one "Johnsonism": "You know how a mule arches up
his back during a thunderstorm, when the hail comes down, and all he
does is stand there? That's the way I feel when I get the kind of pressure
you're putting on me today."

In my Radcliffe dormitory that night, on television, I watched as the
president addressed a joint session of Congress, calling for a Voting Rights
Act: "This great rich, restless country can offer opportunity and education
and hope to all—black and white, North and South, sharecropper and
city dweller. These are the enemies: poverty, ignorance, disease. They are
our enemies and not our fellow man, not our neighbor. And these enemies too—poverty, disease and ignorance—we shall overcome." A tran-
script of the speech quotes Johnson as saying "We shall overcome" only
twice, but I remember him repeating it as a refrain. *We shall overcome:*
none of us could believe he'd used those words. "Wasn't Johnson's speech
GREAT?" my mother wrote. Within days the Alabama federal judge lifted
the restraining order and enjoined state and local authorities from inter-
fering with the march. On March 21, King led three thousand across the
Pettus Bridge under federal military protection, and on the twenty-fifth,
a rally of twenty-five thousand welcomed the marchers to Montgomery.
Newsweek, dated March 29, came out on Monday, the twenty-second, but
because the Russians had walked in space, the photograph of my father
was bumped from the cover. "Mr. Bradlee gave us the proof & you'll flip!"
my mother wrote.

In Cambridge, I was now officially Luke Marston's girlfriend, and *The Threepenny Opera* was a hit. Every night after the show, Tim jammed Luke and me and often a few others into the red leather interior of his white convertible and drove us out Storrow Drive to Ken's of Copley Square, a Las Vegas-like establishment across from Trinity Church where we smoked and drank into the night. There Tim held court, accosting young waitresses with appalling sex talk while conceiving brilliant, fabulous productions of Brecht or Shakespeare as if he were Peter Brook, whose *Marat/ Sade* we had all flown to New York to see, or fabulating, as if he were Orson Welles, how he would next cast "Mrs. Channing," or, as if he were Irving Thalberg, how he would get Donnie Graham to improve the *Crimson* reviewing staff. After speeding home across the Harvard Bridge and down Memorial Drive, Luke and I nervous that Tim was too drunk to get us home safely, we'd arrive at the entrance of my dormitory, hours past curfew, Tim still not content to cease his endless flow of commentary: "Do you know, Marston, your girl is socially prominent"—or when I bought a yellow plaid coat with a dropped waistline—"You know Marston? Your girl is low-slung."

13
Eager

Rain. The river outside the window. The small elevator. The apartment: Kitchenette. Bedroom. Double bed. The summer after my sophomore year at Radcliffe, just eight blocks from where I now live. There was desire, the forbidden dark, the tearing off of clothes, my clothes. We were committing a crime, or at least a sin. Both of us thought of it that way.

But I wouldn't call it sex, what Luke and I did: nineteen, scared, my fin-

gers slippery with spermicidal gel, sitting on the edge of the bed, my back
to him. In spite of my impatience and with Luke's awkward encouragement, I squeeze the rubbery circle, aim, get the thing in, properly I hope.

The gynecologist at the Harvard Health Services, a doctor known as
lenient with birth control, had turned me down: "I don't think premarital
sex coincides with your worldview," he said, hands folded on his desk. I
knew what a worldview was from reading *The Elizabethan World Picture* by
E.M.W. Tillyard for Herschel Baker's course in the poetry of the English
Renaissance. I left Holyoke Center in tears, and when I told him, Luke
cursed. I couldn't ask my mother for help; solving this was up to me. I
walked the Cambridge streets. If I couldn't manage this, I'd lose Luke.
He had a summer movie job in New York, I was going to take art courses,
and we were going to make love. My cousin's wife lived in New York City,
and knew someone there. Fifth Avenue is the street I remember crossing.
This doctor asked no questions, gave no instructions, just handed me a
prescription for a diaphragm, which I quickly filled. I associated the thing
with my mother's bathroom, the half-squeezed tubes that weren't tooth-
paste, the faintly medicinal smell, her body losing its youth, my father on
top of her when I caught them once in the Adirondacks, bursting into their
cabin uninvited: "Poppy and I are cuddling."

Luke reached for me. We left the lights on, or it was still light, or this
happened on a weekend morning. We'd planned ahead. What I remember is that we somehow missed the connection. Our first time had the
mechanical logic that my mother had described to me that time with one
of my infant siblings on her lap—penetration, the eager swimming sperm,
nothing about pleasure. What had happened to how I'd felt with Rick
Warner? Where was the mystery in this thing I had so longed for, holding
back in high school cars while necking and French-kissing? Intercourse
is what my mother called it, and those first times it seemed just what that
utilitarian word made it sound like. A railroad crossing dependent on correct signals. The name of a small town in Pennsylvania, as the joke went.

The movie job fell through and Luke was working at Bankers Trust—
I'd called my grandmother in tears, a position had been arranged. Luke
took the job and bought a new suit, but he resented that he'd let me rescue
him. We'd have breakfast at Zum Zum in the Pan Am Building (later the
MetLife Building), then he'd go to work and I'd take the subway uptown to
the apartment on East Seventy-second Street where I told my parents I was

living, which I shared with two Radcliffe friends. Three times a week I'd go downtown to NYU for courses in life drawing and graphic design, and every day at suppertime I'd meet Luke for the evening. "You sound happy & well," my father wrote at the end of July, "& I envy you the summer in N.Y. with Luke. Mommy & I had a great time there when we dated, doing silly things & going to offbeat places."

That's what made it less criminal: Luke and I would get married as my parents had. I couldn't see me and Chris, or me and Rick Warner, or me and Ben Sachs in a wedding picture, but I could kind of see Luke in a dinner jacket and me in a bride's dress, holding hands, beaming at the cameras. I remember slowly spinning on a barstool at Sparks Steakhouse, as I heard the door open. I was wearing my backless black dress, Luke his new summer suit; we drank Johnnie Walker Red at the bar and then had steak in a candlelit booth. We went to the first Philharmonic concert in Central Park, Mayor John Lindsay's maiden effort to open the park to the city; and for a special night out Luke took me to "21," where I ate smoked salmon for the first time, the lemon tied with cheesecloth so the juice got through without seeds. We went to Lincoln Center for a John Cage concert, the sound produced by Merce Cunningham dancers whirling past electronically sensitized posts, and alone I went to a Giacometti exhibition, my first at the Museum of Modern Art. My drawing teacher, an Abstract Expressionist painter, had explained how the emaciated figures distorted physical proportion but intensified a sense of human presence, how the spherical, whirling pencil lines that surrounded the figure in Giacometti's portrait drawings gave the likenesses a third dimension.

Weekend mornings when we hadn't left the city to visit Luke's parents in Katonah, New York, or his aunt at her beach house in Westhampton, Long Island, or my Uncle Bill and Aunt Mouse on the ocean in Old Lyme, Connecticut, Luke read poems to me, E. E. Cummings and Wallace Stevens, as we sat on the window seat that overlooked the Hudson. One or two nights a week, I think I cooked, and one Saturday we had lunch with Luke's uncle, his father's identical twin, glamorous, mysterious, divorced, who was courting a model from Hong Kong. On his way to Greenville, Mississippi, my father wrote me: "I imagine you are thinking about next year & how it will be in Cambridge without L." Luke had graduated, and I would be a junior; I'd commute to New York most weekends, I thought, and though Luke was fatalistically preoccupied with the draft, I brushed off my father's concern that given the "South Vietnam bit," he might be called up. Luke's friend George Trow, with whom I'd madly fox-trotted at the Spee Club Dance, had joined the Coast Guard to avoid combat; others of Luke's graduating friends were enlisting in officers' training to "get it over with." In March, President Johnson had sent 3,500 marines to China Beach to defend the American air base at Da Nang; by June, there were 23,000 American troops in Vietnam; by the end of the year, there would be 184,000, most of them draftees.

At the end of the summer, Luke and I drove to the Adirondacks. A boyfriend with me, I finally felt like a grownup, though it went without saying that Luke and I slept in separate cabins. We had cocktails with my parents, and, after the kids were asleep, played bridge, my mother making laconic flirtatious remarks, my father acting paternal toward the young man who might one day be his son-in-law. We all talked about the aftermath of Selma, and about Los Angeles—what the civil rights movement had worked so hard to prevent had happened in Watts, Negroes and police rioting for six days, killing thirty-four, streets in charred ruins. And Luke asked my father about the Marine Corps. My father was not yet against the war, in conversation still putting forward a belief that Vietnam had some equivalence to the war he'd fought.

In September, I returned to Cambridge and Luke to New York, where he continued at the bank by day and, at night, ran lights for *Hogan's Goat*, a hit off-Broadway play by William Alfred, a professor we'd both had at Harvard. But in November, believing it was a responsibility, Luke enlisted in the Marines—he wanted, as my father had said of himself, "to be in the thick of it." The one weekend I visited him in New York, I sat in the front window on a Sunday morning, pretending to read Wallace Stevens, trying to look beautiful as I gazed out the window. The atmosphere was tense, and we were no longer making love. "Complacencies of the peignoir . . ." Yes, I was reading "Sunday Morning" and wearing a silky negligee of a shimmery print of pale blue flowers. A few weeks later, on Thanksgiving, I arrived home in Washington to find a letter from Luke, breaking up with me. The following week he returned what I'd left in his apartment in a brown paper bag—the negligee and my diaphragm in its leatherette case. The friend he'd designated courier found me at the Loeb, in the dark, watching a rehearsal.

To keep my life free for Luke and weekends in New York, I'd refused when Tim, wishing to get out of directing *The Mikado* that fall, asked me to replace him. Now my life was a blank, and the only news of Luke, who would soon leave for basic training at Camp Lejeune, came in chagrined snippets from his friends. In my shock, I associated the breakup not with the war but with my own certain defects; something was surely wrong with me, some unknowable, hellish, female flaw. I carried shame for weeks. "I am really sorry for the way I acted earlier today," I wrote my father after Christmas vacation.

> All of a sudden I began thinking how much I would love to spend New Year's Eve with Luke—and in New York and it all came back again and when I started thinking about that, I got ashamed of how I was acting period and mad and so I left the room. I guess that you have to learn some time to stop acting like a child— but it's really hard—and it's becoming harder to control myself period because I think about Luke so much of the time and really feel like crying all that time. But I know that I can't at twenty go on being fourteen or twelve or four forever, but sometimes I just can't not think of myself and instead of not crying I do cry sometimes—and it goes on but I am sorry—and I'm glad that you and Mom are there and will never stop loving me.

It was then that my father told me the story of choosing Seattle, of how cruel he'd been to my mother. But I was not comforted. My father was a great hero, and he and my mother were happy and good; they hadn't committed the crime of sex before marriage. I had thought some magic would render me engaged to Luke by now, freed of any obligation to pursue my own life, that I would be as safe as I thought my parents were, waiting for him to get out of the Marines, for the war to be over, for life to return to normal, but the war was only just beginning, the first wave of soldiers dead, the first reports of massive Vietnamese civilian casualties. I knew Luke was still in basic training, but I heard nothing until one day in the spring when a letter arrived. Just as my parents had twenty-two years earlier, Luke and I reconciled in letters. He wrote of the horrors of basic training, cartoons of yellow faces with slanted eyes pasted above his locker, to be called "geeks." I did not then know that my father had received equivalent instruction; he had taught us "From the Halls of Montezuma" and I

sang it in the same spirit as "Onward, Christian Soldiers." *Geeks.* Was this
my father's Marine Corps? "We had a fine letter from Luke," my father
wrote me late that spring. "Rough for him to sort out good motivation
destroyed by horrid realities. I feel for him. It was so much easier for us in
WW II—motivation-wise. But I look back with horror on my simplistic
reactions & admire guys like Luke who see things more clearly."

As the weeks passed, Luke's leave and our reunion grew closer. Tim
had decided to mount a renegade summer season at Agassiz, a small theater at Radcliffe, to rival what we considered the boring summer fare
across the street at the Loeb Drama Center. I was planning a summer in
Europe, but I agreed to be the producer until I left in mid-July, raising
money from alumni and parents, recruiting techs and costumers, com-
posers and musicians. We opened with Joan Littlewood's antiwar musical
Oh! What a Lovely War, which Tim directed. My mother brought her uncle,
who had fought at Verdun, to the opening, and he wept at the old World
War I songs; we played to packed houses and great reviews, even in the
Boston papers. The second production, *The Bacchae* by Euripides, was to
be directed by Thom Babe, a Harvard graduate legendary among us; days
after he returned in April from two years' study in Cambridge, England,
Tim met with him. "I had dinner with Babe," he said. "He wants to work
with us." Thom was said to be a "great" actor, he wrote poems, and he had
written a play called *A Pageant of Awkward Shadows*. He had a bony, ruddy
face and big hazel eyes and a head that seemed outsized for his narrow
body. Whenever he spoke to you, he seemed to be entrusting a confidence.
I was immediately infatuated, but I had no doubt that as soon as Luke
came home in his marine uniform, he would sweep me off my feet, just as
my father had my mother.

He met me at the house on the beach in Manchester, Massachusetts,
which my parents had rented for the month of July. He was not wearing a
uniform but khakis and a white shirt, and he was very tan, his blond hair
shorn to a crew cut. We walked on the beach. It was a moonlit night, we
lay on the sand, he kissed me, he touched me, he said over and over again
how he'd missed me. I felt nothing but the strangeness of his newly mus-
cular body, and his smile now looked too bright, Thom Babe's face intervening. Someone should have told Luke and me to have dinner first, to sit
across from each other and just talk. When I did not kiss back a second
time, he abruptly stood, pulling me up from the sand, and we walked to

his dark green car. He had a pet name for me, and that is what he used, romantic, still, unsmiling now, standing there. This was not what I had wanted. I needed time to look at him again, to reassemble the parts of his face that I had seen only in imagination for nearly a year. I wanted to forgive his abrupt rejection, the return of the baby blue peignoir and the diaphragm in the brown paper bag. I was crying, trying to kiss him, but he pushed me away, not roughly, but not warmly either. He was supposed to spend the night, I said. My mother was expecting him for breakfast. No. And he got in the car, shut the door, and drove off.

The next morning, a photographer came to take family pictures, all nine of us, one after the other—me the oldest, almost twenty-one, Patience, the youngest, just four, blond and smiley. Except for Paul and Adelia, I didn't really know my brothers and sisters. The little girls were flitting presences—when I'd make a face in the mirror to put on my lipstick, I'd hear Rosie and Marian giggle behind me and turn to see them imitating me. "The children loved ogling their big sister," my mother once wrote. For the sitting, I carefully combed my shoulder-length hair and put on my favorite bright orange turtleneck. The photographs are black-and-white. In the series, which my mother had mounted on eight-by-ten blocks, and which became iconic portraits of the nine of us for the next decade, every one of us but me and perhaps Paul, who was about to start Yale, looks carefree. I'm not smiling. I'm looking at the camera, and, if I didn't know I'd been trying to hide the fact that I'd cried all night and barely slept, that I'd taken a decisive step I had not intended, at least not consciously, I would describe the look on my face as questioning. The trip to Europe would remove my questions and awkwardness, wipe away the last traces of heartbreak. I didn't understand what was in store, that Europe's revelation would be of sensibility—how I looked at things, how I tasted food, how I listened.

In Paris, I had a fourth-floor room under the eaves of a small hotel on rue Monsieur le Prince, pigeons darting at the rooftops, potted geraniums at windows. If I craned to look out, I could see a Vietnamese restaurant across the street. Even though I'd been to Paris with my parents when I was fourteen, this seemed all new. The croissants and café au lait at breakfast, the water running clear in the cobblestone gutters, hearing French on the street. "I miss the HDC Summer Players," I wrote my father, "but I feel absolutely *free*. I can do *whatever* I want." In each place, I spent time with friends, but I was traveling alone. I had a Eurail pass, and after Paris I went to London, then to a cabin in the Alps near Berne where Elly, the Dutch exchange student who had lived with us in Indianapolis, was on vacation with her family. In Florence, I had the phone number of Pam Morton's mother, who ran a finishing school there. In Rome, I'd see a friend of Tim's who was teaching there, and finally, I'd have a few days in Geneva—the visit with Nona Clark. "I have been twice to the Jeu de Paume now & absolutely am feeling quite ecstatic about the Degas, Manets, and Cézannes there—not to mention the divine Monet room! Tonight I am going to *Tartuffe* at the Hotel Sully," I wrote. "Sunday I'm going to the opera to see *Tosca* and at some point to an Ionesco thing and a Camus thing. I find that although I can speak only a bare minimum of French, I can understand quite a lot . . ." It was Italy that undid me. I remember days in the Uffizzi and the Bargello, the first time I saw a Botticelli and then the flatness of Uccello, which I gazed at mystified, and my disappointment when the drastic edginess of the quattrocento gave way to what I considered the decadent sweetness of Raphael. About Donatello, I wrote Grandma Kean, my mother's mother Margarett, who had studied in Florence as a girl, and had been a painter long ago. I spent dark afternoons reading in my room at the Florence *pensione*, Thomas Pynchon ("a crazy book called *V*"), and Ford Madox Ford (*The Good Soldier*): I'd found a bookstore where I could trade in paperbacks. "Read *Lady Chatterley*," I wrote my father, "and cried for hours. So candid.—I've also read *The Rainbow* and *Women in Love* this summer and this is so much less ponderous . . ."

In Cambridge, my aesthetic experience had come through others, chiefly Tim and Thom. They had the courage to do what I was scared of; they took Robert Lowell's poetry workshop, sat up nights drinking with William Alfred, whose lectures on *Beowulf* and Joyce had thrilled me as a freshman. I had been locked out of their secret interior, but now I was entering one of my own. I didn't care what anyone else thought, and, it seemed, I could withstand any fear, the catcalls of Italian men, loneliness on the bus trip I took to Siena, because I would be rewarded: the spectacle of the Colosseum where I could kick a stone that had been there since the gladiators, the Piccolomini Library in Siena where my eye sank through color into the Pinturrichio frescoes, or San Marco in Florence, a monastery where each cell had an ancient fresco, an Annunciation, a Crucifixion. "It's all been so wonderful," I wrote my father, "so much exactly what I wanted it to be. A going out into the cold strange world—having time to think and read and be alone—it's been much happier than I thought it would be—very restful—and exhausting at the same time."

I was truly alone—no easy picking up of strangers for me. My friend Ann had been followed by an Austrian painter in Paris who would not rest until she agreed to sit for him, but I froze with terror when I missed Milan and ended up waiting for a mail train back in a tiny station in Reggio Emilia. Sitting on the lone wooden bench alternately reading Robert Lowell and writing a letter to my mother, I concentrated to avoid my panic. "On my right is an ancient Italian woman, who should be saying her rosary, but who is instead muttering things I don't understand under her breath . . ." Eventually a hovering soldier, tall and in uniform, who looked like Gregory Peck but Italian and my age, approached me. He could not speak English, but he understood my predicament, and waited with me, lifting my suitcases on board when the train came. When I finished the letter home the next day, I made the story a comedy:

> He told me I was a 'bella signorina' & I clutched again—but
> some old man began playing his accordion & we both listened
> & that was nice—only disturbed by much screaming of chil-
> dren & passing through of various Chianti vendors. After what
> seemed like hours, we got to Milan—me 4 hours later than
> expected. He took my suitcases to the taxi stand & decided it was
> time to bid an affectionate adieu. He kissed me on each cheek
> (I involuntarily felt pangs of guilt for having mistrusted this pure
> young man) & then it was all over—hands everywhere—lips—
> tongue—I finally fought him off *"Basta! Basta!"* & then laughed
> and laughed because it must have been such a funny scene.

In London at the end of the summer, I ran into a boy named Howard who had acted the previous spring in Thom's production of Wedekind's *Spring Awakening*. There he was in the lobby of the Old Vic, where the National Theatre was performing O'Casey's *Juno and the Paycock*; afterward, we walked all over the city, talking about the actor Colin Blakely as Boyle, the paycock, Joyce Redman as Juno, Ronald Pickup as the son.

To see these actors we had only read about, who were our gods! "I've seen
nine plays and four movies," I wrote home. Howard was different away
from Harvard, more relaxed I thought, as we sat in St. James's Park talking, taking off our shoes, walking across the grass. We met the next night
at see Peter Shaffer's *Royal Hunt of the Sun* and had supper afterward at a
German restaurant in Soho, and one afternoon we saw *Othello*, sitting in
the highest balcony, afterward talking about the intimacy, the specificity of Laurence Olivier's portrayal, in blackface. The politics of blackface
were complicated, but I allowed art to sweep away all the contradictions so
insistent in 1966. From Paris, where I returned to catch my flight home, I
wrote again to my father, "I want you to know and understand how much
this summer has meant to me. It's been absolutely wonderful. I will always
remember it and love it."

Back in Cambridge and a senior, I entered the last months of my term
as the first woman president of the Harvard (later Harvard and Radcliffe)
Dramatic Club. Tim was in London observing the director Peter Brook, so
I was free of the frenetic pace that working on his productions, irresistible
to me, always required. I was reading Chaucer's *Troilus and Criseyde* in my
honors tutorial, and planning to play the soubrette in a Loeb production,
the North American premiere of Georges Feydeau's farce *A Flea in Her
Ear*—it would be my only appearance on a Harvard stage. In a narrow bed
in his single room in Quincy House, Howard and I had a short affair, two
pale-skinned brunettes making love to Mahler through long afternoons.

My mother had offered me a twenty-first birthday party, and we arranged
it at the Cambridge Boat Club on the Charles River—a dinner for twenty,
a dance for everyone I knew (I would find a rock-and-roll band), and then
scrambled eggs at 4 a.m. I invited everyone, and everyone came—all my
theater friends, my parents, my brother and his friends from Yale, professors, girls from my dorm with their boyfriends, Indianapolis friends at
college in the East, the friends with whom I'd gone to Pakistan. "I am sorry
I can't be present to dance to the Growth Orchestra"—Grandma Kean
telegraphed. The rock band, called Growth, played everything we knew,
and in a long gold dress, I danced happily all night, with Howard my date,
with George Trow in his Coast Guard uniform, with my father, with any
man I wanted to. At the end of the evening Howard escorted me back to
my dorm, kissed me good night, handed me my birthday present, a book
of Daumier drawings.

That spring I took a course in American poetry, a seminar called "Wordsworth, Eliot, Coleridge, and Stevens," and the fiction-writing workshop in which I wrote the story about my father and Nona Clark. Under the tutelage of a graduate student who had taken Robert Lowell's poetry workshop and who wrote quietly in an apartment on Green Street, I was writing poems. "Ah breakfast, t'would delight me," began a sonnet I composed when he canceled a date; "But now my tears do flow profuse / For thou didst disinvite me . . ."

One day that spring, my father met me at the Ritz. In those years, the side door still had a sign above it that said "Not An Accredited Egress Door"—as it had when my parents danced there during the war, as it had, probably, when *their* parents lunched in its vast upstairs dining room. If my father and I had eaten at the Ritz, I doubt the subject of sex would have come up, but we walked to a café nearby. Did I tell him I was no longer a virgin? Or did I simply ask him what he thought about sex before marriage? I sound more brazen than I was—when I asked the question, I mumbled, looking down at the tablecloth. My father said he didn't think it was a good idea, sex before marriage. "Jenny and I didn't go to bed before we married."

I had expected him to speak as if from a pulpit and tell me he thought sex before marriage was a sin, but he did not. If he had, it would have been possible for me to go right ahead without a second thought, but because he didn't, I was left with freedom and confusion. It was the spring of 1967, and girls at Radcliffe were losing patience with the finishing-school ethos— housemothers, milk and cookies on Saturday night for the dateless, signing in and signing out. Freshman year, you had to be in by ten-thirty on a week night and eleven-fifteen on a weekend unless you had special permission to use a rationed "one o'clock." If "a man" was visiting your room, the door had to remain open the width of a matchbook. If you wanted to spend the night with "a man," you had to lie, invent an aunt to spend the weekend with, for instance. Now there was no curfew and you could spend any night you pleased with anyone you wanted to, provided the houseparents had prior written permission from your parents, which all our parents gave. You wrote your name and destination on a card which you then sealed in an envelope and put in a file box on the "bells desk" at the dorm entrance: so the college could be certain in the event of fire that none of the charred corpses was yours. No one considered that the file box wasn't fireproof.

Radcliffe hired a psychologist to discuss sex with its students. I was living in a college-owned "off campus" house for fifteen girls—all upper-classmen who wanted a less institutional place to live. The sex counselor arrived one afternoon in October. He was a youngish man wearing glasses and an ordinary suit, and when we sat down, he introduced himself and gave a delicate speech that concluded with a request for our questions. To break the awkward silence, I raised my hand, putting the question I'd dared myself to ask: "What constitutes promiscuity?" My housemates managed not to laugh. "I'd say, ah, I'd say *ten* partners," the sex counselor offered. After he left, I told my friends I planned to break ten as quickly as I could, and so when a gangly graduate student, who turned out to be studying philosophy, approached me in the new Radcliffe library and invited me back to his parents' empty apartment, I didn't hesitate.

"Honor's Radcliffe graduation, Rosie's Junior High & Dee's High School commencement (as valedictorian) are all three on June 14," my mother wrote Pam Morton the spring of 1967. "We are trying to sift out the actual hours of the events but you may have to fly on as a mother figure!" But the family managed to come to Radcliffe Yard for mine: Mom and Pop and Gami, and maybe a sibling or two, my father standing to take a picture as Mary Bunting handed me my diploma. I wore an ecru lace dress under my cap and gown, and we had a festive lunch after outdoors at the Window Shop, a Scandinavian café on Brattle Street across from Marimekko. I didn't mind that they all immediately flew off for the other graduations. Tim and Thom and I were already planning the summer season: "four plays of war and the city." I was periodically stopping at Tim's chaotic apartment, nagging him as, at the typewriter with coffee or Scotch, he crawled to the finish of his translation of Aristophanes' *Peace*, which was opening in less than a month. Or he would send me on a mission—to cajole the composer, a law school student, to work for nothing: "Fuck him if you have to!" he shouted, turning back to his crumpled drafts as I flinched and strode off in search of Thom, who was kinder.

Days after graduation, again wearing the ecru lace dress, I stood on the stage of Agassiz Theatre on a stifling afternoon to present Alfred Hitch-cock, who was briefly in Boston, an honorary membership in the Harvard Dramatic Club. It was Tim's idea of course, but it was I who commissioned a calligraphed certificate, which I signed as president and which Tim and Thom signed as artistic directors of the Harvard Dramatic Club Summer Players. Licking stamps and stuffing envelopes, begging at the offices of deans, and from parents, we raised $10,000 to put on the four-play season, and Tim hustled three enormous, very noisy air conditioners from his father. Outside Agassiz flew an orange banner I'd had made, proclaiming our season:

> Peace   Trojan Women
> Measure for Measure
> In the Jungle of Cities

Though I was residing in an apartment on Trowbridge Street with two Radcliffe friends, I was living with the graduate philosopher in his parents' apartment on Massachusetts Avenue. He insisted that I come home every night between the day of work and the evening rehearsal; he'd cook me supper, and we would go to bed until I had to drive back to the theater. Tim barely spoke to my new boyfriend, who had volunteered to photograph rehearsals, and after I introduced him to my mother, she told me *she* certainly wouldn't want to have an affair with him. I should have kept this new life private, the delicious suppers and my unruly orgasms, to a soundtrack of the Beach Boys' *Pet Sounds* and the Beatles' *Sgt. Pepper's Lonely Hearts Club Band*.

Each of the productions ran for two weeks, and as the summer progressed and our success grew, we forgot how hard we were working. We were competing again with the Loeb, whose summer season was to culminate with "White House Happening," a play by Lincoln Kirstein with John Lithgow as a humanized president with an illegitimate half-Negro son. On our side of the street, Tim, the showman, and Thom, the poet and intellectual, were a great combination. *Peace*, Aristophanes' antiwar play, became a rock-and-roll musical, and, as Cassandra in *Trojan Women*, Channing, in oversize war fatigues, spoke her prophetic lines in a blaze of white light. Tim did *Measure for Measure* as a comment on the corruption of the city, and Channing was Isabella to Paul Schmidt's Duke—Paul was older than us and a veteran of years in Paris as a student of Marcel Marceau and Jacques Charon. He was a star of Boston and Harvard theater, a friend of New York School poets like Frank O'Hara, and the first man I'd ever known who described himself as "queer" even as he flirted outrageously with women. We considered it a privilege that he showed up for openings, French-movie-star resplendent in the manner of Alain Delon, wearing a white linen suit, so when Tim announced that "Schmidt" was "on board," we were astonished. Tim and Luke and I had seen the Boston Opera's production of Luigi Nono's *Intolleranza* in which the director Sarah Caldwell had used video, then still extremely experimental. Now we rented a video camera, a monstrous piece of machinery on casters, and got our hands on six big television monitors, which the assidous techies secured from Agassiz's nineteenth-century proscenium and balcony. When Paul returned as the duke to Vienna, his entrance was broadcast live to every corner of the theater.

At our triumphant cast party at Tim's parents' house on Cape Cod the Sunday after we opened, we read about ourselves in the *New York Times*: "I had a talk with Tim Mayer, a lanky, shaggy 23-year-old who appears to be the latest example of a recurrent Harvard phenomenon, the genius-director. One of them comes along every few years, puts on a few plays, and becomes a celebrity in the miniature world of Harvard: freshmen look up to him, the *Harvard Crimson* and the Boston papers sing his praises, understrappers rush to execute his orders. Like so many Harvard types, Mr. Mayer plays his role rather past the hilt." The reporter didn't think *Measure for Measure* exactly worked, but he described the duke's televised entrance as a coup de théâtre. "Mr. Mayer is so joyfully, so youthfully, so prodigally, so infectiously in love with his own virtuosity that it seems almost churlish to complain the play has been sacrificed to it."

I'd moved on from the philosopher by sleeping with his best friend, then with a campus figure who strode through Widener in a black cape, who took me to parties in New York where the talk was of Norman Podhoretz's memoir of growing up a New York intellectual, *Making It*. I had been accepted to Yale School of Drama in theater management. I said I was honing my skills for the day when Tim and Thom and I would start a real theater, but really I was marking time. I'd received enough praise in the fiction-writing workshop I'd taken my last semester of classes to believe I could write, but I didn't know how to begin. In New Haven, I rented an apartment in a new high-rise and dressed for the opening party in a flimsy lavender dress. A directing student with dark eyes asked if I was an actress, and I crossed the room to introduce myself to Gordon Rogoff, the head of

the directing department, who was a friend of Paul Schmidt's. I'd bought
series tickets to the New York Film Festival—there was a new Godard and
I planned to drive down. But I had crew, tearing tickets for the Jacobean
melodrama 'Tis Pity She's a Whore by John Ford, which was opening the
professional repertory season.

At Yale, administration meant service, not intense collaboration with
boy geniuses; I had to give up the film festival. I paid no attention to the
little voice inside me that kept insisting I was in the wrong place here in
New Haven—but where else could I go? The press agent for the Yale Repertory Theatre, who thought it was ridiculous that I was tearing tickets,
took interest in me, and included me when he had lunch with Harvey
Sabinson, David Merrick's press agent who taught publicity, and Herman
Krawitz, the assistant general manager of the Metropolitan Opera, who
was head of the theater administration program. That fall, when I visited
Cambridge and the Loeb for the world premiere of a play of Tim's, there
was already talk of the next summer at Agassiz, but in the late spring
Harvey Sabinson got me an interview for a publicity job at the Berkshire
Theatre Festival in Stockbridge, Massachusetts. I remembered the tedium
of begging Tim for completed scripts, of cajoling people into working for
nothing; I was ready to move on. My resignation was seen as a betrayal
and it ended my friendships with Tim and Thom, but that summer, for the
first time, I was a paid professional, having, as my mother put it in a letter
to Pam, "a heady summer as press agent for the Berkshire Theatre Festival,
rubbing shoulders with William Gibson, Arthur Penn, Elaine May etc."
My employer was Lyn Austin, a woman who had been producing plays in
New York for two decades. I put to work the publicity skills I'd learned at
the drama school, and by the end of the summer I managed a great coup:
a photograph from one of our productions on the front page of the Arts &
Leisure section of the New York Times. "They were all so enthusiastic about
her when I went up for an opening," my mother continued in her letter to
Pam. "It made me very proud."

14

The Family Cracks Open

In September 1968, my mother published a book, *The People on Second Street*, the memoir of Jersey City. She appeared on the *Today* show and was photographed for a spread in *Life* magazine, which also included a review of the book by Kim Myers. There were photographs of her returning to Jersey City, photographs of the past in Jersey City, and a portrait of our entire family. She traveled the country giving readings and talks, and the book went into a second printing. Her friend and Washington neighbor Eugene McCarthy nearly won the New Hampshire primary on an antiwar ticket, and Johnson withdrew from the presidential race. My mother spent the spring campaigning, first in Indianapolis, where she introduced the candidate and his wife to her old Democratic friends, and later in several primary states, where she did advance work for Mrs. McCarthy. In Washington, she and my father gave a small party to present the senator to some of their colleagues from the civil rights movement who were skeptical of him. Knowing exactly who his audience was that night, he did not say a word about race. My mother was furious and told him so. My brother Paul, who had also worked for McCarthy, had shifted his support to the McGovern campaign. "I am beginning to feel he is a Montague and I am a Capulet," my mother wrote Pam, "and discovering to my horror that people could break up over such crises!" In August, my mother and Paul had both gone to the Chicago convention, and were gassed outside the Hilton, a spectacle I watched on television in the Berkshires. That year changed my mother's life. She had journeyed out into the world; she now had an identity, she felt, independent of my father's. And, like many, she saw and experienced violence in Chicago that challenged her faith in institutions she had never questioned.

I was in my second year at Yale Drama School, and that spring the black students formed an alliance, and one of them, my friend Pamela Jones, asked me to ask William Sloane Coffin, the Yale chaplain, if we could reserve Battell Chapel as a venue for Bobby Seale of the Black Panthers, who was flying in from California to give a speech as part of a Black Arts Festival. I had never met Bill Coffin, but he knew who I was because of my father and my brother, and he said yes. And my new boyfriend approved. I had fallen in love with Arnold Weinstein, a man almost twenty years older than I was. He was the first older man I'd slept with and the first to make love to me in daring, experimental ways. He used words that scared me like "pussy," but that was not the part of him I loved. I loved his miraculous silvery curls, his button-shiny brown eyes, and how he touched me. He wrote poems and plays and lyrics and opera librettos, and if he wasn't talking in puns and swervy off-rhymes, he was scrawling fragments on scraps of paper that he left all over his turreted faculty apartment. He believed, for instance, that you should write the lines of a play first and then decide what character said them—and so when he was

writing a play he stayed up all night, wild-eyed, looking on the side table
or the bureau or searching the cracks of the sofa for the right little squiggle
of paper. I'd follow him, searching too, reassuring him the scrap of paper
would turn up, until he kissed me, until he put his tender, precise hands
under my short skirt and we fell onto his narrow university-issue bed. He
wore wonderful Italian cashmere turtlenecks, and his beautiful Italian
trousers were held at his narrow hips by a braided cordovan belt with a
shiny brass buckle. But being with him was turbulent, the poetic part of
him often nudged into rage by a small frustration, a professional slight, or
the political situation, which in 1969 supported both his idealism and his
anger. The part of him that ranted also shot up speed and vitamins under
the supervision of a Central Park South doctor, even snorted the odd whiff
of heroin with his best friend, Larry Rivers, the famous New York Pop artist whom Arnold considered "great" and with whom he had once had a
brief homosexual affair.

   I was trying to write Sylvia Plath–like lyrics, often after evenings of too
much drink. I had kicked the diet pills, Dexedrine, that I'd been taking
since Indianapolis—one day after running out, I'd gotten so depressed,
my insides so heavy I could barely walk. Change is the only constant, I
remember saying to myself, looking at the bookshelf I'd painted bright
orange enamel as I tossed the orange pills into a wastebasket. That spring,
an actor, a fellow student, asked to photograph me nude. He had a girlfriend and so, naïvely, I had no suspicion of his motives. The day he came
to my apartment it was raining, and we drank Scotch; he photographed
me, then pushed me down, coming into me. It was that involuntary cou-
pling, rather than sex with Arnold Weinstein, I believed, that made me
pregnant during the spring of 1969; I was on the pill but often forgot to
take it. I managed to get a psychiatrist's excuse and had a legal abortion
at Yale–New Haven Hospital, keeping my secret from Arnold, the photographer, my parents, and all but two or three of my friends. Recovering in
his apartment, I told Arnold I was ill and did not want to sleep with him:
the doctor said I had to keep from having sex for six weeks. When I con-
tracted an infection and got really sick, I told Arnold about the abortion,
though not about the nude photography, and he flew into one of his rages,
this time at me. How could I meddle with something so sacred as a child?
His child! He would have married me!

   The night we had that fight was the night of Bobby Seale's speech, and

I woke up at 2 a.m., Arnold not there, having slept through the enire evening and its aftermath. The murder of a New Haven Black Panther that
night led to the arrest of Bobby Seale and other members of the Black
Panther Party; the ensuing trial would eventually lead to May Day, 1970, a
massive demonstration in New Haven, to which I'd travel from New York
City with my women's consciousness-raising group. But in the spring of
1969, the women's liberation movement, which had begun roughly a year
earlier, had not made its way to the Yale School of Drama—even so, I
knew that I did not want to have the photographer's child, and though I
believed I was "in love" with Arnold Weinstein, the playwright, I understood there could be no domestic tranquillity with him. And I could hear
my mother on the subject of premarital sex: *Don't come home pregnant.*

The abortion was months behind me the day the family began to crack
open. I had quit the drama school and was moving to New York, to the
Chelsea Hotel, to write. It was a morning during August of 1969, and we
were in the Adirondacks. You can't count on sun in those mountains, but
that day was clear and as I walked the boardwalk toward my mother, I
imagined her sunning on the big porch over the boathouse, her skin getting darker and darker, burning into me how pale I was. Two weeks earlier, Arnold had visited me in the Berkshires, lain in my bed surveying
the shelf of books by Mao and Marx and Herbert Marcuse I'd assembled
to impress him, complained that the theater where I worked did nothing
worthy, then turned and fallen into an uninterruptible sleep. The next
morning he departed on the bus to start his new revolutionary improvisa-
tional theater in Chicago, and I hadn't heard from him since. I'd wanted
to go to Chicago with him, but, he said, I wasn't "helpful" enough. Again
I'd made a decision for my independence without meaning to, and so I
was grieving as I approached my mother. But I put a lift in my walk and
pretended I was enthusiastic about moving alone to New York.

My mother was not sunning but standing on the porch wearing long
pants, her back to the green railing. Behind her was Silver Mountain, and
the tree that still juts out over the lake, and of course the lake itself, where
at twilight often you hear a loon call its mate as mist rises off the water.
But it was morning and so the lake was blue, a pale, intense blue. My
father was not in camp, otherwise my mother would never have said what

she did that day. I can't get back much of the conversation, but I remember the sentence and the singular possessive pronoun: "I am having some problems with my marriage." At twenty-three and with limited information, I had facile explanations for her shattering announcement—she was tired of marriage to my father; Senator McCarthy, who often came over for morning coffee, was much more exciting than an Episcopal bishop in a purple shirt. It would be many years before I learned the deepest secret of my parents' marriage, but that morning in the Adirondacks, I learned there was a secret and also that I didn't want to know it, though the fact of it came into my imagination right then, and into my body.

Because I didn't want to believe what my mother said, I focused my attention on the fact that she had used the singular pronoun—*I am having some problems with my marriage*—and since she did not implicate my father in any way, I was angry only at her. Furious. And sad. This was not *her* marriage, it was *our* marriage. Weren't my brothers and sisters and I as much a part of the *our* as she and my father were? Suddenly this woman, my mother, was a stranger. Her tan skin looked pale and there was a dizzy blankness in her blue eyes and the black of her hair no longer called forth words like obsidian or ebony. When I got to New York, there was a letter from my father—"Things are a little bumpy here, as I guess Mom indicated."

That autumn, on the second ballot, my father was elected bishop coadjutor at the convention of the Episcopal Diocese of New York. Coadjutor means "with the right of succession"; "the Episcopal Church," my mother once wrote, "uses a lot of words you have to look up in the dictionary." In three years, my father would run the most urban and most influential diocese in the Episcopal Church—this had been his life's ambition since he became a priest. In the weeks after his election, their differences put aside, my parents traveled to New York for parties, interviews, tours of the bishop's quarters on the grounds of St. John the Divine. That winter, after one of those trips, my mother visited her mother in Boston—the date was January 10, 1970—and on her way home accepted a ride from the airport in Washington with an old friend. At an intersection not far from Newark Street, his Volkswagen Beetle was struck broadside by a car running a stop sign. My mother was thrown forward, the gearshift stick punching her lower abdomen. When she got home, she complained of stomach pain. By the time she and my father were dressed to go out for the evening, she was in agony on their bed. At the hospital the doctors discovered her body cavity filled with blood, and a surgeon cut away the damage, seven-tenths of her liver; the fraction's strange specificity is as I remember it.

My mother spent the next several months in the Washington Hospital Center, first hovering between life and death in intensive care, then recovering in a capacious room in the luxury wing, receiving friends and her children, masses of notes and flowers. She learned how much she was loved, independent of her children and her husband, and she understood it was remarkable that she had survived. For the weeks she lay there, she meditated on her life. There was the family to think about, and my father's career. At the time, divorce for clergy was allowed by the Episcopal Church only in special circumstances and was unthinkable for a bishop. After the move to New York, she would write another book. She would make an effort to repair the marriage. It would be a new beginning.

On a luscious evening the June after my mother's accident, my father met me at a restaurant on Eighth Street in New York City. I was twenty-four and he was forty-nine, not so many years older than my lover, and he was wearing a seersucker suit and a necktie. This is my father, I remember thinking to myself as I looked at him sitting opposite me. Normally he would be wearing a clerical collar and a purple shirt, but tonight he is not, and so somehow he is more present, and I am looking at him, suddenly, as a man. Let's say I am waiting. Waiting to feel what will come in my direction. What do we talk about? It is not the conversation that I will remember about that night in the restaurant that became a jazz club later in the evening. Instead I will get back a *sense*, a sense of my father's presence. He is handsome, I think to myself, handsome and slender, his hair starting to go a little gray, and his haircut is different, his hair maybe a little longer than it had been in Washington. Sexy. I say it to myself: sexy. Yes, my father looks sexy. I was fresh into serious therapy, and I imagined that the next day I would carry this new impression of a sexy father uptown to my psychiatrist like a trophy. I had sought out this psychiatrist when I moved to New York, so sad and confused about what my mother had told me that day in the Adirondacks that I thought I must be crazy like my mother's mother. I said I was writing poems, but the truth was I hardly knew what to do with myself. I couldn't say that to my handsome father, or even, for that matter, to my handsome psychiatrist whose analytic couch I lay on twice a week on East Ninety-sixth Street.

This would be a new gambit: "Look," I could say, "I had dinner with my father and I thought he looked sexy." But what was sexy? There was a sheen to my father that night, a glitter as he looked this way and that, and I thought it had to do with me, his daughter in her twenties coming into sexuality and desire, even beauty. I felt both an uncomfortable charge between us and a new distance, which I ascribed to our new circumstances: I was living on my own, and so was he—my mother and the family wouldn't move to New York until late summer. I had never talked to my father about what my mother had said about the marriage, and so a silence about her hung in the air. It was tempting; here we were in New York City. I finally had my father to myself. The waiter brought our food. I was wearing a very short skirt, crossing and uncrossing my legs. I could feel my new sexual sophistication push it further: my mother had nearly died and my father was *turning me on*. That phrase had scared me the first time Arnold used it, because his eyes got strange as if I were suddenly not who he was looking at. Now, as my father talked, his skin looked different, more alive. Always, when I remembered that night, I would feel a strange silvery nimbus pulling me in, implicating me in something illicit that excluded who my father and I had always been to each other and that caused me to think thoughts that betrayed my mother. Many summers later, when I learned of my father's hidden erotic life, that supper on Eighth Street came back to me.

My mother arrived in New York three months later. Two moving vans carried the possessions of twenty-five years of marriage and of five children north from Washington. "The move was pretty grueling," she wrote Pam, "but accomplished, in that week of 93°, smog, squatters hurling human you-know-what at the Cathedral doors etc." My father's first challenge as coadjutor was a demonstration by squatters in an apartment building owned by the diocese right across Amsterdam Avenue from the cathedral, which was scheduled to be torn down. "But I got through it," my mother continued, "and have arrived at the strength plateau where one night of sleep cures the day's fatigue as opposed to 3 days of hysteria." But she was being optimistic. What no one then understood, including my mother herself, was that she was still too fragile for such a change. It was 1970, and the benefits of a certain kind of post-traumatic health care—vitamins, homeopathy, nutrition, short-term psychotherapy—were not yet generally understood. My mother had always been healthy and athletic—in Washington, she played tennis two or three times a week—and resilient, but the damage to her liver was not an ordinary wound, and recuperating was nothing like recovering from, say, childbirth. After initial optimism, the placement of the children in progressive, integrated private schools, the hiring of a full-time Chinese couple to cook and clean, the glamorous welcomes—Mayor Lindsay and his wife threw a dinner dance for their old friends, the new bishop and his wife and family, a magical evening at Gracie Mansion—it became clear that my mother had not really recovered.

The cathedral on Morningside Heights stood at the center of an almost monastic world. My mother was expected to be the bishop's hostess, while making a new life for herself and a refuge for the five children still at home in two stories of a mammoth stone mansion. The close, as the cathedral grounds were called, was thirteen acres of lawn, gardens, and granite buildings that housed the offices of a nearly entirely male community. Through the leaded windows of the apartment, my mother could see priests walk from office to cathedral, cathedral to office. One of them, bald and bearded, nearly always wore a cassock and an embroidered hat. He was a canon (senior priest) of the cathedral and lived in a cathedral apartment with a rottweiler, which, one day, as my mother watched from a window, attacked a smaller dog, the corgi belonging to my father's predecessor Bishop Donegan, which had been a gift from the Queen Mother. My mother shouted, called cathedral security, and ran downstairs; by the time she reached the scene, the dog had died. Weeping, she berated my father about the canon's carelessness, and the incident obsessed her.

She no longer had the boundless energy required to keep everyone happy, and every day, five children came home from school homesick. A night of sleep no longer revived her. She went first to doctors and then to psychiatrists. She sought out old friends living in New York and took freelance writing assignments for the *Washington Post*. But she began to long for her lilacs on Newark Street, her rose garden, her circle of friends. In my first consciousness-raising group, I was coming to see her predicament as a woman. I was reading whatever women's liberation literature I could get my hands on, and I was one of a group of women raising money to free Joan Bird, one of the two women Black Panthers incarcerated in New York. We were writing about her, flyers and analyses to be published in the underground newspapers that would bring to women's liberation, as feminism was then called, a politics of antiracism. My mother was wary. "Honor," she wrote Pam, "is a little overboard (I think) on Women's Lib. & Black Panther fund raising, but who knows."

She was trying to write again, and I was encouraging her. *The People on Second Street* had sold well and an excerpt had appeared in the *Washington Post*; after publishing several features there, she had a contract for a book on aging. She was forty-seven, she had survived, what came next? She'd done some exploratory interviews with older people, but now she couldn't bring herself to continue. New friends and some people she had known for years—the group included psychotherapists, actors, and playwrights—were meeting, trying to combine prayer and introspection with some of the new thinking about psychotherapy. After a few meetings, though, my mother left the group. She couldn't speak openly, she said; she didn't want to compromise my father. To me her situation was not so complicated: why would she silence herself for a man? I didn't know that she and my father were trying to figure out how to separate. Later I would believe my mother was having affairs on the sly, and that my father was suffering alone. Actually they had agreed to see other people, and he was dating no fewer than five women, among them, Nona Clark. Once that fall my mother surprised me by asking me when oral sex had come "into vogue." I had no idea what to say.

We were sitting in the Palm Court at the Plaza having lunch. The space was open, white floors, high ceilings, palm trees. My mother's face was impassive, seeming almost to look away as I told her about Johnny, the man I was now seeing, who rode a motorcycle. I would go to his small apartment in Chelsea, a corridor of darkness, one room behind the next. He was my age, and he worked in advertising so he had real furniture, a leather sofa, low wooden tables, shiny lamps that had once been tobacco cans or outdoor lanterns or automobile equipment. One day he said, "I'll buy a real Tiffany lamp, keep it for a few years, and sell it at a great profit." My family didn't sell their antiques, and I wasn't used to people who talked like that about money; I spent most of my time with radicals who talked about Mao and the end of capitalism. I remember sitting smoking in the dark, each of us with a glass of Scotch. Perhaps we would go out to dinner to some undistinguished restaurant of the kind common then: booth, burger and salad, red wine. And then on the motorcycle we would ride back to his place and have sex, sex in which the silences were vacant, the breathing athletic. One weekend he took me away to the Delaware Water Gap with a couple of his friends and their girlfriends. Each couple had a cabin; the men did the barbecuing and the women made the salad. In our cabin there were two small rooms; Johnny gave me one and took the other; we didn't have sex, and after that weekend, he never called again. I couldn't tell my consciousness-raising group that despite the fact that another male chauvinist pig had fucked me over, I was sad, and so that day in the Palm Court, I decided to confide in my mother. But as I talked, she sat there without speaking, her hands in her lap, or fingering her glass.

I suppose that while she sat looking at her hands my mother was trying to decide what to say to me about Johnny. Usually she was not at a loss for words, but she didn't say, for instance, "I'm so sorry that happened to you." If she started to talk, it was probably about my brothers and sisters, for instance, how Susanna and Patience, the two youngest, were getting to Manhattan Country School on East Ninety-sixth Street or how she was having so much trouble getting started on the aging book. I didn't know she had a lover and so I did not understand what the significance was when she told me that after lunch she was going to visit a man she had mentioned frequently. Years later I would learn she had been involved with this man and that he was the only man for whom she had ever considered leaving my father. Now, though, he was marrying another woman and she was going to meet that other woman. "This is very important," she said. "It is very important that I meet her, that we become friends." Perhaps she lit a cigarette, or perhaps she was picking at her food. As I fumbled for something to say, I could hear forks scraping and hitting china as waiters moved across the wide spaces carrying serving plates protected with silver domes.

Letters between my parents from this period were anguished. The reconciliation they'd hoped New York would bring had not come about, and my father was mystified, desperate with hope my mother would return to their physical life together. Her letters were alternately angry and desiring of reconciliation: "I want to live with you and be your lover." Beginning to see my mother's suffering, I now had less sympathy for my father, who seemed to me to have all the power. As my mother came to mistrust my father's feelings for her, I felt myself internally withdrawing from him, as if putting him on probation. I was not aware they were again struggling, turning over alternative plans: a dual household with residences in Washington and New York; a scenario in which my father would quit his new job, the position he had so longed for, and they would move the family back to Washington.

Eventually I hear enough from each of them to know all is not well. My mother tells me of her return to the psychiatrist she'd seen when they lived in Jersey City, of lunch with this or that old friend. My father tells me he misses her, her participation in his work. At first, it seems, he will do anything to please her. Does she want to live in an apartment off the close? He buys one on Park Avenue, but she finds it sterile and they never move in. Eventually his pastoral empathy deserts him. He seems to forget she is still in a weakened state; he is angry, even a little vengeful. But she is simply surviving: she has almost died, had lain in that hospital bed for months—what had happened to her life? She meets my psychiatrist at a party: "I met your doctor," she reports. I ask him what he thinks of her. "Your mother is very seductive," he replies.

That October was my twenty-fifth birthday, and my mother asked if I'd like her to give me a party. I could ask anyone I wanted, she said. I invited the members of my women's consciousness-raising group, new friends, and she invited a woman writer whose parents she'd known in Jersey City, Toni Cade Bambara. I was surprised and pleased that my mother wanted to give me a party, but nothing prepared me for her present. Though I didn't think of it at the time, it was as if she was trying to repair what her declaration in the Adirondacks had shattered the year before. The box was enormous, and when I opened it I found four leather-bound scrapbooks—orange, blue, yellow, bright apple green—all identically embossed with gold borders. In them were enlargements of perhaps fifty photographs—of the family, of each grandmother and grandfather, of herself and my father when they were children, teenagers, engaged, a wedding picture. And pictures of me throughout my life. Now, of course, the age of twenty-five seems barely the end of childhood, but at the time I believed I'd had a life and gotten myself to the conclusion of one phase of it and to the threshold of the next. I was amazed and delighted when my mother acknowledged this by giving me those four scrapbooks.

Present-giving is a challenge for a mother of nine children. When does she begin shopping for Christmas? How will she manage to perform the act of imagination necessary to find each child a present that will give him or her the new sense of self we in our family believed a birthday present should represent? Perhaps it seems strange, even melodramatic, this emphasis on birthdays. But think of it. There are nine of us, and there is just one day a year when each is celebrated for who she is independent of the others, and that day is her birthday. You are a child of privilege but one of nine; love is spread thin and so its material demonstrations are especially important. Each Christmas, each birthday as well, you receive several presents, one of which is designated your "big" present "with love from Mommy and Poppy." It is the "big" present that you scrutinize for clues as to who you are, or at least who your parents think you are.

Often, for me, the message was unclear. Our final Christmas in Washington, I had opened with great anticipation a large package. In it, I found sixteen glasses—eight tumblers and eight short glasses. They were rather heavy glass, painted turquoise and gold, and I thought they were hideous. I tried to stretch and distort my mind to find them at least "attractive," a word we used to denote something that partook of our family aesthetic. Turquoise and gold stripes were an aberration, and I didn't understand what my mother meant by them. I must have looked, what, shocked? Disappointed?

"Thank you, Mommy," I said.

"Don't you think they're good-looking?" she said, reaching for the next child's present.

Was I supposed to give cocktail parties? Learn precisely how much alcohol went in what size glass? Or was I supposed to move to the suburbs? Who did she think I was? I wanted to be a writer, and my love life, such as it was, showed no sign of evolving into a suburban marriage. My efforts to disguise my disappointment apparently failed, because, later in the interminable present-opening process—nine of us, one at a time so we could all admire and exclaim, so the list could be kept that ensured a thank-you note went to the correct giver—anyway, sometime after I opened the glasses, my mother disappeared and returned with a small box. "Here," she said. "I thought you might feel gypped." The replacement present was extraordinary, a Victorian brooch I had never seen my mother wear, a butterfly, its abdomen a large baroque pearl, its wing a banner of tiny diamonds and different-colored sapphires. It had belonged to her grandmother.

The jump cut from the ugly glasses to the glorious pin was confusing. It took me decades not to dismiss the butterfly because it was a last-minute idea. The scrapbooks, on the other hand, were remarkable. They represented something I had desired without knowing it, my mother's individualized and particular time and attention. They were also unusual for a "big" present in that they were specifically from my mother. She had arranged the pictures chronologically, and the colors of the books may have been a reference to *The Golden Notebook*, the novel we were both reading at the time, in which Doris Lessing's heroine inscribes her life and thinking in different-colored notebooks. To complete the final book, my mother had snipped out a passage from the end of *The Scarlet Letter*. Hester Prynne, long past her humiliation and suffering, has become the wise woman who assures young women who come to her "of her firm belief, that, at some brighter period, when the world would have grown ripe for it, in Heaven's own time, a new truth would be revealed, in order to establish the whole relation between man and woman on a surer ground of mutual happiness." This she pasted inside the back cover of the yellow scrapbook, opposite a black-and-white photograph of me that Pop had taken the summer before, smiling, long-haired, wearing a swagger of a hat that I remember was salmon pink and a purple band jacket trimmed with gold—very 1970.

The party was in the living room of the cathedral apartment, a nearly perfect cube, leaded windows set high in the walls, a granite fireplace in the Gothic style. You entered the room by stepping down three stairs. I was sitting on a sofa as my father came in, kissed the top of my head, said "Happy Birthday," and tossed into my lap a cheap set of brandy glasses, the kind that come six to a set and are packaged in a light cardboard structure that resembles a six-pack for beer. Glasses again!

That is when it breaks into the open, the difficulty that had been building between my father and me.

As I replay the memory—the tall man, fifty years old, coming down the stairs into the room where his eldest daughter is celebrating her twenty-fifth birthday, and tossing a six-pack of cheap glasses into her lap—what I see is not only the stinginess my psychiatrist suggested it was, but indifference bordering on anger. Anger at what? When my mother announced that day in the Adirondacks, *I am having some problems with my marriage*, I was angry at her, but not at my father. I saw him as victim of her insatia-

ble and inexplicable need for some life independent of us and him. I had
not really understood my mother's situation, and I'd felt terrible for my
father. By the time this change played itself out, I would see my father as
my mother saw him, and he would see me as he now saw my mother, as
a woman who was rejecting him. But I knew none of this the night of my
twenty-fifth birthday; his distance only confused me. Why had he tossed
those glasses onto my lap?

In the years to come, I would learn that my father expressed anger easily but rarely in language, and that he knew how to put a passable spin
on a hostile message. But back to the brandy glasses. He knew I liked to
drink, but he had not stopped to consider whether at the age of twenty-five
I drank much brandy. Actually I drank wine, but the glasses were liqueur
glasses, so, not only were they cheap, they were of no use to me. They
were an insult. "Your father is a little stingy," my psychiatrist explained, "a
little withholding." If your father were generous, the doctor continued, he
would have had some of your poems privately printed in a little book.

What an idea! I still hold that nonexistent little book in my imagination. It has a rust-colored cover, my name under a title my father has
invented. The book is a surprise. Because this imaginary version of my
father had always been so interested in my writing, he was always the
first person to whom I showed a poem. He'd kept them all in a folder he
treasured, and when I turned twenty-five, he'd had this small collection
privately printed, the most wonderful gesture of support a father could
give a poet daughter. The psychiatrist's imagining was not so far-flung:
it had always been my father to whom I wrote what I was reading, with
whom I shared my innermost thoughts, not my mother. So why this sudden shift, this insult? And what did I do with the glasses? Perhaps I had
the nerve to toss them into a garbage bin on my way home that evening,
but it's more likely I kept them, allowing them to gather dust in the back
of a cupboard.

15
Killing Me Softly

At a party in 1969 in the Berkshires the summer after the abortion, the summer I knew Arnold was leaving me, I met a man named Venable. I liked the urgent way he talked to me, saying my name, telling me about himself and the woman he lived with. He had a shock of dark brown hair and blue eyes that were magnified by the round glasses he wore. He looked so young I was surprised to learn that he was forty-two, Arnold's age and eighteen years older than me. Like Arnold, Venable knew more than one language, and like Arnold, he was a playwright, but he also wrote for the movies. To see him again after that night, I invited him to translate from the French for the press conference I had organized for Eugène Ionesco, whose play *Hunger and Thirst* the theater I worked for was presenting. This was an English-language premiere by the famous absurdist, and reporters from all over New England came to interview him, Venable interpreting. Afterward, he and I took the playwright and his wife and daughter to an African restaurant in the countryside. At the end of the summer, Venable came to a party I gave. I begged him just to kiss me. "No," he said, "I can't do that." He was living with Jocelyn, who had black curls down her back. "Can we just have lunch?" "No," he said, "not even lunch."

In September, I moved to New York City, into a room at the Chelsea Hotel with a kitchenette and a balcony overlooking Twenty-third Street. A plaque on the door memorialized Dylan Thomas and a few other dead writers as former residents, but Arthur Miller, the last famous writer who'd lived there, had long moved out. I recognized the painting by Arnold's friend Larry Rivers in the lobby, but not Viva, the Warhol superstar with whom I shared the elevator, nor did I know that the bearded pot dealer upstairs was an Iranian prince who secreted a heroin stash under his sink. I was coproducing the first play by a woman named Tina Howe, an extreme comedy about three girls entertaining their boyfriends in a New York high-rise, and when I wasn't at the office I was sitting in front of my typewriter at a desk facing Twenty-third Street "writing a novel."

No sooner had I settled into a routine than Arnold turned up in New York. We had dinner, and he spent that night, and the next. Soon he was calling his friends, telling them he was "at the Chelsea," in town to translate the libretto of Brecht and Weill's opera *Rise and Fall of the City of Mahagonny*, to be produced on the Lower East Side by the man responsible for their earlier work *The Threepenny Opera*, which ran for years on Christopher Street and whose marquee I saw every time I left St. Luke's School and walked to the Hudson Tube. Were Arnold and I back together? I knew he had nowhere else to go (his apartment was sublet), that he'd never contribute to the rent, and that I couldn't write when he slept half the day, but I wasn't finished with him. He took me to Bradley's for supper and jazz, introduced me to musicians like Paul Desmond and Elvin

Jones, whom he knew from "the old days at the Five Spot" and who came to our table for a drink, and to the proprietor, who also had a girlfriend in her twenties. He harangued me about the play I was producing—"If it has characters, it *can't* be good"—and every few days dove into a doctor's office on Central Park South for a shot of speed and vitamins while I waited at the wheel of my Corvair. At the "Sweet Sixteen" party Larry Rivers gave for his redhead girlfriend, he disappeared into the back room, leaving me to fend for myself. I was too shy to approach anyone in the glamorous mob of Abstract Expressionist and Pop Art painters, New York School and Beat poets, collectors and girlfriends, so I stood there watching Jackie Curtis, the first drag queen I'd seen up close, dab perspiration from the brow of a be-tuxed "Lennie" Bernstein as onlookers gushed and murmured.

Some nights Arnold would go out after supper, promise he'd be back by midnight, and never return. Some nights I sat quietly as he and the producer worked through lyrics for *Mahagonny*, a pianist playing the score. They would draw the Fillmore East audience, Arnold told me; the star would be Linda Ronstadt, whose single "Different Drum" was a recent hit. I thought Arnold and I would marry, I told my psychiatrist, but that came to seem less and less likely. One day, as I wept lying on the psychiatrist's narrow couch, he told me that Arnold was "exploitative" and possibly a "sociopath." He asked what my fantasies were, and I told him that sometimes I saw myself standing near a bed, a pistol in my hand pointed at Arnold as he slept. "Is that a fantasy?" I asked.

By the time Tina Howe's play closed after one night, Arnold was long gone, and I was finally free to throw myself entirely into the women's movement and radical politics, writing the rest of the time. One day that fall, near Union Square, Abbie Hoffman had picked me up. I'd read *Revolution for the Hell of It*, the book he'd published, "Free" his non de plume. It was a manifesto of the Yippies who infused hippie rebellion with politics at events he and Jerry Rubin organized, like a "Be-in" in Central Park. Now he and Rubin and five others including Tom Hayden and David Dellinger, an activist who was my father's contemporary, were going on trial for conspiring to disrupt the Democratic Convention the summer before in Chicago. The group was originally called the Chicago Eight, but when the case of Bobby Seale, one of the defendants, was severed from the trial, they became the Chicago Seven. At pretrial hearings, they had already demonstrated their plan. By taunting the judge and comically twisting legal rhetoric, they would make the trial an epic tour de force of political theater. "You can produce our movie," Abbie Hoffman declared right there on the street. The next thing I knew, I had a date for lunch with him and Jerry Rubin. I'll ask Venable to write the screenplay, I said to myself. Venable had written *Alice's Restaurant*, a hit movie of the year before inspired by Arlo Guthrie's talking blues about being arrested for throwing out garbage and getting out of the draft. The movie's droll touch helped turn draft resistance into a national phenomenon, grist for satire. I called Venable in Los Angeles and told him I was about to have lunch with Abbie Hoffman and Jerry Rubin about a Chicago Seven movie. "Tell them you'll do it if we can write it as an animated film," he said. Over lunch at Max's Kansas City, a place that didn't look good in daylight, Hoffman and Rubin said they didn't see their story as a cartoon.

The following summer, in Stockbridge for a play, I saw Venable briefly, and when I got home to New York, I sent him some of my poems. A few weeks later the telephone rang. It was a Sunday afternoon, and I was lying on the mattress and plank bed Arnold had set up in the tiny bedroom of his apartment, which he had sublet to me as compensation for his departure, his return to Chicago, and his hasty marriage to another brunette in her twenties. But I was thinking of Venable, and here he was. He liked the poems, he said, and he'd rented an apartment just around the corner. Had I ever read Pablo Neruda? Would I like to have dinner? He took me to Casey's, a glamorous restaurant on Tenth Street where I'd gone many times with Arnold, and afterward, back at his apartment, he gave me books by Neruda, and then we went to bed. Or perhaps we went to bed before dinner because I remember light coming through filmy white curtains. I think we had one more evening together, and then he disappeared, back to Los Angeles or to Stockbridge, and I didn't hear from him again.

Some of my political friends were moving to St. Louis to live collectively, take "straight jobs," and do organizing. I was drawn to the people— the woman at the center of the group, just thirty, had five children, and charisma like my mother's. She said I had "great politics." It would be like Jersey City, but centered on Marxism instead of the church. "Come on," she kept saying "come with us. And we'll get you knocked up. Or maybe you want to be with a woman." I didn't move to St. Louis. I didn't want to get "knocked up" nor did I want to "be" with a woman. I wanted to write, but I had such misgivings: most of my friends had to work—what business did I have, a white girl with money, thinking I could just write? But Venable had liked my poems, and he suggested that I use my money to support myself while doing my own work. And so, late that fall of 1970, declaring myself a writer, I dropped out of my political groups. What I had been doing, as important as it was for "the movement," felt like my backstage work in the theater; organizing a demonstration like producing a play. I wanted to put forward something of my own. My poems, I promised my comrades, would be my contribution.

Sometime in the early winter, Venable called again, and, while breaking up with Jocelyn in long agonized telephone conversations, he courted me. He had been in Hollywood writing movies, the entitlement of *Alice's Restaurant*'s hit status still clinging to him; now, in New York, he was writing a play about father-daughter incest. Before long nights of making love, he wined and dined me on his Hollywood money, our evenings a primer in food and wine: Spanish at Granados on Bleecker Street, sushi at Kamehachi on Waverly Place, "eau Perrier" at a sandwich shop on Sixth Avenue, Italian at Portofino, where the chef Alfredo Viazzi and his wife, the actress Jane White, boisterously greeted us. Venable spoke Russian and had married a French writer and fathered her child when he was very young. He wore thrift-shop band jackets, which he dyed, striped shirts, and, always, a bow tie. He talked and talked, about books, about the theater, about French poets, about the advertising business where he had gotten his start, how the viciousness of Edward Albee's *Who's Afraid of Virginia Woolf?* had inspired him to write his own cruel play, *Until the Monkey Comes*, which got him the *Alice's Restaurant* job. Soon I moved out of Arnold's apartment and into Venable's.

By the beginning of 1971, Venable and I were making a life. With Radcliffe friends, I started a new consciousness-raising group—we were aspiring writers, actresses, filmmakers. Everything was going very fast, but not too fast for Venable: he had a vision. One night, he sat me down in a Greek restaurant and told me I was a real writer, that if I worked very hard, I would publish what I wrote, and that I would make my way as a person in "the New York literary world." He had once been an editor of *Chelsea*, a literary journal, and he took me to poetry readings—Denise Levertov, David Ignatow, Jerome Rothenberg. They all greeted him as a returning friend, and he introduced me as Honor Moore, a poet. I barely considered myself a poet, but every day now, watching Venable bent over

his desk, I bent over mine. *My grandmother had a stroke and the dishwasher /
broke down. Neither works anymore,* I wrote when Gami lost her speech to a
stroke. *Those eighty-seven years she owned / are really hers. She is taking them
with her.* Once a week or so, we took the subway uptown and sat around
the living room with my younger brothers and sisters, and my mother,
whom Venable called "Jenny." I was in denial that she was only four years
older than the boyfriend I was so proud to have; my consort, I called him.
Venable gave me a new way to know my brothers and sisters, five of whom
were still at home. He vigorously interviewed every one of them, explaining Freud and Jung, pointing out Oedipal and sexual innuendos in their
dreams, doing their numerology, encouraging their painting and writing.

My mother still seemed unhappy. Just before her birthday in March,
she checked into Mount Sinai for tests. When Venable and I got to the hospital room, she was asleep. "Oh, hello," she said dully, waking up. Her skin
was yellow again, as it had been after the accident. The doctors had found
"nothing," she told us. "I'm very tired," is what I remember her saying as
she smiled at Venable. Venable had a way of taking over any situation in
which he found himself, and usually I liked to let him, but there in the
dark hospital room with my sick mother, his talk about her possible condition seemed too loud and too dire. I wanted to reach out for my mother's
hand, to be the one on whom her eyes rested with the hope of rescue or
understanding. I wanted to protect her, climb into that bed, and pull her
arms around me. Everything Venable was saying and everything she said
or didn't say further shattered the new family I was just getting used to. My
mother was in a hospital bed again, tears in her dark blue eyes, her lashes
very black against dank skin. If only she could go back to Washington, she
said. What would my father do, I thought, rattling around that big apartment, suddenly a man alone? She turned her head away and continued.
She wanted to have a house in Washington again with a garden, life on the
leafy street with the children running in and out.

On one of my romantic wanderings with Venable through the city, I
bought a suit of a big geometric print of maroon and tan jersey, with a fitted jacket and an ankle-length gored skirt. I remember it because one day,
after a lunch out, I fell into bed still wearing it and the telephone jolted
me from a wine-induced nap. Because it might have been Jocelyn, Venable
answered, but he handed the phone to me. It was my father. The doctors,
having found "nothing physical," agreed that my mother was "depressed."

He wanted me to know that she had decided to go into Payne Whitney, the psychiatric ward of New York–Presbyterian Hospital.

A mental hospital! This had been my mother's lifelong fear. Every time she felt a little down, every time she felt the violence of her temper, she thought of her mother's years in sanitariums, courses of electroshock doing no good. I shared that fear: it was why I had never taken LSD, why I was now seeing a psychiatrist. My mother, with her buoyant energy, charisma, and presence, had always been my hedge against it. When I hung up, I went right to sleep, not bothering to change out of the suit or turn out the light. Eighteen hours later, I woke up. I tried to pretend that nothing had changed, but everything had changed. My hungry sexual abandon abruptly ceased, and I began to wonder what I was doing, living in an apartment that wasn't mine with a man almost twice my age whom I barely knew.

I saw my mother once at Payne Whitney, was let in through the locked door, led to what you could only call a cell. She sat at the edge of her narrow bed on a gunboat gray blanket wearing a cardigan and pants. She looked up, her teeth bright but her eyes mournful. I was with Venable, to whom this all seemed inevitable. But it did not seem inevitable to me; I was scared of this creature my mother had turned into, and fighting to keep my tears in. Venable talked to her as I looked on. I kept thinking of her on the telephone in Indianapolis, hearing the latest about her mother: after she hangs up, she painstakingly explains that Grandma Kean is sick, but in her head. Now she herself was sick like that, no longer possessed even of the force with which she slapped me that day in the room with the cherry wallpaper, shouted at me to neaten my room, or wrote letters in that distinct, upright hand, *We love you very much.*

It got harder for me to hang on to the mother I had known. During the weeks she was at Payne Whitney, she could get mean. On her first day pass, we had a family dinner at a Greek restaurant. When I reached for dessert, a piece of chocolate cake, she told a story she'd heard from a mutual friend about the poet Muriel Rukeyser, overweight, eating an entire chocolate cake at one sitting. "Can you believe it?" my mother exclaimed. Did I know Rukeyser's poems? Did I admire them? I'd better be careful. This kind of assault was new, and Venable and my psychiatrist wanted to protect me, but they had not known the mother I had always adored, the woman who could turn any room into a theater, everyone laughing, then suddenly still, attentive to what she'd say next.

The sun is out, the sky as blue as a sailor's pair of trousers, and I walk from the shadowy dark of the mental hospital cell, of the chocolate cake aria, into a past where her smile skews a room's geometry, noon sun hot and crystalline, its reflection off the lake brightening her teeth, the whites of her eyes, darkening her black-rimmed irises, throwing her tanned skin into shadow. If she is distracted, I bring her back: "Good evening, dear mother, breeze of the summer afternoon," I say in an actressy voice. And then one of the little ones runs to her, climbs onto her lap, and I watch her fingers move through child-short hair, her engagement diamond blinking in bouncing shards of light.

When I think of her in that room, another memory crowds in. We all sit at lunch, one lazy Susan at my end of the table, the other at hers. Absently I nudge the one at my end and watch as the cut-glass sugar bowls, one of brown and one of white sugar, pass me, slowly spinning toward my brother Pip, who sits across from me. I remember my mother at the head of the table, the sun out, the wind rustling all those millions of leaves, the lake shivery blue through the windows, the island in the corner of the lake a giant pincushion, and now there's a lull in the conversation, her smile, her head tossed with laughter at someone's good line. Except for my brother Pip, we are not a family in which anyone tells actual jokes, so my mother is laughing at a characterization or a turn of phrase, a remark that exposes absurdity. We had all competed for that laugh and now someone has won it, and she has thrown her head back.

"Mom," I hear myself say, "when you smile, it lights up the room."

There is silence. I remember reflection from the lake dappling the walls.

"Why, thank you, sweetie," she says, awkward.

No, on second thought I don't remember her saying anything. I remember silence, just pure silence, though I can't swear the room was really silent. A space opens between us, a path as straight as a chute, the path I lost when my first sibling was born, the path whose entrance receded further every time my mother and I fought, every time another child pushed out of her and she brought it home. But now it was opening again, that true path from me to her.

And then someone broke the spell. "I'll bet you never thought of yourself as a lightbulb, Mom."

I can't promise that was the sentence that actually began the ridicule, nor do I remember who said it, but a chorus of teasing, a sequence of that sort of remark, burst like pandemonium and obliterated the light, the chute, the path, the momentary view of heaven I had cleared through our history. *I have a war with my mother,* I wrote in a poem when I grew up. *It is longer than the longest war in history, / longer than a hundred years.* But when I return to that moment, as I do now, I am at that table again, the willow plates, sunlight fractured by the green mullions of the French doors, the expanse of lake, the mountains, the wide sky, and the fading image, my mother's tall body folded into the big chair, her laughing face, and me spinning the lazy Susan, watching the cut-glass sugar bowls, waiting for that lull in the conversation.

We are driving, my father and I, down a road somewhere. The landscape is not familiar, but it seems to me that we angle left onto a road whose surface is the color and texture of sand. It's hot and he's telling me how sad he is, that he doesn't know what to do, that he doesn't know what he's done, he's lost her, she won't talk to him anymore, she keeps saying she wants to go back to Washington. I don't want to hear how serious it is. Alone, he wrote notes to himself, an inventory of his feelings which I now have: *How do I feel about J. Very angry. Hurt. Feels like I have a hard ball inside— sometimes inside my spirit & sort of in my mind, a hard ball you can't unravel just then. And sometimes in my chest, hurting hurting hurting.* In the car that day, I could feel that hard ball, but unable to apprehend my father as hurt, I felt him as weak. What was I to do? I knew I felt something about how my mother was behaving—sadness, confusion—but to call it anger and join him in it seemed too dangerous and not my business. Instead, I spoke as a go-between, asking questions, representing my mother's point of view in the warmest language I could come up with, what she'd put so clearly, writing to me after Payne Whitney: *to see if I can hone down my conscience to live more of a life, and I keep fighting the failure syndrome not really in terms of the life I've led because I've done that well—but much of it, other than child-bearing & nurture, was not me, i.e. the backbreaking Xtian concept of immolation for everyone else. The great sadness is that I seem closed-in and undemonstrative, when under certain conditions (and I don't mean merely sexual), that is not the way I am at all.*

Now questions that had been unleashed during the summer of

1969—the summer my mother said *I am having some problems with my marriage*—and quieted that fall by my mother's near-death in the automobile accident and my father's election as bishop of New York, were reignited. It seemed crazy to me—the life in Washington had closed down, the house had been sold—but my mother was desperate. She was insisting that my father buy another house in Cleveland Park. She needed time to recover. She needed her old friends. In Washington, she was already a person in her own right; at home there, she could make her way. My father resisted. What about the children? He was their father. "I think the person who wants to leave should do the leaving," he wrote in the inventory of his feelings. Was he actually supposed to quit his job? If he didn't, it would seem to the children that "I put my career first." By midsummer, a decision was made. My father would buy a house in Cleveland Park, and my mother would move back with the five children who still lived at home. My father would commute for two days a week; Washington would be a second residence.

In a public letter to the diocese, he framed the separation as they had agreed: *I wish to thank all of you for your prayers and thoughtfulness over the last few months of Jenny's illness. It has been a rough winter for our family following last year's accident and hospitalization. After consultation with the doctor, we have concluded that Jenny should be in a quiet, familiar place where she can regain her strength and where it is easier to take care of the children.* The new house was diagonally across the street from 3400 Newark Street, where we'd lived when my father was suffragan. My mother redecorated 3319, built on a large living room, planted a rose garden, and installed a sprinkler system. The children were enrolled in local schools. My mother was profoundly relieved and grateful: *My life alone—and relationship with Poppy—are reconstructed in a way I never dreamed possible—albeit somewhat Jamesian and I feel an inner joy and clarity—*

Was it true what I remembered? That after near-death and the rages of long sadness and anger in Payne Whitney, that after she entered her new independent life, the mother I had never been able to trust made her way toward me in friendship? *Dear Honor, I tried to call this evening but no answer—really to hear your voice and tell you that I love you. You've been so*

generous with your brothers and sisters this year which has been so fragmented
for all of us . . . It must be hard to think of us all leaving after you've established
yourself so deeply and well in the family. I feel so right about it at this time that
there seems to be no other course of action to take, but we will all miss seeing
you as naturally & casually as we have this year . . . you have taught me a lot
by your courage, unerring sense of your direction—and your tireless search for
yourself . . . Do know that I will always come flying if you need me or want me
to . . . She was writing a play and had "unearthed" ten thousand words of
a novel she wrote before the accident: *I'm thunderstruck at how well it reads.*
And she had applied to the master's program in writing at Johns Hopkins—
because I think getting really out will help my double mother writer life. She flew
to New York for a poetry reading I gave: *I loved being there last night and I felt*
you did an excellent job under conditions hardly human—distance & darkness
of audience etc. . . . I really do want copies of those you'd like to have me have,
& especially & soon the last one you read about "the life I live" for my bathroom
bulletin board.

She was also looking to married women friends who had made creative
lives, like Toni Bradlee, Ben's wife, who made sculptures she found *stern*
and quite beautiful—white concrete on wooden blocks—and she does every bit
of them herself (by that I mean the carpentry as well as the casting). And she
was reading—Woolf, de Beauvoir, the first issues of *Ms.*: "Have you seen
the latest issue?" she asked in a phone call. "Something called *Combat in*
the Erogenous Zone by a young writer named Ingrid Bengis? So courageous.
Do you know her?"

As I made my way with Venable, my mother made hers without a husband, but late in 1972 she wrote me in confidence that she was having a
love affair. She didn't mention that she and my father had again agreed to
see others, nor did she tell me who her lover was. I now know it was Artie
Trevor, also married, "whom I would have married if it hadn't been for
your father." I opened the letter of announcement, now lost, at my desk on
Twenty-second Street, in my study in the duplex Venable and I had moved
into together. I was looking out at the trees, at the backs of the brick houses
across the garden. Of my cautiously supportive reply, also lost, my mother
wrote, *I loved your letter (a) because it was honest (b) because it was so clear*
and intelligent . . . on the "high risk" we are very careful—never have dinner in
town etc. etc. Also, he has an apt. so no motel-life is needed . . . In New York my

father was dating a few women, but in Washington he cowered, desperate to please my mother, though to me it seemed clear she didn't want him around. I was sure of my parents' good intentions, but not certain how good their awkward visits were for the children still at home.

At its convention in the spring of 1971, the Diocese of New York had taken initial steps toward the ordination of women to the priesthood, and one night after supper in Washington, my father and I began a conversation about it. It will happen, he said, but it is important to go slowly, not to "rock the boat." If we wait until the boat sails in calm water, I said, we'll wait another two thousand years! The women's movement, I argued, is nothing less than a reconfiguring of exactly the kind of hierarchy the church represents. "I hear you," my father replied, restrained and pastoral. I wanted him to come to a radical position, and I was about to push further when my mother, who had been quietly listening, began to pound the table with her fist. "Why would women *want* to be priests?" she shouted. I began to explain how I imagined the nature of the church would be changed by women's ordination, but my mother wasn't listening. She was in a fury. "The church," she said, almost hissing, "the church is just second-rate," and then, weeping, she left the room. My father said nothing. Their differences were clearly deeper than I imagined.

In September 1972, Bishop Horace Donegan retired, and my father was installed as diocesan bishop of New York, with my mother, in spite of her ambivalence, and most of his children in attendance. For its Christmas issue, *Newsweek* celebrated by putting the new bishop on the cover, photographed in color in a red cope and miter, holding a gold crozier or bishop's crook, stained glass behind him. He looked like a Christmas card. In the photograph, his face looks a little sad, and there is something close to the bone about the cover line, "The Church Faces Life," and about the title of the article, "An Activist Bishop Faces Life." The "life" under discussion was not that of our family, but the new reality the Christian church faced with the end of the heady 1960s. The article opened with a description of my father's installation service and went on to discuss the uphill battle the new bishop faced in his huge diocese and his plan to launch major fund-raising efforts for ambitious initiatives in urban work. "In the Cathedral's soaring Gothic nave," the reporter wrote, the cast of the rock musical *Godspell* danced and sang through the traditional Anglican Holy Communion service. Outside 5,000 well wishers—blacks and Puerto Ricans from nearby Harlem and the WASPish well-to-do from Wall Street and Park Avenue picnicked on the broad Cathedral close. Promptly at 3 p.m., the most solemn moment of the day began. With a fanfare of trumpets, the great bronze cathedral doors swung open to admit a procession of prelates in brightly colored vestments. When it was all over, a rock band joined the choir in a joyous Gloria in Excelsis from a mass written by the composer of *Hair*, and the Episcopal Diocese of New York had a new bishop—the Rt. Rev. Paul Moore, Jr.

Accompanying the article were photographs of my father performing a confirmation in Harlem, marching with Martin Luther King Jr. for Home Rule in Washington in 1968, fleeing tear gas at a Saigon peace rally in 1970. Of my parents standing together at my sister Adelia's wedding in the Adirondacks two months earlier, and a game of touch football in the Washington yard, "with Jenny and the children." The family's unconventional living situation was ascribed to my mother's having "collapsed and ended up in a psychiatric clinic" after nearly dying in an automobile accident. "I obviously couldn't cope with New York City and five kids under 17," my mother told the interviewer. "It was too big a burden to carry." My father was characterized as a "commuting father."

"I was 'on' with the *Newsweek* article," my mother wrote me from Washington in January after attending her first consciousness-raising meeting; "not its results but the conflict of being interviewed for it—& feeling I had to 'protect' throughout . . ." On my twenty-seventh birthday that October, she came to visit. Venable and I had taken over the house in Kent as a weekend retreat and, in lieu of rent, we were restoring it. My mother arrived the day before my birthday, a Friday, with a painted tin box about eight inches square, which she immediately put into the refrigerator. On Saturday, my birthday, she took the box out and opened it. In it was a walnut torte she had baked in Washington and transported on the plane and in the rented car she'd driven up from LaGuardia. She whipped some cream and slathered it on the cake. After supper, she presented me with a package in which there was a flimsy magenta binder. I opened it, and in it, awkwardly pasted on loose-leaf pages, were pictures of roses she'd cut from a garden catalogue. Ten of them. "The bushes will arrive in March," she said, "and you and Venable will plant them."

At breakfast the next morning, she and I discussed where I might put my rose garden. "You'll want to be able to see it," she said, "when you're working in the kitchen." We decided on a place out back, just outside the screen porch. As we washed the lunch dishes, she noted my lack of silver flatware—for my sister Adelia's wedding present, my mother had collected antique silver, rather than "a boring old set from Tiffany's." She knew that Venable was not yet divorced, and that we were "against" marriage. "But that's no reason you shouldn't have silver," she said. "I'll start looking." After lunch, Venable carried her suitcase down the front steps, and after we kissed her goodbye, we stood on the porch under the ancient twin wedding maples as she got into her white rented car. We were waving, and then she drove away, and as I watched the car disappear, I began to cry, and I couldn't stop. "Don't worry," Venable said, putting his arm around me. "She'll come back."

My father gave my mother a fiftieth birthday party that March at the F Street Club in Washington. At the very long table were seated many of their close friends. Venable and I flew down from New York; I wore a long navy blue wool dress and a sapphire bracelet my mother had given me. Standing, I sang the words I'd written to the Kurt Weill–Ira Gershwin song, *Jenny made her mind up*, and my father his to Irving Berlin's "Cheek to Cheek": *Heaven, we're in heaven / And her heart keeps beating so that she can hardly speak / For we seem to find the happiness we seek / Now that Jenny Moore / Has finally reached her peak.* There were toasts and dancing, and toward the end of the evening the pianist struck up "Cheek to Cheek," and my parents turned toward each other. Soon they were the only couple on the floor, my mother in a long, brightly flowered dress, the nine gold bangles on her wrists, my father in a suit and necktie, the two of them smiling. In spite of all I now know, I like to think that dance was when they decided to try to reconcile. "It will not be easy but we must have faith in each other," my mother had written my father a year before. "I need to lie in your arms & tell you everything . . . I want to be in Washington for a time in order to grow—and *not* to escape from you—I want to be whole & to be your wife and lover." And he had written her, "I want to retract my part of the conversation about the future. I am going to hang in, as it were, for the foreseeable future."

Days after the party, I got a thank-you letter. My mother loved the towels I'd given her for the house in Virginia, and my song. She hadn't been feeling well at the party, and was going to have more tests. *Am nervous about the hospital—it ticks off so many eras—some pleasurable like babies, others—*the final page of the letter is lost. She and my father spent the weekend after the party together in the house she'd bought with her book royalties in the country in Virginia, talking about the future of their relationship. The following Friday, Venable and I drove to Kent and spent Saturday planting the rosebushes. Late that night, I was wakened by a call from my father. My mother had cancer of the colon which had spread to her liver. I flew to Washington and in the following days we learned that she had six months to live. There was no chance chemotherapy could save her life and little chance it would give her more time.

"Everything was just starting," my mother said, weeping, as I sat with her, helplessly, in the hospital. Another public letter was sent to the diocese, and my father took a leave and spent some months, the spring and the summer, seeking out alternative cures all over the country. My sister Rosemary was in Washington, living with a boyfriend, and she and a nurse and friends of my mother's who arrived for weeks at a time, produced wheatgrass juice from a juicer and administered pills under the care of a medical doctor who had converted to naturopathy when he cured himself of cancer.

Often that summer, she was very well. "Mom really looked beautiful in the turquoise caftan & turquoise beads. God I hope she doesn't die. I almost can't keep my hands off her," I wrote in my diary. Some evenings, as we sat on the porch after supper, her childhood friend Ben Bradlee, now editor of the *Washington Post*, would arrive with tantalizing hints of what the paper would break the following morning about the evolving Watergate scandal, and one afternoon my mother and I watched Billie Jean King beat Bobby Riggs in "the tennis match of the century." The surgeon who had proclaimed there was no hope was amazed at her strength, and the naturopath said that if he could keep her alive till mid-October, she'd survive.

But one night in Kent in late September, an inordinately heavy wind raced through the limbs of the giant maples, and Rosie called to say my mother was in the hospital and that this time it was different. Venable and I packed the next morning, jumped into the car, and were on the shuttle by evening, a bouquet of roses from the new garden in my arms. During the days that followed, my mother slipped in and out of a coma, and one day all nine of us and my father stood around her hospital bed. "See you tomorrow," I said the next afternoon, kissing her goodbye.

"I don't think we need any Custers," she answered.

"Custards?" I asked.

"No, Custers." And then, "Goodbye, darling."

The October 3 entry in my diary reads, "Mom died 4:45 a.m. Pop called me at 5:20 & we went over to the hospital." She'd had her last stand by herself, with the night nurse.

"Room peaceful. Purged," I wrote.

The funeral was in the National Cathedral. Already I was carrying my mother inside me. She had been slender as a girl those weeks at home in the big double bed, raising her arms in the air "conducting" as Roberta Flack sang "Killing Me Softly," which she got us to play again and again, the sound of her fingers brushing against each other like dry grass. *Whish.* The service she planned would be an "Agape," an early Christian rite; everyone, not just confirmed Episcopalians, could greet each other, drink the wine, and eat the bread, which was carried down the aisle in huge baskets. The cathedral was full; aunts and uncles and cousins, friends from all over, busloads from Indianapolis and Jersey City. My mother's mother, Margarett, swathed in black lace in a wheelchair; Dorothy Day, now very old, who had taken the bus from New York; my old boyfriend, Luke Marston. One of my friends imagined my mother sitting at the foot of the altar in blue jeans, watching as the men who were her close friends—Bob Potter, Ben Bradlee, Artie Trevor, her writing teacher Astere Claeyssans, Blair Clark, and Roger Wilkins—bore her pine coffin down the aisle.

There is a newspaper photograph of all of us on the steps of the cathedral before the funeral, my father's long hair lifted by the wind as he holds on to the younger children. Some days before my mother died, I had found myself alone with him in a hospital waiting room. "I remember her on the sheets," he said, "she was so beautiful." And then he wept and wept, and I held him.

16
Art and Life

The roses my mother sent survived the winter and bloomed again the following summer. I saved the tin box she'd brought the cake in, and the four scrapbooks she so lovingly put together exist outside the charged realm of imagination I reserve for the things of which I've been deprived. All these years later, their leather covers—orange, blue, green, yellow— are perfectly intact: I've never lost them, have always meticulously replaced the photos I've removed for any purpose. They are strangely buoyant, these large, brightly colored books, and, with the butterfly pin and a particular letter, are evidence that her love for me came to have substance: *I often think of you in the early morning—Susanna and I have a half hour before everyone else gets up. She feeds Lucy—and we eat and talk—about things like the branches against the light of winter sky—and that her favorite colors are "bright black and silver"—She reminds me of you—and I wish I'd had the peace and composure to talk in those days when you were twelve. I remember we made coffee cake in Jersey City—and made artificial flowers but not under conditions of a bright winter sky! There are so many times in life when you really don't know what you're doing!*

In her will, written the last weeks of her life, my mother left me her writings. I was to use or develop them in any way I saw fit. I took this bequest as her blessing of the life on which I was already embarked, the life of a writer, and when I left Washington after her funeral, I rented a car for the journey home, loading it with cartons of her manuscripts. Not only, I believed, had she left me what she had started to write, she'd left me her ambition, her dreams, her imagination. In my top-floor studio in Chelsea, I found refuge. Carefully, I filed her manuscripts and stored her letters to me in an Italian-paper document box.

But what would I write now? Looking for women writing about their mothers, I found Simone de Beauvoir, writing of her mother's death: "as violent and unforeseen as an engine stopping in the middle of the sky." I was at the edge of a crater rapacious with darkness, at my typewriter holding on to its keys, beneath me my great-grandmother's Chinese rug. I wrote my first attempts with purposeful melodrama: *How will it impress itself on this cruel world that I am bereft of my mother?* And in dreams, she returned, black-haired, breathing the death rattle from the dark of her hospital bed, or radiant, enthroned in a bright green field. And I dreamed of myself, on the lawn in Kent, trying to fix the dishwasher. *The dishwasher broke down / My grandmother had a stroke.* Now it was my mother I would approach in writing: *a series of poems, taken from this journal, about Mom,* I wrote in my diary that week after her death. *First get it out, then give it form.*

The four children still at home stayed on in Washington, my father with them, still on leave from the job in New York. A weekend after the death, I visited to help my sister Rosemary clear out my mother's bureau and closets. My father was bereft, at a loss as to what he should do. How could he uproot my two youngest sisters again? They were ten and twelve, and their mother had died. But could he resign his job and live in Washington? One morning, I walked into the guest room where he was staying— no one was sleeping in the bed wreathed with baby pictures, the room my mother died from. My father was bending over, putting something into a suitcase. I asked a question. "Do you think you'll marry again, Pop?" He looked up. "I don't want to marry again quickly," he said. "It's so easy to get caught."

In my dreams, my mother became insistent, night after night turning toward me, her face gaunt. Or reaching for my hand, hers in the cuff of a white Irish sweater, and I would wake, waking Venable. "Just go upstairs and write," he would say. I read and reread Adrienne Rich. "A woman in the shape of a monster / a monster in the shape of a woman / the skies are full of them." And then one day, I began. On a shuttle to Washington right after my mother was diagnosed, I had written, *Ladies and gentlemen, my mother is dying*, imagining myself walking the airplane aisle, past business travelers bent over newspapers. Now I made a poem, then poems, my friends offering support. One sent a silver letter opener that had belonged to her mother, dead when my friend was in her teens; another framed a photograph of Gertrude Stein. Paul Schmidt, who had stayed in the apartment over the summer, wrote: *As I always do when I've been to your house, I come away very peaceful and full of strong literary resolve. Tell Venable his prodding has so far produced 15 pages which I am tempted to call a memoir—the inner me, in English at last.* Venable had encouraged him to write the truth about his bisexual life. Now Venable was prodding me, too.

12/23 Washington. I am not sure that I am any more able to go pick out a gravestone for Mom than Poppy is. My father had asked that Rosemary and I go to the cemetery and decide between marble and granite. He was turning away from my mother, and, as I turned toward her in my writing, I could feel him also turn from me. Was he leaving me because I still loved her? Had he forgotten the day I remembered so clearly the week before she died? They had reconciled, he'd told me, radiant. Had found each other again. But now, he no longer talked to me about what he was feeling. In this way, my writing, the dimension in which I was most alive, the part of my life in which my mother was present, came to exclude my father.

12/24 Washington. I feel as if I must have full time for writing—and I don't.

I must go back and write every day or else, which the holidays, the terrible mill-stone of the family has helped me let slip . . . Irritation. Sickness. My poem. The most terrible missing of Mom. It is almost grotesque to sit around the table with-out her. The whole thing is undynamic without her, static. Cleaning up the vari-ous living rooms. The debris of death choking everything. At the typewriter, my fingers slipped from the keys. "Why are you doing something so private when you are such a public person?" asked a friend from Yale, a public woman herself. "It is difficult to write poems about one's dead mother," proclaimed the distinguished poet, a man who had been my mentor. "Keep going, Wonz," repeated Venable, using his nickname for me. "You must do this," said the older woman writer I barely knew. And I walk around my studio, my feet bare, Granny Moore's Chinese carpet soft under my feet, its blue and creamy colors vibrating in the early winter light. Again I press the keys: *If she could only sleep.* Condense. Count syllables. Make poems.

For a reading in mid-January, I chose not only "My Mother's Mous-tache," my triumphant just-published poem, but the unfinished new ones about her death: *Ladies and gentlemen, my mother is dying,* I read, *If she could only sleep . . .* As I continued to read, silence thickened in the dark, and when I finished, there was prolonged clapping. Afterward, in the gather-ing of my excited friends, something like a scene from a Hollywood movie: a woman approaches, asks if I might like to see these poems on the stage, with music? Yes.

Reading my journals now, I am in search not of the story of my mother as I was in 1974, but of the story of my father and me. I find it, embedded.

The morning of my mother's funeral, I stood in the kitchen, next to my father. Making coffee? Washing dishes? Suddenly my sister Adelia, mar-ried a year before, burst into the room and announced to him that she was pregnant. My father, turning, said something like, "Oh, how wonderful," and leaned to hug and kiss her. I stood back and watched the embrace, her smile, his effort to be present. Why had she not been able to wait another day? What did I have to offer on this day of burial?

I took this tangle of rage, envy, and grief to my therapist, who after introducing the idea of "the good daughter," told me he found it *difficult to imagine someone of my temperament without a child.* Within days I had a dream, which I recorded in my diary: *I see Paul Schmidt in a field. He says*

he always goes to bed with the wrong person. I tell him I've had a dream. In it
Hecuba is lying in a bed in a dark room, fat, distended, diseased, the mourning
mother. Athena/Minerva (My-nerva) stands & transforms from dark to blond. I
do not go to bed with Hecuba; it is Minerva who knocks me out. I go to bed with
her. At the time, in the wake of my psychiatrist's remark about my suitabil-
ity for motherhood, I thought the dream spoke to my vocation as a writer.
Hecuba had mothered fifty children, her sons had died in the Trojan War;
I choose to be a childless woman, born from the brain of my father—from
my own brain. But could it be that even then I knew of the turbulence in
my father's spirit? That this other Paul, Paul Schmidt, who loved men and
had loved and married a woman, was a stand-in? That it was my father
Paul who was always *going to bed with the wrong person?*

I had encountered, and repressed, the fact of my father's homosexual
desire only once. I was in college, home in Washington for a vacation, and
it was an evening after supper. Perhaps my parents were out, because I
walked into their bedroom. The giant bed was on the right as you came in,
and in red frames, arranged around its semicircular headboard, the baby
photographs of their nine children—an altar to the generative power of
my parents' marriage. Though the room was not off limits, I rarely went
into it except to talk to one of them. Why was I alone there? I could have
been looking for a safety pin or a Kleenex, but this night, the light in my
father's study, an alcove off the large bedroom, was on, and suddenly,
mysteriously, I was in search of something else. First I looked at the little
shelf above the built-in desk where my father kept small objects brought
back by his grandmother from her trips around the world, two of which
he later gave me. One of those he gave me was a lapis elephant, the other
was a small Chinese figure carved of white jade—two men, one on top of
the other, heads and feet at opposite ends so that the sculpture is of four
men, the third and fourth, each squatting, composed of the head and feet
of one of the others. A beast of two backs. Four backs?

Then I turned to leave. I don't remember if the book of photographs was
already open, or if I opened it, but the image it was opened to was unlike
anything I'd ever associated with my father. The photograph, in black and
white, was of a young man, naked, standing on a stony beach. The texture
was almost grainy, and the youth was beautiful, dreamy, almost sullen. I
remember that he stood, three quarters turned from me, facing out to the
sea so his genitals were obscured. I understood that if I turned the page,

there would be another photograph like this one, that this was a book of such photographs, but I did not want to see another photograph like this one, nor did I want to be caught looking at the book, even though it was out there, maybe even open, on the neatly painted white surface.

It was soon after I saw the book of photographs, the photograph of the naked young man, that my mother became certain my father had lovers outside their marriage, and that the lovers were men. She made the discovery, I was told by a friend in whom she confided, not as the result of a single event, but from putting things together—a series of suspicions suddenly becoming in her mind enough of a certainty for her to consider leaving my father, for her to make a dramatic announcement to her oldest child during the summer of 1969: *I am having some problems with my marriage.* Until she reached that conclusion, she had not seriously considered that my father had been unfaithful to her, or that he might have another sexual preference. She confided her new belief only in her sister, her brother's wife, and Bette, a woman she became close to before her death.

My mother had struggled with what she and my father agreed were their sexual problems, and he had gone to a psychiatrist, my mother assumed for depression related to the war. In fact, I learned years later, the psychiatrist my father had first seen was Bertram Schaffner, homosexual himself, a pioneer who had counseled gay men drafted into World War II on how to avoid the draft or to live undetected in the armed services and one of the psychoanalytic profession who had worked hardest to get homosexuality removed from the *Diagnostic and Statistical Manual of Mental Disorders*, which happened in 1973, the year my mother died and a few years after I saw the open book of photographs. But my foray that night into my father's study took place before my mother's announcement of her discontent, and so I was ignorant of the fissures that would eventually break my parents' marriage. There was no context in my conscious mind to conclude, from seeing the book of photographs, any new information. I believed that my parents took Christian marriage seriously, and I assumed they did not argue with the commandment "Thou shalt not commit adultery."

I learned that my mother's dissatisfaction with her marriage had a sexual element sometime after her announcement in the Adirondacks. I was in Washington to visit once in the early 1970s, just after she had gotten out of Payne Whitney and moved back, but before we started to become friends. It was a spring day, April or May as I remember the light, but mild, the edge off the cold because it was Washington. The Roma was not a fancy place, but a big neighborhood trattoria that was quite empty at lunch. The maître d' took us to a table in the back. In the shadowy darkness, splashes of light from the few windows fell across red-and-white-checked tablecloths. We sat down, an unlit candle in red glass on the table between us. My mother was on one of her perennial diets and she had no gray in her black hair and no wrinkles on her long face. We rarely looked directly at each other, so I saw her face turning aside and looking down, her fingernails, as always, bitten to the quick. I was still wary of her, but I was trying to respond to her overtures of friendship. We both ordered wine, and then she looked up at me. I don't remember how the conversation began, but suddenly she was saying, "I didn't have an orgasm until I was forty." I had no reply. "And when I finally did," she continued, "Paul said, 'What's the matter, Jenny?'" Venable, who was just four years younger than my mother, had introduced a new discourse of sexual candor into our family, an ease with Oedipal conclusions, ardent talk of Freud and Jung. But this, like the picture of the young man in the book of photographs, was nakedness I did not want to see—my father, fumbling and insensitive as a lover, my mother new to pleasure in her forties.

Night after night, the summer after my mother died, I watched the characters I had made from my mother and father, from myself, from my sister Rosemary and her boyfriend, from my mother's doctors, reenact the six months of my mother's terminal illness. *Ladies and gentlemen, my mother is / dying*, said the actress-daughter. *What has happened to all the cures?* asked the actress-mother, in white light, startled from her coma, *The miracle wheat sprout juice / they gave me hourly. / . . . The predigested protein which tasted like melted muscles.* I allowed the mother to say what I feared my mother had believed. *You have all betrayed me*, she rages when she realizes the remedies are exhausted. But I didn't allow my father to rage. I did not know my father well enough to imagine his grief.

He spent July in Europe, so he missed the play. By the time he returned, there were reviews—"intense, yet detached, somewhat as if Emily Dickinson had written Noh plays"—and a producer, teamed with the women who mounted the play in the small tent theater in the Berkshires, had made plans to bring it to New York. By the end of summer, I had made minor revisions, and *Mourning Pictures* was scheduled for a November opening at the Lyceum Theatre on Broadway. I was twenty-eight. What was it like for my father to see this play? From his oral history, I learned that he had "quite a lot of ambivalence about it," but that on balance he thought "it was a lovely job." At the time, I was sure he was angry at me. I had made him a minor character and I felt guilty about it. But he proudly acted the part of the doting father, trekking down to West Forty-fifth Street to photograph the Broadway marquee with my name on it, and he came to the play, once with Susanna and Patience, my two youngest sisters, and a second time, to the opening.

In the wake of sold-out houses in the Berkshires and rave reviews from such critics as the venerable Eliot Norton of Boston, I thought the play was invincible. I ignored those who questioned the wisdom of the producer in moving such an intimate work to Broadway, where, in 1974, no one had yet seen a character speak openly about cancer or watched a young woman's last months with her mother unfold at the center of a play. And I reveled in the glamour of my new prominence. But rehearsals were difficult, and at one point, with barely any directing experience, I was drafted to take over rehearsals. I knew even in previews that the revised production lacked the simplicity and power of the original, but I did not expect the chorus of hostile and uncomprehending reviews that descended, all in one day, or that the play would close after a week of previews and one performance. An interview in the *Washington Post* was accompanied by an enormous photograph of me wiping tears from my eyes, but I took solace in the fact that my father understood what I had made—"It was a liturgy, liturgically done," he said—and that *The New Yorker* declared that I was "a very good writer." I had left room within my text, Brendan Gill wrote, that put him "in mind of passages in Eliot's *Four Quartets*." But I was humiliated, and now, with my mother no longer alive each night on a stage, I was faced with the actuality of her death.

In Europe that summer, my father had visited Nona Clark: I thought of the tall, willowy, red-haired woman I'd met at twenty, and I remembered his saying that morning in Washington, *It's so easy to get caught.* Would Nona become my stepmother? I had no idea she was just one of five women my father had been seeing and that another one of the five was only two years

older than me. My father had performed Brenda Eagle's marriage, and
recently, after just two years, Vernon Eagle's funeral. In her twenties, she'd
lost a first husband to a sudden, aggressive cancer.

"How are you, Pop?"

"I'm fine."

"What have you been doing?"

"Last night I went dancing with Mrs. Eagle." Mrs. Eagle. My mother,
who had been a friend of Mr. Eagle, had once briefly mentioned meeting his new wife; now my father spoke of Mrs. Eagle with romance in his
voice. Nona would never marry him, I thought; she was much too sophisticated and worldly. *Mrs. Eagle. Eagle.* Crowding in came a story my father
liked to tell of my childhood. We were in Kent and he'd taken me for a
walk across the road, deep into the fields, down toward the river. "We're
going to look at birds," he said. He had binoculars around his neck. He
took my hand. It was a hot, clear morning.

"What kind of bird do you want to see?"

"I want to see a bald eagle."

"Okay," my father said, knowing full well that eagles rarely came to
that part of New England. But at the river, suddenly, there appeared in
the sky a dark speck of bird. My father lifted the binoculars and looked
through them, and then he placed them over my eyes, and there gliding
across the blue sky was the eagle I had imagined, its head silvery in the
bright sun.

I first met Mrs. Eagle in the Park Avenue apartment her husband had
been given when he was the director of a small foundation. At dinner
there, with my father, we sat in half darkness, the large dark leaves of
houseplants dramatic against the white woodwork. She was from Richmond, Virginia, the daughter of a Cadillac dealer; her first husband had
been a diplomat with whom she was posted to Ethiopia. All Virginia had
vanished from her speech; she was slender and small with dark hair; she
was not beautiful like an eagle or like my mother, but she had energy; and
a sense of humor. On December 15, I wrote, *Met Brenda Eagle, Pop's amour.
Very pretty. I liked her enormously tho felt shy.*

The second time I met Brenda was at a family supper at the cathedral;
by now she wore the emerald and ruby intertwining engagement rings my
father had presented to her in Central Park. We talked about furniture. I
asked her where I might get a table refinished. "I'll take you," she said. "I

take all my antiques there. I'm going to take Paulo!" My father laughed,
but I flinched. Brenda's looks, I realized that night, were the result of hard
work. She had a disciplined waist and a face that had been pushed to prettiness. Soon I heard a rumor from Washington: over breakfast somewhere,
she'd pointed at my father's photograph in the *Washington Post*: "I'm going
to marry him." Stories like this began to make me nervous, but my father
seemed madly in love. "She has bedroom skills," Venable quipped, and
I asked him to shut up. She certainly seemed to love my father, and she
knew how to describe herself as a perfect wife for him. "I wanted you to
know, before the wedding," she wrote Gami,

> . . . the real joy and happiness that Paul has brought to my life.
> I was extremely happy and very much in love with my late
> husband Vernon Eagle. As we suffered together in his long and
> impossible fight against cancer I used to think that when it
> was over, I would be empty and capable only of the most mediocre
> feelings. I didn't think that I would be able or entitled to love
> someone so deeply again. It still seems incredible that Paul has
> come into my life and brought me an even warmer and deeper
> feeling of closeness and love than I thought possible or dared
> hope for.
>
> That he is a very, very special person, must be an old refrain
> to you. He is the most wonderful and loving father with his
> children (and his congregations) that I have ever seen. He is tough
> as nails when he goes to work for a cause or against some social
> injustice. And he is an exuberant, funny, peaceful and loving suitor.
> I so look forward to being a good friend to the children whom I
> love dearly. I also adore going with Paul to his Sunday services . . .

The wedding was in May 1975, a year and a half after my mother's
death. Among the wedding pictures—my father tall, his hair long in the
fashion of the 1970s; Brenda in a short white dress, holding a bouquet—
there is a shot of me, all smiles and dressed in turquoise, bending over
the newlyweds, who sit at one of the round tables placed in the cathedral
azalea garden for the bridal supper. But I was still fighting wariness. During the short outdoor ceremony, the garden garish with coral blooms, the
seven of my father's children who could be there and my mother's sister,

brother, and sister-in-law had stood as my father, having kissed the bride, said, at least twice, "This is the happiest day of my life."

After Brenda moved with my father into "the Manse," as Venable and I called the vast cathedral apartment, everything that had to do with my mother was quickly removed. Brenda reminded me of Natasha, the woman from the rising middle class whom the brother marries in *Three Sisters*, Chekhov's uncompromising metaphor for those who sweep away the past to create a new order. Brenda painted the headboard white, threw the baby pictures with the red frames into a box, and put them in the attic. Away went the bean pot used as a kitchen sugar bowl ever since Jersey City. Nothing was offered to us. Familiar pictures, except those that were valuable, came down, and what she referred to as "my collection" went up—on every wall, it seemed, hung the mournful works of the Polish postwar painter that her second husband had collected. Then my father informed me that he and Brenda would be removing certain family objects from the house in Kent, which they now shared with Venable and me on alternate weekends: the trophies of real gold that my great-grandfather had won racing four-in-hand, various paintings, and sets of china. A moving truck was dispatched for most of the furniture, including Nathaniel Moore's four-poster that Venable and I slept in. In short order the house was emptied of everything of value and aesthetic appeal as Brenda furnished the enormous bishop's residence and "my house on Martha's Vineyard," left to her by Mr. Eagle. I had thought these were family things, and, while I now understood they actually belonged to my father and that he was entitled to them, I felt pillaged.

"What are you doing, Paul?" my father's old friend Bob Potter asked him. "Stripping the joint?"

It was as if Brenda had suddenly come upon a shop at which she was the sole and favored customer and everything was free. But my father saw it differently: "She reminds me of Great-granny," he said, recalling his adored grandmother, as "the Manse" gained baronial splendor. From Brenda's point of view she was simply deconstructing the frayed remains of another woman's residence and making it her own, something I would certainly do, I kept telling myself, under the circumstances. I had barely recovered when, one June Saturday, a month after the wedding, Venable and I were in Kent. The morning was close and cloudy, and I was in my study trying to write when the telephone rang. "Your sister Marian," my

father said, "has been in a motorcycle accident." Marian had just finished
her sophomore year at the University of California at Santa Cruz. On a
bike . . . behind a boyfriend . . . coming down a mountain. The words
seemed to float in the humidity of the small room. "She's broken her leg in
several places," my father continued.

"Will she be all right?"

"I've talked to her, Paul is there." (My brother Paul lived in Oregon.)
Now Venable was standing behind me, his hand on my shoulder. "And
also," my father continued, "I want the rug back."

"The rug?" I was still thinking about Marian, six feet two, one of her
unbelievably long legs broken in three places, her marvelous smile, her
long blond hair.

"Granny's rug."

"Granny's rug?" As if I didn't know what he was talking about. And
then, "But Mom gave it to me."

"Brenda and I want to put it in the attic office." The attic?

"Mom gave it to me, Pop."

"It was *my* grandmother's, and I want it."

In the letter I wrote him announcing my refusal to give him the rug, I
invoked Virginia Woolf, enclosing, inscribed, my copy of *A Room of One's
Own*. I believed that the rug belonged to me. I remembered the phone call,
my mother's offer to have it cleaned before it arrived, her excitement that
I would have something of my great-grandmother's, Venable and I unroll-
ing it on my study floor.

The first headache I can place in time came that day. Think of my skull
bones as an open flower, think of my father's words swirling, of the bones
closing on the flesh of the brain, and staying there. Years later, I would
stop drinking alcohol and eating certain things, and then find remedies:
the laying on of practitioners' hands, acupuncture, migraine medication,
medication for allergies, further medication. Now on the rare occasions
when I have a headache medication does not reach, I take a hot bath, can-
cel appointments, lie down, apply ice, and begin. I have learned how to
separate my thinking and emotion from the physical pain, to follow its
trajectory backward to its origin, a fine point of throbbing force. Digging
my fingers into the cavities around the jaw, at the edge of the occiput, I
can calm it, even celebrate its power to vanquish me. If I'm lucky, I'm able
to take those hours as the visitation of all that remains snarled and unre-

solved, as an expedition to a far edge of my thinking, even an encounter with the suffering of others.

But in 1975, I thought only of myself. Each headache was evidence of my imperfection, punishment for failure to align my life with an ideal I believed possible, and its hours were hours of shame. I knew only palliative care. Take a bath, Venable would say, and I would, and then, wrapping myself in a towel with a hot washcloth on my forehead, two Bufferin quickly swallowed, I'd lie down. Perhaps I'd fall asleep, and, if I was truly fortunate, when I woke up, the headache would have gone, leaving only its shadow. The day of the phone call about Marian's accident, about the rug, I went to sleep in the attic room at the back of the house so I wouldn't hear cars snap by on the road or trucks bang down the hill. The bed was an extra-long mattress; my father had slept there when he came for weekends before my mother died, before Brenda, when I thought being in love with Venable would make me permanently happy. But now I had "terminated" therapy, my mother was dead, and the gathering pain offered nothing but the most violent inchoate truths. I could barely consider the suggestions that presented themselves: leave this house which after all is your father's house; make your way to understanding so that even the worst pain won't confuse your thinking.

Venable tried his best. Sometimes he brought tea, other times, misjudging, he aggravated the wound, cursing my father, ridiculing Brenda, analyzing my need to keep hold of my dead mother, fetishized now in a Chinese carpet. Even his admiration hurt. I was heroic, he kept saying, for holding my ground. I saw no way to another choice, but unlike Venable, who as a child had suffered the abuse of a violent stepfather, I had no experience of a life under siege. I was frightened of the future. My dreams became a sequence of spectacles: a pyramid of discarded fetuses, each wrapped in tinfoil; the collapse of the log cabin, an outbuilding next to the house in Kent where I'd camped out as a child. Another night I dreamed I went to a surgeon who recommended cuts to each eye. One would extend the eye opening so I would see better; the second cut, a more risky procedure, would free me, entirely, from my family. I chose only the cut that would make me see better.

All these years later, it was a surprise to read in my journal of my father's repeated approaches. His acknowledgment of the letter and of the book by Virginia Woolf. His request that we talk about the rug. His second request that we talk about the rug. But I was frightened of this new father and his new wife. I visited Marian at the hospital in Santa Cruz, and when Rosemary moved to New York to become a writer, she rented an apartment in our neighborhood and became part of the life Venable and I were making. But I shut my father out, except for formal encounters at the cathedral on Christmas and Easter. I watched him celebrate and preach, went back to the Manse afterward, exchanged with him the customary brief kiss, watched his life with Brenda evolve, feeling in his tall presence, and over and over again, the loss of him.

Part III

———◆◆◆———

REVELATIONS

17

Women and the Kingdom

In July of 1974, before he was engaged to Brenda and before we fought about his grandmother's rug, my father, traveling in Venice, received a telephone call from his old friend Bob DeWitt, the bishop of Pennsylvania. Eleven women were to be "irregularly" ordained priests the next morning in Philadelphia by three retired bishops. The news reached me in Kent when, outside the market in a newspaper rack, I saw what I remember as front-page headlines of the *New York Times,* the *Daily News,* and the *Hartford Courant* announcing the event, and, on the front page of at least one paper, a photograph, a woman priest vested, kneeling, bishops bent over her. Shaking with excitement and barely able to hold back tears, I bought the newspapers and raced home.

Days later in the Adirondacks, my father just back from Venice, we began to talk about the ordination. I was surprised by the power of my reaction, I told him. It felt as if the earth had shifted on its axis. But he could barely listen. He was "damn mad." With DeWitt and a few of the women who had been ordained, he told me, he had been working toward bringing the issue of women's ordination to the floor of the General Convention of the church two years hence. Working within the legislative processes of the church, he believed, would make the acceptance of women priests easier; before breaking for the summer, the group had rejected a militant action such as this ordination. My father felt betrayed. It wasn't ego, he said—he genuinely believed those opposed to women priests would overreact and that the conflict would ultimately set back the cause. "I cursed Bob DeWitt," he told me later, "and called him a sonofabitch and God knows what." His old friend said simply, "I know how you feel, Paul. We just wanted you to know." Now, in preparation for an imminent emergency session of the House of Bishops, my father was working at damage control.

"We're fighting two thousand years of tradition!" he argued at the supper table.

"I know that, Pop, for God's sake!" Feminism had long since dissolved my childhood disdain for the women of the altar guild, at the submissive posture of the nuns in Jersey City. In 1971, I had been part of a service at St. Clement's at which each woman had read, then burned a biblical or theological statement of women's subjugation; when I saw the ordination photographs in the newspapers, my reaction had been visceral. How differently I would have seen the world if I'd grown up with women priests! These Anglican amazons were my sisters, the bishops who ordained them heroes. I remembered my mother at the dinner table in Washington: *The church is just second-rate.* I wondered what she would make of these women who had dared translate their anger into action. "Jesus was a revolutionary," I argued, appropriating my father's rhetoric. "Surely he would have been in favor of women's ordination!"

"I have six daughters!" my father shouted back. "Of course I'm in favor of women's ordination!"

"But these women did it without your permission!"

"The church moves slowly," he insisted. He and others had been work-ing "for years" on this issue.

"Oh, Pop," I said, "what if Martin Luther King had waited?"

The next morning my father left for the emergency meeting of the House of Bishops, all 153 bishops summoned to a small meeting room in a motel at O'Hare Airport. It was the last weekend in August, the Chicago day was hot and humid, and the motel, as my father later described it, was "depressing." The bishops were angry—some at having their vacations cut short, others dead set against women ever becoming priests. The debate was rancorous, old friends on opposite sides maintaining courtesy. There was the apostolic succession to consider! If Jesus had wanted women apos-tles, the twelve would not have been all male! But, my father argued, Jesus had spoken of the priesthood of all believers: one could argue, he main-tained, that all worshipers are priests.

At this meeting, though, the task was not to settle the argument about women priests, but to decide whether the Philadelphia ordinations should stand and if the offending bishops should be censured. In the end, when the question was called, the rebel bishops were merely scolded, but the mea-sure to invalidate the ordinations carried and a committee was appointed to study the situation; my father was in the minority that refused to nul-lify the ordination. Whatever he felt about taking such an action outside of canon law, he said later, "the Holy Spirit" had certainly been present in Philadelphia. That's more like it, I thought to myself.

Within hours of the vote, Charles Willie, a Harvard professor of soci-ology and education and the highest-ranking black man in the Episco-pal Church, made a public statement, drawing parallels between how the church had treated black people before the civil rights movement and what the House of Bishops had now done to women. "And I hereby resign my office as Vice-President of the House of Deputies," he said to a bank of microphones, "and all other positions I hold in the national church." I got a telephone call from Ms. magazine, then in its second year of publication. They planned to put the Philadelphia ordination on their December cover. Would I interview Charles Willie? My article appeared in the December 1974 issue—"When you're fighting oppression," Willie had told me, "the time is now."

* * *

The first time I'd heard the phrase "women's liberation" was in the spring of 1969, before I left Yale, and so, when I moved to New York that fall, I was in search of feminism. In the spring of 1970, I joined a consciousness-raising group which came out of the Left, and then in 1972, started the group with Radcliffe friends, actresses, filmmakers, and writers. We talked about Sylvia Plath as having broken barricades against speaking as a woman in poetry, as having paid with her life when she couldn't change her situation. Now I was reading Adrienne Rich, June Jordan, and Diane Wakoski, and when I became involved with a poetry series at the old Manhattan Theatre Club on East Seventy-third Street, Sonia Sanchez and Rich were the first poets I invited to read. Downtown, women were convening readings for women poets, and at the first, at the Loeb Student Center at NYU in December 1971, I took my turn, reading my poems to a roomful of women, except for Venable. By 1974, when I was writing *Mourning Pictures*, I was part of a community, a cultural movement of women.

Sometime that spring, I went to a reading by Judy Grahn, a radical lesbian poet from California, at Westbeth, the artists' residence in the Village. I had been given her first chapbook, *Edward the Dyke and Other Poems*, by a Harvard friend, Andrew Wylie, who had a tiny bookstore on Jones Street. In person, Grahn was small and pale, dressed in tattered jeans and a leather jacket. To a hushed room of barely fifty women, she read the urgent, furious, devastating epic poem "A Woman Is Talking to Death," in which the lesbian poet's witnessing on the Bay Bridge of a late night accident in which a young white man on a motorcycle is killed by a black man driving a car becomes an opportunity for a meditation on the marginality of the lives of women, particularly the lives of lesbians. Afterward, trembling not only from the power of the poem and the reading but because of the company, I joined a group at Mother Courage, a feminist restaurant nearby. There I was introduced to Kirsten Grimstad and Susan Rennie, two young women who had resigned as junior faculty at Columbia and were assembling *The New Woman's Survival Sourcebook*, a sequel to their best-selling *The New Woman's Survival Catalogue*, for which they had traveled the country, documenting the new world women were making—women's centers, rape crisis centers, women's publishing houses and music companies, bookstores and restaurants, credit unions and academic programs. A month later, they invited me

to a party—the first I'd been to announced as "for women only"—to introduce the women of New York to the founders of the Woman's Building, a
cultural center for women in Los Angeles.

Alone and timid, I climbed the stairs to their Bowery loft, a harmonic
rumble of women's voices growing louder as I approached the open door.
In two enormous rooms, one giving onto the next, were easily a hundred
women, some of whom I'd only seen from a distance at readings or never
at all: Adrienne Rich was there, the poets Audre Lorde, Robin Morgan, and
Susan Griffin, and the playwright Megan Terry, who put her arm around
me and said hello with an inviting smile. The culmination of the evening
was a presentation by Arlene Raven and Ruth Iskin, art historians who had
started the Feminist Studio Workshop, the art school for women housed at
the Woman's Building, and by Judy Chicago, who showed slides of her work
and described the process of "making art" with "a form language" integral
to her identity as a woman. She had changed her surname to mark her
departure from "the dominant culture," she told us, though she remained
married to her husband, also an artist, who was "very supportive."

It was not enough, she explained, to make abstract images, as she had
in a series called *Reincarnation Triptych* that hung on Susan and Kirsten's
walls, giant radiant pinwheel-bursts of color representing three great
women—Madame de Staël, George Sand, and Virginia Woolf. The lives
of these women had to be reconfigured, the women themselves "reincar-
nated" to take their places as avatars of the new consciousness women
were now creating. Bordering the image for Virginia Woolf were the words
"Virginia Woolf—first woman to forge a female form language in literature. Conscious to the point of agony, she controlled her anger, yet did not
emerge undamaged from her struggle to balance the excesses of masculine
culture with female values."

What I heard that night thrilled me. I was attempting that very kind of
reframing as I wrote *Mourning Pictures*, I thought to myself. In my play, the
autobiographical character participates in the action as a daughter, but she
comments on it as a woman poet, shifting the emphasis of the narrative
so that the story told is a new, woman-centered version of the relationship
between mother and daughter. After the party, I wrote in my journal that
the evening had "made me feel that, rather than being an effluence of diseased narcissism, my poems could be meaningful to women."

I found it reassuring that Judy Chicago was married. In 1974, in New York

City, every woman my age whom I knew, whether she lived with a man or not, had either slept with a woman, was considering sleeping with a woman, or was definitely not going to sleep with a woman. All of us, in other words, had addressed the issue. It made sense: we were in consciousness-raising groups together, forming theater groups, editing magazines and newspapers, making music together, writing poems in which the newly powerful "I" was female. For some, living with men had become an impossible contradiction— sleeping with "the oppressor." Others simply fell in love: "In those years, all the young women began to sleep together," the novelist June Arnold, a lesbian, remarked once to me, "like puppies." Some believed that instruments of female vanity like makeup and brassieres were marks of women's servitude and dressed plainly, eschewing skirts, even pants cut for women. Others theatricalized their lesbianism, affecting the sapphism of Vita Sackville-West, Natalie Barney, or Romaine Brooks by wearing black velvet, high heels, long black capes, rings on every finger. I began to alter my style. I would be a sapphist in my imagination, but in life, a political and philosophical lesbian, what we called a "woman-identified woman" who continued to live with a man, Venable.

I remembered the first lesbian I ever met. I was nineteen, and she was older. She came to our table to say hello to one of the men I was with at a small bar near Boston University. As she slid in to sit with us, I took note of her self-possession, which I observed in silent fascination. Later, when she left, the man who knew her spoke of her using the word "lesbian." This woman—I never saw her again or learned her name—was not what I then expected a lesbian to be: a woman who looked like a man. She was elegant, her gestures were casual, and she seemed more powerful than any of us, as she spoke of the theater, of Bertolt Brecht and the alienation effect, laughing, her eyes green, or maybe brown, her lashes dark and long. I remember she was wearing forest green, almost black. She could not have been older than twenty-two or -three, brushing a lock of dark opulent hair from an olive cheek, throwing back her big head and laughing, contralto, lush, her conversation a combination of warmth and sophistication. In her presence, I felt callow. She was a woman; I was a girl.

I met Sonia, the first lesbian I really knew, when I was at drama school. We had been friends for months when one afternoon she called and asked if she could come over, as if she were making an unusual request, which was strange since we often talked on the phone or met casually for lunch or supper or drinks after class. "Are you all right?" I asked.

"Yes," she said, "I just need to talk to you for a few minutes."

"Of course," I said, and when she buzzed from the lobby, which was also unusual, I said, "Come up. Come up!" meaning to be reassuring. When she arrived, she wouldn't sit down or take off her butter yellow car coat, and she didn't look at me as she began to speak.

"I never want to see you again," she announced. She was standing in the middle of the room. I was still sitting.

"What's wrong?"

"I find you very attractive and I never want to see you again," she repeated. My eyes filled as I tried to take in what she was telling me. I'd had no idea.

"Sit down, Sonia."

"I don't want to sit down," she said firmly. "You're too good. I won't do this to you." And then she lifted her hand in a half salute, smiled with half her thin mouth, turned, and left.

Grasping to make sense of something I was too naïve to understand, I realized that our conversations had never been the usual girl talk about boys but discussion about ideas, or about the play she was directing that I was producing. She had been an unusual friend because of her seriousness, and now I had lost her because of something she felt about me. At first I felt sorry for her, sorry that she had this—what? affliction? deformity?— but also I was self-conscious. What was it about me that she had seen? And angry. What she had said seemed a strange way of expressing love, or attraction. She hadn't even given me a chance to respond, though I had no idea what I would have said if she had.

The next day I sought out a friend of hers. Had I done something wrong? I asked him. Of course not, he said, and he told me to respect what Sonia had said, and so I took her at her word, avoided her at school, tore up without reading them the love poems she left in my mailbox. Hadn't she said she didn't want to "do this" to me? From a distance, I watched as she talked to others in the greenroom, scrutinizing her to detect evidence of this new identity she'd presented. There was something unforgiving in how her bangs were cut, in how she moved her hands, an awkwardness I had first ascribed to intelligence but which now, with the cruelty of fear,

I associated with her desire for her own sex, for me. She was nothing like the gay men I had come to know and love at the drama school. Nor like the woman in the restaurant booth that night in Boston, the woman with the beautiful big head she threw back, laughing. Or the girls in my teenage bed for whom I'd stretched my body until it curved like a bone, rubbing against them until the night tilted and banged, altering the texture of the darkness.

Now, in 1974, I found myself in a dream realm of women, which I imagined superimposed on, or interspersed with, real-life Manhattan, a gossamer Isle of Lesbos whose residents recognized each other in code, in gestures that had one meaning in the real life, another in this domain I now found myself part of. Now I understood Sonia's awkwardness and regretted my ignorant response. What she had discovered about herself in a hidden world now seemed the revelation of many of the women I was coming to know. We found each other everywhere, introduced ourselves to each other with solemn respect. Our friendships were alliances, our encounters significant. We were changing the world. Toward the end of the decade, glamorous French feminists began to cross the Atlantic. Having read Monique Wittig's apocalyptic *Les Guérillères,* I watched with fascination as, wearing a brown slouchy hat, a creamy shirt open at the neck, and riding boots, Wittig mounted a platform at a conference to give a paper. Now established poets like June Jordan and Carolyn Kizer were joining our NYU women's readings. I would read "My Mother's Moustache," wearing black, and Fran Winant would read her droll, marvelous epics, "Christopher Street Liberation Day, June 28, 1970" and "Dyke Jacket," and when the glamorous Rita Mae Brown, then of the Washington, D.C., collective the Furies, declaimed a poem that culminated with the line, "an army of lovers shall not fail," we ululated like the women in *The Battle of Algiers,* rocking the room with applause.

It worried me that there didn't seem a place in those readings for love poems to Venable, but in any case, I couldn't seem to write one. Instead I wrote a poem about an encounter with a sexist sales clerk called "Conversation in the Eighth Street Bookstore," and a poem that began, "This is the poem to say Write Poems Women, / because I want to read them," which, in order to dodge accusations of propagandizing, I titled "Polemic #1." Was it that my relationship with Venable lacked the passion these young women celebrated in love poems to each other, or was it that I was falling out of love? When I tried to talk about my lack of sexual excitement, Venable, with the wisdom of a man in his forties, argued that intensity came and went. But I was restless. What were we together for? Venable would not consider marriage or having a child with me—his daughter was close to my age. I considered marriage a patriarchal institution oppressive to women, and I was pretty sure I didn't want to have a baby, but I felt his refusal to consider either constituted a limitation on his feeling for me, which I increasingly thought had more to do with his need for security than with love. "We have beautiful places to live and work," he would say. "What more do you want?"

In my journal, I wrote of frustration about my writing, but not of the terror of being alone, which I tried to deny. One night when Venable was late coming home, I stood at the window watching for him; after an hour I was so tense I could hardly breathe. What was I afraid of? I was horrified at the power of this terror and embarrassed by my weeping when he returned. Neither his reassurances nor my tears got at the root of my anxiety. We began to have fights about the financial imbalance between us. I was too young and too privileged to understand the impact of his continuing inability to get screenwriting work, and I found his rages at those he considered more successful than he was overwhelming. In the fall of 1976, we took a trip to Russia, and there was something about the landscape that "opened me up," as I put it then. I began to have a new ambition which I called "the romance of alone." If I was to live a writer's life, the life of an artist, I couldn't be standing at the window weeping when my lover was an hour late. The poets I admired, like Adrienne Rich and Judy Grahn, seemed to face down their fear. What kind of poems would I write if I were "alone." I was accepted at the MacDowell Colony for a month; the week I left, I noted in my journal my fear of upsetting the relationship with Venable, which had reached, with the successful publication of his biography of James Dean, a new calm.

At the first breakfast at the colony, I noticed a man, an American painter who lived in Paris. Daniel, pronounced the French way, had also lived in Moscow, I found out. He was fluent in Russian, knowledgeable about Russia's history, and had made documentary films in the Soviet Union. I told him about the trip Venable and I had taken and described how powerfully Russia had affected me. Daniel understood: "Yes! Yes!" he said, waving his arms, looking down at me in the snowy dark. As we walked the frigid New

Hampshire forests, he told me of his Uzbek wife, whom he had gotten out of the Soviet Union, and when I described Leningrad, the brilliant gold domes, buildings that looked like French palaces painted yellow, green and orangey pink and reflected in canals that crisscrossed the city, the dark of Dostoevsky's apartment, the paneled elegance of Pushkin's, and how, after sunset, the darkness seemed to rise from the ground, he would turn to me and say, "You! You *understand* Russia!" Then he told me he had fallen in love with me, and very soon his passion, his extreme physical beauty, and his romantic manliness swept me up. I imagined traveling with him to the Greek island where he had a house with a blue door on a narrow street and baking bread in bare feet. My writing? I wasn't sure. "I want to get you pregnant," he said, kissing me and lifting me from the snowy forest path. He left the colony before I did, and as I stood shivering on the platform, watching the train grow smaller and disappear, a sickle moon hung orange in the sky.

At home, no viable writing done during my month away, I closed the door of my skylit studio and read Daniel's letters, watched the telephone, willing it to ring, conjuring my lover calling from Paris. Have Daniel's child? Bake bread barefoot in a tiny house in Greece, the Aegean sparkling below? I no longer took tea breaks with Venable. "When you left for MacDowell, you were one person," he finally said after days of stilted silence, and burst into tears. Horrified at what I had done and that I had hurt him, I tried to tell myself that Daniel was a passing fancy. Venable really did love me, but when he asked what had happened, I couldn't tell him. "You can do whatever you want, Wonz," he said as I cried, too, holding him tight. A month later, Venable asking no questions, I met my paramour in the south of France. His wife was having another child, he told me, and went out alone to the film production meetings he'd promised to take me to, leaving me in the hotel. "I don't want any gossip," he said. In bed, he turned away from me—the great romance, such as it was, was apparently over. Chastened, devastated, embarrassed, I went home to Venable. Downstairs in our bedroom, I was desperate to get back what we'd once had; upstairs in my studio I wrote poems, an epic inspired by the Russian poet Marina Tsvetaeva's "Poem of the End" in which a line of mine played with one of hers: *Did you think love was just a chat at a small table?*

I was looking for ways to get *Mourning Pictures* produced elsewhere, and I'd heard of a woman director who'd done an extraordinary evening of

Sylvia Plath in Los Angeles. We began to talk on the telephone. She would be very interested in directing my play, she said after reading it. Victoria Rue was her name, and she and her lover, Jeremy, also a woman director, had both left Roman Catholic convents for the theater—Victoria had been a novice, Jeremy a nun. Based on a combination of her low voice and the look of the nuns I had known in Jersey City, I formed an image of Victoria as a mousy, dowdy character; that spring, I traveled West to meet her. My first night in Los Angeles I was taken to a performance by prison inmates that Victoria and Jeremy had directed. Standing in the courtyard before the play, I saw, across the crowd, a tall woman with black hair and a blazing smile. "Is Victoria here?" I asked the friend who'd brought me. "There she is," she said, pointing at the woman with the black hair. Again, I went home to Venable, but I was haunted by my two-hour meeting with Victoria, the vividness of her intelligence, the silkiness of her hair, blacker than my mother's, the glancing fun in her dark brown eyes.

Nothing happened with Victoria's plans to revive *Mourning Pictures* in Los Angeles, but six months later I heard that she and Jeremy had broken up, and that spring when she visited New York, I invited her to stay at Twenty-second Street. "Have you ever had a relationship with a woman?" she asked one afternoon as we sat talking, sitting at opposite ends of the bed in the guest room. "No," I said firmly, and launched into the story of Daniel, the snowy woods, the south of France, and, half lying, told her that Venable and I had managed to repair our relationship, and that we were very happy. That fall, 1977, Victoria moved to New York to pursue her career in the theater, and she came to visit Venable and me in Kent.

All weekend, I looked at her, trying to imagine what it might be like to go to bed with her, not being able to imagine it, so palpable still was the dream of Daniel, whose letters from Paris now only fitfully arrived, bringing back the athletic hardness of his body, a rebuke to Venable's warm softness. But Victoria's question, asked playfully, in her low, velvety voice, reverberated. One night I took her to a women's dancing party in Brooklyn to introduce her to some of my lesbian friends. In Adrienne Rich's poems now, and in the lives of many of the young women who read her, the monster in the sky was finding herself transformed in the face of her woman lover. Victoria and I danced, and when she danced with another woman, I found myself jealous, Not long after, in a loft bed in her sublet on Waverly Place, we made love. Very late that night I went home to Venable, but the feeling of Victoria's body, a woman's body as strange, unknown terrain, had illuminated a new dimension of my imagination.

In the days that followed, I met Victoria when I could, feeling exhilarated as we walked the city. What could be wrong with this? I asked myself. Why shouldn't I be able to freely love whomever I wanted to, I wondered as, climbing the stairs of the Fifty-third Street subway station, I boldly put my arm around Victoria, kissing her as she turned to me with that smile. I wasn't sure I would love another woman aside from Victoria, but I knew I had to tell Venable what had happened, and I began to know I would leave the life we had together.

Ms. had another assignment for me: Would I write about what it was like to have a father whose loyalties were divided between the church and his family? Certainly, I said. It was November 1977; this would be the first conversation I'd have with my father since our battle over the Chinese carpet. The interview, in his office, took place a week after Victoria and I became lovers, and, in a coincidence I took as a sign, the most recent controversy to surround my father involved a lesbian. A year before, in 1976, as he'd predicted, the issue of women's ordination had come up before the General Convention of the Episcopal Church, and two favorable resolutions had overwhelmingly passed—one reinstating the validity of the irregular Philadelphia ordinations, the other clarifying canon law to allow women to be ordained priests and consecrated bishops.

My father's first ordination of a woman to the priesthood took place on January 9, 1977, at the cathedral and passed without controversy, but on January 10, at the Church of the Holy Apostles in Chelsea, he ordained two more women, one of whom had been honest about her lesbian orientation. I was not at the ordination, but I read the prominent newspaper coverage—the diocese had not publicized the event, but a right-wing priest who'd left the church in the 1960s over the issue of integration sent out a press release.

Nothing my father had ever done had caused so much controversy. Ellen Marie Barrett was honest about her orientation, but not actively gay. My father, as bishop, and the standing committee, a quasi-judiciary panel of four clergy and four laypeople elected by the diocese which had to approve candidates for the priesthood, had found her "spiritually, mor-

ally, and intellectually qualified." Many gay people who kept their orien-
tations secret had been ordained. Why should a candidate be punished
for being honest? But no matter how many times my father declared that
Ellen Barrett had been selected in accordance with canon law, opposition
to her ordination continued to build. My father returned to the standing
committee and asked if they wanted to withdraw their approval, but the
chair was outraged even at the suggestion. The ordination was to go forward. "I have never felt that it was the responsibility of a pastor to protect
his people from the confusion that comes to them from the World and the
Church," my father wrote in *Take a Bishop Like Me,* the book he published
about the controversy. His responsibility was, he continued, "rather to
give them strength and wisdom and compassion to deal with that confusion. Compared to the hurt and confusion of homosexual Christians over
the years, the quandary of a few insecure and respectable people seems
minor."

By the time he and Brenda traveled to Florida for the annual meeting
of the House of Bishops eight months after Barrett's ordination, talk was
mounting that my father would be censured for ordaining her, an action
that could lead to his being stripped of his orders. His opponents accused
him of breaking faith; the bishops had laid out a timetable to discuss the
ordination of gay people. My father stood by his argument: Why should
a person honest about her orientation be penalized? He and Kim Myers,
now bishop of California, were in despair as to what to do when Brenda
wondered aloud what on earth had happened to the courageous radicals
she'd heard so much about. That night, with her help, my father drafted a
defense. "I have broken no canon law," he proclaimed, reminding his fellow
bishops that Ellen Barrett had been found qualified for the priesthood.

> Please carefully listen to the possible consequences of this pro-
> posed action. Aspirants for holy orders who sense a vocation within
> themselves will be encouraged to lie to their psychiatrist, Standing
> Committee, Ministries Commissions, and bishop. Ordained clergy of
> the church who have declared themselves to be gay will be left won-
> dering when charges of deposition will be brought against them. The
> Episcopal Church may become the scene of a McCarthy-like purge,
> rife with gossip, charges, and counter-charges . . . There has been
> much talk here about freedom of conscience . . . Given this principle

. . . do you then proceed to censure or deplore a Bishop and Standing
Committee acting with full canonical scrupulosity in ordaining someone whom they believed qualified and whom most of you have never
met? I think such an action is outrageous . . .

My sisters and I, together for a weekend in Washington, heard that our
father was in danger of being defrocked, and sent a telegram of support.
He called to tell us he had received a long ovation and that the resolution
to censure him had been voted down, but the controversy about inclusion
of openly gay people in the ministries of the Episcopal Church was just
beginning.

When I sat down in his office two months after the Florida meeting,
my father was still putting out fires stoked by the ordination. I was looking forward to hearing about his adventures, but I had also prepared a
list of questions. The editor at Ms. had assumed conflict between us, but
now, for the first time since the end of my parents' marriage, we seemed
to have no differences; there seemed to be no gap at all between the father
I desired and the father I had. Our talk was an interview, but it was also
a reunion and a reconciliation. Listening to the old cassette thirty years
later, I hear first our formality—he declares himself "very proud" of me
"professionally" and I respond in kind. Since Ms. wanted to know about
my relationship to a bishop-father, I first asked what he felt about the fact
that none of his children had a relationship to the church. It had disappointed him, he said, that none of us were active Christians, but he'd come
to realize that what was more important was that each of us had serious
vocations—mine, for instance, poetry, but also social action as a feminist.
"It would have been fun, though, if one of you had been in the clergy," he
said wistfully.

When he began to talk about Ellen Barrett's ordination, the formality
gave way to the familiar pleasure of hearing my father tell a story. He and
Brenda had arrived at Holy Apostles to find the Chelsea street mobbed with
television cameras and were led through a back entrance. He told me about
the simple power of the service itself; the thousand letters that had poured
into his office, two-thirds of them against what he had done; the parishes
that threatened to withhold their contributions to diocesan work. When I
asked how he'd managed to bear up, he described his visit to the Church
of the Ascension three days after the ordination to preach for Integrity, the

organization of gay Episcopalians. Seeing the church full, he presumed for another service, he found the parish hall empty, and panicked that he had the night wrong. "We're expecting you, Bishop," said a man who suddenly appeared and led him into a church packed to capacity.

Some of the protest had been so vicious my father was gun-shy: he'd requested no publicity and had expected a small, easy group. "Don't worry, Bishop," he was told. Word had spread that he was coming and that Ellen Barrett would be there. The congregation was gay people and their families and supporters of all faiths, Roman Catholic priests, rabbis, women and men and their companions, children, old men with, he said, "years of anguish" on their faces. Wanting to steer clear of controversy, he preached about love and suffering, how close the two are, concluding, as he often did, by reminding his listeners of the Resurrection, of "the new life that follows after redeemed pain, how the Church would be filled with new life when we were finally able to love everyone as he or she was made." His voice filled with the wonder I remembered from childhood as he described the sacred feeling of the Eucharist that night, how people took their time receiving communion, how his purpose as a bishop and pastor came back to him in the midst of the love he felt, and in what people said to him afterward. One man pulled him aside. "Until now," he said, "the church has only offered to 'help' us. That is the very worst insult of all. We don't want to be bundled off to a psychiatrist. Now someone in the church, a bishop, our bishop, has ordained one of us. It's beautiful, man, beautiful."

I asked him about his first knowledge of homosexuality, and he talked about being a late bloomer at St. Paul's, and a terrible athlete: "It was *agony.*" And the panic when two boys were discovered having sexual contact. "The *worst* thing you could be called was a sissy," he said. "Which, of course, I realize now, had to do with fear of homosexuality. And, of course," he added, "there was Fred Bartrop. You answered the telephone . . ."

Immediately I knew the call he meant. "That was Fred Bartrop?"

I was five or six, and it was Sunday, after mass, in Jersey City, the cocktail hour at home after the coffee hour in the parish hall. "Hello?" A twisted, barking voice. "Is Father Moore there?" I ran to my father. I was used to these phone calls—he got them from people who wanted money, from people whose houses had burned down, women whose husbands had gone to jail, from people who were hungry or sad or drunk. He went immediately to the phone, sat down, turned toward the window, the receiver to one ear, a finger in his other, all the grownups drinking sherry. My mother was there and Freddie Bradlee and Joanna Smith, who wore wide belts and full skirts and was acting the lead in the church play. When we sat down for lunch, my father was still on the telephone. Roast chicken, let's say. The grownups were laughing, doing what my parents called "setting up gags." A couple of seminarians, some old friends from New York. When my father finally hung up, he slipped into his chair at the head of the table and rejoined the conversation.

Now my father told me the voice had been Fred Bartrop and that he had been drunk. I could hardly believe it. The Fred I knew was courtly, silver-haired, always beautifully dressed, a gold watch on a chain in his waistcoat I played with as he balanced me on his knee; he looked right at me and spoke carefully, the way people who love language do. I knew he had been my father's teacher. I did not know then that he had once been a priest, the chaplain who encouraged my father to make his first confession, to whom he first confided his conversion; that he had been a teacher my father was so close to he called him "Bear." Now my father was telling me that Fred Bartrop had been defrocked, court-martialed, and kicked out of the army. On an evening walk, he had reached out, "in loneliness and love," my father said, and the soldier had reported him. To my father, then twenty-four, homosexuality was a moral failing, like drunkenness. "People shouldn't despise, but pity," he had written my mother about Bartrop in 1943. "When he took holy orders, he was taking on a tremendous fight, bravely, because he knew the strength of his temptations . . . I can never repay him, none of us can—for the thing on which we will live our whole lives. That stuff is dynamite."

I had my father back. I was stunned and moved as I walked up Amsterdam Avenue after the interview to meet Victoria for Greek food at the Symposium. I told her everything he had told me, how he now believed he'd been wrong about the Philadelphia ordinations, that he now felt the action had been a good thing because there had been time for deep discussion before the convention vote. I told her, too, because it was the most powerful thing he said that night, how he believed that in the human psyche, religious emotion and sexual feeling come from "the same mysterious, undifferentiated source," how "the human life of love and the divine life of love," as

he wrote later, "are not separate, but part of the scope of God's love that
sweeps through His creation. The love of a man for a woman, of a parent for a child, of a man for a man, a woman for a woman . . ." Victoria
knew exactly what I was talking about. She'd left the convent when she
was forbidden to go home for her grandmother's funeral. Decades later, as
a dissident Roman Catholic, she would integrate her lesbian activism and
theater work with worship. In 2005, she would become a "womanpriest,"
ordained on a ship in the international waters of the St. Lawrence Seaway
by women bishops from Germany and Austria who had been consecrated
in secret by rebel Catholic bishops in Europe who believed the ordination
of women should be in the hands of women.

At home that night, I wrote in my journal: "Quite wonderful interview
with Pop. Felt really warm after. Think it's really extraordinary how open
he is: he said he wouldn't have any negative reaction that he knows of if
one of his daughters were a lesbian."

I still hadn't told my father about my new life when he went to India
in February to preach at the Maramon Convention, an annual gathering
in the province of Kerala. These were Mar Thoma Christians, whose tradition is that Doubting Thomas, one of the apostles, had traveled to India
to found a church fifty years after the death of Christ. My father was to
preach a series of sermons on Christianity and social justice. Beginning
weeks in advance, canopies of bright-colored silk and cotton were erected
in a dry riverbed, and as the opening day approached, hundreds of thousands gathered, camping at the site, dressed in hot pinks, blues, and reds
and greens, bearded, veiled, chanting hymns, and every morning before
the sun got too hot, my father preached. Bob Potter, my father's longtime
friend and the chancellor, or lawyer, of the Diocese of New York, and his
wife accompanied my father and Brenda on the trip, and one day at lunch
"Potter," as my father called him, leaned toward my father and said, "Hey,
Paul, did you know that Honor has a girlfriend?" His goddaughter whom I
knew slightly had heard the news and passed it on, and when he got home
from India, my father had asked my sister Rosemary if it was true.

But he never asked me. I had been waiting to tell him. Waiting until I
was sure. Waiting until Venable and I decided what to do. But now we had
made our decision. I never had a serious conversation with my father about
this great change in my life, and because of that, the new sense of connection between us dissolved. Venable and I split the apartment. I moved

upstairs into my studio and the adjoining guest room, and Venable stayed downstairs. About a year later, I moved again, and it was in that new place that I introduced my father to Victoria and there that he and I came to an accommodation about his grandmother's rug. I'd bought a renovated loft in Tribeca, the only requirement in the search a space large enough for my magic carpet, 14½ by 22 feet. We sat on my inherited Victorian furniture which I had reupholstered sea blue velvet, and I served cookies and espresso in delicate antique cups given to me by my mother. When I passed the tray to Brenda, she knocked her cup from its gold-edged plate, shattering it on the rug. We all laughed, Brenda quickly gathering up even the tiniest shards and promising to have it repaired. It took two years, but she returned the cup, cracks invisible, virtually like new.

Now, living alone, I had an enormous room of my own where light spilled through huge warehouse windows onto a creamy ground where indigo and cerulean grapevines and flowers spiraled and intertwined. I had both solitude and my beautiful black-haired lover with whom I spent most nights. Here, in a pioneering neighborhood close to the world of artists, to which I carted groceries from blocks away, I would renew my writing life. I would make more serious poems, and, to inure myself and other women against the costs of the bold life on which I and many of my friends were now embarked, I would write the life of my mother's mother, an artist who had gone mad when she stopped painting, a woman who had had many lovers, of both sexes, a woman I had always been said to resemble.

"Are you sure you're not making this place for someone else's approval?" Venable asked when he visited and we sat on Aunt Lily Hanna's Victorian settee, which with its companion chairs looked quite odd in the enormous space. Perhaps he knew me better than I knew myself. There were tasks at hand beyond the ones I acknowledged: to mourn the loss of a man I had loved but with whom I no longer wanted to live, and, at the same time, to establish myself in a new sexuality. I all but ignored them as I set forth on my "romance of alone." In the years that followed, as my new world of women deepened and evolved, fractured and split, and as I wrote the life of Margarett Sargent, I created, in spite of my loneliness and my desire to find an ideal love, a way of living on my own.

18

Discovery

In 1984, I left New York and moved to Connecticut. I could not write the book about my grandmother in the city. Or that's what I told myself. I would leave for a year, sit alone in the house in Kent; even if I wrote just a page a day, it couldn't take more than a year to produce the book. But my life came with me, and my sadness. I had left behind a broken history of lovers. I hadn't been able to make a commitment to Victoria, or to Diane, whom I left her for. I left Diane for a woman who lived in California, who spent much of her time traveling as a performer and who declared herself unwilling to be monogamous. I didn't believe her, and the obsession lasted for years. But in Connecticut I found a new life, and new friends. In particular, I became close to a couple a generation older than I was, both accomplished artists. By watching them and coming to know them, I learned what an enduring life of creative work required.

In the early years, my father visited once or twice a year, and I gave spectacular dinner parties, inviting my new friends, proffering my amazing father. When he and I were alone together, I tried to keep our conversation away from family controversy. It had become clear that Brenda was an alcoholic, and she had made it clear she only barely tolerated my father's children. Now, for instance, my father came to the Adirondacks by himself. Perhaps because I had stopped drinking alcohol, I began to notice that my father's charming tipsiness often had a slightly out-of-control quality. "We've switched to vodka," he joked once. "Gin fights are just too vicious." Brenda began to gain weight, the prettiness of her face to coarsen. Now when I saw them or anyone in my family, I could feel disturbance roiling beneath the surface. As my siblings and I passed through our twenties and thirties and into our forties, Brenda still treated us as adolescents, and my father allowed her to rail against us, often in the presence of friends who told us about it later.

Sometimes my father's need to please Brenda took the form of disloyalty to my mother—he had taken to psychoanalyzing her, denigrating her, particularly to the younger ones who had been so young when she died. Once he told a friend of mine it worried him that I idealized my mother, that she had been, at the very least, an indifferent parent to me and often even cruel. I was willing to listen to my father's stories about my mother when he took responsibility for his part in the difficulties of their marriage, but it enraged me when he blamed her, and because he consistently blamed her, I defended her. She became my cause. It was then that I took out my mother's letters and reassured myself that whatever had happened between us during my childhood, she had made amends before she died. And then, once when he visited, my father turned on me in a rage. I was explaining the point of view of one of my sisters in a family fight, trying to make peace, and he began to shout, even curse. I asked him not to speak to me that way, and he quickly apologized, begging me to keep his outburst between us. "Please, please don't tell them," he said. Now my feeling for my father included fear of that temper.

. When I moved to Connecticut, the AIDS epidemic was intensifying, and the world I had been part of in New York was under siege. In early January 1986, I went to an AIDS memorial service at the cathedral. It was a Eucharist, a requiem, and as part of the liturgy, names of the dead were recited, a process that took more than an hour. As I listened, I heard the names of friends, actors and poets and artists I had known, and then my father preached. In his white chimere and crimson rochet, he climbed the pulpit and began. It was a sermon about sexual freedom, about the lives these dead men had lived, about the presence of Christ's sacrifice in human suffering. This was not a new subject for him, but I had never heard him so fierce, so passionate, so loving. What came to me was this: Here is where I can come to find my father's love. There is, I told myself, magnificence in how he can give, opening his long arms, practically weeping on behalf of these men dead of a plague: here in his preaching I can be close to my father. In 1988, when my first book of poems was published, I dedicated it to him, taking it uptown and making a presentation. After his death, I found a note he wrote me then but never sent, "You are a VERY GOOD POET. Someday we'll talk about them."

The following spring, my father announced that he would retire two years later, after twenty-five years as bishop of New York. I remember, when he gave me the news, seeing a kind of resigned sadness cross his face; it seemed strange to me that he would give up what he loved most, what gave him life. He was getting old, he said, but he was only sixty-eight. Even when I reflected that twenty years was a long time, I couldn't get the expression I'd seen on his face out of my mind. He had that beaten look, which I associated with his domestic life but never with his priesthood. He convinced me, though. He had books to write, other things to do; he wanted to spend more time with Brenda, traveling, which was when they had their best times together, and at the house they'd bought in Stonington on the Connecticut coast after giving up Martha's Vineyard. Also he wanted to get to know his grandchildren.

In New York, he and Brenda would move to the small townhouse in Greenwich Village they'd bought a decade before with the proceeds from the sale of a painting by George Caleb Bingham which my father had inherited. Brenda had begun the renovation. The details of their moving plans came to me and my siblings from their accountants. Brenda, who was studying antiques appraisal, had inventoried every possession they planned to "deaccession" and listed it in a crisp twenty-page document, along with cash values. A cover letter informed us we could purchase any piece we wished, in advance of a public auction.

There had always been a tradition in the Moore family of passing things on; now, apparently, that had changed. My father and Brenda led a luxurious life, and he had always been a magnanimous philanthropist, but could their finances be that bad? The list included pieces of both actual and sentimental value, antiques we had grown up with and furniture from the house at Hollow Hill which had been dismantled when Gami died several years before. Also listed, at a wildly high value, was the wire head of my mother as a child done by Alexander Calder, who had been a great friend of her artist mother; my mother had left it to my father in her will. A sick joke, we all thought—Brenda puts her predecessor's head on the auction block.

Some of my sisters and I decided to try to buy it, but when I called to make an appointment for an independent appraisal, Brenda answered. Immediately she put my father on the phone, and he hung up on me before I could pose the question. It seemed that every time I reached a new accommodation, another impossibly sad and enraging predicament would arise. In spite of years of trying to understand the dynamics of alcoholism, of trying to accept Brenda for who she was and my father for who he had become, I was still embroiled in a melodrama that never seemed to end. Each of my father's children had a way of dealing with it. I'll face this after I finish, I said to myself as I struggled with the book about Margarett. I was also teaching writing workshops in my living room in Kent, and as my students wrote, I wrote with them, producing pages and pages about my mother, about my father, about the past. It never occurred to me that these strange reversals in the way my father approached the world were the consequence of real suffering of which I had no knowledge.

One day in April 1990, I was standing in the Washington kitchen of my mother's friend Bette, who lived in our old neighborhood in Washington. For years I had confided in her my disappointment in my father, bringing forth the latest Brenda outrage. Bette was wonderfully patient, and like most of my mother's close friends, she saw my point of view. She was also able to manage compassion for my father, even though, as a woman who would never deny her children anything, she found his behavior incomprehensible. It was helpful to talk to her—during our conversations I felt

I almost had my mother back, undistorted by what had happened in our family since she died. By now, these talks with Bette required little ornament. On this particular day, I remember that she was filling the teakettle, and I said, "What did *she* think about *him*?" And Bette, knowing the *she* was my mother, the *he* my father, turned from the sink and said, "She thought he was the most unhappy man she had ever known, and she thought he was homosexual." I tried to take in what she said. It had been almost twenty years since my mother's death, and I was hearing this for the first time. I guessed Bette thought I was ready.

"When did she tell you that?"

"Toward the very end." Bette lived close by; only a five-minute walk through a neighbor's yard and she could be at my mother's bedside. She had grown up Communist and Orthodox Jewish in Michigan, and when she met my mother, she had no use for her. "Another rich girl," she said. But in the last months of my mother's life, they became close friends, and since my mother's death, Bette had become family to me and to my brothers and sisters.

"Was it something he told her?"

"No," Bette said. "It was something she put together, something that became clear to her over time."

"Do you remember when it was that she said it became clear?"

"I would say before her accident." The news did not shock me, but also I couldn't quite take it in. Instead, I shelved it, adding it to the chaotic morass of feeling I was putting off until later. Another fact, I thought, to include if I ever undertook to make a portrait of my parents' marriage.

During the summer of 1990, I went to Europe for the first time in years. I traveled with friends in Ireland and visited others in London—it was the summer Iraq invaded Kuwait. When I got home to Kent in August, there were messages on my answering machine from two of my brothers. I decided to call them back the following day, but the next morning, before I got to it, the telephone rang. It was my father: "Are you by yourself?"

"Yes," I said. It was an unusual question.

"I have something to tell you."

"I'm here," I said, wondering at the shakiness in his voice. There was a silence, and then he spoke.

"It's come out that I've had gay affairs," he said.

How to describe the moment—I was not remembering Bette's announcement, so what my father said came as a shock, my stomach turning over. It embarrasses me, but what I first thought was that this forced admission of his would present us with the opportunity to talk intimately again, for me finally to know my father. And then I thought of him, of the terrible pain of living a double life.

"Do people know?"

"Only in the family," he said. "It is *not* public, and," he said with a nervous laugh, "you are NOT going to write a short story about it." I was so disoriented, all I could think was, Doesn't he know I don't write fiction? And then he said, "I'd like to come see you and talk about it."

"Oh yes, yes," I said. "I would like that."

And then, "Does Brenda know?"

"Yes, Brenda knows. She's very hurt and it's pretty rough, but I hope we'll work it out. I'll tell you more when I see you." I told him how sorry I was that it was so rough, that I knew he'd get through it. He named a date in September for his visit.

Jet lag gave me an excuse to spend that day in bed. And the next. Lying there, my father's contradictions came crashing in, blurring any clarity I'd had about our family past. I knew I wanted to protect him, so I confided in only one close friend. I remember telling her it was as if the light which had been pink was now green—I meant the ambient light through which I saw the world. Pink and green! If you wore pink and green on Thursdays at Shortridge High School, you were definitely "queer"! How impossibly sad and painful, to live a whole life torn in two, to move forward as husband and father while kept from another kind of desire. And as a priest! Every angry feeling I'd ever had toward my father dissolved, but then, as I considered what he'd withheld in our so-called intimate conversations, a new anger rose up. My father a liar? My father, the priest, a liar? And then I saw his guilt, his weeping when my mother died, how he said of Brenda, *She's very hurt, and it's pretty rough.* And I thought of Brenda's adoring love of him, her nicknames, her eyes sparkling, how she looked after him.

And the conversation with Bette came back, and with it, in spite of my effort to hold it off, anger on behalf of my mother. And he blamed her for the difficulties in their intimacy? I thought of her in Payne Whitney, of her admission over lunch at the Roma, of her struggles to be honest and kind during their separation. He blamed her? In telephone calls with my sisters and brothers, I gathered new information that continued to shatter the emotional chronology I had so painstakingly constructed in the years since my mother's announcement in the Adirondacks. I watched the light play on the ceiling, turned to sleep, to waking, unable to believe what I now knew. That my mother had known my father's secret when I walked toward her in the Adirondacks: *I am having some problems with my marriage.* That in the painful years she spent separating from my father, she never confronted him or betrayed his secret to us, in spite of the agony it must have caused her. And I remembered her cheeks wet with tears, her rage that women might want to be Episcopal priests, how, nearly spitting in anger at my father, she had shouted, "The church is just second-rate," pounding the dining room table.

In memory I saw the book in my father's study, the black-and-white photographs of young men. The white jade figure. "For as long as he can remember," my sister said on the telephone from the Adirondacks when I asked how long my father had known this about himself. Had he had "gay affairs" in the Marine Corps? At Yale? I remembered how Venable, a little drunk, would suggest, joking, that my father loved wearing "those long skirts." "They're vestments," I would say, firmly tamping down the confusion and discomfort I'd feel, in spite of myself. Now my father himself had told me he was bisexual. And wanted to talk to me about it. Was it possible that when he came to visit "in a few weeks" we would, for the first time since my mother's announcement in the Adirondacks, for the first time since he married Brenda, for the first time ever, speak with real intimacy? After all, wasn't that all I'd ever wanted, to approach him as his true daughter? His firstborn who was living her own searching sexuality—sexuality that somehow, I was suddenly thinking, I had inherited from him?

I remembered our interview at the cathedral, all those years ago, my father gesturing to include his body when he told me that he believed that sexuality and religious feeling came from the same place in the psyche. I hadn't found my way that day to questions I wanted to ask, questions about his desire and sexuality, and now I understood why—there was a crucial fact I hadn't known, and it was that fact about his own nature, not his relation to God, that kept our relationship unsatisfactory. The piece was "too general," the *Ms.* editor had said when she rejected it; it was "general" because I didn't know my father's complicating truth. "There is no conflict," my father had said that day, "between ordinary life and what is 'divinely ordained.' It's all connected." My own experience of sex took me to a place I considered sacred, but I never imagined, when my father said those things, that he was talking about himself. *I'll tell you more when I see you.* I had so many questions: When did you first sleep with a man? What was it like for you? Was it like sleeping with a woman the first time was for me? The searing opening of a closed part of the brain and consciousness, the dark forbidden bed, as if it were a reunion? Holding, being held naked, close to a body like one's own?

I thought of the gay men I had known in the 1970s, before the epidemic, their stories of nights of sex in trucks parked under the West Side Highway, in the bars that lined West Street. I thought of how men I knew to be poets and intellectuals, men with refined and delighted sensibilities, dressed in cowboy jeans and plaid flannel shirts; how they squired their younger lovers to literary parties, only to disappear with them later. I remembered the dinner with my father on Eighth Street after my mother's accident, the alien excitement of his smile, that silvery nimbus I hadn't been able to identify. What had he done after we parted that night? When one of my sisters expressed concern about HIV, my father reassured her: "No tricks or hustlers." And so I would not have to imagine my father in the vast warehouse spaces along the river, dancing among disco throngs as I had with Victoria, or finding his way to the bathhouses that were now, in the wake of AIDS, closed. But I wanted to know what my father's gay life had been. I wanted to know how he had loved and whom he had loved.

As the days passed, there were more calls from the Adirondacks. My father had arrived, Brenda accompanying him, to face his children. Bits of the story were communicated, some peculiar tale of a speakerphone left on, a receiver not quite hung up as the source of Brenda's discovery. Of Brenda one night on Martha's Vineyard, intoxicated enough, after my father had gone to bed, to tell a visiting stepchild her agonized secret, how word had been passed until all of us knew, how I was the last to hear because I had been in Europe. His whole life. No names. What would you say, Brenda had asked her stepchild, if I told you your father was gay?

He came to visit on a quintessentially beautiful September day. The sky was saturated blue, the green beginning to turn gold. We drove the familiar roads past Kent School and up Skiff Mountain. We parked the car and began to walk. The khaki trousers, the frayed Shetland sweater. He seemed nervous. I wanted to help. After some conversation about how difficult it had been for him in the Adirondacks answering questions about a life he had never wanted to reveal, we began to talk, and after a while, I asked the only question that concerned me.

"Did you love any of them?"

"They were all nice people," he said.

Did he mean he hadn't loved them, or was he just dodging the question? I didn't want to believe he hadn't loved them. If, as he taught, one's existence was inextricably bound up with the liturgy, and if he had lived his life with the attention to the life of Christ that his preaching always evidenced, how could he now deny those he had sexually loved? Saint Peter in Gethsemane: *Art not thou also one of this man's disciples? He sayeth, I am not . . . Did not I see thee in the garden with him? Peter then denied again.* I wanted to know that my father had experienced passion, that he had known love. The life my father had lived had brought suffering to my mother and to Brenda, but I had no judgment of his infidelity to his wives. I understood desire. But if my father had sacrificed the happiness of the two women whom he had married and now his children's trust, I wanted to believe that he had loved these unidentified men.

"Did you love any of them?"

"I don't want to talk any further about it. I would never have chosen to have this thing come out."

Silence.

"I have some trouble with it, Pop," I said. "Not with what you did. But with the deception. It will take some time to—" I was going to say "adjust to this new reality," but suddenly my father was shouting.

"Well"—he was furious—"you haven't had a perfect life! You had affairs with women when you lived with Venable." What I wanted him to say was something tender. I wanted him to say, I am very sorry the lie has hurt you. I did the best I could. I tried to keep it a secret so your mother and Brenda wouldn't suffer. I tried to change, but I could not because I love men. Instead he was accusing me of deception in order to justify his own.

"No, I did not have affairs with women while I lived with Venable," I said. "I told Venable two weeks after I fell in love with Victoria, and then

I left him. There is nothing in my life that compares to what you've done, nothing at all."

By then we were sitting at the round table in my kitchen in Kent. It was dark. We had watched television, the Ken Burns Civil War documentary, because I hadn't wanted to talk anymore. "I don't feel we're quite finished," my father said when we returned to the kitchen. He wanted me to forgive him, by which he meant erase what I was feeling, erase how hurt I was. I poured him a Scotch on the rocks. I don't remember what happened next, but I do remember turning away from him in my chair, so angry I didn't know how sad I was. If he would only tell me something really true, something that would allow me to know this part of him, I could forgive him. I was so disappointed, looking at him cowering there in the darkness of the kitchen, and so sad. He wanted forgiveness, but offering forgiveness would mean giving something for nothing, and I didn't have anything left.

"Why did you get married again?" I finally asked.

"I fell in love with Brenda," he said.

"And you've stopped having male lovers now?"

"Yes."

"And how is that for you?"

"It's okay. Sometimes on the street I get that feeling, but I just don't act on it."

"And that's okay?" I said, feeling at last some sympathy.

"It was an addiction," he said. "I loved your mother, and I love Brenda."

Why did having loved my mother or Brenda make his love for men an addiction? Now I felt revulsion, his self-loathing enveloping me. "You're talking about feelings at the center of my life," I said, using my disgust to say something dignified. But as I said it, a complicating truth presented itself, something inchoate I deftly pushed aside. In time I would recognize it as another dream, a desire more painfully close to the center of my longing than my love of women—a desire for a man who was not like my father, who was, rather, a man who fully loved women, who loved me as a woman.

"I fell in love with your mother," he repeated. I was thinking to myself, He looks at her and wishes she were a boy. No, it wasn't that clear.

"It was something different with men," he said. "It was like an addiction."

I had found a therapist who was willing to witness a conversation between us, and in a phone call before his visit, I'd asked my father if he would participate and he'd said yes. That night, though, he said that he had rethought my request and that he didn't, after all, want to come to therapy with me. "I have my own therapy," he said. "That's enough."

At the time I took his refusal as another rejection, but now I understand the decision. His life was torn apart, he was working at keeping his marriage, he was going to lead a life without secrets. He was appalled at having hurt Brenda, suffering again the guilt he'd always had about "how I was made." The sadness I'd seen on his face when he talked about resigning as bishop had in it Brenda's discovery of his hidden life just before the announcement. He had begged her forgiveness, promised never to touch a man again, never to be unfaithful again. But could he forgive himself?

When my father had left office the year before, it was as if the ritual of succession became tangled in the turbulence of his private life, as if forces long held in check had abruptly surged to life, their energies erupting randomly, with an odd but distinct violence that seemed uncannily directed.

In the Episcopal Church, bishops are elected at diocesan conventions, and going into the convention called to elect my father's successor, there were five candidates. The front-runner was Walter Dennis, black and a suffragan bishop who worked with my father, behind whom many liberal, African-American and West Indian delegates, and the gay caucus had united. The other candidates included two white priests, also liberals and both from the Diocese of New York, and a priest from California. The candidate of the conservatives, those who for instance opposed women's ordination and those who wanted a break from the activism my father personified, was Richard Grein, the bishop of Kansas. Early in the balloting, Dennis was far ahead, and as voters filed to the machines to cast the decisive ballot and he stood, beaming with the probability of his victory, he fell to the floor.

Janet Kraft, then a seminarian at General Seminary, was in charge of the balloting, and she was standing next to my father, who leapt from his chair, bounded to the dais, and crouched next to Bishop Dennis, cradling his head. Call 911, he said forcefully to a young priest, then he asked another priest to call Dennis's doctor, whom he knew by name and who was at St. Luke's Hospital, close to the cathedral. "The EMT guys got there," Janet Kraft said, "and your father said, 'Take him to St. Luke's Hospital.'" The driver said that legally EMT had to wait for orders as to which hospital to take him to. But Bishop Dennis had a known heart condition, and there was no time to waste. My father rose from his crouching position to his full height and, raising his voice, spoke firmly to the orderly. "Take him to St. Luke's Hospital. I am a very important man in this city, and if you don't do as I say, you will be in serious trouble." Janet remembered the exact language, she said, because the tone of voice in which my father delivered this order was so striking, so unlike the bishop she knew. My father, in his memoir, *Presences*, recorded a different, but no less dramatic threat: "If you don't take him to St. Luke's Hospital right now, I will lie down in front of your damn ambulance."

"Yes sir," the EMT orderly replied, and then my father grabbed a young priest.

"You," he said. "You go along. In the ambulance. Make sure they get him there."

After Walter Dennis was put on a gurney and wheeled out of Synod Hall and was safely en route to St. Luke's Hospital, my father returned to the business at hand. The African-American caucus asked that the voting be stopped, that the convention be canceled, that the whole nominating process be repeated. The decision was my father's, and as sternly as he had insisted EMT take Walter Dennis to the hospital, he declared the voting would continue, a decision that seemed hasty and out of character to people who knew him well. And so the election did continue, new candidates were put forward, others came forward themselves, and still others dropped out. The supporters of Walter Dennis held out all day and into the evening, and it took until the tenth ballot and the early hours of the morning for my father's successor to be chosen. Though Richard Grein was known as conservative, he was not an archconservative, and he pledged to continue the process of bringing women equality in the priesthood and to sustain certain other progressive initiatives within the diocese. He was, my father told me, a bishop who saw as central to his mission being a pastor to his priests. "And that can't be bad," my father said.

In fact, my father reported over the succeeding years, Bishop Grein reversed many of his initiatives—decentralization of power in the diocese, the establishment of regional governing bodies within the diocese so that churches could keep a closer eye on each other. These changes had been the fruit of my father's decades of work on how best to make parishes effective in the contemporary life of New York City. When I saw him in the months after Bishop Grein succeeded him, my father did his best to be philosophical. He was no longer bishop, he would say when I asked if the changes made him angry. But another time—I remember we were crossing the street—he said, "It just makes me so goddamn mad."

"I'm so sorry, Pop," I said.

"Well, what can you do? I just feel so badly for all those parishes, all those people who did all that work." Or words to that effect. And he was moving on. In the late 1980s, he and Brenda were asked by Human Rights Watch to visit East Timor, where they met Bishop Carlos Filipe Ximenes Belo, the great bishop who would be cowinner (with José Ramos-Horta) of the Nobel Peace Prize in 1996 for his successful effort to stem violence by teaching and employing passive resistance toward "a just and peaceful solution" based on self-determination for the people of East Timor, an estimated third of whom had lost their lives due to starvation, epidemics, war, and terror as the result of Indonesian aggression. On the way, they stopped in Guadalcanal, visiting the battlefield where my father was wounded in 1942. Eventually, after two more visits and after East Timor won its independence, my father organized a partnership between the graduate schools of medicine and of management at Yale and agencies in East Timor to rebuild the devastated infrastructure there. When he told me about this, I saw some of the old excitement in his face, and when Belo received the Nobel, my father and Brenda traveled to Stockholm to witness the speech and celebrate.

But Brenda's alcoholism was progressing, and weeks in a few rehabilitation centers had not worked. Then, in a freak horseback riding accident, she broke her pelvis. Though she was just over fifty, drinking had cut into her health, and her recovery from the accident was very slow. My sisters and I intervened with my father; we were worried about *his* drinking, but we were even more concerned about Brenda—I was certain that if she didn't stop drinking very soon, she would never recover her health. As it turned out, the accident was the beginning of her decline, difficult years in which, more and more, my father became her caretaker.

*   *   *

It was during those years, in May 1994, that the part of the family living on the East Coast, including my father, gathered for the graduation from high school in Hartford of one of my nephews. Pop did not look well—he had a tooth gone, a front tooth that had been missing for almost a year. No one could understand why he hadn't replaced it, and when I joked with him about it, there was some story about an infection preventing replacement. It was a period of time when we were barely speaking—it was my failure. I was still angry at him for his refusal to come to therapy after the revelation of his homosexuality, his inability to talk to me about it, and, though my continuing anger was at odds with how I believed people should behave, I couldn't help myself. After the commencement, we all sat around the kitchen table celebrating the graduate, my sister Adelia's second son, having lunch. Afterward, when I made a move to leave, my father stood up and said, "I'd like to talk to you for a minute." He had a begging look on his face, and the black emptiness where his tooth should have been exaggerated it. We left the kitchen. The house was Victorian and there was oak paneling in the front hall, and near the carved oak doorway, a shallow built-in bench. My father and I sat down there.

He said that what he wanted to tell me he would rather not have to tell me, or anyone, but that he was quite sure I would hear about it by other means, and he wanted me to hear it from him. He'd already talked to most of my brothers and sisters, he said, and by the end of the week would have talked to all of us. A priest in the Diocese of New York with a job complaint had gone to see Bishop Grein's chaplain assistant, and in the course of the conversation had revealed that he and my father had been briefly sexually involved. The chaplain took this information to Bishop Grein, and, my father said, the priest with the complaint was encouraged to put forward an accusation of sexual harassment within the disciplinary mechanisms of the church. In preparation for a meeting with my father and the presiding bishop of the Episcopal Church, Bishop Grein called in several friends and colleagues of my father's—one was asked, he later told me, about "Paul Moore and men." This man, an Episcopal priest, also told me that he had known my father very well, and had never known about this aspect of my father's life; his first reaction, and, he told me, that of many around the cathedral, was that what Bishop Grein had implied was not true.

When the summons came for the meeting with Bishop Grein and the presiding bishop, "Brenda was just wonderful," my father said. Not only did she encourage him to bring a lawyer to the meeting, she came along as well. The investigation produced no evidence that my father had been guilty of anything but a consensual liaison—there were no grounds for defrocking, for stripping him of his orders, no grounds even for censure. In spite of that fact, my father continued, he had been "inhibited" from celebrating communion and from performing confirmations or ordinations in the Diocese of New York for a period of two years. "Inhibited," a medieval ecclesiastical term, meant that my father was not permitted to exercise his orders in his home diocese. He was not, either, to preach at the cathedral. Later, a priest who was then working at the cathedral told me that my father had once been disinvited from celebrating a funeral there of one of his friends. The bereaved arrived to find that my father would not be officiating; some excuse was made. At least one New York City parish flouted the bishop's orders and invited my father nonetheless.

The reason that my father was telling his children this story in detail was that news of the investigation, which he had assumed and expected would be kept confidential, had not been kept confidential, and facts about his life that he had tried to keep private were now known in church circles. He had refused on principle to discuss Ellen Barrett's personal life. I remembered, too, as a child, understanding that there were confidences my father kept as a sacred trust. It was almost impossible for me to imagine that someone in the church had been so careless with the reputation and feelings of a colleague. That day in Hartford, my father refused to speak against anyone, but I was angry.

"This must make you hate New York," I said.

"It makes me hate the Episcopal Church," he said.

I thought of his love for the church, what he had given the church, his tolerance for its shortcomings. I thought of all the sermons in which he promised the Savior's forgiveness, of his arms opening in welcome as he looked down at a congregation. But right now my father was not opening his long arms, he had made himself small. In spite of my own shaky sense of self where love was concerned, I felt stronger in that way than he then seemed. Oh my sweet one, I thought. What change would this experience bring to the man who had always found in the tangle of human weakness and cruelty a path through to the succor of what he understood as God's love? Now his head was bent in shame—how excruciating for him to have to make a confession like this to his children. Feeling the familiar, sickening inability to take him in my arms, I touched his hand. How could they have done this to my father? Followed by, Why not? Why should he be spared what others were not spared?

I remembered a call from a pay phone. I was dead asleep. Her plaintive voice, Would I pick her up? She was my lover, on and off, and this night she had driven from Kent, where she lived, to New Haven with a friend of ours, a gay man, who had wandered off with a trick, leaving her in the bar. Now it was after midnight, and she was at a pay phone on a deserted street. I drove the ninety minutes and picked her up at the intersection we'd agreed on. It was 2 a.m. We parked the car in an illuminated lot next to a bar and then took a walk to see if we could find a shop—cigarettes, matches, a place to sit down. Nothing open. When we returned to the bar parking lot, there was a message scrawled in the dust on the trunk of the car. DYKE. KILL THE DYKE. We took it in, the violence of the epithet and the threat. There were no further consequences of my driving out in the night to meet my woman lover, but in that parking lot in New Haven I was subject to what any woman who has sex with another woman is subject to. And now my father had been subject to what any man who has sex with another man is subject to.

But this is not what I said sitting next to the old man with the missing tooth that day in Hartford. What I said was, "I am so sorry that you have to go through this." And I repeated it over and over, taking in his white hair, his sadness, and his shame. "It makes me think of Fred Bartrop," I said, thinking of his unrecognizable voice that long-ago Sunday in Jersey City, and how my father had told and written the story. Now I thought of the silver communion set his mother had given Bartrop all those decades ago at St. Paul's, how Fred had returned it to my father when he was stripped of his orders, how, years later, my father had seen to it that Bartrop was reinstated as a priest, how he'd had the communion set refurbished and engraved, returning it as a gift when Bartrop celebrated his first Eucharist in twenty-five years, how he had chosen "Bear," newly reinstated, as one of the presenters when he was consecrated bishop in Washington. The darkness where my father's tooth had been was the mark of his kinship with his old teacher, with the men to whom he had given communion that night at Integrity, with those whose names he'd read at the AIDS requiem.

And it was evidence, evidence of his vulnerability to forces I'd imagined him free of, us free of. Although my father looked terrible and sad, he had no intention of leaving the priesthood. He would ride it out.

When I got to my car, I sat for quite a while before starting the engine, tears burning my face in the close June heat. If I had not had a headache earlier, I got one then; all I wanted was not to have seen my father in a condition of such suffering. "Gay and proud," came the words out of my mouth—not a locution I'd ever uttered about myself or about my father—but now I took the phrase in. I had understood for some time that there had been tentativeness in my own homosexual existence. Whatever I am, I must make my way to it, I thought to myself, pulling into the traffic. In spite of my openness about my relationships with women, I felt in myself an avoidance, a turning away from forces that moved in my spirit, an angry wanting I kept secret even from myself.

My father had not kept his equivalent desire secret from himself, but the events he recounted to me on the bench in Hartford were vindication of the precarious wisdom of the choice he had made to keep his homosexual life secret from others. He had not exaggerated when he imagined the worst consequences of revealing the entirety of who he was. This terrible consequence was central to the story of the bargain my father had struck. As I drove the familiar Connecticut roads, all my rage at him about his secrecy and deceit now seemed small, even sentimental. If I continued to sit in judgment of him, then I was no better than his enemies.

19
Wayfarers

When I sat in tears that day in my car in Hartford, thinking of my father's lost tooth, making a pledge to come to terms with my sexuality, I did not expect I would return to men. But that winter, after years of intermittent flirtations with men that always unsettled my relationships with women, a man began to pursue me, and we went out for several months. Eventually I found myself free to fall in love. I met Raphael when

I moved back to New York in late 1998, and we saw each other for nearly a year. In retrospect, I see that he was both available and unavailable; in the end, he turned cruelly from me, but our months together were filled with pleasure, and hope. It was the collapse of that relationship that took me back to therapy, and that therapist who said one day, as I wept at some twist in a story I was telling, "You must once have loved your father very much." And that day that I shouted, "No! Absolutely not."

"Okay," the therapist said.

And I fell to weeping again, remembering the feeling of possibility I'd had with Raphael, the wonderful dinners we made for friends at his house on Martha's Vineyard, the laughs, hours spent in New York museums as we talked and talked about his childhood in Rome, his architectural study at Harvard, his interest in my writing. In the rush of its beginning, this love seemed a solution, a way to repair all my years of failure with men and with women. Perhaps, with Raphael's protection, I might even repair my relationship with my father. And so, when the love affair ended, I was faced with everything I had put aside. When I tried to write, I could write only fragments and transcriptions of dreams. It was as if I had to make myself all over again. I had time and no alternative, and so I committed myself. After several months of work, my therapist suggested I try again to bring my father in for a few sessions.

"Why do I have to do this?"

"You don't have to," the therapist said gently. "But I think it would help you."

"How? He'll just shout at me."

"But I'll be here. I think you'll be able to say what you need to say."

There were reasons I was still so angry. During the summer of 1997, my father had sent each of his children the galleys of *Presences*, a memoir of his life and career to be published the following December. I remembered when he began writing it; we were in the Adirondacks and he was reading the published version of John Cheever's diaries in which details of the writer's gay life are recounted. "I'm afraid I can't be as candid as Mr. Cheever," he said when I asked how he liked the book, and turned back to it like a boy to an adventure story. As time went on, we had periodic conversations about how his writing was going. His editors, he told me, kept asking him to make the book "more personal." At least once, I suggested that if he told the truth about his sexual conflicts, his book would be profoundly "personal" and a great culmination of his ministry. I said I'd learned the power of self-revelation from him. "I just can't," he said. He had hurt Brenda so much, and there were his brother and sister to think of. At the time, I was disappointed in his lack of courage, but after our conversation in Hartford, I realized that perhaps I had been asking too much of him. I could write what I wanted to, but I was from a different generation, I had no spouse or children, and, most important, I did not have a public life as a religious leader.

But when I read the actual text in bound galleys, I saw that, under pressure to be personal, my father had disclosed painful details of my mother's life—her collapse after the accident, her time in Payne Whitney. I was furious. Without disclosure of his own sexual secret, his description of my mother made her seem selfish and irrational. He did not admit to having been unfaithful, therefore it was inexplicable that she had banished him from their marriage bed. "Even now I do not know what came between us," he wrote. She'd had a great life as a mother, had been a friend to many and a partner in his work—why did she feel her life had been worthless? I found his account of their life together utterly self-serving, and so did many of my siblings. How could he lay bare our mother's vulnerability without taking any responsibility for his part in the collapse of their marriage? She was not here to tell her side of the story, and furthermore, she had protected him! For years she had known of his sexual relationships with men, but, in pain herself and sensing his suffering, had never confronted him. Nor had she betrayed him by revealing what she knew to any of us. Our collective anger, held in check the years since our mother's death, rose in a tidal wave of fury. In the end, he removed some details but not others.

Now, six months after the book's appearance, I was living in New York and my father was calling. He wanted to see me, but I was still angry and I didn't return his calls. "He's just an old man," one of my friends said. "Call him back." I felt threatened. Still in pain at the loss of Raphael, how could I risk that abrupt barking anger of my father's? In therapy, I was putting together the loss of Raphael with the history of my relationship with my father, and I was beginning to go out with other men. I dreamed of my father standing with me, the house in Kent disintegrating, submerged in floodwater; of Raphael returning, of myself unable to choose between women's clothes and men's clothes, of men with female bodies, of women with male bodies. If my New York phone rang, I'd pick it up, terrified it would be my father, and, sitting in restaurants, I'd see a man I was sure was Raphael talking animatedly with another woman, and then he'd turn his head. People my age whom I passed on the street looked old; I felt old and defeated. So much that had been familiar turned alien; the therapist's tiny office was my only refuge. I came to understand that I had moved to Connecticut not only to write my book but to escape the confusion of my sexuality and of my relationship with my father. I was learning that I spent days in bed not from exhaustion but from sadness, from depression, that my headaches were apt to follow family phone calls or visits. I cried for hours at a time.

It was also a difficult time for my father. He was beginning, at least intuitively, to understand that Brenda was leaving him—not walking away, but drinking herself away, falling down, her broken bones never healing, lying on the sofa at Bank Street or in Stonington, just lying there, drinking, her face set in unhappiness. My father felt guilty and responsible and he missed her ebullience and humor. The last time I saw her was at a family Christmas party. She looked seventy though she was only fifty-six; she had shrunken back to her bones. I had found two tiny objects for her, a miniature green wire basket, a tiny Chinese ceramic bird. I watched her open them, barely able to work her fingers, and then she looked up, lifted herself, and stumbled over to me. "Oh, you know me so well. It is so extraordinary to be known so well," she said, and kissed me, her hot breath dense with alcohol.

Eventually my father's persistence wore me down. "I just wanted to be sure you'd gotten the message," came his voice on the answering machine. One day, I decided to write him. I admitted I had been avoiding him and asked if he'd come to therapy with me. He quickly agreed.

To the first session he wore a garish black-and-white tweed suit, a mustard-colored shirt, a matching handkerchief fluttering from the chest pocket. He was very solemn, greeting my therapist as "Doctor" and giving me a kiss of greeting. The therapist spoke quietly, announcing to my father that there were things I wanted to say, and then he said, "Perhaps you can tell me, since I don't know you, something about the history of your marriage and of your relationship with Honor."

My father began to talk like a movie voice-over. I looked at my therapist, intent as my father told the formulaic story, falling in love with my mother after he was wounded, his decision to go to Seattle, how his decision to marry my mother was reached on his trip home, the details, as familiar to me now as certain sequences from the Book of Common Prayer.

When the therapist asked me to speak, I told my version of our story and my mother's story, integrating the fact of my father's bisexuality. I spoke of my anger at his refusal to take responsibility for his role in the breakup of his marriage to my mother, his insistence since her death on blaming her, painting her in his memoir as a depressive lunatic, all to keep his complicated secret. And then my father began to shout.

"Please don't shout," I said quietly.

"If you weren't so GODDAMN oversensitive."

"Yes, I am sensitive. Please don't shout." And then he was weeping. I reached for him.

I remember being able to speak clearly, and I remember that he listened. Of course, my father was used to listening—but after a while he didn't seem to be listening like a pastor. I said everything that had hurt me, the words flowing out of me in sentences, paragraphs. I saw across what seemed a long distance that my father loved me and that he had missed me. It had hurt him when I withdrew after my mother's death, he said. That didn't surprise me. But what he said next amazed me. Why hadn't I come home to take care of the youngest children after my mother died? When I answered—"Pop, you never asked me! And I had my own life!"— he looked bewildered. What comes back so clearly from those ten hours is looking at him, reaching for him as he cried, and coming to understand who it was I was going to have to love if I was going to love my father. And the relief I felt that he hadn't given up on me.

Summer was coming, and I asked for some time. We had torn down the old house and dug up the field. In the fall we would begin again.

But then Brenda became very ill, and then she went into the hospital. My father was so beset, I thought the last thing he'd want was a therapy session with me, and so, characteristically, I didn't bring it up and, equally characteristically, neither did he. By the following spring, it was clear that Brenda was dying, of liver failure. When I got to the hospital with my youngest sister, Patience, she was unconscious, thin, yellow, a husk. Within a month, she died. Days after the funeral, I took my father out to dinner at a French bistro on MacDougal Street. I wanted to let him know that I was with him. We talked about what he was planning to do. He'd thought about leaving Bank Street, he said, but he was too sad, it was too soon—he was going to stay "for the time being." And then he asked about my love life. "There are a few men," I said.

"Men?" he said. "I'm surprised," and he leaned back, the evening sun playing off his face. He'd met several men I'd seen. He'd met Raphael. How could he have forgotten?

"Yes, men. I am seeing men, now."

"Well," he said, lifting a glass, "to the future!"

Our reunion was short-lived. The selling of the Kent house and the end of my Connecticut life in the fall of 2001 just weeks after 9/11, a new teaching job, deaths of friends, all combined to postpone a return to our therapy, and at the end of 2002, when my therapist and I were talking about trying again, my father, unable to recover from a long bout with pneumonia, had a chest X-ray. A spot on his lung, and on New Year's Eve, a diagnosis of melanoma. But he had no intention of dying. "They'll have to shoot you at one hundred and fifty," was a remark he liked to repeat, something a doctor said after a physical he had in his late seventies. The diagnosis gave him a new lease on life. It was as if he were Henry James's Lambert Strether, the hero of *The Ambassadors*, freed of all restraint. Yes, I *will* live all I can. It *is* a mistake not to. As his children muttered in awe, my father sped around the country, even the world. *It doesn't so much matter what you do in particular, so long as you have your life. If you haven't had that what have you had?* Lambert Strether proclaimed to his young friend Bilham. My father postponed a brain scan so he could go fishing in the Amazon, a lifelong dream. "Don't you think I should go?" he asked. "Of course you should," I said. He hired a guide and went by himself. As a precaution, the doctors had given him Decadron, a drug to prevent swelling should he have tumors in his brain, to keep him from having seizures—Decadron's side effect is euphoria. And my father was euphoric, sending home wild, misspelled, miscapitalized e-mails, "countless peACOCK BASS. BUTER-

FLY BASS, PIRANHA, CAIMEN (cROCODILES), PARROTS MONKEYS
MACAWS sTORKS, ETC ETC lOVE pop."

On his return he had a brain scan, and days later my sister Rosemary
and I sat with him in a consulting room at Columbia-Presbyterian, listening to a surgeon trying to be gentle. The doctor told us that when he
looked at the MRI of my father's head, he stopped counting at six. Six sites
of melanoma, and they were continuing to spread—replicate—across my
father's brain. Something like spiderwebs, or mold, the cancer's origin a
cyst removed from behind his ear—"just a little something"—two years
earlier.

"These conversations are theological, not medical," the surgeon said,
and my father laughed.

"We should get along very well."

Between radiation sessions to arrest the tumors, my father hit the road
again, his Decadron-induced euphoria fueling his appetite to respond to
every invitation. A columnist in the Metro section of the *New York Times*
had noted in a profile that he was fighting an aggressive cancer, and letters
of support arrived at Bank Street by the score. He traveled to Chicago to
give the keynote at the annual meeting of the Episcopal Urban Caucus, an
occasion that was a reunion of those whom he had inspired for decades in
their work in the church and city. There was a standing ovation. "I've never
felt better in my life," he kept saying as he bought another airplane ticket:
a visit to my brothers and sisters in California, a sermon in Washington,
a week in Antigua with great friends. My brother George predicted that if
our father was to die at all, it would surely be in an airport line. "Such a
great man," people said as I moved through my life in New York. "I'm so
sorry about your father." And then there was a day when he no longer felt
like traveling. I took him to the theater one night and he was suddenly
feeble, for the first time looking his age. I was grateful for the gloss of formality; touching him with authentic affection was still difficult; as if all the
years of distance had irreversibly calcified, or had acquired an independent dynamism. I could take his arm to help him up the marble steps to
the dining room at the Century Club, or to the curb for a taxi, but I held
myself in when he embraced me.

But as the days went on, I could feel something returning to life, something from long ago, like the familiarity of a house in a dream. I began to
burst abruptly into tears, and there he would be, young again, rowing a

golden guide boat through black water, telling me a story. I want to love my father again, I said to myself as into each day came the new reality of his dying. The doctor had said he had four months. I didn't have much time to make it right and I didn't know how I possibly could, but now I could hardly bear being apart from him. One night I called my sister Marian, who had come in from Minneapolis to take care of him. She is ten years younger than I am. "I can't stand this," I said to her. "I'm so sad for him."

"I'm so interested," she said, tentative, compassionate, "that you're in this place . . . He's very happy about where he is with you," she continued. I told her about our last dinner out together, when he'd told me about his conversion—his big hands pushing off from his head, his arms opening. "I felt the presence of God. It changed my life," he said. "And I could always return there, and during the war, what came to me in battle when I was among the dying, the Crucifixion—that was where I could go with my questions, with my . . ." Here was the man whose ring they kneel and kiss. A man who had actually lived something he called faith, something implacable, certain, unassailable.

On March 19, 2003, the United States invaded Iraq and there were demonstrations all over the world, and four days later my father preached at an evensong for peace at St. John the Divine. Mark Sisk had succeeded Bishop Grein, and this was one of the first sermons my father had been invited to give at the cathedral since he had been inhibited. Listening to the tape now, I hear that my father's voice was weak, but I also hear the familiar preacher as he forcefully poses a question. "What kind of Christian," he asks, "is a man who prays alone in the White House before proceeding with a war that millions across the earth of all faiths have protested? What are we going to do?

"I don't know," he said, answering his own question, and in that *I don't know* was the knowledge that he would not live to find out. "But no sermon can end without hope," he continued. "No sermon is complete without hope. Some hopes are just dreams. Some have reality. This is one of my most favorite, from the Book of Revelation.

And I saw a new heaven and a new earth: for the first heaven and the first earth were passed away; and there was no more sea. And I John saw the holy

city, new Jerusalem, coming down from God out of heaven, prepared as a
bride adorned for her husband. And I heard a great voice out of heaven say-
ing, Behold, the tabernacle of God is with men, and he will dwell with them,
and they shall be his people, and God himself shall be with them, and be their
God. And God shall wipe away all tears from their eyes; and there shall be
no more death, neither sorrow, nor crying, neither shall there be any more
pain: for the former things are passed away.

And then, on the tape, I can hear the sound of rustling papers, and my
father giving a concluding blessing. "Let us in silence pray that these dark
times will pass. Pray that we will have the courage and the freedom to
stand against death and destruction, pray that our leaders will turn from
their course. Pray that our loved ones will be protected. Pray that this
great land will again be a land that lives out our principles and a land that
people come to with peace and joy. Amen."

There is a video of the aftermath of that service. My father is sitting in
the nave of the cathedral, and people are coming up to him, and I stop
counting when the number of those who kiss him and whom he kisses
and embraces passes one hundred. "I love you, Bishop," over and over, or
he grabs at the hand of a nun, "Will you come see me, so we can talk about
old times?"

In early April, at the yearly family meeting in New York about the Adirondacks, my father begs us to care for "that exquisite . . . exquisite . . .
place . . ." and unable to find the next word, tears coursing down his face,
exclaims, "It's my . . . brain . . . my . . ." After the meeting, eight of his children and a few of his grandchildren celebrate him around a big table at the
Waverly Inn, each toasting a quality he's passed on. "Your love of life," I
say, raising a glass. And the following week, in the enormous gallery at the
Century Club, there is a party, my father sitting in an old-fashioned bent-
wood wheelchair surrounded by more than a hundred friends and family.
Imagine! A going-away party before one's death—off-color, sentimental,
and heartfelt toasts, my father's face happily large and placid, bowing like
a great balloon.

At Bank Street, the telephone rarely stopped ringing, my father making
dates still, in his inevitable tiny black book, visitors arriving to take him

out to lunch, to have tea, cocktails, supper. They call ahead or just arrive at the door begging to see him, and he sits there, praying with those who come to pray, smiling and nodding with old friends from Indianapolis or Washington. "You can't see him," I say once to a caller. And the prominent man in his eighties bursts into tears. "Never again?" And so I write him into the book for the next morning. And so the days pass and I teach, ride the subway, sit in a café reading student papers or writing, everyone walking past outside as if the world were a normal place, as if the blue sky were actually blue, as if my father were leading an Easter procession again, in his white brocade, following the gold cross, the dry, heated air pungent with incense.

One Tuesday morning, Rosemary and I hired a town car and took him to Columbia-Presbyterian Hospital. He had been having radiation for eight weeks; if the tumors had decreased in size, then it would be possible to attempt further treatment—in other words, there would be a chance of survival. We wheeled him into the doctor's small consulting room, Rosie and I each taking a chair. "How are you?" the doctor said.

"Weaker," my father said. The doctor was looking at the sheets on his clipboard, lifting one, and then another. "What I really want to know is what's going on up here," my father continued, pointing to his head.

"It's worse," the doctor said. "It's going to progress at a relatively rapid pace."

"A week? Three weeks?" Pop asked.

"Weeks," the doctor said. "How many I don't know." I saw my father look a little dazed, and so I filled the silence.

"Would it have been worse without radiation?"

"Much worse," the doctor said.

"Well," my father began, "my brother came to see me two days ago. I knew what I wanted to say, and then, well then I just forgot it!" I looked at Rosie.

"There will be more incidents like that," the doctor said, as if he were talking about a problem with a furnace or a car. "Also more sleepiness and seizures."

"What do we do now?" my father asked, and the doctor said that the only treatment possible now was palliative care and the continued use of Decadron. "There's nothing else?" my father asked, and the doctor continued his emotionless monologue.

"My own outlook is to be very aggressive in treating this disease, but to be realistic, treating it aggressively when such treatment will have no effect just makes the patient miserable."

"So I'll just gradually get worse until . . ."

"It's not going to be gradual." My father looked at the doctor, his eyes filling. The doctor looked away, and then my father's head dropped as if he were a heartbroken child.

Back in the waiting room, when Rosie left for a moment, he looked at me and said, "I sort of knew, didn't you?"

"Sort of," I said. Then, to change the subject, I asked him his latest thoughts about an afterlife.

"I don't know," he said. "I think I'll just go to sleep," and then, "Well, no one has really come back from the afterlife."

"No one except Jesus," I said.

"And he was a little"—there was a pause—"maybe a little nuts." His mystified expression was like a big cartoon.

"I don't think it was as bad for Jesus as it is for you," I said. He looked at me as if I were crazy and held out both his hands, palms up.

"But he had *pain.*"

"But don't you think," I said, "that the pain was so great he might have stopped feeling it?" Pop looked at me and I at him, and then we began to laugh.

Two days later when I arrived at Bank Street, my father was in the living room, facing the window in his big chair. He had been scheduled to preach the previous Sunday, Palm Sunday, at St. Mark's in-the-Bowery, had climbed the pulpit only to find he had brought the wrong notes; the congregation had broken his fumbling silence with applause and chanting, "We love you, Bishop Moore." He had become what the hospice worker called "confused"—he talked like a poem or like a character out of Samuel Beckett: "Three gentlemen came, we had the luncheon, that was all." In fact only one man had come for lunch, and Pop had sent him away. The day was beautiful, and so I wheeled him out the front door onto the stoop, and we sat there for a while, watching the new buds on the trees.

I stayed for supper. We ordered food from a place called Mama's, and at the table that had once been in the Kent dining room, we ate turkey and mashed potatoes. Halfway through supper, he began an inventory of his children. He was looking at me, his white hair, his wide-open blue eyes, and it was dark in the room. When he got to me, he paused and took a breath.

"That therapy we had didn't work," he said.

You must once have loved your father very much. The light in the therapist's small office came back.

"It worked for me," I said. "Why do you say it didn't?"

"We didn't finish," he said.

"Brenda got sick, I didn't think you would have wanted—"

"It didn't bring us back together." *Together.* The word wrenched my heart.

"But I'm here," I said, filled with sorrow that I had failed him again. Then, abruptly, he seemed somewhere else.

"And why was it that we went to therapy?" he asked. I forgot that he had tumors in his brain, that he was losing thought and memory, that he was dying. I was angry that he didn't remember as I did. Cold and angry.

But I couldn't stay angry. Two mornings later, a call from Bank Street: He'd had a terrible night. He was incontinent and frightened. "His brain function has further deteriorated," I wrote my brothers and sisters when I got home that evening. "His memory is utterly blasted and his verbal capacity near zero; the same with his comprehension. This was not expected to get better, though if he rested, it could uptick a little." Oxygen was brought into the house, and a supply of liquid morphine. Rosemary and I met with the hospice nurse, who delineated certain milestones that mark the way to death. My father was not yet picking at his bedclothes, there weren't yet "changes" in his skin. His heart was still strong. But I put a message on his voice mail saying that he was no longer accepting calls.

The next morning, however, I arrived to find my father had slept very well—twenty hours straight. With the nurse's help, he had showered and put on his red silk aviator jacket, one of his favorite presents from Brenda. Rosie and I sat down with him and the hospice nurse, and Pop very clearly said he wanted to stay at home "for the duration," as if he were asking our permission.

"Yes," we both said. "Yes, of course."

The next day, Good Friday, I arrived after lunch. We did his mail, and as the sun fell and the room darkened, we were having what conversation his sputtering synapses allowed. On an impulse, I went over and sat on the chair next to him, snuggled up to him, and said in a little-girl voice, "Oh, Poppy, will you tell me a story?" I hadn't called him that in years, and I expected he'd cuddle in return, but instead, violently, he drew back.

"I love you," he said, an expression of terror and distaste on his face, "but not . . . so . . . close." He tried to recover himself. "I mean I love you, but . . ." I had been helping finish his sentences, and so I helped him complete this one.

". . . not that much."

"Yes," he said, holding himself apart, "not that much."

It was my turn to draw back. I stood up and moved in the darkness to the sofa across from him, holding tears in. This time I wouldn't flee, I told myself. I would sit right through whatever came. I watched him turn toward me and settle back into his chair, and I settled into mine and considered how to reconfigure the conversation.

Suddenly I heard him say, "Once upon a time . . ." And then he stopped, embarrassed.

And I said, like a child again, "Oh, tell it . . ."

"I think I'm too—" He couldn't find the word, so he tapped his head.

"Please," I said into the darkness.

"Once upon a time," he said, "there was a little girl who lived by herself in a house in the forest. Every night she dreamed of a wonderful man who would come and save her." He said "wonderful" as his mother would have, bouncing from syllable to syllable, the sound of the word becoming a world of tenderness and wonder. "Night after night she dreamed of this man, oh, how she wanted this man." My father was inside himself, not looking at me. "And then one night she heard the sound of footsteps outside." And here he tapped his chair with a finger. Tap tap tap. "Footsteps through the forest. The little girl was frightened. What was it? Who was it? And then she heard a knocking at her door." And Pop knocked on a table, hard: the bishop knocking on the doors of the cathedral, the storyteller sound effect that thrilled me as a child. "Should she go to the door? She couldn't tell if it was a mean man or the dream man." A mean man or the dream man! I leaned forward, and he continued, no problem with the sentences. "She was so scared. But she heard the knock again." And my father knocked again on his table. "And this time she went to the door and opened it and there before her stood the most extraordinary man she had ever seen, dressed in white armor and carrying a sword and a spear."

This was a new story, nothing I'd ever heard him tell. How could he know I was falling in love, right then. Falling deeply in love with a man who was also falling in love with me? How could he know that in the darkness of these extraordinary months, my question had been exactly the one he was now asking for me: *A mean man or the dream man?* It was as if this father of mine had walked the terrain of my dreams, had found there the thread of my story, a story he was now, at the brink of death, weaving from what had gone unsaid all our years together. Soon the girl and the man were dancing, he was saying, and I could see us, whirling around the room. "And then, then," my father said, with an exhalation of relief, "then they went to bed together!"

"Pop," I said, "what about breakfast?" My father hesitated, and then he smiled, a glint of delighted mischief in his eyes.

"I can't tell you that now."

One morning the following week, I climbed the stairs to my father's room, opened the bedroom window, and pulled up a shade. The room had low ceilings and took the entire width of the house, four windows, sunlight coming in through all of them. His bed was queen-size and quite low, and there he was, lying on the coverlet, a pale mint green embroidered elegant thing. I rearranged his pillows so that he could hold a glass of iced tea and drink without spilling. He'd allowed me to help him, to be tender with him. I'd brought him some French blue cheese and crackers, because blue cheese was always his favorite. Sometimes, late at night in Indianapolis, he'd pour himself a glass of milk and cut a piece of Roquefort, and I'd sit with him in the kitchen. He'd be wearing khakis and a flannel shirt, just as he was today in the sunlight on the bed in which he would die. It was this late night cheese that he gave up whenever he wanted to get back down to his usual 185 pounds, and now he still looked beautiful, the black eye he'd got falling a month before still there, but diminished, his skin healthy. He was clean and shiny, the same physical body I knew as a child.

I wanted to hold his hand and he didn't resist, so I took it. Now there were not many sentences he could make. He would begin and then, when he couldn't form the next word, say, "Oh shit," and we'd giggle. But he had one remaining sentence: "What do you think?"

And now he said it to me. "What do you think?"

"That I love you very much," I said, squeezing his hand, feeling him squeeze back as, sad, I said, "I'm sorry it's been so hard," meaning our life together, which is I'm sure what he understood. I kept hold of his hand, his long, slender fingers, the sun in the room making everything beautiful. He tried to say something else, "We—" and then all he could do was mumble, but he kept looking at me, and I kept crying, which felt safe. This moment will always bring tears, I thought to myself, because in it was the lost land, the place we could have had a life together as father and daughter all our lives. Perhaps what is meant by the land of milk and honey is this room with the sun falling across my tall, lanky father, catching the white of his hair. Time was shifting, the years of obstruction falling away. We race to the house on Bank Street as if we are still, or have become again, the children who are proud to tell our friends that our father is six feet four and three quarters, who love to see him in his vestments sweeping down the aisle.

And then one night, after helping him to the bathroom, bathing and changing him, putting him to bed, my sister Susanna and the hospice nurse left his room for just a moment, and he bolted from bed, falling, crushing the mahogany rocker, the last piece of furniture from his grandmother's big house in Chicago. Now, for the first time, he had pain, and for it, liquid morphine. "The surge of life," is what the hospice worker called his great leap, another marker of the nearness of death.

It was May 1, May Day, festival day of revolutionaries, signal of emergency. I was startled awake at six-thirty. It was a teaching day. I don't remember how I got up to Columbia, but I had an office hour, and then forty-five minutes into class, my cell phone rang: "They say it's imminent." I leapt into a taxi. When I got to his room, Pop was laboriously breathing, his skin chalky, no more radiance. My sister Patience was in a chair next to the bed. I kissed her hello and took his hand. The blinds were pulled against the light, no chance of another trip downstairs, no sentences left. Patience left the room, and Rosie came in, then Abdillahi arrived. Rosie and I left Abdillahi alone with Pop for a few minutes—Abdillahi, a Somali from Kenya, an unofficial adopted tenth child for the last forty years.

After a few minutes, Rosie and I came back into the room and Abdillahi left. Then my father spat something up, and I wiped his cheek. Rosie left the room to call a friend who was going to a Tibetan prayer service, to ask her to pray for Pop, and then I noticed his chest had stopped rising, that he was not breathing. I was holding his hand. I wondered if this was death.

And then he breathed again. And I said, "I really love you, Pop. We all really love you. And we love each other. We really do, and we love you." Then, wanting to tell the truth, "You taught us love . . . in all its colors." What I meant was, even the dark, cruel colors. "And we will be all right." I couldn't tell if he could hear me, but I said it anyway. "And so you can go, when you're ready."

And then he took a big breath, like a baby opening his mouth for a breast. And he didn't breathe again.

The living room was getting dark. My brother Dan was standing against the wall, I was sitting down, Marian was sitting down, and Rosie was on the sofa. The funeral people, Tommy and Anita, were small. "Is there anyone else coming?" Marian asked when they arrived. We wondered how these two little people would get our father's long body down the stairway. We'd foraged his closet for vestments and I'd chosen his rochet and chimere—the scarlet overvest that fell to the ground over the flowing white chemise, long sleeves gathered at the wrist. He looked beautiful in that, and I found a black tippet and a white brocade stole with *IHS* embroidered in gold and black and crimson. I remember so well Pop solemnly explaining those initials as Greek letters signifying Jesus, but now they looked tender and familiar and small.

Downstairs we waited. There was light on the wall along the stairwell, the creamy yellow of incandescent electricity, and the narrow balusters cast faint shadows. First we heard it, a thumping, and then between the white of the balusters and the ghostly creaminess of the bare wall appeared the black of a body bag, a very long body bag, nosing down the carpeted stairs, my father in a black plastic bag in a slow fall, the stripes of the balusters a ripple between all of us waiting there and him leaving us, shiny and black against the bare white wall.

20

Andrew Verver

M y father died in May, and in early November, a truckload of boxes
and a few pieces of furniture were delivered to my apartment on
Riverside Drive. The apartment was small, but in spite of my having chosen, I thought, a minimum of things from the estate, there were many
boxes to be unpacked. As the day went on, I developed a horrific headache. I continued unwrapping china anyway, filling the sink with hot,
soapy water, washing Staffordshire pitchers which had gathered dust for
decades, first at Hollow Hill and later at Bank Street. It felt a little like
Christmas. Out of a flat mirror box came a big watercolor of the living

room at Hollow Hill, in which I could see the very pitchers I was unwrapping lined up on the shelves of a tall New England cupboard. Now I was
thinking of Gami racing toward me down the steps, sun streaming into
the entrance hall, and of my father as a child packed up and waiting in
that same entrance hall for the chauffeured car that would take him to St.
Paul's. And of my grandmother later, her language lost to a stroke, sitting
on the sofa in that living room, her darkly freckled hand reaching for me,
wedding diamond sparkling, the gold necklace I now wear resting in the
folds of her old-fashioned flowered blouse.

Overcome by the headache, I lay down in my bed and looked up at
the bookshelves—the green leather-bound Buxton Forman Keats my
father gave me when I read Keats as a junior at Harvard, the bright look
on his face, as if he were handing me a treasure. He *was* handing me a
treasure. The pressure of the headache and slight nausea cut into my
thinking. When had I last eaten? When had I last read Keats? I thought
of getting up and taking one of the books from the shelf. The headache
must be sadness. The headache must be an allergy to all this old dust, all
this memory.

As it happened, it was my father's birthday, and my father's absence
still sailed through me like a dark ship, alternating with images of his
dying, the visceral sense of his love that afternoon in his sunny bedroom
days before he died, when I sat watching him, along with Rosemary and
Adelia, all of us imagining what our family might have been had we always
had the love from him we felt that day.

Then the telephone rang.

"This is Andrew Verver." He had a confident voice.

Andrew Verver was the only name in my father's will that was unfa-
miliar when we sat in the lawyer's office the day before the funeral.
The moment had passed without comment, but later Rosie identified
Andrew as the man who had gone with my father to Patmos the summer
before. "I need someone to look after the tickets, you know," my father
said at the time.

"Yeah, right," said Marian when we talked about it.

"How was the trip, Pop?" Rosie asked after he returned.

"Great."

"How was Andrew?"

"He worried about his girlfriend the whole time."

"Yeah, right," I said to Rosie. Then laughter. And sadness: Why couldn't he tell us the truth?

"This is Andrew Verver," said the voice on the telephone.

Two months earlier, I had gone to the cathedral press office to pick up copies of my father's obituaries, and among them had been a letter from Andrew Verver dated the day after the funeral. He had been a "very close" friend of my father's for nearly thirty years, he wrote in a crooked but clear hand. Thirty years? Yes, thirty years. He would like to visit my father's grave. He would like to see the videos that had been shown at the reception after the funeral.

Reading the letter, I'd felt like I had when my father was dying—nothing in my body or mind but a pull translating to *Take care of him*. What if this man on the telephone had been my father's lover? How would it be for me if I had been the secret lover of a "great man," of a man as protected as my father was? Suddenly there is no access. Had Andrew Verver come to the funeral? Alone? How far back had he had to sit? And afterward, who had been there for his grief? I wrote him back that day. *Of course you can visit Pop's grave—I will try to get directions for you—I would also very much like to meet you. I'd love to hear about the trip to Patmos. My # is . . .* He had not called in September, but now it was my father's birthday, and here he was.

His voice was soft in texture.

The beginning of the conversation was formal.

"Your father was a close friend of mine."

"Yes."

"For almost thirty years."

"Yes. You said so in your letter—"

"I'm sorry I didn't call sooner."

"I was just about to—"

"I had . . . feelings."

"Today is his birthday!"

"Yes. Oh, I didn't know that. Right. His birthday."

Andrew had been a student at Columbia, a Roman Catholic. "I was considering being received into the Episcopal Church," he said. "I went to your father for advice. He was very helpful. At first it was a pastoral thing," Andrew continued, "and after a while, we became friends." He had an accent I couldn't place. Boston? Near Boston, it turned out. "We were very close friends," he repeated. "Paul came to my father's funeral. My family knew him. He even came all the way out to Brooklyn, to my new apartment."

Rosie and I had laughed about that. "Where are you going, Pop?" she asked him after a lunch on her birthday. "I'm going to visit a friend in Queens." "Queens?" "Yes, I'm going to visit a friend there, who's a teacher." When Rosie repeated this to me, I had an image of my father, his tall, white-haired, black-suited self, on the subway, then walking down a narrow street lined with row houses, bending to ring a doorbell. I couldn't visualize the man who opened the door, but I saw the inside of the apartment. Modest. Afternoon sun. A cup of coffee offered. My father carrying a small package, a house gift. Of course, I didn't know then that the man had just moved into the apartment, that this was the first time my father had visited Andrew at home, that the package was a jar of very good black caviar, or that it wasn't coffee that was offered but vodka.

"He even came to my new apartment," Andrew repeated.

"I'm so happy to be talking to you," I said.

"I would have called sooner—"

"I understand," I said. Then there was silence. "I want to hear about Patmos," I said.

"I had been there before," Andrew said, "but Paul hadn't. I had had a spiritual experience in the cave, where Saint John wrote the Book of Revelation. And Paul wanted to see it, so we went there."

Should I write this down? Though my headache was almost unbearable, I had no desire to hang up. I reached for a notebook, and a pen. Andrew was silent, but I could hear him there. I couldn't get over his humility, the calm in his voice. And how he could wait through a silence.

"Your father was a good friend to me," he said.

"I'm so glad," I repeated. *Good friend*, I wrote. We had been talking for about twenty minutes. I kept being afraid he would hang up, that he would stop talking about my father, telling me these things. Oh, please don't hang up.

"Your father told me a great deal," Andrew said in that gentle voice, that accent with the broad New England vowels.

"Yes," I said. And then suddenly I realized I should take advantage of talking to this man who was so close to my father.

"Did he tell you about us? About . . . me?"

"You had some problems with each other."

"Yes," I said, "we did."

So my father had had someone to talk to, someone with whom he had talked about his children who was a tender, sympathetic person. Had this man been my father's lover? The fact that my father had bequeathed Andrew his bedside table seemed almost too bad a joke.

"Tell me more about Patmos."

"It was wonderful. I couldn't keep up with Paul." I loved the way he said Paul. As if he had loved him. "We climbed the volcano. He ran up the hill. There he was, in his eighties, and I could hardly keep up with him. We went to the cave. Your father was carrying the book around, of Revelation, preparing. 'This guy is crazy,' he said." Andrew was laughing, not with derision or even amusement. It was the laugh inside a secret, the kind children laugh, the kind you laugh when you share something with a lover.

Now there was another silence. "We should get together sometime," I said. And he gave me his phone number. "We could go to his grave," I said, "together."

This man had loved my father, whom he had no obligation to love. This man missed my father, whom he had no obligation to miss. I missed my father.

"That would be great," Andrew said.

"Sometime after Christmas," I said.

"We were so close, your father and I. He told me a lot of things." He didn't want to get off the telephone either.

"About—"

"About your family. About his life. We missed our boat to Patmos, and we had to spend the night on Samos, another island. Something about the missed connection freed Paul, and we really talked that night. It was a beautiful night, we sat outside, we ate fish." I could hear Andrew breathing. I could imagine this man holding on to my father's hand with the tenderness with which he was staying on the telephone, waiting. The silence opened, my headache throbbed. All over the floor was the crumpled newspaper.

"Did he talk to you about his sexual life?" Two men in Greece in the bright evening sun.

"I was his sexual life," Andrew said.

"You were?" We both began to laugh.

"For a long time."

"I am so happy he had someone like you," I managed to say.

"Of course there were other men," he said.

Andrew, a student at Columbia, had been having trouble with the Catholic Church. Young, gay, tired of the church's hypocrisy about homosexuality. "I thought the Episcopal Church would be better." I laughed.

"Was it?" He was laughing too.

"A little."

It was 1975. Andrew, having read about my father, wrote to him at the cathedral, and my father wrote back—*I would be glad to see you but it may take me 2–3 weeks to open up an appointment because I'm pretty clobbered right now . . . However, if you want to see somebody more quickly than that, I can recommend one of our clergy.* But Andrew, I would learn, is a determined person. He wanted to see my father and eventually it was my father whom he got in to see, and after several meetings, long conversations about Andrew's anger at the Catholic Church, in which Andrew revealed that he was gay, they became friends, and one day, Andrew said, "He asked me to go to bed." That quiet laughter again. I held on to the telephone. Nineteen seventy-five was also the year my father married Brenda. The friendship became an affair. Which continued.

"Your father met my family," Andrew said. "He came all the way to Massachusetts for my father's funeral. After he died, my brother said, 'Paul really loved you.'" And then, again, as if he had to prove something to me, Andrew said, "My family knew him."

Nothing Andrew was saying upset me. On the contrary, it made me terribly happy.

"Your father was just getting to know Brenda then," Andrew said.

It surprised me that my father had been able to choose someone kind. I would have expected someone with a harsh sense of humor, like Brenda, even like my mother. This man was witty, but he was also gentle. I had forgotten that tender part of my father. I knew from the will that Andrew was "a teacher and therapist." After years in the school system, he now worked with autistic children, he told me. Children under three years old. He had dropped out of Columbia, coming to terms with his homosexuality, his family's disapproval. When he talked to the university therapist about his anger at the Catholic Church, at the priests who had seduced

him as a teenager and then refused to acknowledge it or help him when he
himself was coming out, Columbia referred him to the Catholic chaplain
on campus. "Can you believe that!?" Andrew said. It was then he called
my father. At the same time that he met my father, he told me later, he was
working for Allen Ginsberg, and he laughed.

"After a while I thought to myself, Which of these two men shall I get
to know? *Two roads diverged . . . I took the one less traveled by . . .* It was like
the Robert Frost poem, it really was! Paul Moore, I decided," and again a
peal of that laughter.

"Did you feel pushed when my father asked you to go to bed?"

"Yes, I did, but, you know, I'm a strong person."

"What made you say yes?"

"Your father was a hard man to say no to," and Andrew laughed again.

"Did you want to say no?"

"No," Andrew said.

"You saw him while he was married to Brenda."

"Yes, and then for a while, no. She didn't understand," Andrew said.

"She didn't know, and then she found out," I said.

"Your father didn't believe that making love with a man was cheating
on his wife," Andrew said. "He believed it was a different thing."

"And so you saw each other."

"We saw each other when we could. I often went with him on Sundays when he went out to churches. That was how we worked it out. Even
though I couldn't drive. He always took someone along to drive, and he
told me to say, if anyone asked, that I was his driver." I, too, had driven
my father to confirmations. I could hear it made Andrew happy to tell me
these things.

On those Sunday trips they talked of theology and homosexuality, and
about whether Andrew should be received into the Episcopal Church. At
first my father thought Andrew should work things out in his own church.
But Andrew was a serious gay activist, and he couldn't bear how Catholicism shut him out.

"I began to go to St. Luke's, in the Village," he said. "And then, one day
I wrote to your father that I thought it was time for me to be received."

You can't imagine how happy this makes me, my father replied in a letter
Andrew later showed me.

"But he also talked to you about the family."

"Yes, he did. I didn't always agree with him, you know," Andrew said. "I sometimes took your side, or the side of one of your brothers and sisters. Sometimes I'd argue and argue and then your father would say— you know what he was like, he'd get very stern, wave me off and almost shout at me, 'I don't want to talk about it!'" My father enraged when disagreed with—shouting, even cursing. That part of him, which terrified me, seemed to amuse Andrew.

"Was there any significance to the table my father left you in his will?"

"Only that it was next to the bed!" he said, and we laughed. "Your father had a sense of humor. We were on the sofa once talking," Andrew continued, "and Paul took off his bishop's ring and put it on my hand for a minute. The New York bishop's ring has windmills on it, and your father smiled and said, 'I'm your Dutch uncle.'" My father, this man my age, whom I have never seen, next to him. Playfully, tenderly, he slips the heavy gold ring from his finger and puts it on Andrew's. The Dutch uncle as lover—twenty-five years of letters which support, respond, confide, reach out, extend invitations, encourage, advise, convey affection, gratitude, desire, even love.

In one of Andrew's silences, I remembered the day Raphael announced abruptly that he was returning to Los Angeles, that he did not want me to come with him, that he was considering reconciling with his wife, that he had never intended romance with me. We were having lunch at our favorite restaurant downtown—a reunion: I'd been away for three weeks writing. It seemed so sudden! We'd been seeing each other for a year, he'd been out of touch with his wife for months, they hadn't lived together for two years. "People are assuming," he declared, "that you are coming with me to Los Angeles. As if we were having a great romance," and then he paused. "I hope you don't think so." How far this cold man with the strange contorted face was from the man whose opulent mouth I loved.

My therapist was very pragmatic. He nursed me through months of agony and encouraged me to meet other men, which I gamely tried to do, dreams coming that confused Raphael with my father, dreams in which he was present but just out of reach. Finally, when I began to see another man who seemed to have no ambivalence whatsoever, Raphael began to call again.

It was nearly two years after the breakup that I had lunch with Harold, an old friend from Harvard who was gay, who was like a brother to me, who had helped me to give up alcohol, a process during which you can have no secrets. After a while our work became mutual, me telling him my life, him telling me his. Sometimes he had startling intuitions, as when a few years earlier he'd said, "You'll be ready for a new sweetheart soon," and I'd said "Yes," and he'd said, "It'll be a man, you know."

I'd blushed. "Yes," I said. How had he known that? It was still just a feeling, something I'd barely let into my own mind, much less spoken of.

But now that was years ago and Harold and I were catching up, our conversation a ripple of disclosure and giggles, when, abruptly, he went silent and looked at me.

"I have something to tell you." It was unexpected for Harold to get solemn like this; usually our conversation erupted in cascades of laughter. I was unnerved. Perhaps he was going to tell me he wanted to borrow money or that he had AIDS, or that his mother, at long last, had told him what she really thought of his sexual preference.

"I love you, Honor," he said, "and I don't want to hurt you, but I think this will help you." Something about my father? He wasn't looking at me, just talking. He'd had dinner just days before with a friend of his, a gay man recently left single, who, after months of grieving, was beginning to meet men, in particular men he met on the Internet. It was still early as far as Internet dating was concerned, and Harold, who always declared himself "a Luddite and proud of it," was intrigued. "What kind of men do you meet there?" he wanted to know. "Interesting men," his friend said, the most recent, an independent curator from Los Angeles.

"Oh my God, is what I thought," Harold said, "and then I asked the name. Raphael Benedict."

Raphael Benedict. My stomach turned, my eyes filled.

"And so," Harold continued, "I asked some questions." Raphael, the friend said, was "very passionate." Apparently it hadn't been the first time for him; he had been with men on and off his whole life, even while he was married. He had wanted to see Harold's friend again, but the friend hadn't wanted to see him. "He said Raphael was too confused, too ambivalent."

I could hardly believe it, but I felt oddly relieved. I wanted to laugh. After all this time, all the hours of tears, of incomprehension. I remembered having suspicions, when Raphael was so hot and cold about sex, that he might be gay. The thought had faded away, though, when, after the initial breakup, we began to see each other again when he came to town from Los Angeles. But now I remembered something. After the lunch when Raphael told me he did not want me to move to Los Angeles with him, he stayed behind at the restaurant bar for a quick meeting. I was still there when the man he was meeting arrived, and Raphael made introductions. But his focus entirely shifted. I hardly recognized the man I knew in the small talk he made with this man who was "a venture capitalist," an art collector, and a former Olympic swimmer. As they talked about hotels in Eleuthera and golf courses in Scotland, I meekly said I had to leave, and truly, as I slipped out, trying to keep my composure, I felt I was hardly noticed.

"You found the perfect man with whom to work through your relationship with your father," my therapist said when I told him the news. At the dawn of the twenty-first century, I had managed to choose a man who lived a hidden gay life identical to my father's. If therapy were graded, I thought to myself, I'd be an A+ student!

Andrew was still there, on the other end of the line. "Your father told me that you were a lesbian," he said.

"Did he tell you I'd gone back to men?" I asked.

"Yes," he said.

"Ten years ago," I said.

"Your father could never accept it," Andrew said. "His homosexuality."

"I knew that," I said, remembering the end of one of our therapy sessions, the one to which he'd worn the terrible black-and-white suit with the mustard-colored shirt and matching handkerchief. He looked so tall in that suit, I remembered, too big for the chair. People would come up to him, he said, after he'd given a reading from his memoirs and congratulate him. "You've had such an extraordinary life," they'd say. As my father reported this, the saddest, most disgusted look came over his face. "If only they knew the truth," he said, eyes reddening, bending his head to his hand, pulling the handkerchief from his pocket, trying to recover himself.

"Your father could never accept that he desired men," Andrew Verver repeated.

"Even at the end?" I remembered the male ballet dancer who'd moved in "to take care of things" at the end of his life, rumors my brothers and sisters had heard.

"At the end, he was becoming more gay. And I," Andrew said, "I was going in the other direction." Now, his voice quiet, he was telling me about the woman he was engaged to marry.

"A woman?" No one will ever believe this story, I thought to myself.

It was late July, and Rome was erotic with decay, oleander and wild lavender, towers and gleaming store windows, and I could still feel his mouth, Raphael's luxurious mouth, the body I'd left behind when I left for Italy, what I had seen on his face the first time his hand fumbled down my cheek.

A middle-aged woman, returning to Rome after decades. I was walking down a street with my friend Emily. She was newly in love, finally happily, with a woman. We were telling each other stories about falling in love, she with Lauren, I with Raphael.

It was our first afternoon and the late sun burned a slant of white cut sharp by the orange buildings, leaving the portion of sidewalk in shadow nearly black.

"You're quiet, sweetie," Emily said. I didn't like it when she called me sweetie. It reminded me of the embarrassing moment when she had announced that she was in love with me, just at the time I was beginning to leave women.

"I'm preoccupied," I said. "I'm sorry." I didn't want to talk.

"Do you still consider yourself a lesbian?" Emily had a way of blurting things out, like a child.

"I can't think that way," I said, nervous. I was going to have to learn how to answer these questions.

"Don't you feel disloyal?" she said.

I crossed the narrow deserted street, stopped at the curb, and turned back toward her. Emily was almost invisible in the glare. "I'm the same person," I said.

"In a way you've betrayed us," she said.

"If you believe that, then you don't know me," I said. The shade gave no refuge. "I have lived with women for fifteen years. I have given my life to women." I was shouting.

"But sweetie—" She crossed the street and put out her hand.

"Don't touch me."

"The lives of lesbians are dangerous," she said. I remembered the night in New Haven, the words fingered across the trunk of my car.

"A woman who loves a man gets raped and killed as easily as a lesbian," I said.

And a woman who moves from a woman to a man, what do they do to her?

My father had led a complicated life, I was thinking after Andrew Verver and I hung up. But, I realized, so had I. I was again looking at the ceiling of my apartment, at the green and gold leather-bound Keats, and now my eye caught a cross of my father's, red-painted wood on red, green, and yellow wooden beads. I'd recovered it when we scavenged Bank Street after the funeral and hung it on my doorknob. It had been years since those days I'd spent in bed the week after what I'd come to call "the revelations." I thought of the conversation on the carved oak bench at Adelia's house in Hartford, of Fred Bartrop's unrecognizable voice on the phone in Jersey City when I was a little girl. And I remembered my question to my father that September day, *Did you love any of them?*

In the months following Andrew's call, reading my parents' letters, my father's oral history, and rereading his books, I began to put together the evolution of his sexual attitudes and to make out the path of his questioning search. To my Marine Corps father, homosexuality had been a moral failing, but after Jersey City and ministering to people there whose sexual mores he described in his oral history as "rather free" and undertaking psychotherapy with Bertram Schaffner, he became less judgmental about sex, and, one might say, about his own sexual nature. "And yet," he wrote of himself then in *Take a Bishop Like Me*, "I still believed that all sexual activity outside marriage was *per se* sinful. This conflict between my intuitive understanding and moral conviction continued. I held them in tension, but it became increasingly difficult." Later, he was able to say that even those who had sex outside of marriage did not "offend against the commandment of love, as long as no one was being betrayed or hurt by their sexual acts." I remembered the sermon he preached in Jersey City in 1999, on the fiftieth anniversary of his ordination. Christ is incarnate among us, he said, with us if we are poor or sick, if we are suffering or confused, when we celebrate or mourn. Christ is present, he declared, with a woman in the agony of giving birth, in the infant's cry, and in the act of loving sex.

On the first anniversary of my father's death, Andrew and I drove to Stonington, and after finding the place where his gravestone would be installed, next to Brenda's, we drove to the house that had been my father's and parked the car. Next to it is a large town green that gives onto the Long Island Sound, and we walked through the gate and down to the water. From where we stood, we faced the funny ruffled awning Brenda had installed over the deck where she and my father sat out in the evening with their martinis. After some time, we both turned away. "It's too sad to look at the house," I said. Andrew nodded, and we stood in silence watching the small waves lap at the sand, foaming up, and then Andrew climbed out on the rock breakwater that extended into the sound. He stood for a while, then he came back.

"Are you sad?"

Andrew nodded. "I stayed with him here. We'd drive up from the city in that Volkswagen, and I'd take the train back." And then he said, "Are *you* sad?"

I'd thought it would be dramatic to come back here with Andrew. I thought I would feel my father's presence again, but instead, I felt empty.

"Let's go to lunch," I said. And we got back into the car and drove to a café. When we sat down, Andrew pulled out a thick folder of letters, and I began to leaf through.

Glad to see you've come back to life—a line in my father's handwriting jumped out.

"What is this?"

"We hadn't seen each other for a while," Andrew said. "There was a mistake. My name was on the list of those dead of AIDS read at that mass in 1986, and Paul heard my name, that I had died. It was a mistake. A friend of mine had died, and I'd submitted his name."

"What happened? Did you go up to him afterward?"

"I couldn't get to him, but he called me that night."

I had been at that service, and it was during the sermon that night that I'd felt my father almost transfigured in the power of his preaching. It was also that night, years before the discovery of his hidden life, that, feeling the love coming from him as he preached, I had decided to accept who he was, to take the love he gave when he was his truest self, when he was preaching. Now I'd learned that my father had preached that night believing a man he loved had died.

21
Complexity

It was not until my father was dying that I took in the full weight of what he said bitterly in one of the therapy sessions, looking away, "I can't help how I was made." I could hardly bear the sadness. What was wrong with how he was made? I remembered a passage in my own sexual grief. Looking out the back porch in Kent at a hillside of trees, their leaves turned bright yellow, their black branches gnarled and jagged, I suddenly understood that what had created those trees, so ragged in their beauty, had also created me. Looking at my father bent in sobs, I reached for his hand, tears blurring my sight. Hadn't he taught me all creation was perfect?

I wanted to say everything to him, to want to say everything, but something held down my chest.

"Fear?" the therapist had suggested.

"What I have to say is all that I am; if I say it to him, I will be nothing."

"That's what he's taken away from you."

And now my father is actually in the room with my therapist and me, and looking at him, at the long legs bent at the knee, the socks slightly loose at the ankle because his legs are very thin, the weird shiny loafers with their floppy tassels, I feel sadness which then becomes nothing more than childhood memory of khaki, how it creased and wrinkled, became battered, lost its polish. But this was black-and-white tweed, the mustard handkerchief bursting from his jacket pocket, a rebuke to the elegance of khaki, of battered penny loafers, of worn athletic socks.

That his hair was white never ceased to surprise me.

We were talking about my mother. "We didn't have a very good time in the sack," my father said, "but we had a great partnership"—and then he looked at me—"and all you children." He was starting to cry. "I was very angry at her. I didn't understand why she left." He was describing the weekend in 1969, just before her announcement to me at the Adirondacks, when she asked to sleep separately. "Of course sex was something we never, never talked about when I was a child," he said, lifting his face to the therapist, as if this should explain everything.

"How did your homosexuality affect your life with Honor's mother?" the therapist kindly asked.

I knew my father found this entire mode of discourse barely tolerable, but he forged ahead. He talked about his overprotective mother, his distant father, the voice-over again. I became impatient—there are, after all, many men with distant fathers and overprotective mothers who don't become homosexual—but I watched him try to explain.

"Jenny never talked to me about it," he said. "She didn't know."

"She did know," I said.

"She never talked to me about it."

"She knew," I repeated. He turned to me angrily.

"She didn't know."

"I'm telling you she did know. I know that she knew because she told a couple of close friends, who told me. I'm telling you that if you can place her knowledge of your homosexuality in the frame of your life together, you might be less angry." He looked at me, earnest, speechless, and then repeated that sentence, "We didn't have a very good time in the sack." Didn't he understand that it was all over now? That when she reached for him from her deathbed, she was forgiving him?

"She loved you," I said. "She was protecting you."

The note was in blue ink on white notepaper. She would love to have lunch, supper, would love to see me. It was a year after my father's death, and I went to Boston to see her. I had reserved at a French restaurant on Beacon Hill. I got there first—the room was small, bright, and painted tawny yellow—pine tables, amber-colored wood floors. There was a garden out back, visible through French doors, and because the walls were bedecked with Chinese-import porcelain, the room could have been, as Emma and I later agreed, a breakfast room in one of our family houses. I hadn't seen her since the funeral, hadn't talked to her since I held her in my arms, both of us weeping, the sunny morning she'd seen my father for what turned out to be the last time.

She asked me about the book I was writing. "He told me he was ambi—" she said, "ambidextrous." (She meant bisexual.) I was surprised my father had been so intimate with her. Emma Black was a woman whom he had known since he was young—my mother mentions her in letters written during the war. She had been married to a Yale classmate of my father's who had become an authority in medieval history and a professor at the University of Wisconsin. There are names of family friends that evoke the whole dead world of my parents' pasts, the war, Jersey City, my childhood. "Emma Black" is one of them; and she is one of the fierce, intensely alive survivors. When I gave readings in the Berkshires, near where she spent summers, she always turned up. She was not a woman I saw simply because she was one of my parents' friends; I found her fascinating. Her marriage to the medievalist had been unhappy and eventually, after three children, they divorced. She'd become a philanthropist, a writer, had "years and years" of therapy and family therapy with her children. A second husband had died a decade ago.

"He told me he was 'ambi—'" she repeated.

"I'm glad he could tell you," I said.

She asked if I was planning to "tell everything" in my book, this book, and when I replied that telling the story required breaking the silence about my father's hidden life, she said, "Of course, he never would have wanted you to." In that restaurant room, so aesthetically redolent of all the familiar blankness, the old repression surged up, and all my hard-won thinking dissolved. I kept looking at Emma's face, her scarlet lipstick, her honey blond 1940s pageboy, the large, deep diamond on her hand, her old-fashioned blouse. I felt my hands folded on the table, and as I told her calmly that I disagreed with her and that I believed in my story, I felt callow and over-earnest. What did I think I was doing?

"He said it embarrassed him," Emma said, "shamed him." I could see them sitting in the capacious Stonington living room, or on the porch in summer at sunset, respective vodkas in their hands, him telling her this. I didn't want my father to be embarrassed and it still hurt that he was ashamed.

My father and I had many conversations in which he communicated a desire to tell the truth. "I've thought about it," he said at lunch at Le Refuge when I encouraged him to do so in *Presences*, "but I don't want to hurt Brenda." And at dinner, after Brenda died, "I've thought about it, but I don't want to hurt Polly and Bill," his surviving brother and sister. And another time, "I wish I could."

"He told me he'd never been in love with a man," Emma said, and waited for my reply. I did not mention Andrew Verver, or the other men with whom I now knew my father had had relationships, or at least relations. Instead, I explained to Emma that I had been with women for fifteen years of my life and that telling the story of my father and myself was necessary to my understanding him, to altering the pattern of sexual unhappiness that I had inherited. I told her that I believed sexuality to be a crucial aspect of existence, that my father had considered sexuality and faith to coexist in the same realm of the spirit. I told her I had struggled with whether or not to tell this story since I learned it, that I had written it in pieces for years and years, but that no narrative became clear until the days before he died when I was able to tell my father I loved him.

I thought about his letters to Andrew Verver: *I love you*, my father had written to a man with whom he was physically intimate. What does "in love with" mean anyway?

"You're with men now?" Emma Black was asking. I had almost forgotten I was in the restaurant.

"Yes," I said.

She looked genuinely mystified. I explained that I had fallen in love with a man nearly a decade before, fifteen years after my first lesbian affair, and as a result had returned to therapy to resolve what had been, during my years with women, a duality I'd hidden from, a nub of confusion and pain that I was never free of. I had been in love with women, authentically, but almost always, simultaneously, there had been desire for men, usually a particular man—a married man, the husband of a friend, a man who lived far away. I kept the seriousness of these crushes secret, even from myself, as in fantasy I enacted them.

"Are you, I mean, do you," Emma asked, "still think about women?"

"Only as part of a past life," I said. How strange it was to be having this conversation with Emma Black, whose wedding picture had hung in one of those red frames over the bathtub in Jersey City. I explained to her that while I had sincerely fallen in love with women for those years, I hadn't understood, until I knew about my father's secret life, the alienation that always disquieted my commitment to them. I told her about the men I'd dated in Connecticut, and about Raphael, how shattering that breakup had been, how in therapy since, I had grappled with the difficulty of my relationship with my father and the fear of my desire for men, and how gradually that fear had fallen away. I told her that when I learned that Raphael himself had secret relationships with men, I came to understand that my own sexual development was inextricably tied up with my father's complicated erotic life, and that I thought that story important for me to understand. I said that because I was a writer, understanding meant telling.

"So you have to write this for your integrity," Emma said.

"Yes," I answered. When the waiter came, we ordered, and then Emma began to talk about her own father, how remote and unknowable he'd been, and then, seeming to contradict her disapproval, she said how lucky I was to have known anything at all about my father's interior life.

Exquisite plates of salad were placed in front of us. "I can't get over this place," Emma exclaimed, delighted, looking around at the porcelain-hung walls, the mere five tables.

"And you," I said. "Are you alone, or is there—"

"The only man for whom I've felt anything since Rob is your father." She looked at me, then down at the table.

I was stunned. My father's life as a Shakespearean problem play? My father as the sexual trickster! I wanted to laugh, but I could see that for Emma Black, my father had been, if not a great love, a serious one. As I recovered my composure, I remembered embracing her at the foot of the stairs at Bank Street a few days before my father died. She had been wearing an aubergine suit—I could feel the roughness of the bouclé as I held on to her and she shook with sobs. "He was such a lovely guy," I remember her saying. Now I realized that for a woman like that, an upper-class WASP of my father's generation, using the word "guy" carried desire with it; her sobs had expressed more than the loss of an old friend. "We were going to England together in June," she had said, plaintive and weeping, "to look at gardens."

"Was your friendship with him a romance?" I asked her now.

"Yes, it was," she answered. "We saw each other in Stonington. I stayed there often."

"Yes," I said.

Did you love any of them?

"He told me he'd never fallen in love with a man."

It was an addiction, my father had said that night we talked in Kent after the revelation to the family of his bisexuality, disgust in his voice both for his own homosexual life and, I felt, for mine as well. Emma Black was a woman of depth and substance; I was surprised and impressed my father had loved her. The morning she'd come to see him while he was dying, I'd instinctively backed out of his bedroom, wanting them to have privacy. Would they have needed privacy if she had been a mere family friend? It was one of those sunny days, and I watched from the doorway as she bent over him. After she left the room and I returned to him, he lifted his arms from the bed surface. "We have to—we have to—g-g-g-et her—come back," he said, arms falling back onto the bed, as if relieved of great exhaustion, and I'd run downstairs and Emma had come back, and as she bent over him a second time, I backed again out of the room.

*   *   *

After Brenda died, my father had begun to "date," as he sardonically put it. The worldly among my friends joked that "every woman in New York" of "a certain age" would be "lined up for Bishop Moore." But my father, when asked, said that he didn't know if he wanted to marry again. I was relieved, thinking that he might find his way freely into his homosexuality; in fact he had not been able to keep his pledge to Brenda—he and Andrew had resumed their hidden relationship after a while. But after Brenda died and he was seeing Andrew and other men more freely, he came to family events—a sister's concert or play reading—with a woman on his arm, always, it seemed, a woman he had known in the past, the widow of a priest he had known, the divorced wife of one of his oldest friends. "We had fun," he might say if I asked about one or the other. Or, alternatively, "There was no chemistry." He even went to Mexico, and then to Switzerland, to see Nona Clark, and she came to Stonington to see him. "How was it with Nona?" I asked. "We're friends," he said, "wonderful friends."

In the years of Brenda, my father and Nona were sporadically in touch. I knew that he had gone to see her the summer after my mother died, and in going through letters after his death, I learned that he'd begun an affair with Nona in 1971, even before my mother got sick, in the wake of her discovery of his love affairs with men, her announcement to me that the marriage was no longer working—that anguished period when both were seeing other people. The tenor and abundance of Nona's letters, and how my father talked about her, made it clear that they were seriously involved from 1971 until after my mother's death. What I imagined now made sense, that by the end of his life, Nona had become a dear and close friend, and, I assumed, nothing more.

"I think I understood more than most people about your father's conflicts," Nona said. We were talking on the telephone when I called to tell her he had died—I hadn't seen her since that long-ago visit to Geneva. To me "your father's conflicts" meant the split in his sexuality. I imagined that since Nona was in her late seventies and he in his early eighties, their recent closeness had not included going to bed together. I pictured them sitting looking at the sea, talking over old times. I remembered the quality of sympathy Nona had, her ability to listen, to draw one out. I thought of my father, white-haired, reclining, his long legs stretched out, on the beach, and I pictured her, red-haired, protecting her pale skin from the sun in some filmy silken thing.

I was curious about this friendship that had endured for more than sixty years, and so, two years after my father died, I went to see Nona in Crans-Montana, in the Alps above Sierre in French Switzerland, where she now spent springs and summers. It was early August, a clear day, and her concierge, Monsieur Dragon, picked me up in a Mercedes for the half-hour drive up a steep road to her apartment on the side of a mountain. As we pulled into the driveway, she waved from the balcony, and when I emerged from the elevator, she opened the door as she had all those years ago, and immediately showed me to a small guest room and bath in the modest apartment, out its window a view in the close distance of a wall of mountains, snow in the crevasses and already gathering at the summits. Nona had the same laugh that had charmed me all those years ago and the same look of sympathetic inquiry, the same intelligence in her blue eyes. "You are much more beautiful than you were then," she said, having taken stock. "Then" was when I was twenty!

"Thank you," I said, ascribing her illusion to a Greek tan, the five-week break from life in New York.

"No, no, no," she insisted, "it's something in your face. You've become a woman." Her way of speaking English, marked by forty years speaking French in French Switzerland, and her sincerity disarmed me. Imagine what she might have said to a lover! To my father, for instance, a man certainly vulnerable to admiration, and to sincerity.

"Do you want anything?" she asked. We had a cup of tea.

Nona did not dress like a woman of eighty-one, which she now was. In our planning phone call, she'd told me she'd broken her back in a fall, but I saw no evidence of it. I remembered the conversation we'd had when I called to tell her my father had died. "At the end, we worked everything out," she said. That night, as we drove down the mountain to dinner, we began to put together a chronology. Yes, they had seen each other in 1971 for a couple of years, when he and my mother were separated, and again after my mother died. And after Brenda died, they saw each other twice in Mexico, in Connecticut, and a few times in New York. She herself had never married again, never wanting "the burden" of a domestic relationship. Instead she'd had several enduring affairs with distinguished European men and one prominent American politician.

"When Paul came to Mexico the first time in 2000," she said, "we made love, and afterward in bed, he said, 'You're so forgiving.' 'Well, Paul,' I told him, 'I've had a wonderful life.'"

Now as she drove the curving switchback down into the village, I was marveling. *A wonderful life.* In that sentence were confidence and self-possession. I remembered my father saying of another woman he courted after my mother died, "She doesn't need a man." Was it self-possession that confused him in a woman? That confused him in me, his eldest daughter, who had made a life as a writer, without children, a woman without "a family of her own"?

Montana, the next town over from Crans, Nona explained, had opened a casino which she pointed out as we drove past, a building that looked like a cross between a luxurious motel and a Los Angeles health club. Crans was more traditionally Swiss, chalet roofs, balconies. "It's perfectly beautiful in winter," Nona said as we parked in front of the restaurant, a large open place crowded with August travelers.

"I miss your father," Nona said, "and so it is wonderful to have you here." She leaned toward me.

"I remember clearly the time I saw you last," I said, "our conversation on the balcony, and wasn't your dressing gown pale green?"

"How do you remember that?"

"I wrote about it then, and I still have the story." Her eyes widened. "I know that you and Pop continued to know each other, and you said you thought I should talk to you, because you felt you understood his conflicts." She had sounded proprietary when she made that declaration.

"Yes," she said.

"You said that you had worked things out with him at the end." She nodded and then, almost abruptly, spoke again.

"What about Brenda?" She took a sip of wine. "Were they happy?"

"Well, she drank," I said.

"Were they happy?"

"I think in the beginning, but then—"

Even later in the evening I couldn't get back what question of hers prompted what I said next. "So he told you he was gay?" She didn't acknowledge what I'd just said. She hasn't heard me, I thought, though not from any impairment of her hearing. She leaned forward a little. "That he was gay," I repeated. I saw her face shift, first to confusion, some fear, a shudder.

"Your father was——"

"He was gay, or bisexual. I thought you knew. I thought he must have told you at the end, that when you said you understood his conflicts, that's what you meant."

"No," she said, looking down, then looking again at me. "But this explains a great deal. You see, we lived together in Mexico in 2000"—she meant they shared a bed. "When we had our first reunion after all those years, we felt great love. I remember him in the hallway after dinner the night he arrived, holding me and saying over and over, Nona, I love you, I love you, I love you. The mask was down. It was as it had been after the divorce——"

"Divorce?"

"From your mother."

"They never divorced. They separated."

"Yes, separation. Our bodies worked together then. We traveled together to Paris, and he came here, and to Geneva, and I saw him in New York—and Connecticut. We went to a motel, a wonderful motel in Connecticut."

"Before my mother died."

"Yes. And he came here that summer, and we began to talk about going on together, to make plans to see one another again. And then"—she looked down and then up again, the surprise still on her face—"he called and said he was marrying someone named Brenda."

"The same thing. He did the same thing again!" I exclaimed, and she nodded, and we almost laughed. Now we were women together.

"Yes," she said, "but now I understand."

"You would eventually——"

"I would have known. He wouldn't have been able to hide it from me."

"Why did you see him again after Brenda died?" I asked.

"I loved him," she said with a half smile, both of us understanding that particular helplessness. "But after the first time in Seattle, when I cried for weeks, I never let myself be hurt like that by him again. Or by any man."

When I was twenty, she hadn't told me she'd cried, and I hadn't asked,

not wanting to intrude or look any more closely at the impact my father
had on a woman other than my mother. Nona had seemed to me then
above ordinary female suffering, and in spite of what I took to be fragil-
ity, seemed, in her independence, to have triumphed. Of course, in 1965,
I had no understanding beyond instinct of the notion of a woman's independence. Now I stepped out of myself to watch us there in the resort
restaurant, each nearly forty years older than when we first met and she
opened my imagination and curiosity to the fact that my father had a life,
a sexual life, outside the realm of his relationship with my mother, outside of the family. In all the years since, I'd held an image—Nona tossing
her head and laughing, her admirer leaning toward her as I, twenty years
old and innocent of that kind of flirtation, studied her from across the terrace, and as I had studied Garbo in *Camille* when I was sixteen watching
Frances Farmer Presents at Andra Crawford's, eating pizza. I had not seen
a woman like that before. Robert Taylor as the young lover returns to the
bedside of Marguerite, his courtesan mistress, the lady of the camellias,
and she is dying of tuberculosis. His father had importuned her to reject
the young man so he could make a proper marriage, and out of love for
him she had agreed, but now as they reunited, tears were streaming down
my face. I couldn't have articulated then that what I saw in the way Garbo
tossed her head or heard in the catch in her throat was a kind of dignity
and power.

At twenty, I'd thought of Nona in relation to my mother. With her long,
slender body, her delicacy, her pale redhead skin, she seemed to me the
fragile one. I was intrigued that she wore the motherhood of five, lightly,
almost gaily. My mother, with nine children, seemed more serious and
strong, with her raven hair, her fierce inquiring mind, her conscientious
direction of the lives of her children. But now, forty years later, I understood that Nona was the survivor, that the intensity of my mother's relation to experience which had seemed so strong to me as a girl, actually had
made her vulnerable.

"Did he act on it? I mean, did your father have male lovers?" Nona was
asking. By now we were back at the apartment, sitting at the dining table
in the near-dark, having a cup of tea.

"There were many men, but there was one man with whom he was involved for thirty years. His name is Andrew." A look of relief came across Nona's face. "Oh, Honor, I'm glad he had that."

"Yes," I said.

"When did you learn of this part of his life?" she now asked.

I told her the story—my return from Europe the summer of 1990, the unusual urgent messages from my brothers, the awkward call from Pop: "You see I was with women then," I continued, "and so I thought that this new discovery about him would bring us closer." And then I described our visit that September, how hopeless and angry I'd felt when he refused to talk about love.

"I can see how this has been terrible for you," Nona said.

"And terrible for him," I said. "But also I am grateful to have had a father who lived his passion."

She laughed. "Well, certainly he did that."

"And terrible for you," I said.

"Good for me," she said. "Good that you told me. Helpful."

In the morning, I emerged from my bedroom to find Nona in the living room, already stylishly dressed in slacks. "Honor," she said, "I am *reeling*." She stretched out the *e*'s as an onomatopoeia, and I imitated her.

"*Reeling*. Yes," I said.

"I have been thinking," she said. "I remember something. When your father came to Mexico the second time, he invited himself. I was happy he wanted to come back, and of course I welcomed him, but I told him that the son of a friend would join us after a few days. Two things happened. When James arrived, your father's attention shifted. This was a very beautiful young man, of about thirty. And then after dinner, in the hallway, he took me in his arms and said he hoped that James's visit wouldn't prevent our being together—he meant sleeping together. But it wasn't the same after that."

I always believed my father when he said, "I was in love with your mother." And I believed what Emma Black said in the restaurant, that he'd told her he'd never been "in love" with a man. "In love" is what a man is with a woman. Even before I knew about my father's homosexual relationships, I remember his taking the position that homosexual love was "something else," that the sacrament of marriage sanctified the relationship between a man and woman. This was a conversation we would have had had he lived into 2003 for the Massachusetts Supreme Court decision, the sacramental festivity of the gay marriages the subsequent February in San Francisco. As my father lived his sexuality with men, it certainly was "something else"—something that moved beneath the surface of the life he lived with his wives, with his children, with parishioners and colleagues; something that moved between the interstices of language in the charged realm of desire, of imagination, of relationship with the unseen, informing his theology and his compassion.

If my father had disclosed that existence to his wives and children, he would have had to give up one life or the other—which is what eventually happened. After Brenda found out about his homosexual relationships, my father met Andrew in Central Park to say goodbye. Andrew should write him only to his retirement office at General Seminary. One of my father's replies to Andrew during that time reads, "I wish I could see you, but I can't—such is life."

22
Footsteps

There are no bins in the train station in Wiltshire. Because of the July 7 bombings, is what the woman at the café tells me; no place to drop my empty water bottle, and so I stand there, holding it. It is a cloudy summer day in 2005, and I am waiting for someone I have barely met— one conversation at the edge of the Thames, a tall, handsome Anglican priest of my age, smiling and saying that, with the election of an openly

gay man as Episcopal bishop of New Hampshire, the Anglican communion is confronting further revelation of the nature of God. It was a blus-
tery November day, and I wrote furiously in my notebook as he stood
there, blue-eyed, smiling intently, insistent in his belief, which seemed not
only Christian faith, but the integration of his own sense of the meaning
of existence with a belief in the force of the unseen, the movement of the
divine. Now, nearly two years later, I have tracked him down, and he is
on his way to my train, which, I have telephoned to inform him, is thirty
minutes late. As I stand on the platform, I wonder again what on earth I'm
doing in search of my father's hidden life. Perhaps those friends of his who
have heard rumors of what I am writing and now barely speak to me are
correct: This is no business of mine. Let the dead rest.

But for me my father is not at rest. I can still see his long frame, his head
in his hand, myself sitting on the therapist's sofa in a rage of grief that anyone should have to suffer that degree of pain. *If they only knew the truth*, he
had said just seconds earlier, his body moving in large waves of sobbing.
Now there was silence except for the roar of his sadness which took me
full in the chest. I understood I was incapable of taking away his pain, but
I hoped he understood I wanted to be in it with him. How could any truth
be this painful and unrelieved? It was he who had preached his understanding of the Resurrection, that such darkness is transfiguring. *If only
they knew the truth*, he had said, thinking of people who praised his life. I
had always felt my father's need as a pull downward, a threat to my own
existence, but now, in the modesty of my therapist's office, he was humbled and human, and so was I. I reached out my hand and touched my
father's arm, then his knee, tentative, asking, and he put out his hand.

The news of the election of an openly gay man as Episcopal bishop of New
Hampshire came to me exactly five weeks after my father's death, while I
was on retreat, writing. My cell phone rang—it had to be urgent: everyone
knew I needed this solitude. The priest, a man named Gene Robinson, had
stood at the front of the church with his partner and his two daughters, my
friend Carolyn tells me, her voice filled with wonder. My father was still
powerfully with me, and of course I thought of him, of the life we might
have had if that openly gay bishop had been him. But could I visualize my
father moving Andrew or another male lover into Bank Street? Not really.

"He is a prince of the church," a priest and lifelong friend of my father said, days before his death. And some months later, Louie Crew, who founded Integrity, the gay Episcopal organization, "Your father was born into a certain time, came to maturity after the war. He had certain ambitions about what he wanted to do in the church, and marrying is what one did. Or becoming a monk. Don't judge him for that." I had taken the train to Newark to have this conversation. "And what you told me your father said, 'They were all nice people.' For a man like your father, that was a powerful announcement. It means that he had relationships."

Carolyn began to send me press coverage, first about the American bishop, next the news of the appointment by the archbishop of Canterbury of an openly gay man as bishop of Reading, near Oxford in England. In the ensuing days and weeks, the protests mounted, not only from within the United States and the United Kingdom, but from many Anglican provinces in other parts of the world—Africa, South America, Pakistan—where tolerance of homosexuality has no place in ordinary life. By the middle of September, Rowan Williams, the archbishop of Canterbury, a man whom my father greatly admired, had called a special meeting at Lambeth Palace, his London residence, of all the primates of the Anglican Communion, and I had managed to get *The Nation* to send me there as a reporter. It was on that assignment that I first met Colin Coward.

On the south bank of the Thames in the shadow of the palace, red stone fourteenth-century walls, a barricaded archway, within it the green grass of a courtyard, the flash of Episcopal purple, then nothing. I positioned myself behind the bright yellow police barriers and introduced myself to a clutch of BBC reporters, cameras on backs, mobile phones in hand. Soon a crowd began to gather, and with them, throughout the day, I moved from one side of Lambeth Palace Road to the other. It was cold, and often we gathered in a small jerry-built cafeteria where the tea was hot and the sandwiches were wholesome. Men and women in clericals, journalists evident in their informal, even hip, work clothes, men in ties and Turnbull & Asser striped shirts whom I later learned were conservative American laymen, moved up and down the river, some striking poses for television cameras, others, like me, engaging in conversation. I spoke to many people, a Trinidadian woman priest attached to nearby Southwark Cathedral; the tall dean of Southwark, a progressive; an American priest from the Diocese of Utah, to whom I introduced myself by name.

"Are you . . . ?" he asked, looking into my face.

"Yes," I said. "I'm Paul Moore's daughter." He embraced me.

"Your father was a saint in our church," he said. I smiled, tears coming. Would he change his judgment if he knew the truth about my father's life?

"Why are you here?" I asked him.

"I am here to bear witness to this extraordinary moment in our church. I thought it was important that those who support Gene Robinson's election be here, as well as those who oppose it."

My father's shame, it seemed, was not shared by those coming up behind him in the church; the progressive forces my father rallied for so long were again moving forward. "The American church has thrown the tea in the harbor," a gay British theologian had said to me earlier. I said goodbye to the American priest from Utah and moved through the crowd. It was as if my father were still alive and I was searching out stories to tell him when I got home, listening carefully so that I could report in his language, the language of theology, that the life he had lived had been a courageous one, that the truth of it needn't bring him shame. And there, suddenly, was a tall, blue-eyed priest, a man my own age. When I got home, I found the notes I'd taken talking to him. The more, he said, that the church comes to include homosexuals and women as priests and bishops—that is, to accept "us" as fully human—the more clearly the image of God is revealed. This was a sentence that echoed much that my father had written in his defense of Ellen Barrett's ordination. Shame is powerful, I thought to myself, in the force with which it can divide us from what we know.

When I met Colin Coward that day at the edge of the Thames, he was dressed in clericals; now, coming toward me, he is wearing shorts and a ratty shirt. It's raining and I carry an umbrella I've just bought in Paris. It seems extraordinary to me that this man, who could barely remember meeting me and who had never heard of my father, is willing to give me time on a summer afternoon. Colin introduces me to the young black man who accompanies him. "Here from Ghana," he says, and the younger brother of his partner. "Oh yes," I say, remembering Colin that day on the Thames, describing the happiness of what was then a new love. But now, he tells me that his partner was killed a year before in an automobile accident on a trip home to Ghana. As I give my condolences, I tell him how vividly I remember his description of his beautiful African lover, and he smiles, thanking me. When we are finally seated, our food in front of us, I explain to Colin that it is his theology, as he talked about it that day two years before, which has brought me here. And I explain why, outlining my father's life, what I've told here, including my father's hidden sexuality, its impact on his life, my life, the life of our family. The food is modest, the day hot, and I am a bit self-conscious, but as I continue, I feel Colin Coward's listening intelligence.

Our conversation goes on for four hours, first my story and then my father's, then Colin's—the understanding in childhood that he was gay, his study to become an architect, his eventual vocation as a priest. At first, he was curate of a parish in Southwark, and then a vicar. During those years he was not open about his sexuality, but when his first partner died of AIDS, "the people in the parish went through that suffering with me." Eventually, in 1998, he was invited to help represent the progressive position on gay and lesbian ordination at the Lambeth Conference, the once-a-decade convocation of Anglican bishops from all over the world. Out of his work at that conference, he was "called" to the ministry he now pursues in Changing Attitude, the organization he founded that sends people, including gay men and lesbians, who support inclusion of gay people at all levels of the church, into parishes to answer questions and form friendships—to change attitudes toward gay people at the grass roots.

"What a different world my father lived in," I say. Colin takes note of my inquiring expression.

"You might understand," he tells me, "that your father had to make a choice. It seems to me that he understood that he could accomplish his work only with that concealment." The waitress brought more tea, two more sandwiches. I had been thinking that surely Colin must have other things to do, but now I understood that I was part of his ministry, and that he was giving me answers I had been seeking.

What had always seemed to me a pragmatic choice with terrible consequences now seemed instead a bargain with the circumstances of the time in which my father entered his ministry. What Colin offered echoed what Louie Crew had said, that Pop could never have accomplished what he did, had he come out as a gay man.

But what of the suffering? It was my father's sacrifice and his gift. It was, as he had once told Andrew Verver, what kept his ministry alive, what made his faith necessary. When I asked Colin Coward about suffering, "about Jesus, if you will," he winced.

"I haven't quite worked that out," he said.

"Well, try," I said.

"Crucifixion, resurrection. The death of Christ in that humiliating way is a constant reminder that we all must die," he said. "And resurrection tells us that everything can be transformed. Think about art—that's the way you do it."

Yes, I thought, my father's work is barely comprehensible without knowledge of his suffering. If only I had been able to tell him so that day in the therapist's office. If only I had been able to communicate what I now understood, that to me his living of his passion was heroic. Isn't it just inevitable, I might have asked, that such courage comes at a cost? Isn't that what it is to be human? Don't we just do the best we can, and don't we sometimes fail?

I was in search on that summer journey of a way into the hidden truths of my father's life. Before I left for Europe, I'd asked Andrew Verver again about their time in Patmos the last summer of Pop's life.

"I'd like to take you on a trip," my father had said to him. "Where would you like to go?"

"Patmos," Andrew said. So Patmos had been Andrew's idea, and the trip had been my father's gift to him.

Once in the hired car, baggage in the trunk, tickets in hand, on the way to the airport, my father looked at Andrew and said, "This is pretty wild!" It was the first trip they had ever taken together.

The journey to Patmos is arduous. There is no airport on the island and the ferry schedules are notoriously difficult to procure in advance. I flew from London to Athens and then to the island of Kos, from which I planned to catch a hydrofoil to Skala, the port town of Patmos. At the hotel in Kos, where I arrived at midnight after a delayed flight, there was no one to help carry my bags, packed for six weeks, up the stone stairs, and in my frugal room, the fluorescent light turned on when you put your key tag in a slot near the door. When morning came, the sun was halogen-bright, and I sat for my buffet breakfast on a terrace shaded by an overhang. I had been told the "Flying Dolphin" would leave for Patmos at ten-thirty. I reached the pier an hour early, only to find that the boat promised for ten-thirty had left at eight and would *arrive* in Patmos at ten-thirty! In the café where I settled with my bags, I was told another boat would not leave until one, or perhaps two. The Moldovan waitress smiled sympathetically and brought first eggs and then yogurt with honey and nuts.

My father and Andrew Verver also had an adventurous journey. They flew from Athens to the island of Samos, where they missed the last boat to Patmos. "We had a wonderful evening there," Andrew told me. They checked into a hotel and went out to dinner, and sitting on a terrace overlooking the sea, they talked for hours. "Paul was very relaxed," Andrew said.

Imagining my father's excitement in Greece, I wished I had taken that trip, any trip, with him as an adult. I would never have asked—after he and Brenda married, they took a series of extraordinary trips, sometimes alone, sometimes with friends. There seemed to be no end to the places they traveled—Russia, the South Pacific, a cruise up the Turkish coast, a barge on the Rhine, the Nile, all over Europe. My father had a boyish enthusiasm when he talked about a trip, a delighted vivacity like his mother's when she led you through the rose garden at Hollow Hill. He'd begin an anecdote, and suddenly it would be the moment when light and smell hit you in a new place, before your mind engages, before you start to think, before you begin to worry if you'll find the hotel. I imagine that was how my father was with Andrew that night in Samos, his first vacation with a male lover—but the stories he told Andrew that night were from a part of his life he never opened to me. Of his desire for men, its dawning at St. Paul's when ordinary sexual play brought erotic dreams not of girls but of boys, of his first experience with a male pickup in Paris before the war, his first love affair with a man, a married instructor at General Seminary. Of his marriages, how he did not consider his sexual relations with men adultery. By then he and Andrew had known each other for more than twenty-five years, and had talked of many things. Now they were outside of time. My father was not married and no longer the bishop of New York, was in fact considering inviting Andrew to live with him. But Andrew had made an important decision, a decision he shared with my father. He had met a woman he hoped to marry.

*   *   *

Patmos is known to be "a sacred island." Even now, if you build a hotel you are required also to build a church, and so on an island ten miles long and five wide, there are said to be 366 churches, one for every day of the year, and a spare. My hosts on Patmos were friends of mine who had never known my father, a couple much younger than I, with a ten-month-old son. Christoph's Austrian parents had first come to the island in the 1950s when his uncle, an archaeologist, had given Christoph's mother "a ruin" in the hill town of Chora as a wedding present. The "ruin" was now a simple but capacious house in the shadow of the fortress-like monastery of St. John the Evangelist, first built in the eleventh century. Standing on one of its terraces, looking down, the monastery behind you, you see first the town of Skala, and the harbor, beyond it in the blue mist the mountainous expanse of the sea-horse-shaped island, and in the distance smaller atolls. On a clear day, you can make out the coast of Turkey, what, in his stories from the pulpit, my father referred to as "Asia Minor"—Ephesus, where Saint Paul preached, to whose congregants he wrote the Epistle to the Ephesians.

If I imagine him with me on Patmos, my father is wearing a seersucker suit and sitting, lanky and eager with us on the terrace, which has a view of the harbor and the mountains beyond that rise where the island curves. He is drinking a vodka, charmingly asking questions. Christoph and his wife, Marie-Charlotte, a devout Catholic, smile back as my father, very much a bishop on holiday, inquires first about their lives, then about the truth of the Apocalypse. Do those on the island believe that Saint John and his secretary, Prochorus, actually worked in the cave which is now the chapel? Did John write his gospel there, as well as the Book of Revelation? Christoph shrugs, laughing. Yes, that is what those on Patmos believe, though there are scholars who disagree. And in return, he asks my father if he, the bishop, considers the author of the Apocalypse John the brother of James, John the Apostle and author of the gospel, John the Evangelist, or, as most contemporary scholars would have it, another John altogether? My father thinks the latter, but, he says, the truth doesn't really affect his feeling that this is a sacred island. And then I ask which John it is who is called "Saint John the Divine," and my father, exasperated at the profusion of saints named John, throws up his hands, and we all laugh, and I promise Christoph and Marie-Charlotte that I will take them to the cathedral at 110th Street the next time they come to New York.

Not for a week do Christoph and Marie-Charlotte and I begin sightseeing, first at the monastery, which is a short walk up a narrow stone street between whitewashed walls, the wares at icon booths flashing in the sunlight as we wheel baby Johannes over the stones, pulling and pushing the stroller up several sets of stone stairs. I am thinking what I would tell Pop—how the ancient, unbroken Greek Orthodox tradition infuses the atmosphere, more integrated and yet lighter than the Catholicism of Italy; and the other sense I have, that the Holy Land is so close, that while there is no record of Saint Paul on Patmos, he certainly could have come here, since he visited Ephesus, easily reachable by boat. Of course that is true, my father would say, reminding me that the New Testament was written in Greek.

My reverie is interrupted as Christoph, Marie-Charlotte and the baby, and I enter the courtyard of the monastery, stone arches curving over us, the surprise above us not the vaulted ceiling of a nave, but an open, piercing blue sky. The Greek Orthodox monk standing at the entrance to the chapel speaks American English, strange in contrast to the icons the sun illuminates, their Byzantine formality, which usually seems so stiff, strangely animated in the daylight. When Christoph asks if I think about my father when in such places, I deny it, remembering a moment on my first trip to Italy with Venable, when he accused me of an obsession with churches because of my father. "No," I had protested, "the churches are where the art is."

But how could I not have been thinking of my father when I gazed at frescoes in which his tellings of New Testament stories came so vividly to life? And now that he is dead and I am confronted with the austere faces of the Byzantine saints, their long necks, their solemn, penetrating eyes, the colors of their vestments, how am I not somehow in his presence? In the chapel, I light a candle for him—even if I don't believe, this is an ancient tradition, sacred purely through the repetition of this gesture by hundreds of years of supplicants.

With us in the chapel are a group of tourists, and sitting, bent on priedieux, several Greek men. "Here is the skull of Saint Thomas," Christoph says, leading me to a vitrine in which a tiny skull, darkened with age, rests next to the supposed sandals of Saint Christodoulos, the founder of the monastery in which we now stand. I scoff, but Christoph is insistent, "Research has been done," he says.

The first time I met Andrew in person, he brought his fiancée Zofia with him—she had come from Poland two years before, and he had met her through his teaching. His decision to open himself to women had come gradually, and he had found it possible. "I did not want to continue as a gay man," he said. "There was no life for me there." Zofia nodded with a smile as Andrew introduced me. "We are getting married this summer," he said. I ordered a cappuccino.

"Can we talk?"

"Yes," Andrew said, taking Zofia's hand. "She knows everything." I smiled at her again, and she smiled back. "She's learning English and I'm making my way with Polish!" From his briefcase, Andrew pulled an album of photographs which he laid on the table and opened. He flipped pages. "Here's Paul," he said. And there they were, Andrew and my father in Patmos—standing together in front of the entrance to the Cave of the Apocalypse where John was said to have written the Book of Revelation, each in shorts, my father holding a guidebook.

Looking at the funny, modest photograph, I was suddenly embarrassed to witness my father's private life. I turned the page. "This is the night in Samos," Andrew said. His face is in near-darkness, the photograph certainly taken by my father as they dined at sunset on that terrace overlooking the sea. Another of Andrew, the dying sunlight on his face. These were the photographs you take, one, then another and another, as if to sear the lover's face and that moment into your memory.

I closed the scrapbook and looked at Andrew's wistful face, his gray eyes. "Your father had desire right up until the end," he said. "I could hardly keep up with him." Pop had told my sister that Andrew had talked about his girlfriend the whole time they were on Patmos. I looked at Zofia. "Were you involved with Zofia when you went to Patmos?"

"We had just met," Andrew said. So my father had been telling the truth.

I looked again at the scrapbook. "On Patmos I couldn't keep up with him," Andrew repeated. "He raced up those steep paths, and I was behind, out of breath." I remembered that about Pop, his long legs taking him up Silver, the highest mountain on our land in the Adirondacks, faster than anyone else. And now Andrew laughed. I'd taken a mountain hike on Patmos, and from the path I had seen the great stone at Petra, where monks retired to meditate, fasting, drinking only the water caught in the small cavity when it rained.

On our last day on Patmos, Christoph and Marie-Charlotte and I drove to the Cave of the Apocalypse, bringing the baby along because his name is Johannes, German for John—all week in the midst of German speakers, I had heard the author of Revelation called "Johannes." Again we climb stone stairs in the blazing sun, the sky stark blue, a south wind bringing humidity into the air. Into the vestibule, past the white drinking fountain with its bright blue fixtures, into the dark chapel where a tour group is being told, in Greek-accented English, the legends of Saint John's authorship, first of the gospel—"In the beginning was the Word"—and then of the Book of Revelation.

The room is small, actually a cave, pale granitelike stone forming a wavy ceiling above our heads. I want just silence, to stand in the shadowy stillness, but Christoph is pointing out a round hole in the stone, the aperture decorated with silver relief. This naturally occurring cavity is where John is said to have rested his head, the better to hear the words of Christ reverberate through the stone. In spite of myself, I am taking the story in. Next to it is a smaller hole, also braceleted with silver, in which it is said Saint John put his hand to pull himself up from his knees. A bit further along is a naturally formed stone shelf, an ancient book resting there on an altar cloth: it is here that Saint Prochorus is said to have placed the papyrus while taking down the evangelist's words.

I think again of my father—of the attention with which he would have scrutinized all of this, and of the tenderness with which he always directed me to look at such marks of the invisible, the finally unknowable. We would both have been in a condition of amazement, he at what remains, I at the idea of a religious tradition that includes a writing surface. And of course we would have discussed the discrepancies—the certainty that Prochorus lived in the fourth or fifth century, not at the end of the first when John, in exile from Domitian's scourge of the Christians, lived and worked on Patmos. "Does it matter?" I imagine asking him. "Isn't the ledge what matters?"—I point to the book, to the altar cloth resting on the stone—"That it was, at some point, recognized as bearing resemblance to a writing surface?" I am standing in front of it, extending my writing hand to see if the height works.

Now I turn toward the corner of the cave where John knelt, and looking again at the smaller of the two silver-lined apertures, I think not of the hand of the evangelist lifting himself from his knees those thousands of years ago, but of my father's hand—holding the bishop's crozier, the shepherd's crook, lifting the chalice to my lips, his hand trembling just slightly as he places the host in my hand, my father in red and white, the vestment in which I chose to have him cremated. What is the sacred but evidence of the repetition of meaningful human gesture? And what is the silver-rimmed cavity in a wall of stone but a reminder that a man who has knelt for hours does not rise to his feet with ease?

"And here," Christoph interrupts, a bit of nervousness in his voice because of my earlier dismissal of Saint Thomas's remains. He is pointing to a triune crease in the stone ceiling of the cave, "the sign of the Trinity, which was supposed to have come when Johannes had his revelation."

What if I had taken such trips as this with my father? Would I still have become this ersatz pilgrim following his elusive trail, or would I have stayed at home, contented to reenact such gestures as the cooking of food or the laying of a table for supper? Instead I come half around the world, climb stone steps in the late July heat of Greece, gaze at Byzantine faces, some worn away by sun and wind, others darkened by candle smoke, some so vivid you lose track of time. Andrew has told me that neither he nor my father had a spiritual experience when they visited the cave together that last summer. Was that because of a crush of tourists? Or was it that neither Andrew nor my father was in a condition of sufficient longing to overcome temporal interruption, the baroque overlay, the too obviously human legend?

In the chapel of the Apocalypse, I light a candle for my father, and another for my work on this book. When I am out of range of the sand-filled container where the candles flicker, looking at the altar, at the sarcophagus of Saint Christodoulos, the eleventh-century founder of the monastery, I see out of the corner of my eye the tall, black-clad monk blow out the candles of the pilgrims, barely burnt. He pulls them from the sand and tosses them into a bin.

* * *

At the closing of my father's funeral, the celebrant gave the blessing, and nearly five hundred priests and deacons and bishops and nuns and monks, men and women, and acolytes and choirs, filed up the aisle of St. John the Divine, and at the end of the procession, slowly moved the pallbearers carrying the plain pine coffin, my father's grandchildren over fifteen, all boys but for one girl leading, the grand organ thundering a recessional. The service had lasted three hours, the cathedral which seats three thousand had been packed. My father's brother, Bill, and some of his old friends who had flown in had to leave before it was over. I was in the dream of it. I had spoken from the pulpit, five of his children had. "My father wore robes of crimson and gilt, of green, of purple, of black, of white and gold," I'd said, summoning my little-girl sense of this great figure, summoning too my father on his deathbed, passing along our last moments together, making of the release of his death what he might have had he been preaching, a kind of lesson.

Now as his coffin passed me, I stepped out into the aisle and joined the crush of family—there are nearly forty of us now. The organist was playing Bach, a saxophone spinning a descant into the dark reaches of the arched Gothic ceiling, faces from my whole life whirling in my peripheral vision, and then I look up, and the cathedral doors, the doors that open only at Easter for the bishop's entrance, are now wide open, throwing a shaft of light onto the pale surface of the pine coffin, the waxy shine reflecting daylight radiance.

And as we move out through the doors, the coffin leading us, I see that the stairs of the cathedral, scores of stairs that spill downward from the arched entrance, are crowded with bishops and priests and nuns and monks, in their vestments and habits, their red and their white, their African or Asian vestments, their Trappist and Franciscan habits and rope sashes, their tippets, cottas, surplices, and cassocks, and they are clapping as my father's coffin is borne slowly down the stairs, clapping, not applauding, and not exactly rhythmically clapping either, solemnity on their faces, as if a medieval guild were bidding farewell to one of its own, their hands coming together, the sound both very loud and barely audible, as I stand there, eyes burning, and the coffin, the light of the white sky blazing from it, slides into the open trunk of a black hearse.

And then I understand that this is the end of my father, that inside the coffin is his body, and that when I see him again he will be ashes, and so, as the clapping continues, I fly down the final steps, the attendants moving away from the open doors of the hearse, and I touch the wood, alone there I touch the coffin, at the same time seeing myself in black, a woman bending toward a coffin, her hand reaching.

NOTES

Quotations from Paul Moore are from my diaries, my memory of our conversations, and from his books or his oral history unless otherwise noted. Quotations from the Episcopal liturgy are from *The Book of Common Prayer* (1948), and hymns are from *The Hymnal of the Protestant Episcopal Church* (1940).

1: Prophet's Chamber

page 23: in the diary my father kept PM's St. Paul's Diary is in the Archives of the Episcopal Church (hereafter cited as AEC).

page 33: his notes notebook, AEC.

2: Guadalcanal

page 35: Marine Corps citation AEC.

page 36: "the medal for the whole platoon" Unattributed clipping in family papers (hereafter cited as FP).

page 43: The New Start and *A Marine Speaks of War* FP.

4: Holy Matrimony

page 65: "Things very near my heart" Undated letter from Fanny Hanna Moore (FP).

5: Firstborn

page 90: "*Wisdom about our destiny*" Reinhold Niebuhr, *The Nature and Destiny of Man, Part II* (New York: Scribner's, 1943), p. 321; quoted in Elisabeth Sifton's valuable book about her father, *The Serenity Prayer* (New York: W. W. Norton, 2003), p. 228.

6: Becoming a Priest

page 99: "*Puerto Ricans we had seen*" My mother's quoted recollections in this chapter are from *The People on Second Street* (New York: William Morrow, 1968).

page 100: "*We were trying to overcome hatred*" Dorothy Day, *Loaves and Fishes* (New York: Harper & Row, 1963), p. 47.

page 102: "*Everybody just takes a little less*" Dorothy Day, *Loaves and Fishes,* p. 73.

7: My Jersey City

page 110: The King of Kings The Cecil B. DeMille version, 1927.

8: Four-in-Hand

In compiling the red book, the scrapbook keeper snipped away the newspaper sources of most of the clippings I used to construct this narrative, and those citations are now virtually irretrievable, but the names of some of the newspapers escaped his or her scissor: the *Chicago Daily Tribune,* the *Chicago Times-Herald,* the *Sunday Inter-Ocean,* and the *New York Herald.*

page 123: Years after making a bronze portrait . . . Katharine Weems diary and Paul Moore letter quoted in Louise Todd Ambler, *Katharine Lane Weems: Sculpture and Drawings* (Boston: Boston Athenaeum, 1987), pp. 42–44.

page 131: "*You have been in politics long enough to know*" Quoted in Matthew Josephson, *The Robber Barons* (New York: Harcourt, Brace, 1934; copyright renewed 1962), p. 353.

10: Light and Dark

page 159: "*. . . You couldn't go next door*" Jervis Anderson, "Out There on the Issues," profile of Paul Moore Jr. in *The New Yorker,* Apr. 28, 1986, pp. 73–74.

page 160: "*The Tea Shop*" Ezra Pound, *Selected Poems* (New York: New Directions, 1957), p. 37.

12: In Public

page 193: "*where the suffragan Episcopal bishop . . .*" Jenny Moore, "Bishop Paul Moore's Wife Looks Back at Six Years in Washington 'with Confusion and Love,'" *Washington Post, Potomac Magazine,* Sept. 20, 1970.

page 193: "In a blunt address . . ." "Courts Fail Children, Bishop Asserts," *Washington Post*, June 23, 1964, p. C2.

page 194: "My ogling at powerful figures . . ." Jenny Moore, "Bishop Paul Moore's Wife Looks Back," p. 43.

page 199: "a leader of the new breed" Benjamin Bradlee, "Bishop Moore: A Leader of the New Breed," *Newsweek*, Mar. 29, 1965, p. 77.

13: Eager

page 215: "I had a talk with Tim Mayer . . ." Julius Novick, "The New Talent May Be Here," *New York Times*, Aug. 27, 1967, sec. 2, p. 4.

15: Killing Me Softly

page 242: "In the Cathedral's soaring Gothic nave . . ." Kenneth L. Woodward, "An Activist Bishop Faces Life," *Newsweek*, Dec. 25, 1972, p. 55.

16: Art and Life

page 248: "as violent and unforeseen as an engine . . ." Simone de Beauvoir, *A Very Easy Death*, trans. Patrick O'Brian (New York: Putnam, 1966), p. 106.

page 249: "A woman in the shape of a monster . . ." Adrienne Rich, "Planetarium," *The Will to Change: Poems 1968–1970* (New York: W. W. Norton, 1971), p. 13.

page 253: "intense, yet detached . . ." Laurence Senelick, "In Boston," *After Dark: The National Magazine of Entertainment,* vol. 7, no. 5 (Sept. 1974).

page 254: "in mind of passages . . ." Brendan Gill, "Mighty and Dreadful Death," *The New Yorker*, Nov. 18, 1974, p. 113.

17: Women and the Kingdom

page 265: "When you're fighting oppression . . ." Charles Willie, *Ms.*, Dec. 1974, p. 48.

page 275: "I have broken no canon law . . ." Quoted in Paul Moore, *Take a Bishop Like Me*, p. 128.

18: Discovery

page 293: "a just and peaceful solution" Press release, Nobel Peace Prize, 1996.

A NOTE ON SOURCES

This is a work of memoir, with elements of biography and autobiography. I have been aided in remembering by my parents' letters, my own correspondence and diaries, my parents' writings and my own, and conversations with friends, with friends and colleagues of my parents, and with members of our family. For historical and social context, I have consulted works of history and the journalistic record of the time. In spite of my best efforts, I am sure errors remain, and for them, I alone take responsibility.

One's memory, on the other hand, is a document with its own character, and like its companions, dream and imagination, comes with its own beautiful distortions. I have been careful to correct for gross inaccuracy, but I have happily employed memory's riches in the composition of this narrative. Also, in order to protect the privacy of some of the people who appear as characters in this book, I have changed some names and places and omitted or altered personal details. As I say in the dedication, each of my siblings has another story; this one is my own.

I have consulted and sometimes quoted from my father's three published books, *The Church Reclaims the City* (New York: Seabury Press, 1963), *Take a Bishop Like Me* (New York: Harper & Row, 1979), and *Presences* (New York: Farrar, Straus & Giroux, 1997). I am grateful to Columbia University for permission to consult and quote from my father's oral history ("The Reminiscences of Rt. Rev. Paul Moore, Jr.," 1979–1989, in the Oral History Collection of Columbia University). My father's papers, deposited in the Archives of the Episcopal Church (Papers of the Rt. Rev. Paul Moore. AR 2003.101, Archives of the Episcopal Church) have also been invaluable.

It was my mother, Jenny Moore, who first told the story of our family in Jersey City, and I have consulted and quoted from her memoir, *The People on Second Street* (New York: William Morrow, 1968). The family scrapbooks she kept for the duration of her life with my father provided me with an almost cinematic chronicle, as did the family photographs my father assiduously took all his life. My parents' letters are owned in common by our family, and I am grateful to my sisters and brothers, in particular Marian, Rosemary, Susanna, and Paul Moore, for providing me with copies. I am also grateful to Pamela Morton, Andrew Verver, and David Challinor for sharing their correspondences with my parents.

For material about my great-grandparents, including letters, clippings, and the red scrapbook referred to in the text, I am grateful to my father's older brother, William H. Moore. For Moore family history, I also consulted *William Henry Moore and His Ancestry* by L. Effingham DeForest and Anne Lawrence DeForest (New York: DeForest Publishing Company, 1934) and "Ada Small Moore: Collector and Patron" by David Ake Sensabaugh and Susan B. Matheson (*Yale University Art Gallery Bulletin* 2002 (December 2003), copyright Yale University Art Gallery, New Haven, Conn., pp. 30–49).

"My Father's Ship," a selection from my journals, which has been folded into chapter 19, was published in *The American Scholar*, vol. 72, no. 4 (Autumn 2003). My debt to Anne Fadiman for her intuitive first reading of what became the germ of this book is great, and my gratitude to her and the staff of the magazine is heartfelt.

ACKNOWLEDGMENTS

For the time, space, and resources required to write this book, I have many to thank.

First I am grateful to the John Simon Guggenheim Memorial Foundation for a fellowship which not only supported me for a year during the writing of this book, but also enabled me to enlarge its vision and scope. In that regard, I am also grateful for conversations with Edward Hirsch, president of the foundation, and an e-mail correspondence with Jack Miles, of its selection committee.

For time out of time, I am grateful for fellowships from the Corporation of Yaddo, the MacDowell Colony, and the Rockefeller Foundation's Study and Conference Center at Bellagio. For residencies, I am also grateful to the UCross Foundation, Medway Plantation (Bokara Legendre), and Elixir Farm (Lavinia McKinney). For hospitality, I thank my friends Roxana and Hamilton Robinson, Wendy Gimbel and Doug Liebhafsky, Christoph and Marie-Charlotte Meran, Claudia Weill and Walter Teller, and Fanny Howe. For time and a work space in the Frederick Allen Room at the New York Public Library, I am grateful to the library and to Wayne Furman, and for hospitality in London, I thank the guest house at St. Matthew's, Westminster, Rona and Bob Kiley, and Diane Gelon and Gillian Hanna.

For their forbearance, generosity, and support during the composition of this book, I thank my colleagues in the writing programs at the New School and at the Columbia School of the Arts, especially Robert Polito, Richard Locke, Lis Harris, and Patricia O'Toole. I also thank Susan and Roger Hertog and the Columbia School of the Arts for awarding me a Hertog research assistant in 2004, and I am grateful to the remarkable Sarah Smarsh for her work in that capacity and for our many conversations. Roslyn Schloss read the manuscript and made valuable suggestions, and Tayt Harlin not only fact-checked but offered useful advice. For their thoroughness and hard work I am most grateful. Thank you as well to the New School and its president, Bob Kerrey, for extending my benefits during time off for writing. For technical help at the last minute, I thank Tanya Selvaratnam.

For important conversations, I thank Louie Crew, the Very Reverend and Mrs. James Parks Morton, the Reverend and Mrs. Ledlie Laughlin, Nona Clark, Andrew Verver, Nell Gibson, Colin Coward, Joel Gibson, John George Robinson, Daniel Webster, Frances FitzGerald, Geoffrey Kabaservice, Michael Roberts, Kirsten Grimstad, Diana Gould, Brad Gooch, Benjamin Taylor, David Leeming, Janet Kraft, Isabel Potter, Ruth Lord, Emma Black, Victoria Rue, and Robert Leleux. And last but not least, for particular friendship and support during the writing of this book, I am indebted to Marian Moore, Stanley Siegel, Carolyn Forché, Catherine Ciepiela, André Bishop, Fanny Howe, Victoria Redel, James Lapine, Wendy Gimbel, and the late Arthur Miller—thank you.

At the Wylie Agency, I thank Sarah Chalfant, Andrew Wylie, and Edward Orloff for their extended attention and encouragement. I am, of course, enormously grateful to W. W. Norton & Company, and I particularly thank my editor, Jill Bialosky, for her shrewd readings and buoyant support, and Don Rifkin and Paul Whitlatch for their marvelous attention to detail.

PHOTOGRAPHS

CHAPTER 18: Discovery, p. 281
My father at the Cathedral of St. John the Divine, at the Blessing of the Animals, St. Francis Day celebration, c. 1988. Credit: Collection of Moira Kelly

CHAPTER 19: Wayfarers, p. 298
With my father on Martha's Vineyard, c. 1980. Credit: Photograph by Victoria Rue. Used with permission.

CHAPTER 20: Andrew Verver, p. 314
The cave of the Apocalypse, Patmos. Credit: Photograph by Ellen Warner. Used with permission.

CHAPTER 21: Complexity, p. 328
In Antigua, 2003. Credit: Photograph © Inger McCabe Elliott. Used with permission.

CHAPTER 22: Footsteps, p. 341
The guide boat, on the lake in the Adirondacks. Credit: Photograph by James McKean Whalen. Used with permission.

THE BISHOP'S
DAUGHTER

Honor Moore

THE BISHOP'S DAUGHTER

Honor Moore

HONOR MOORE ON WRITING
THE BISHOP'S DAUGHTER

For many years, in pieces, I wrote about my father—scrawled pages I stored away, for a book I never thought I'd write: A description of him celebrating Holy Communion or rowing a guide boat across the lake at our family's summer place in the Adirondacks. Dreams that replayed moments from my childhood. Something funny from our family life. An imagined conversation between my parents during the early days of their marriage. Enraged tirades I never delivered, letters I never sent. Only after his death was I able to understand our life together clearly enough to make my way into telling our story.

My father was a man of contradictions: A sincere man of God who cursed like the marine he once was and loved a stiff martini and a tough tennis game. A visionary social activist who lived and worked with the poor, but relished the trappings of luxury. A genius at the intimacies of pastoral work who only awkwardly navigated the closeness of family life. A husband and the father of nine children who led a second life—a secret existence with lovers who were men.

Much of our life together was spent in stilted silence, but in taking care of him during the weeks before his death my feelings about my father were suddenly transformed. One moment my emotions were so inchoate that I could see nothing at all, and the next my perspective miraculously shifted—I could see the whole of our years together and love him as the firstborn daughter I had always wanted to be. That freedom brought a new way of thinking about my father's life as an Episcopal priest and bishop. I began to liken his spiritual calling to an artist's vocation. Thinking of him as a kind of artist, I could disentangle the strands of his complexity and identify with his suffering, his shortcomings, his errors. And in comparing his sexual search at the beginning of this century with my own in the heyday of sexual liberation in the 1960s and 1970s, I found new respect for his difficult choices.

I began to ask questions. Was my father's choice to become a priest predicated on his altruistic desire to help people or spiritual desire to become closer to God? Or was it the only avenue available for a man like him? Unlike some of his generation and class who chose the ministry to escape their passions, my father became a priest to dive deeper into life, to venture much farther than he would have had he become the banker or lawyer his father expected him to be. My father's vocation brought him great satisfaction, carrying him to the highest echelons of religious and political power in America, but his secrets caused suffering for my mother and later my stepmother, and for his children and himself.

During the four years I spent writing *The Bishop's Daughter*, I saw my father's life anew. I read the letters he wrote to my mother in the early days of their courtship and met many people who credited him with a dramatic influence on their lives. My childhood sense of my father's greatness returned, now seasoned by my own experience as an adult. At times, I felt as if I were accompanying my father and mother as they lived their lives, all the while revisiting my own experiences as a child and a young woman. To my surprise, writing the book, while hard work, was also an ecstatic experience. I had wandered in my own confusion and pain and had thought about these people and events for years. Now things began to fall into place, and I was telling a story that seemed larger than my own, filling in the blanks, with memory rising through my dreams and thoughts, bringing revelation and tears but also laughter.

Alfred Kazin, the literary critic, once told me that what he adored about being a writer was that when he finished a book, he found himself "an entirely different person." After turning in my first manuscript to my publisher, I asked him when he thought a book was finished, and he answered, "When you stop thinking and dreaming about it all the time." Now that I have stopped thinking and dreaming about *The Bishop's Daughter*, now that this story is out in the world, I find myself free of the shame and sorrow that accompanied much of my life. But, surprisingly, I also find that I miss my parents more than I ever have. Released from their story, they float through my days, and I'm forever thinking of things to ask them, imagining that when the phone rings it's one of them and that we can start all over again, now that I understand.

DISCUSSION QUESTIONS

1. In the prologue, Honor Moore writes, "it took me decades to escape the enchantment of my father's priesthood." How does Honor describe this feeling of enchantment, and how does it change as she grows up?

2. In crafting the book's prologue, Honor includes a scene that depicts her childhood perspective of her father, along with a brief conversation she had with him shortly before his death. Why do you think Honor chose to juxtapose these two scenes?

3. Honor notes that her father, Paul Moore, was born as "the beneficiary of vast wealth"—a fortune his grandfather, as "one of the Moore brothers," made through corporate mergers in Chicago in the early twentieth century. Her mother, on the other hand, came from wealthy roots but was also the daughter of a pioneering American female artist, the painter and sculptor Margarett Sargent. What role do these two influences—wealth and art—play in the lives Honor's parents lead, and how do Paul and Jenny Moore try to control their influence? Does Honor suggest a parallel between her life as an artist and her father's vocation as a priest?

4. Her father tells Honor that his primary reason for joining the

priesthood was to satisfy his longing to celebrate the Eucharist. And yet, like his friend Dorothy Day, Paul Moore's spirituality seems grounded in an effort to solve concrete problems of living. How did Paul Moore directly engage his ministry with the world, and how did it make him a household name in the Episcopal Church and later in the city of New York? How does Honor view the differences between her father's personal spirituality and his practicality as a civic-minded religious leader?

5. Honor describes her years in Jersey City as the best time of her childhood. What about this period in her life does she grow to cherish? What influence does her time there seem to have on her later life?

6. What effect does Nona Clarke have on Honor during Honor's trip to Europe as a college student? How does Nona complicate Honor's view of her father both in 1967 and later, when Honor sees her in Switzerland after nearly forty years have passed? How does Honor seem to view Nona's assessment of her "wonderful" life?

7. What role do letters and letter-writing play in *The Bishop's Daughter*? What does Honor mean when she describes the letters between her parents as "unrevised by the decades"? How would your understanding of the book be different if Honor had chosen not to include excerpts from letters?

8. Besides her parents, what are the other major influences on Honor during high school and college? What factors does she cite in the emergence of her political and sexual consciousness in the 1960s and '70s? What is the importance of theater to Honor's life when she is a young adult?

9. Why does Honor remember the dinner she had with her father on 8th Street in 1970—when she was twenty-four and he was forty-nine—so vividly? What role does psychotherapy play in Honor's relationship with her father when she is an adult?

10. How does Honor describe the memory of finding in her father's study a book of photographs open to a page depicting a naked young man? Later, when she finally learns of her father's affairs with men, how does Honor react? Why is Honor "furious" when she reads a copy of her father's book *Presences*?

11. How does Honor's relationship with her mother evolve after her parents' separation? How does Honor feel as her mother begins to open up to her about sexuality and her marriage with Honor's father?

12. After her mother died, Honor turned the experience into art, writing poetry and the play *Mourning Pictures*. How does Honor describe these artistic endeavors in relation to her grief over her mother's death? What is the effect on Honor of the critical failure of *Mourning Pictures* on Broadway?

13. Honor writes, "in 1974, I found myself in a dream realm of women." Later, she writes of trying to "establish myself in a new sexuality." What is the relationship between the awakening of Honor's feminism and her same-sex love affairs? How do both Honor and Paul Moore's sexual lives operate outside the boundaries of traditional sexual labels such as "gay" and "straight"?

14. How does Andrew Verver and what he reveals about his relationship with Paul Moore affect Honor's understanding of her father's sexuality? How does Emma Black further complicate this picture? Does Honor reach any conclusions about her father's sexuality?

15. The book's dedication reads: "For my siblings, each of whom would have another story." What does this dedication suggest about the story Honor presents in *The Bishop's Daughter* and the nature of self and memory?

ABOUT HONOR MOORE

Honor Moore is the award-winning author of three collections of poems, *Red Shoes* (2005), *Darling* (2001), and *Memoir* (1988). She is the author of the biography *The White Blackbird: A Life of the Painter Margarett Sargent by Her Granddaughter* (1996), which was a *New York Times* Notable Book and published in a new edition by W. W. Norton in 2009, and of the play *Mourning Pictures* (1974), produced on Broadway. She coedited *The Stray Dog Cabaret*, a collection of translations of the Russian Modernist poets by Paul Schmidt (2006), and edited *Poems from the Women's Movement* (2009) and *Amy Lowell: Selected Poems* (2004), both for the Library of America. Since 2000, she has taught in the graduate writing programs at The New School and Columbia University School of the Arts, and from 2000 to 2006 served on the board of PEN American Center. She lives in New York City.

HONOR MOORE'S SUGGESTIONS FOR FURTHER READING

Swann's Way by Marcel Proust
Minor Characters by Joyce Johnson
The Lover by Marguerite Duras
Go Tell It On the Mountain by James Baldwin
Notes of a Native Son by James Baldwin
The Border of Truth by Victoria Redel
The Emigrants by W. G. Sebald
My Father and Myself by J. R. Ackerley

*Available only on the Norton Web site: www.wwnorton.com/guides